Victorian Liberalism and Material Culture

Edinburgh Critical Studies in Victorian Culture
Series Editor: Julian Wolfreys

Visit the Edinburgh Critical Studies in Victorian Culture web page at www.edinburghuniversitypress.com/series/ECVC

Also Available:
Victoriographies – A Journal of Nineteenth-Century Writing, 1790–1914, edited by Julian Wolfreys
ISSN: 2044-2416
www.eupjournals.com/vic

Victorian Liberalism and Material Culture

Synergies of Thought and Place

Kevin A. Morrison

EDINBURGH
University Press

Edinburgh University Press is one of the leading university presses in the UK. We publish academic books and journals in our selected subject areas across the humanities and social sciences, combining cutting-edge scholarship with high editorial and production values to produce academic works of lasting importance. For more information visit our website: edinburghuniversitypress.com

Edinburgh University Press Ltd
The Tun – Holyrood Road, 12(2f) Jackson's Entry, Edinburgh EH8 8PJ

Typeset in 11/13 Adobe Sabon by
IDSUK (DataConnection) Ltd, and
printed and bound in Great Britain.

A CIP record for this book is available from the British Library

ISBN 978 1 4744 3153 8 (hardback)
ISBN 978 1 4744 3166 8 (webready PDF)
ISBN 978 1 4744 3165 1 (epub)

Contents

List of Figures

Series Editor's Preface

'Victorian' is a term, at once indicative of a strongly determined concept and an often notoriously vague notion, emptied of all meaningful content by the many journalistic misconceptions that persist about the inhabitants and cultures of the British Isles and Victoria's Empire in the nineteenth century. As such, it has become a byword for the assumption of various, often contradictory habits of thought, belief, behaviour and perceptions. Victorian studies and studies in nineteenth-century literature and culture have, from their institutional inception, questioned narrowness of presumption, pushed at the limits of the nominal definition, and have sought to question the very grounds on which the unreflective perception of the so-called Victorian has been built; and so they continue to do. Victorian and nineteenth-century studies of literature and culture maintain a breadth and diversity of interest, of focus and inquiry, in an interrogative and intellectually open-minded and challenging manner, which are equal to the exploration and inquisitiveness of its subjects. Many of the questions asked by scholars and researchers of the innumerable productions of nineteenth-century society actively put into suspension the clichés and stereotypes of 'Victorianism', whether the approach has been sustained by historical, scientific, philosophical, empirical, ideological or theoretical concerns; indeed, it would be incorrect to assume that each of these approaches to the idea of the Victorian has been, or has remained, in the main exclusive, sealed off from the interests and engagements of other approaches. A vital interdisciplinarity has been pursued and embraced, for the most part, even as there has been contest and debate among Victorianists, pursued with as much fervour as the affirmative exploration between different disciplines and differing epistemologies put to work in the service of reading the nineteenth century.

Edinburgh Critical Studies in Victorian Culture aims to take up both the debates and the inventive approaches and departures from convention that studies in the nineteenth century have witnessed for the last half-century at least. Aiming to maintain a 'Victorian' (in the most positive sense of that motif) spirit of inquiry, the series' purpose is to continue and augment the cross-fertilisation of interdisciplinary approaches, and to offer, in addition, a number of timely and untimely revisions of Victorian literature, culture, history and identity. At the same time, the series will ask questions concerning what has been missed or improperly received, misread or not read at all, in order to present a multifaceted and heterogeneous kaleidoscope of representations. Drawing on the most provocative, thoughtful and original research, the series will seek to prod at the notion of the 'Victorian', and in so doing, principally through theoretically and epistemologically sophisticated close readings of the historicity of literature and culture in the nineteenth century, to offer the reader provocative insights into a world that is at once overly familiar, and irreducibly different, other and strange. Working from original sources, primary documents and recent interdisciplinary theoretical models, Edinburgh Critical Studies in Victorian Culture seeks not simply to push at the boundaries of research in the nineteenth century, but also to inaugurate the persistent erasure and provisional, strategic redrawing of those borders.

Julian Wolfreys

Acknowledgements

Acknowledgements pages often end with references to those with whom we are closest, usually along the lines of 'Last, but not least . . .' Since this project would have been inconceivable without them, something like 'First, and most especially . . .' seems more appropriate. I am lucky to count Michael, Jean and Cole Thompson, Jennifer, Kieron and Justin Chapa, Betty J. Fisher and Jack Bowers, and Paul and Peter Morrison as family. For his unwavering belief in and support of me and my work, I am grateful to my father, Gary. When my mother, Gayle, started reading my work more than two decades ago, she would change commas, correct split infinitives and save me from dangling modifiers. Over the years, her knowledge of the Victorian era grew, and she has since become a tireless and indispensable interlocutor. Thanks is hardly recompense for reading and rereading virtually every word I have ever typed (except these acknowledgements), but I hope she recognises that I am a far better writer and thinker for her efforts. Although I study the past, Camden is daily teaching me to live in the present. I am singularly privileged to inhabit the world of ideas and the realm of daily life with Audrey, whose unreserved love, unstinting patience, emotional generosity, sparring prowess and unmatched acuity inspire my every step. I would call her my soulmate, but she continually reminds me that this attributes to fate our choice to spend each day together. You are my one and only love.

It is a pleasure to recognise the individuals and institutions whose assistance has made this book possible. Helena Michie and Robert L. Patten were incomparable mentors and remain indefatigable supporters. Thad Logan introduced me to the study of material culture and has, over the years, given liberally of her time and knowledge. A number of friends, colleagues and conference attendees contributed in ways large and small to this project. Many thanks in particular to Derek Alwes, Walter L. Arnstein, Sarah Berry, Elisha Cohen,

Mike Davis, Tracy C. Davis, Ross Forman, Melissa Free, Catherine Harland, Rosemary Hennessy, Linda K. Hughes, Joshua King, John Kucich, Scott Lewis, Jock Macleod, Jennifer McDonell, Jed Mayer, Michael Snediker, Marta Straznicky, Asha Varadharajan, Robyn Warhol, Phyllis Weliver and Martin L. Wiener. Anonymous referees, including one whose feedback is unequalled, helped me to reconceptualise or clarify aspects of my argument as I neared the finish line.

Although this project originated in a dissertation, it is essentially a new work, incorporating small portions of that earlier project. Nevertheless, for their support at an earlier stage, I thank the South Central Modern Language Association for a graduate student dissertation award (2009); the Rocky Mountain Modern Language Association for a graduate student research travel grant (2009); St Deiniol's Library, Hawarden, Wales, for a residential fellowship (2008); Rice University's English Department and the Centre for the Study of Women, Gender, and Sexuality for significant travel funding; and the Midwest Victorian Studies Association for awarding me its Walter L. Arnstein Prize for Dissertation Research in Victorian Studies (2008). In more recent years, the Armstrong Browning Library at Baylor University, Waco, Texas, invited me to spend a month as a visiting scholar and has offered help ever since. Thanks to Rita S. Patteson, Jennifer Borderud, Cynthia A. Burgess, Christi Klempnauer and Melvin Schuetz. Librarians and archivists at the Athenaeum Club; the British Library; Wandsworth Heritage Service; Queen Mary University of London; the National Archives (UK); Geffrye Museum of the Home; Bodleian Library, Oxford; History Centre, Surrey; West Sussex Records Office; Worthington Reference Library; Kensington and Chelsea Local Studies and Archives; and the Royal Institute of British Architects facilitated access to needed materials. At Syracuse University's Bird Library, Diane W. McKenney saved me from all manner of trouble.

Finally, I would like to thank the editorial staff at Edinburgh University Press with whom it has been a pleasure to work.

Abbreviations

The following abbreviations are used in this book:

BC   R. and E. B. Browning (1984–), *The Brownings'*
       Correspondence
EIC   East India Company
IOR   India Office Records and Private Papers
JSM   John Stuart Mill
MA   Matthew Arnold
RB   Robert Browning

Introduction: Frames of Mind

'Behind every man's external life, which he leads in company', the mid-Victorian journalist and economic adviser Walter Bagehot observed, 'there is another which he leads alone, and which he carries with him apart' (1965a: 195). To further characterise the distinction between the individual's innermost private space and the outer world of sociality, Bagehot formulated one of his many trademark quips: 'We all come down to dinner, but each has a room to himself' (195). In his evocative phrasing, which locates in the deep recesses of the mind the privacy that secures individuality, Bagehot employs a metaphor that refers to one domain of experience (thinking) in terms of another domain (space). He was not alone in conceptualising the mind in these terms.

For the intellectual heirs of John Stuart Mill, Bagehot among them, spatial metaphors were a way of defining liberal individuality as founded in a possessive relation to mental privacy. In classical liberalism this possessiveness had been presumed to originate in ownership of private property. The liberal subject emerged in a private sphere of intimacy (the home) before joining the public sphere of civil society to debate in a disinterested manner various matters of general interest. Property ownership, because it freed one from either patronage or influence, ostensibly facilitated the ability to detach from self-interest when participating in these deliberative exchanges. But Mill redefined this relation to privacy. To the extent that one had recourse to an inward space of thought and reflection, one possessed the capacity to produce in private the individuated, liberalised ideas that would be expressed publicly as opinion.

Mill had not been raised to valorise individuated privacy. Instead, from an early age, he was shaped as a proponent of utilitarianism, a school of thought that originated with Jeremy Bentham, a family friend. He was also trained as a subscriber to the theory of associationism promulgated by his father, James Mill. Associationist psychology assumed that the building blocks of an adult's cognitive architecture were the mental impressions – rudimentary ideas or images – generated from sensory data and perceptual stimuli experienced in childhood. In the elder Mill's view, when combined through the association of recurrence, simple ideas formed more complex ideas and complex ideas formed duplex ideas. James Mill writes:

> Brick is one complex idea, mortar is another complex idea; these ideas, with ideas of position and quantity, compose my idea of a wall. My idea of a plank is a complex idea, my idea of a rafter is a complex idea, my idea of a nail is a complex idea. These, united with the same ideas of position and quantity, compose my duplex idea of a floor. In the same manner my complex idea of glass, and wood, and others, compose my duplex idea of a window; and these duplex ideas, united together, compose my idea of a house, which is made up of various duplex ideas. (1878: 115–16)

Although indebted to John Locke's notion of the mind as a blank slate (*tabula rasa*), associationism, as elaborated on by James Mill, took the brick-and-mortar house as one of its principal figures of the mind. The mental operations that construct ideas through association are likened to the physical acts that, by combining materials, enable construction of a physical edifice.

Because associationist theory posits the self as the product of its environment, with ideas, no matter how complex, ultimately traceable to simple sensations, it accords well with the utilitarian goal of maximising happiness and welfare by altering the circumstances in which people's lives are led. The foundational tenet of utilitarianism is that humans are intrinsically predisposed to maximising their pleasure and minimising their pain. Thus, to secure the greatest happiness for the greatest number, it is necessary, Bentham and James Mill argued, to work towards removing external barriers to the pursuit of happiness. Nevertheless, to moderate the selfish propensities of individuals, social and political institutions should be reconstituted to foster social feeling. To effect positive social change, therefore, the right kinds of associations must be cultivated: all social good needs to be associated with pleasure and obstacles to the good associated with pain. Practices of thought, sentiment and belief are merely consequences, not engines, of social change. Indeed, as one-time Benthamite Robert Owen insisted, because character is entirely the product of social circumstances, individuals cannot be held accountable for their actions (and the desires directing them). To produce civic-minded, sociable beings, the total environments in which children are raised should be controlled (Owen 1970: 99–108).

At the onset of his well-known mental crisis of 1826–8, John Stuart Mill recognised aspects of his upbringing in Owen's approach. Only through a process of re-educating himself by reading literature and immersing himself in historical thought would Mill conceive of a way to escape the narrowly constructional implications of associationism. In his 1843 publication *A System of Logic*, which exerted a powerful hold on generations of Victorian intellectuals, Mill sought to specify the extent to which intellect and emotion were part of the original 'furniture of the mind' and 'what part [through experience or inference] is constructed out of materials furnished to it from without' (1974: VII, 8). Mill maintained that, although one's desires and beliefs may be causally determined by prior experiences, within the interior spaces of mental reflection one could forge individuated desires and reconstitute one's character through self-amendment.

Instead of utilising the metaphor of a brick-and-mortar house, John Stuart Mill codifies an understanding of the mind in spatial terms by likening it to an interior, private space where one formulates, before expressing, the thoughtful and individuated opinion that is a key characteristic of liberal individuality.[1] Linking individuality to the possession of character, which in turn underwrites freedom to pursue one's own mode of living, Mill would later assert in *On Liberty*, that 'one whose desires and impulses are not his own, has no character' (1977d: 264). Character, in his view, depends on the interior space of individuated privacy – an 'inward domain of consciousness' where 'absolute freedom of opinion and sentiment on all subjects' resides (225) – defined by specific techniques of thought production (abstraction, induction, devil's advocacy).

If the recesses of the mind can be likened to an 'inward domain of consciousness', however, did such spaces not display disparate elements? Did they have crown mouldings or sash windows? Were they filled with bric-a-brac? If the analogy to dwellings holds, might not the liberal mind, despite its implied singularity, represent diversity in its details? Emphasising plurality, *Victorian Liberalism and Material Culture: Synergies of Thought and Place* argues for the essential significance of architectural space and decorative interiors in studying nineteenth-century liberalism. It seeks to transform understanding of Victorian liberalism's key conceptual metaphor, that the mind of an individuated subject is private space, by attending to the actual environments inhabited by four Victorian writers and intellectuals. By delineating how John Stuart Mill's, Matthew Arnold's, John Morley's and Robert Browning's commitments to liberalism were shaped by or manifested through the physical spaces in which they lived or worked, this book foregrounds the centrality of embodied experience to Victorian political thought.

Lived Liberalism

Although historians and literary critics think and write about Victorian liberalism in diverse ways, they often share a desire to impose order on an otherwise 'contingent, malleable, and protean set of beliefs and practices' (Brown 2009: 23). Historians have focused principally on the Liberal Party, providing accounts of its formation, activities in the constituencies and manoeuvrings in Parliament.[2] The formal establishment of the Liberal Party is often dated to 1859, when representatives of diverse interests gathered on 6 June at Willis's Rooms in St James's Street, London, and agreed to unite behind Lord Palmerston in their bid to topple the Conservative minority Derby administration. This coalition included advanced and moderate Whigs (those, on the one hand, who had been inclined to share office with Conservatives and those, on the other hand, who embraced their independent oppositional status); Radicals, who favoured parliamentary reform; and so-called Peelites (disenchanted Tories who favoured free trade and, under the leadership of Robert Peel, broke from their party over its protectionist policies). While the Derby administration was indeed ousted in 1859, the meeting at Willis's Rooms only formalised an anti-Conservative coalition that had been taking shape for two decades (Parry 1993: 1). Historians dispute which election constituted the first Liberal government: John Russell's in 1846 or Palmerston's, either in 1859 or 1865, when the appellation 'Liberal' was first used. But all agree that the general election of 1868, when the party won under the leadership of William Gladstone, was crucial.

Another group of political historians have focused less on formation of the party than on Gladstone's dominating role.[3] From 1868, when he steered the Liberals to a resounding victory over the Conservatives, until his retirement in 1894, Gladstone and the Liberal Party were virtually synonymous. The policy successes of his first two administrations (1868–74, 1880–5)[4] belie the tensions among the party's many factions, which Gladstone's charismatic – some would say heavy-handed – leadership attempted to manage. By 1886 even Gladstone could not keep the party from weakening over the question of Irish home rule.

Other Victorian scholars have looked beyond institutionalised party politics to press for reconsideration of liberal culture by utilising concepts drawn from political theory, moral philosophy and science. Despite differences among them, these studies are consistent in their vigorous insistence on the need to move beyond the reductive or reflexively suspicious hermeneutical models that have prevailed in literary studies. Although Victorian intellectuals have been frequently associated with the pernicious aspects of Enlightenment modernity, such as the way detachment enables a denial of one's situatedness or an assertion of false neutrality or an interestedness disguised as disinterestedness, Amanda Anderson (2001) and David Wayne Thomas (2004) have argued on neo-Kantian grounds that Victorian liberals were motivated by a desire to objectify aspects of modern life and were critically engaged with forms of power.

Anderson does not deny that the detached view is always situated, yet she simultaneously contends that dismissing detachment out of hand disregards its many virtues. Against postmodern, pragmatist and feminist critiques of critical rationality and scientific objectivity as illusory, historically contingent, fully imbricated within the matrices of disciplinary power and fundamentally masculinist, she maintains that 'cultivated detachment', or the examined life, represents 'an ongoing aspiration and incomplete achievement' (A. Anderson 2001: 33). For her, 'the cultivation of detachment involves an attempt to transcend partiality, interests, and context: it is an aspiration toward universality and objectivity' (33). By subjecting to scrutiny routine customs and habits and calling into question the narrowness of much that passes for thought among contemporaries, liberal writers and thinkers struggled to free themselves from the motivations and contingencies of their situated interests.

If Anderson's partial redemption of the Victorian cultivation of objectivity is informed by proceduralist political theory, especially as it has been developed in Kantian fashion by Jürgen Habermas in *The Structural Transformation of the Public Sphere: An Inquiry into a Category of Bourgeois Society*, David Wayne Thomas's is informed by a neo-Kantian view of reflective agency. Contemporaneous habits of critique, he submits, have obscured the positive potentiality of what he designates as '*liberal heroics*' or self-overcoming (D. W. Thomas 2004: 7). Concluding that 'Victorian liberal culture reads self-discipline as heroism, as an overcoming of self that counts as another and better kind of self accomplished', Thomas explicates two corresponding ideals of agency: substantive and regulative (10). The foundational assumption behind both is 'an ambition to fulfill oneself by denying oneself' (9). Yet, although substantive and regulative agency are aspects of liberal heroics, the former is fixed ('something that one might [definitely] embody'), while the latter, which he endorses, serves as an 'aspiration to critical self-reflection in moral agency' (11, 22). Regulative agency is 'a reflective locus of purposeful self-understanding and action' (158). That is, this form of agency requires an ongoing commitment to critical examination of and reflection on the self. Precisely because it is reflective, regulative agency manifests itself in a 'disposition to consider alternative vantage points in private and public issues' (26). This disposition, an 'aspiration to many-sidedness', typifies, in his view, 'the period's liberal ideal of cultivated agency' (26).

Self-overcoming is also at the heart of George Levine's effort to relate liberal formulations of agency and sociality in the writings of key Victorian thinkers to certain features of the Enlightenment. Levine agrees with Anderson, whom he quotes, in saying that Victorian disinterestedness is part of the '"genealogy" of our own relation to detachment, to the objectivity that manifests itself so often in the form of dying to know' (Levine 2002: 175). The title of his study, *Dying to Know*, captures the struggle to overcome various obstacles, including the self, in the pursuit of knowledge. Formulating 'an implicit attack on the view that all attempts at objectivity are disingenuous and politically suspect', Levine traces the way in which this ideal of selfless knowledge emerges coevally with scientific study and its idiom of impartiality (13). 'Because it has always seemed to offer otherwise unattainable possibilities for human improvement', he maintains, disinterestedness is closely associated with various forms of altruism (231). For Levine, therefore, 'those impossible strivings toward disinterest' serve, much as they do for Anderson and Thomas, as an aspiration for social betterment (13).

Where Anderson, Thomas and Levine pursue a balanced but recuperative approach, Daniel Malachuk offers a full-throttled and emphatically presentist defence of Victorian liberalism. Its 'core conviction' – 'that human beings, with the help of the state, can achieve an objective moral perfection' – is of continued utility (Malachuk 2005: 2). Thus, Malachuk reaffirms this aspiration against critiques of objectivity and reason, which he sees as misguided. He also reinterprets a long scholarly tradition that posits key Victorian intellectuals as anti-statists, asserting that they saw the potential for the state to facilitate individual strivings towards moral perfection by creating an environment conducive to active civic participation, including systematically eradicating many injustices and inequities.

In an effort to revivify interpretive practices they perceive as having become all too routinised, these four critics, to varying degrees, eschew historicist protocols. Anderson has called for altogether jettisoning history in favour of political theory as the privileged interlocutor of (literary) Victorian studies (A. Anderson 2005: 196). The move away from history, however, is inherently risky. In so far as liberalism is, in Wendy Brown's phraseology, 'a nonsystematic and porous doctrine subject to historical change and local variation' (1995: 141), one cannot step away from analysing context and change without forfeiting precision and coherency.

The studies I have just mentioned are in no sense wrong, but they are partial. Indeed, as Lauren Goodlad has compellingly argued in *Victorian Literature and the Victorian State*, scholars of liberalism cannot do justice to its 'pervasive tensions and paradoxes' by refusing to recognise its multiplicity, and they cannot adequately or accurately analyse liberal 'ideals, vocabulary, and assumptions' by separating them from the circumstances in which they emerged or their variability over time (2003: viii).[5] A history that understands liberalism to be synonymous with the Liberal Party might therefore include Mill, who was elected to Parliament on the Liberal platform, although he was generally thought of at the time as a Radical, and Morley, one of Britain's premier journalists and politicians. But it would exclude Browning, who spent many years outside England and showed little interest in party politics, as well as Arnold, who, despite being approached for a possible run, never served in Parliament. Liberalism understood as the achievement of disinterested thought and calm reflection might well include Mill, Arnold and Morley. Browning would be a harder sell.

Thus, my approach in *Victorian Liberalism and Material Culture* shares affinities with those studies concerned with the contextual and mutable nature of liberal discourse. One laudable tendency of this sort of work has been its movement beyond familiar personages and texts. Eugenio Biagini's scholarship, which recovers the political thought of plebeian Liberalism, is particularly exemplary (1992, 2003). Biagini compellingly maintains that 'if we really are interested in the context of [Victorian] political thought we must go beyond traditional concerns with the "canonical" texts and look at its social environment' (2003: 55). Yet I contend that we must also consider the physical environments in which liberal ideas were conceptualised, elaborated and lived. This necessitates not jettisoning canonical texts but re-evaluating them in light of the embodied experiences of their authors.

My interest in the body and its relationship to architectural space, decorative interiors and the technologies of everyday life may call to mind for some readers Michel Foucault's writings on governmentality. A small but growing number of historians have in recent years examined the ways in which the liberal subject was shaped and governed by quotidian powers and technologies. Although the places where disciplinary power is practised – such as the prison, the confessional booth and the mental asylum – are well known, far less attention has been paid to 'the positive, catalytic qualities of spaces, places and environments' in forming liberal subjects (M. Huxley 2007: 195). Voting booths, for example, were designed and introduced; and halls that replaced pubs and open-air polling stations in parishes, towns and counties were constructed. These served to narrow the social, potentially destabilising dimension of politics while attempting to realise a more individualised and representative political system.[6]

Urban infrastructural and public architectural projects from the middle of the nineteenth century forward can be seen as attempts to draw out the rational, self-governing citizen. Thus, ordered spaces of recreation, such as municipal parks and swimming pools, provided opportunities for liberalising individuals to exercise and refine their abilities to self-govern (Rose 1999: 104–7); public baths and domestic bathrooms created more favourable conditions for subjective individualisation (T. Crook 2006; Joyce 2001: 65–75); and libraries and museums, while enjoining respect and civility towards others, also facilitated self-help and self-culture (Joyce 2001: 98–143; Bennett 1995: 59–101). Vast metropolitan improvement projects, by materialising forms of indirect rule, attempted to forestall anarchy, the outcome feared by many in what was otherwise seen as an inexorable transition away from monarchical and aristocratic governance and towards democracy.

Governmentality is a particularly attractive concept for studies concerned with the relationship of place and self. Yet in much of this work actual people are absent. To be sure, bodies populate the pedestrian streets, parks, libraries and museums in these accounts. But they exist principally in abstract form – the liberal subject, the shrewd consumer, the newly enfranchised voter, the library reader – as objects on which technologies of power exert their force.

Abstracted embodiment is precisely the focus of Elaine Hadley's *Living Liberalism* (2010). Critics' long-standing insistence that liberalism repudiates the significance of bodies, Hadley posits, has blinded us to modes of embodied life that are essential to liberal subjectivity. Amanda Anderson, too, seeks to call attention to the importance of embodiment, showing how liberals gave critical reason ethical weight by figuring it as an ideal of temperament (tact, moderation, composure) and character (sincerity, conviction, impartiality). But Hadley makes embodiment central to her study of liberal cognition. In her account, the formalised mental attitudes of liberal cognition that produce privately conceived ideas – including objectivity, reticence, disinterestedness, conviction, impersonality and sincerity – work in tandem with public modes of abstract embodiment, such as the individual, the signed opinion piece, the voter and the liberal politician. Through distinctive cognitive practices, liberalism aimed to replace 'situated and habituated bodies', among which were 'gendered and classed bodies', with 'abstracted bodies thinking disinterested thoughts in an abstracted time and place of serene meditation' (Hadley 2010: 13). Liberal cognition, she affirms, relocates 'the generative site of rationality from the highly idealized public sphere of collaboration, debate, and circulation to an equally idealized private sphere of cognition, mental deliberation, and devil's advocacy' (2010: 50). Yet to make this claim Hadley must bracket the perseverance of certain republican political ideals, not the least of which were public discussion and debate, that existed well into the mid-Victorian period she analyses.[7]

Although I share with Hadley an interest in its lived dimensions, my book looks at Victorian liberalism from a different but related perspective. It addresses, as an essential component in understanding nineteenth-century liberalism, the interaction between liberal thinkers and their places of work. By analysing the complex relations among place, self and text, *Victorian Liberalism and Material Culture* seeks to reposition, within historical accounts of liberalism, the human body as corporeal being, rather than merely an abstraction or representation, and bodily practices as an aspect of the quotidian production of knowledge.

In his *Recollections*, as he looked back on the Victorian era, John Morley remarked – purposefully echoing his parliamentary colleague Augustine Birrell – that 'Liberalism is not a creed but a frame of mind' (1917: 127). It is my contention that physical space profoundly mattered to the construction and maintenance of this mood and that, just as spaces share similarities and reveal differences, so too did the liberal outlook. The title of this introduction, 'frames of mind', with its reference to the plural 'frames', is therefore intended to underscore how the material culture of workspaces affects modes of liberal embodiment and thought that no singular formulation of liberalism can encompass. In the aesthetic disciplines of architecture and art, the term 'frame' may refer to the foundational support of a building, the encasement for windows or the border of a painting. For human physiologists, 'frame' refers to the corporeal body, especially its build or constitution. But the interaction of these two realms, as it occurred in historical eras, rarely invites analysis. Although the anthropologist Paul Connerton was unconcerned with this interaction, a remark of his suggests a reason for this lack of analysis. The 'physical existence' of individuals from the past, he insists, is too often erased by historians in so far as, owing to their investments in textual and canonical sources, 'the life of human beings, as a historical life, is understood as a life reported on and narrated' (1989: 101).

Liberal Workspaces

We know relatively little about the workspaces of major liberal writers and intellectuals compared with non-liberals of the period. The artistic life in practice has been the subject of many fine studies of Tudor House at 16 Cheyne Walk, London, which belonged to the (largely) apolitical Dante Gabriel Rossetti, and of the socialist William Morris's Red House in Bexleyheath and his Kelmscott House in London.[8] Also well known are houses, now open to the public, belonging to several literary figures: the conservative art critic John Ruskin, at Brantwood, overlooking Coniston Water; the Whig writer and social theorist Harriet Martineau, at Ambleside; and the Tory historian Thomas Carlyle, in Chelsea.[9]

Seeking to address this deficit, I chose to write about Mill, Arnold, Morley and Browning for five principal reasons. First, each conceptualised the mind in similar ways. Mill, as I have noted, described an 'inward domain' where 'absolute freedom of opinion and sentiment on all subjects' resides and also spoke of the 'furniture of the mind'. Arnold referred in spatialised terms to 'a frame of mind' and to thoughts as 'furniture' of the mind (1965a: 221, 97). Morley contrasted the mental capaciousness and serenity of the liberalising individual – which the specific techniques of thought production Mill championed were intended to produce – with the 'cramped' and 'narrow' mind of a dogmatic thinker (Morley 1878: 5). Browning referred to the mind as an 'inner chamber of the soul' where truths and falsehoods wrestle for legitimacy (1999: 209).

Yet this commonality alone is not an adequate basis for comparison. From Bagehot, who likened the mind to a room in 1853, to

L. T. Hobhouse, who called it a 'citadel' in 1911 (1994: 13), spatial metaphors abound in, and of course are not limited to, writings by liberal thinkers. My second reason for focusing on Mill, Arnold, Morley and Browning, rather than many others about whom I might have written, is that, despite defining liberal individuality as founded in a possessive relation to mental privacy, these writers did not privilege private cognition and mental deliberation at the expense of public exchange and debate. They were not proponents of possessive individualism or liberal atomism. Instead, they were public moralists, to use Stefan Collini's term, who, in attempting to 'persuade their contemporaries to live up to their professed ideals' (1991: 2), did not uncouple private thought from public exchange.[10] Seeking to 'promote virtue among citizens' and 'to build character and promote social betterment by collective means of some kind', which were persistent ideals of seventeenth-century civic republicanism (Goodlad 2015: viii), each of the four stressed to varying degrees the interconnection of individual freedom and active citizen participation.

My third principal reason for choosing these individuals is that each turned to the study of history in attempting to promote character building. Mill thought of his age as a period of transition, following an era of stasis, in which a bewildering array of theories, philosophies and religions competed for hegemony. Through working at India House, Mill developed an objectivising stance that, he believed, facilitated a dispassionate assessment of distinct claims. Arnold, who found himself overcome by 'the multitude of voices counselling different things', sought to cultivate at London's exclusive Athenaeum Club a disinterested intelligence founded on study of the ancient world (MA 1960c: 8). By doing so, Arnold believed, the individual was placed at a sufficient distance from the controversies of modern life and therefore 'under the empire of facts' (1960c: 13). Morley denounced Christianity for inhibiting humanity's capacity to gain clarity by contextualising religious, social and political thought beyond the present moment. The 'vital doctrine of the brotherhood of men' was 'virtually confined to a sense of the brotherhood of contemporaries', which disenabled an understanding of history's sequentiality and a sense of connection with 'all our precursors' (Morley 1871b: 296–7). By contrast, Browning thought artefacts from the past may serve as evidence of the workings of providence in history. Many of his poems set in earlier periods of transition, when he thought it possible to glimpse God's purpose for humankind more clearly, were written while he contemplated these objects.

Fourth, I felt that focusing on four men would prove particularly fruitful in thinking about formations of liberal masculinity. At an early stage, I contemplated writing about the Priory, George Eliot and George Henry Lewes's home near Regent's Park, where they held their famous salons, but Kathleen McCormack beat me to it.[11] When masculinity was less central to my concerns, possible contenders included the writer and traveller Annie Brassey, who built up a massive natural science collection that she displayed in her home and opened to visitors.[12] Another was the painter Pauline Trevelyan, who transformed Wallington Hall, her prominent Liberal family's Northumberland estate, into an intellectual and artistic salon. But Hadley's work on processes of abstracted manliness convinced me that additional and different claims might be made about the relationship of the male body to cognitive processes.[13]

Fifth, I was attracted to the challenge of writing about these particular individuals because each repeatedly insisted he did not want his life documented. Of course, Mill wrote an autobiography. Living 'in an age of transition in opinions', he thought the work might be 'both of interest and of benefit in noting the successive phases of any mind which was always pressing forward, equally ready to learn and to unlearn either from its own thoughts or from those of others' (1981: 5). He therefore set out to elucidate his efforts to develop his individuated intellect. Mill's remarkably impersonal but seemingly thorough account, combined with retention of his papers until the 1920s by his stepdaughter and niece, inhibited others from writing much about his life. With the exception of the reminiscences Alexander Bain published in 1882, which W. L. Courtney drew on in the only other lengthy nineteenth-century biography, issued in 1889, nearly a hundred years elapsed after Mill's death before substantive biographies appeared.

Arnold, who renounced writing subjective, personal poetry and championed in prose 'transfer[ring] the natural love of life from the personal self to the impersonal self', made clear to his family his 'express wish' that his biography not be written (MA 1968a: 334; G. Russell 1904: vii). The family honoured this request, simultaneously satiating a desire among the reading public for an account of his life by commissioning George William Erskine Russell to produce a selection of Arnold's letters, published in two volumes in 1895–6 (G. Russell 1895: vii).[14] The letters, among other materials, and a new volume of correspondence collected by his grandson Arnold Whitridge, published in 1923, provided a foundation for the first significant biographies of the twentieth century: Lionel Trilling's

Matthew Arnold in 1939 and Park Honan's far more encompassing *Matthew Arnold: A Life* in 1981. But it was not until the 1990s, coinciding with the Herculean publication of nearly 4,000 Arnold letters, that several more studies appeared.[15]

Although Morley was one of the most prolific Victorian biographers, he vigorously disagreed with the eighteenth-century approaches to life writing that were still dominant. The essayist Samuel Johnson thought that only by leading readers 'into domestick privacies, and display[ing] the minute details of daily life, where exterior appendages are cast aside', could a man's character be best discerned (Boswell 1826: 6). Morley held another view: discerning the truth or falsity of a published opinion, and of that opinion's relationship to 'the main transactions' of the time, was more important than understanding the character of its author (1865a; 1867b: vi). It is no wonder that Morley, who sought to live in an impersonal manner, which I document in Chapter 3, is almost silent on the details of his marriage and family life in his two-volume *Recollections* (1917). He went so far as to mandate that his executors not cooperate with biographers. 'As it is possible that some person may desire to write a memoir of my life which I regard as wholly superfluous, I enjoin upon my executors . . . to refuse to aid or encourage any such design', Morley wrote in his last will and testament, 'and not to allow any person to have access to any of my papers whether personal or acquired in the course of official duty for perusal or otherwise . . .' (1923a). Making an exception for Francis Hirst, who had served as research assistant on Morley's monumental *Life of Gladstone*, Guy Morley, one of the executors, turned over his uncle's correspondence and diaries soon after his death. In 1927 Hirst published the two-volume *Early Life and Letters of John Morley* in which he remarked, presumably with Guy's blessing, that, while Morley 'would have detested a cumbrous biography', he would not have minded a selection of letters that spoke for themselves, interspersed with occasional commentary (1927: I, xvi, xvii). Until the staff of the Bodleian Library at Oxford catalogued Morley's papers, which they received in 2000 as part of Hirst's collection, researchers had to rely on Hirst's work and a handful of biographical vignettes written with Morley's consent during his lifetime.

Like Morley, Browning recognised the need to grant an occasional interview or submit to a rare profile to satisfy readers' interest or stave off unauthorised investigations by journalists. But he was even more vociferously opposed to divulging personal details. He burned miscellaneous papers, letters and early drafts of poems and dismissed any suggestion he might write what he derided as his 'reminiscences' (Hood 1933: xi; RB 1933: 294–5). The poem 'House', which centres on the front of a domestic residence sheared off in an earthquake, exposing the interior to prying eyes, reveals some of Browning's attitude towards privacy. From the objects on view ('Odd tables and chairs', 'musty old books') and the home's interior layout, observers make snap judgements and superficial comments ('His wife and himself had separate rooms', 'the pagan, he burned perfumes!') (RB 1995: 173). Rather than dismissing biographical considerations altogether, however, the ninth stanza takes a different tack: 'Outside should suffice for evidence: / And whoso desires to penetrate / Deeper, must dive by the spirit-sense . . .' (1995: 173). Getting beyond shallow observations requires employing different 'optics' (1995: 173) by activating one's 'spirit-sense'. The term 'spirit-sense' captures the peculiarly embodied engagement with historical objects that Browning prescribed to readers and, as I will show, cultivated in life in decorating his home – an engagement that begins with sight, an imaginative perception he links to the soul, but involves the somatic body at a multisensory level.

Although they shared a common vocabulary and a background as public moralists, Mill, Arnold, Morley and Browning differ enough from one another that analysing them can tell us something about the diversity and variability of liberal discourse, as well as about changes in liberalism over the course of the nineteenth century. In addition, Browning's and Morley's liberalism was religiously inflected, formed by their Nonconformist upbringing. Arnold's was, too, although he was raised in an Anglican household, which shaped his views in significantly different ways. Mill was raised an atheist. Finally, each associated himself with the Liberal Party, but even here were fundamental differences: Mill was a Radical; Arnold, a professed 'Liberal of the future rather than a Liberal of the present' (MA 1973a: 138); Morley, a Gladstonian Liberal; Browning, a republican in his youth but a unionist towards the end of his life.

Evidencing Interiors

Having narrowed my focus to these four individuals, I began with an initial set of questions. How were Mill's ideas about liberal individuality and opinion formation, expressed in such texts as *Principles of Political Economy* and *On Liberty*, cultivated by his spatial experiences of India House, the headquarters of the East India Company, where he wrote the majority of his essays and books? How were Arnold's notions of culture and perspectival breadth, articulated in *Culture and Anarchy*, shaped by his habitual bodily practices within the Athenaeum Club, where he penned the bulk of his social and political essays? How were the white walls and seemingly spartan interiors of Morley's homes, which have been repeatedly described by biographers but never before interpreted, connected to the lived liberalism he prescribed to others in his periodical pieces and biographies? How were Browning's well-known decorative practices at home related to both his poetry – particularly his most famous collection, *Men and Women* – and his politics?

My initial motivation in seeking answers to these questions was to participate in the ongoing reappraisal of liberalism to which scholars in the disciplines of literature and history have contributed. Although Mill, Arnold, Morley and Browning were contemporaries, spanning two generations, born into families of comparable standing among the professional middle classes, quite knowledgeable of, and often engaged with, each other's work, they have never been extensively studied together in the context of liberalism. One factor inhibiting such a study is a pervasive tendency among scholars, including myself at an earlier stage,[16] to isolate a single strand from an otherwise multivalent liberal discourse and present that part as the whole. Thus, despite a now burgeoning corpus of scholarship on the topic, which I have discussed, liberalism has often been defined in ways that fail to capture its bewildering complexity.

Yet my interest in historically lived lives soon led me to a second aspiration. I wanted to contribute to the growing body of work demonstrating that through the use of floor plans, home-decoration manuals, inventories, account books, lists, probate records, photographs, paintings, letters and diaries, cultural historians can 'uncover' the uses and experiences of Victorian interiors (Hamlett 2010: 11). Burrowing through one archive after another in a dogged effort to answer these questions, however, I continually ran up against the limitations of the archive. As Amanda Vickery notes apropos of her study of Georgian domestic interiors, 'The backdrop of a life is rarely the fodder of diaries or letters, just as routines are less interesting to record than events' (2010: 3). Historical scholars interested in architectural space and material culture must be particularly resourceful, scouring institutional archives for legal records and carefully reading each letter or diary entry, because a room's layout and furnishings rarely invite comment except in moments of great calamity or bliss.

Based on extensive research in British and American archives and utilising recently unsealed records, *Victorian Liberalism and Material Culture* is also indebted to work inside and outside my field that focuses on historical material culture. Among scholars of the Victorian period, Deborah Cohen (2006), Judith Flanders (2004), Jane Hamlett (2010), Thad Logan (2001), Judith Neiswander (2008) and Andrea Tange (2010) have published wonderfully stimulating accounts of middle-class domestic spaces and objects. As Tange persuasively argues, middle-class identity was essentially shaped by the physical characteristics of dwellings:

> The way a house was designed to distribute people through space helped establish the personal and social identities of everyone who entered. In short, British middle-class identity from the 1830s through the 1870s was clearly architectural. It was carefully constructed from the building blocks of family name and gentility, and it was maintained primarily through the vigilant creation of a house that would be not just a home but also a stage for displaying the successful achievement of middle-class identity. (2010: 6)

Thus, Victorian families were concerned less with the size of their dwellings than with acquiring furnishings and exhibiting decorative objects that disclosed both the ideals to which they subscribed and the extent to which these had been realised. The aforementioned studies offer insights into the relationships among interior spaces, gender and class. Almost without exception, however, scholars of the period's material culture have shown little interest in political discourse or politics, especially surprising given how adherents across the political spectrum expressed their ideological commitments through the display of decorative objects in the home.[17]

Victorian Liberalism and Material Culture is also informed by recent work on the material culture of other literary eras. Nicole Reynolds (2010) and Victoria Rosner (2005) have considered the discursive connections between domestic architecture and the literature of historical periods that bookend the Victorian: in Reynold's case, Romanticism, and in Rosner's, Modernism. Amanda Vickery looks further back, to Georgian England, to consider 'the determining role of house and home in power and emotion, status and choices' (2010: 3). Diana Fuss ranges across time periods and national literatures to reflect on significant personages of intellectual history – Sigmund Freud, Helen Keller, Emily Dickinson and Marcel Proust – who were fascinated by both their domestic interiors and the concept of interiority itself (2004). As with other work on Victorian material culture, these studies have said little about political thought, although Vickery notes in passing the long figuration of the household as a microcosm of the state in political theory (2010: 7).

In addition to pursuing a rapprochement between material culture studies and political theory, my book differs from these accounts in considering both domestic and institutional material culture.[18] For well over the past decade, the home has been a primary object of interest for scholars of material culture. As Vickery argues, 'Universal but unexamined, homes are implicated in and backdrop to the history of power, gender, the family, privacy, consumerism, design and the decorative arts' (2010: 3). Whereas the term 'home' in historiographical narratives of the nineteenth century has often been synonymous with a domesticity elaborated and maintained by women confined to the private sphere, recent studies have been eager to show how material inquiry can complicate the notion of separate spheres and of men's relationship to the home.

Although the Victorians were deeply invested in an ideal of separate spheres that distinguished the feminine private realm of the home from the masculine domain of work and commerce, scholarship in the past few decades has called attention to the ways in which such an ideal was unrealised in practice. Many studies extend John Tosh's perceptive argument that the privilege reserved for men was that they could move freely between and through '*both* spheres' (1999b: 230). While a clear demarcation between home and work may have been an ideal, in reality many men, from owners of family businesses to schoolmasters at instructional institutions, worked where they resided. 'Family life in homes where men worked from home, then, was often infused by the world of work, which could transform the atmosphere of home', notes Hamlett. 'The public world frequently permeated the private, and any distinction between the two was highly complex' (2010: 40). Even men who worked principally outside the home received visitors to their places of residence, where, in the confines of a gentleman's study, matters of business and politics were discussed. Thus, it stands to reason, men were also 'domestically minded' (Hamlett 2010: 89). They often collaborated with their spouses in decorating the home or even 'determined the arrangement of interiors', as Deborah Cohen puts it (2006: 90).

The recent focus on the physical spaces of the home has further complicated a neat divide between the public and private realms. As Hamlett contends, 'Public and Private were often inseparable, linked through objects and images, through visitors in the drawing room and below stairs.' By means of the 'presence of male work', the concerns of one sphere thoroughly pervaded the other (Hamlett 2010: 29). Tange shows similarly how the home was 'physically constructed and managed, not only to contain and privilege the feminine, but also to enhance the public positions and respectability of the entire family' (2010: 66). In this way private domestic spaces also had public purposes.

But public spaces also had private purposes. Because the home has been the focus of scholarly inquiry, places such as the gentlemen's club and the office have been relatively neglected by material culture scholars.[19] While studies of the home have shown how the private sphere was thoroughly permeated by elements of the public world, *Victorian Liberalism and Material Culture* considers in Chapters 1 and 2 the ways in which public spaces in this period were often, to varying degrees, domestic. This may suggest a narrowing of the public sphere of collaboration, debate and circulation, as public spaces take on the characteristics of private dwellings. But these settings afforded Mill and Arnold a degree of privacy that, at various times during their most prolific years as writers, they found themselves unable to experience at home, while also equipping them with the accoutrements of reading and writing, endeavours they recognised as forms of political activity.

In addition to considering quasi-domestic but not truly private spaces, my book differs from other accounts by reflecting on the theoretical and practical difficulties contemporary researchers confront in using images and texts to reconstruct material culture. An earlier generation of work on architectural spaces focused principally on paintings and photographs as windows into lived experience. Peter Thornton goes as far as asserting the primacy of visual over textual evidence: images are 'far more eloquent than any descriptions of mine can ever be' (1998: 9). Other scholars have been less willing to accept the idea that photographs, paintings, drawings and illustrations facilitate unmediated encounters with interiors. As Thad Logan argues, graphic and linguistic representations alike are 'partisan, strategic, and embedded in history' (2001: 2).

In any attempt to write about how people long since dead inhabited buildings or decorated rooms, one way of addressing the evidentiary problems images pose is to read them alongside textual sources, including letters, diaries, inventories and last wills and testaments. But such sources pose their own challenges. As I worked with the materials on which this project is based, I was confronted with numerous problems. In some cases, such as the interiors of Morley's residences that I address in Chapter 3, the visual evidence seems to contradict written accounts. In other cases, such as the upper floors of India House discussed in Chapter 1, there are no visual records of the interior spaces described in various documents. If written accounts complicate or counterbalance the visual, or if visual evidence is absent, should one rely unhesitatingly on textual descriptions of objects and spaces?

Absence can sometimes be liberating. Anyone who has engaged in historical inquiry has inevitably confronted the problem of what Carolyn Steedman might call 'too-muchness': the sheer excessiveness of the documentation left behind, which leaves one stymied (2007: 8–10). On learning only about a dozen diaries and a commonplace book of a clergyman whose life she was investigating had survived, Steedman confesses to a feeling of elation: 'I was happy to have so little.' She notes: 'less is often more in the historical game, and some of us like nothing so much as writing within the strictures of absence' (2007: 8).[20] I often longed for such strictures while researching Chapter 1, which required me to make my way through Mill's voluminous output in an attempt to track subtle changes in his multifaceted thought, to read a massive body of scholarship on his life and work, and to master to the best of my ability Britain's complex and long-standing commercial involvement in and imperial administration of India. But despite the substantial published and archival material on Mill, answers to the many questions about his workspace with which I began continued to elude me. Although paintings and illustrations of the public spaces of India House abound, there are no extant depictions of the building's upper floors, where much of the company's everyday work, including Mill's, was done. Only a handful of sketchy written accounts exist. The building itself was demolished in 1861.

However much I sympathise intellectually with the argument by some material culture scholars for incorporating the embodied first-person experiences of researchers, I was unable to heed the call fully. Jason Edwards and Imogen Hart have urged others 'to accept the inevitable subjectivity, embodiedness and time-specificity of our encounters with interiors' and to forego the search for 'an objective, "real" interior [that] exists somewhere beyond the frames of our visual, and the pages of our textual evidence' (2010: 17). Embracing the 'immersive, aesthetic, affective, haptic and somatic experience' of the researcher, Edwards and Hart call attention to 'the historiographic potential of a more nuanced account of the problematic, but powerful, potential relationship between embodied, present-tense, first-person accounts of interiors at particular moments and more obviously historical forms of evidence' (18). With less rhetorical flourish but similar investments in first-person experience, Charlotte Gere and Claire Zimmerman document some of the benefits of visiting the sites about which one writes. For Gere, the pay-off is in the details. The researcher can 'glean a good idea of the original colours and textures, which are not always easy to make out from even the most meticulous of paintings' (1989: 97). For Zimmerman, whose focus is on the interplay of twentieth-century architecture and photography, onsite research can be nothing short of revelatory. 'The experience of the building itself', she remarks with respect to a particular site, 'comes as something of a surprise, largely because of an apparent dimensional difference between space occupied and space depicted in photographs' (2004: 336).

Only two of the spaces about which I write were accessible to me. Browning's house at 19 Warwick Crescent survived India House by a century but was demolished in the 1960s, and although a plaque identifies 29 De Vere Gardens, the house is not open to visitors. Morley's home in Putney has long since been demolished. His residences in Elm Park Gardens, South Kensington, though still standing, have been renumbered and changed in other ways. Determining which units were his is one thing. Being able to enter them, let alone experience them as he did, is another. The current occupants were unlikely to greet me as the architectural scholars Charles Rice and Barbara Penner (2004) were welcomed by the last owners of Red House, before it was acquired by the National Trust, or the literary critics Helena Michie and Robyn Warhol (2015) were received at Knole, Vita Sackville-West's ancestral home, where George Scharf, the subject of their recent study, had dined and stayed.[21] The Athenaeum Club and Casa Guidi posed fewer challenges, in so far as I had access to them, but their interiors have changed considerably, as I discuss in Chapter 2 and the conclusion. Even an examination of these spaces raises methodological questions.

My interest in Mill's, Arnold's, Morley's and Browning's workspaces as a way of thinking about living liberalism, therefore, also affords opportunities to think through meta-archival questions of knowledge-creation. The term 'frame' is frequently used by scholars of film and photography in reference to both the visible image and what is excluded from the field of view. This, too, seems a fitting evocation. Reflecting on my negotiation of the archives on which the book's arguments are based (what remains and what is, as it were, out of frame), the following pages also explore how cultural historians move from textual evidence to conclusions about interiors that either no longer exist or have been fundamentally altered.

Thus, although this book is about the interaction of four liberal intellectuals with the places in which they worked, it also narrates the process of researching historical interiors in public and private archives. In this respect my book contributes to efforts by scholars of literature and history to evaluate critically archival reading practices – the epistemological, ideological and identificatory expectations one brings to bear on material one examines – and, therefore, the interpretive acts that produce sometimes partial, sometimes conflicting, knowledges.[22] How do scholars of Victorian material culture reconcile the differing information about architectural spaces and domestic interiors available to them? How does one deal with the epistemological conundrum of too little information? What are the theoretical and practical difficulties of relying on visual images and written sources to reconstruct material culture? In evidencing historical interiors, how might we attend not just to presence but also to absence? What are the epistemological problems of moving from textual and visual traces to the architectural spaces themselves?

As a way of grappling with these questions, *Victorian Liberalism and Material Culture* develops an account and an integrated methodology that deploys close textual, material, biographical and historical analyses and, on occasion, speculation. When I run up against the limits of the archive, I acknowledge what I can only infer from the available evidence before embracing what the historian Natalie Davis calls 'conjectural knowledge and possible truth' (1988: 574). I suspect some readers may find unsettling the moments in which confidence about what I know gives way to speculation about what I do not know. I hope readers will recognise the usefulness of speculation to historical material culture studies in enabling one to avoid either of two pitfalls: advancing an argument that makes claims about the interaction between individuals and their environments that cannot be substantiated, or accumulating a tremendous amount of local details about interiors and objects that may be highly interesting, while failing to probe larger implications.

Frame by Frame

The chapters that follow show how Mill, Arnold, Morley and Browning depended on their emplacement in specific workspaces and how the materiality of these sites inflected their thinking. In his *Autobiography*

Mill makes only passing reference, in a single, brusque paragraph, to his thirty-five-year career with the East India Company (1981: 248–50) and, as at least one commentator has noted, has remarkably little ever to say about place.[23] Yet Chapter 1 details how Mill's views on cognitive individuation, a culture of merit that might nourish it and, ultimately, the production of truth through rational debate were not simply responses to unreformed associationist and narrow Evangelical conceptions. These arguments developed in accord with a system of rank and apportionment according to intellect and merit that Mill experienced while employed by the East India Company.

Chapter 2 explicates the material environment of a clubhouse dedicated to Periclean Athens, as Arnold would have experienced it, to show that many of his key ideas were shaped by his embodied experience there. It demonstrates how Arnold's election to the Athenaeum was a watershed for him. He found the club, as he wrote to his sister Jane Forster (whom he calls 'K') in March 1856, 'a place at which I enjoy something resembling beatitude' (1996: 336). His access to the club's vast library holdings placed in easy reach 'the best which has been thought and said' (1965h: 233), and by studying these writings Arnold reconstituted himself through his conversion to culture.

Whereas Mill and Arnold had relatively little control over the venues in which they worked, John Morley and Robert Browning created environments in line with their thinking. Evangelicalism, whether Anglican or Dissenting, was a religion of the home, and both men, as they recognised, had been profoundly shaped by the movement.[24] Each possessed a great 'love of domesticity' – akin to the emotion described by John Clive in his discussion of the youthful Thomas Babington Macaulay, the future historian, who suffered a 'keen sense of deprivation . . . whenever he was away from home' (Clive 1975: 39). Like Macaulay, Browning and Morley were reared by evangelically inclined parents in fervently religious counties. Nevertheless, Browning's and Morley's approaches to decoration differed markedly.

Chapter 3 analyses Morley's suburban residences from 1886 to 1923 as reflections of his belief that the home should be inhabited in ways that nurture an optimal liberal life. Morley sought to effect a highly controlled environment that, largely shorn of bric-a-brac, ensured 'a large and serene internal activity' (1867e: 170). Such serenity, he felt, was crucial to maintaining cultivated detachment. This arduous practice, which I call 'impersonal domesticity', attempted to make the abstractions of detachment, which may otherwise seem sterile and disembodied, part of a meaningfully lived experience.

Browning's Casa Guidi could not have been more different from Morley's residences. Spontaneous, experiential and exhibiting Browning's characteristic predilection towards history and openness to other worlds, the interior decoration of Casa Guidi reflected an approach to his surroundings that had been cultivated in his childhood and youth and through his republican political leanings. Chapter 4 rereads Casa Guidi's interior not, as has been traditionally understood, as exemplifying middle-class Victorian decorative practices but rather as a religiously inflected liberal space – liberal in so far as, in the process of acquiring, arranging and displaying objects, he sought to recognise their individuality and particularity, and religious inasmuch as the objects signified for him the universality of human historicality.

Instead of organising my chapters strictly on the basis of chronology, I focus on commonalities in the spaces I study. By considering the effects of institutional material cultures on Mill's and Arnold's liberal thought, I demonstrate that, although liberal ideas had material consequences, they also have material genealogies. My third and fourth chapters contribute to the burgeoning literature on the complexity of men's relationship to their dwellings by considering how liberal ideas in turn moulded domestic space.

Organising my study in this way also enables me to juxtapose Mill, Arnold and Morley with Browning. Although deeply responsive to the political and social events of their time, all four frequently engaged in what Morley calls 'the first effort of the serious spirit': 'to disengage itself from the futile hubbub which is sedulously maintained by the bodies of rival partisans in philosophy and philosophical theology' (1873: 470). He explains:

> This effort after detachment naturally takes the form of criticism of the past, the only way in which a man can take part in the discussion and propagation of ideas, while yet standing in some sort aloof from the agitation of the present. (470)

For Elaine Hadley, this statement by Morley, which she glosses, encapsulates one of the formal principles providing ballast to the (singular) liberal frame of mind: an 'ability to think abstractly in the present and thus to simultaneously be in the moment but think outside it' (2010: 11). Yet, we might ask, what about those individuals whose lived liberalism did not include an aspiration for disinterested thought? Whose notion of viewing something properly involved proximity, not distance? Whose approach to history was intuitive rather than analytical? Eschewing objectivisation (Mill), distantiation (Arnold) and impersonality (Morley), Browning allowed the epiphany to inspire his imagination of fictional personages in their historical contexts. Unlike the modes with which Mill, Arnold and Morley were concerned, Browning's suggests that seeing properly requires restraining the overdeveloped mind to allow the fusion of sensory experience and emotion to serve as its own kind of knowledge.

Notes

1. This is not to say that, before Mill, the mind was not understood in these terms. 'The domain of physical space has always been a common source of metaphors for the domain of consciousness', Sylvia Adamson contends (1990: 512). Against this trans-historical formulation ('always'), my inclination is to develop a historically nuanced understanding of how spatial metaphors and associated modes of thinking function differently in various periods.
2. As starting points, see Vincent 1972 and T. Jenkins 1994.
3. Numerous studies focusing on Gladstone include Parry 1986, Matthew 1986 and Winstanley 1990.
4. Gladstone also briefly served as prime minister in 1886 before returning to Downing Street for his final term (1892–4).
5. Although covering roughly the same era, my book differs from Goodlad's deft analysis of the fraught relationship between the individual and the state. She demonstrates that accounts of the period relying on Michel Foucault's early work on panopticism have failed to recognise the inadequacy of their analytic methods in accurately describing the British political context. Characterised by decentralisation, anti-statism and flourishing networks of private philanthropy, British liberal culture is more properly analysed, she contends, through indirect forms of governance. Yet we are both interested in 'promoting a more rigorous and expansive understanding of liberalism' than either recent critiques or recuperative approaches have allowed (Goodlad 2003: ix).
6. See Vernon 1993: 1–14, 331–9 and Crook and Crook 2007.
7. For a pellucid foundational argument on liberalism's incorporation of republican values, see Burrow 1985. Biagini has since claimed, 'Victorian liberalism was both individualist *and* "republican" at one and the same time. There was no opposition between these characteristics, because, rather than being opposed, they were merely different facets of the same tradition' (2003: 58).
8. On Tudor House, see Prettejohn 1997. On social and aesthetic experiments at Red House, see Helsinger 2008.
9. On Carlyle's house, see Picker 2003: 41–81; on Martineau's, see Easley 2006; on Ruskin's Brantwood estate, see Hanley 2015.

10. C. A. Bayly and I share an interest in the relationship between mental deliberation and public collaboration, debate and circulation, although his work is in the context of nineteenth-century Calcutta and Bombay (2012). Those who subscribed to, transformed or were otherwise engaged in developing liberal ideas on the subcontinent, Bayly claims, were not simply establishing institutions, such as learned societies or educational foundations, or developing robust party politics; they were also 'initiating a new code for living one's life; a new way of being human' (2012: 132). Thus, studying the 'lived life of ideas', or the 'performative aspect of liberalism', is imperative because it 'provides the intermediation between intellectual and social history' (Bayly 2012: 132).

11. In *George Eliot in Society: Travels Abroad and Sundays at the Priory*, McCormack locates Eliot and Lewes's home at the centre of an international social circle. Her discussion of the Priory's architectural and decorative aspects and their relationship to intellectual production is brief (2013: 30–3).

12. After Brassey's death, her husband, Liberal Member of Parliament Thomas Brassey, built an extension to their home as a museum in her memory.

13. The forms of abstract embodiment Hadley identifies and delineates are theoretical constructs that do not, as she readily admits, 'fulfill the material requirements of actual, "real" subjecthood' (2010: 18). Thus, the forms of abstract embodiment she analyses are not 'physical bodies per se, at least not primarily physical bodies, but are always in a complex relation to them' (2010: 16).

14. George Russell also drew on the letters to pen a short sketch of the author's life, *Matthew Arnold*, published in 1904.

15. See, in particular, Hamilton 1999, Machann 1998 and Murray 1997.

16. In Morrison 2010 I tracked the emergence of a wounded masculinist liberal subject through analysing *Wuthering Heights* and *The Mill on the Floss*, two novels focused on slightly different phases of a historical transition in which the new bourgeois property-owning class secures its hegemony. In retrospect, I treated liberalism generically and ascribed to it many of the tendencies accompanying tumultuous economic changes that some strands of liberalism resist. For a persuasive reconsideration of 'what a more robust engagement with certain liberal ideas . . . might contribute to the radical enterprise', see Goodlad 2008: 9.

17. Judith Neiswander's study is an exception in so far as, according to her, 'The ideas that emerge from the decorating literature [of the period] cluster around the concept of cultural liberalism' (2008: 7). But Neiswander focuses almost exclusively on a few phrases of Mill's, which she sees as authorising the expression of individuality in one's choice of domestic goods and furnishings. In addition, she makes only passing mention of the existing scholarship on liberalism, when, in quoting David Wayne Thomas, who has attempted to recuperate aspects of the Victorian liberal legacy, she misreads him – or inadvertently leads her readers to do

so – as criticising liberalism 'as a dangerous ideology, assumed "to encode a baleful atomistic individualism and to perpetuate dominant interests of gender, class, race, and nation"' (Neiswander 2008: 7).

18. Generally, institutional material culture has been neglected in favour of domestic culture. However, recent books – such as Susan David Bernstein's *Roomscape* (2013), which elaborates, through an examination of the British Museum Reading Room, a notion of exteriority (in contrast to the dominance of interiority) – have begun shifting that emphasis. Although unconcerned with practices of reading and writing, Jane Hamlett's fascinating *At Home in the Institution* explores domestic residences within institutional settings (2015).

19. Indeed, these places have only recently drawn the attention of historians more generally. On clubs, see B. Black 2012 and Milne-Smith 2011. Although studies of the office as it appears in popular culture have been published, we still await a definitive history.

20. Steedman, however, is soon plunged into a 'crisis of too-much' when she learns of the existence of 'voluminous' sources 'quite unknown to the West Yorkshire Archive Service and to the National Register of Archives' (2007: 9).

21. Rice and Penner visit Red House as part of their investigation into 'the role of images in constructing histories of the interior' (2004: 271). Michie and Warhol travel to Knole to see for themselves 'the private spaces we knew from [George] Scharf's diaries' (2015: 189).

22. In addition to Michie and Warhol, from whom I have drawn inspiration over the years, see A. Burton 2006, Steedman 2002, H. Bradley 1999, Koven 2014 and Lepore 2001.

23. William Stafford remarks on this peculiarity: the autobiography 'lacks almost all sense of place; of all the houses and neighbourhoods in which Mill lived, only Forde Abbey [a Cistercian monastery in Dorset where Mill had been a guest] is described' (1998: 53).

24. Tosh discusses the commonplace phrase 'religion of the home' (1999a: 36).

Chapter 1

John Stuart Mill's Ascent

Londoners had never seen anything quite like it. After extensive reconstruction during the late 1790s (Makepeace 2010: 17), East India House, located on the south side of Leadenhall Street, a principal thoroughfare in the City of London, reopened in April 1800. Designed in the Hellenic Ionic style, the headquarters of the East India Company was approximately 200 feet long and 60 feet high. It consisted of two austere wings offset by a balustrade and a hexastyle entrance portico crowned by a pediment. On a pedestal above the apex of the pediment was Britannia, spear in hand, riding a lion. Flanking Britannia on pedestals on either side of the pediment were the figures of Europe and Asia, riding a horse and a camel respectively. Many considered the building 'the most faultless structure of the kind in London', as one admirer described it (J. Anderson 1835: 340), and numbered it 'among the most magnificent [public structures] in the city' (Lewis 1831: 131). Its effect on passers-by was arresting (Figure 1.1).[1]

The East India Company, tracing its roots to a private maritime trading organisation formed by royal charter at the beginning of the seventeenth century and a subsequent merger between rival merchants, had operated from this site since 1648, the year it became a permanent joint-stock organisation. Its previous two headquarters on the site were impressive.[2] But this headquarters was distinguished by the tympanum of the pediment, which towered over the principal entrance: unlike the tympana of similarly stylised buildings, it was not plain. Contemporary commentators could cite no other example in the United Kingdom of a tympanum enriched by sculpture.[3] (Until the construction on Pall Mall in the late 1820s of the Greek Revivalist Athenaeum clubhouse, the focus of Chapter 2, the expensive technique of adding a bas-relief frieze to a building's exterior would not be tried again in London.) The frieze, designed by the noted sculptor John Bacon the Elder, proclaimed British magnanimity

Figure 1.1 East India House. Source: T. Malton, *A Picturesque Tour through the Cities of London and Westminster*, 1799; Trustees of the British Museum.

and benevolence. It depicted King George III, dressed in Roman armour, safeguarding commerce in the East with figures representing Order, Wisdom, Religion and Justice by his side. The figure of the king suggested a defensive rather than a militarily aggressive posture. He held a downturned, possibly unsheathed sword in one hand. With shield in the other hand, he protected Britannia and Liberty, locked in an embrace. In the background were Industry and Integrity, standing near a city barge and other symbols of London. Asia, surrounded by various symbols of commerce, including Mercury and Navigation, and by tritons and seahorses, poured forth her treasures at Britannia's feet. The barge's proximity to Integrity and Industry emphasised the munificence of the mission of the East India Company, whose ships had docked for centuries in Blackwall in London's East End, with their cargo then barged to the City of London ('East India docks' 1994). In return for India's riches, Britannia emancipated Asia from all that is superstitious, primitive and oppressively traditional by bestowing on her the qualities Britannia herself exemplified. The pediment was, in material form, the essence of an argument advanced since the seventeenth century: 'trade depended upon liberty, and . . . liberty could therefore be the foundation of empire' (Armitage 2000: 143).[4]

Beyond its ornamentation suffused with symbolism reflecting prevailing cultural assumptions, India House was a working environment that, through habitual use, contributed to shaping the dispositional knowledge of its occupants. John Stuart Mill – beginning as a junior clerk under the tutelage of his father, James Mill, who had recently been appointed assistant examiner of Indian correspondence – passed under the pediment each weekday morning to draft and, later, to oversee drafting of authoritative policy statements and official guidance to the governing bodies in India. Like his father, John Stuart Mill would rise through the ranks to become examiner of Indian correspondence, the second-highest position in the East India Company's home service. But their trajectories differed. James Mill, a mature man in his mid-forties, was hired largely based on opinions about how the company might more effectively rule the subcontinent that he had recently expressed in a weighty, three-volume work, his *History of British India*. He occupied key positions that enabled his implementation of these opinions: assistant to the examiner (1819–21), second examiner (1821–3), assistant examiner (1823–30) and examiner (1830–6). Conversely, John Stuart Mill entered East India House as a teenager in May 1823, holding an unsalaried clerical position in the Examiner's Office; transferring in March 1825 to the Correspondence Branch immediately after it was established within the office; becoming a modestly salaried clerk there in 1826, on completing his three-year period of probation;[5] then, beginning in 1828, being promoted to a series of senior management positions; finally, becoming examiner nearly thirty years later, in 1856. He was the first employee recognised, through internal transfer and promotion, under a new system of quasi-meritocratic advancement established within the office in 1825. This scheme sought to reward and, more importantly, nurture the ethical competency necessary for rendering privately conceived and disinterestedly formed opinions on policy matters, a direction towards which the company had been inclining for decades.[6]

The position of examiner of Indian correspondence and records was established in 1769 by the company's Court of Directors, whose twenty-four members were subject to annual election by shareholders and term limited to four consecutive years.[7] As I will elaborate, the immediate context for this decision was the growing backlog of correspondence between London and officials in India, especially Bengal, which the company had annexed in 1757. But, in creating this position, the directors tilted the basis of company decision-making from interest to opinion: shareholders' concerns with maximising profit through trade were to be tempered by the judgements of a company employee, insulated from public opinion and from having to please shareholders, who immersed himself in Indian affairs and acquired the expert knowledge necessary for policymaking.

Throughout the late eighteenth and early nineteenth centuries proponents of different rationalities of government, vying for moral authority, floated competing policies for India's governance.[8] Orientalists, predominantly Tory, pursued a strategy of engraftment: the slow blending of Western knowledge and practices with traditional learning and languages. Anglicists, mainly Whigs and later Liberals, sought to impose the British model of westernisation. Utilitarians, political reformers at home, endeavoured to reform Indian laws and institutions predicated on utility, the greatest good for the greatest number. Each of these rationalities of government was tied to a particular mode of seeing. Orientalists and Anglicists championed an embodied, on-the-ground relation with India.[9] The instrument of this relation was sight: the Orientalist gaze, with its fascination with an exoticised Other, and the missionary gaze, with its ambiguous mix of repulsion and attraction.[10] James Mill, who championed utilitarian reforms, subordinated the physiological aspects of sight to a schematising inward vision. The historian, he famously thought, could gain more knowledge of India by reading about it in 'his closet in England', therein 'extracting and ordering the dispersed and confused materials of a knowledge of India, once for all', than by spending his life in the subcontinent or learning its languages (J. Mill 1840: I, xxi, xii). In his opinion the Orientalists, who had influenced company policy for decades, had allowed themselves, while living in India, to come under the sway of phenomena that had left strong sensual impressions on them. Mystical rituals, rites and ceremonies were multisensory affairs that threatened the ability to control the data flowing into one's mind. Immersion in the cultural milieu, he believed, compromised impartiality.

John Stuart Mill's objectivising approach to Indian affairs, which relied on distancing oneself from an object of study, was in some respects akin to his father's mode of seeing. The younger Mill, who never visited India despite a thirty-five-year career dedicated to its reform, referred to his father, whose multivolume account of British India included trenchant criticism of Anglicism in addition to Orientalism, as 'the historian who first threw the light of reason on Hindoo society' (JSM 1985a: 320). Yet John Stuart concluded that, for reasons I will explore later in this chapter, the impartiality to which James Mill aspired was incompatible with the partisan, sectarian tendencies of utilitarianism, the philosophy to which he subscribed

(JSM 1985c: 210). The younger Mill would instead advance 'a relatively disinterested paternalism' (Goodlad 2015: 53), premised on opinion and discussion, which evolved coevally with his more general views on liberal subjectivity.

As John Stuart Mill rose through the ranks of the Examiner's Office, he began to articulate positions at variance with his father's. The growing difference in their thinking, several historians have contended, started with the younger Mill's well-known mental crisis of 1826–8.[11] Some of these scholars have depicted this episode of depression followed by psychological restoration as a protracted Oedipal struggle that finally resulted in his breaking with his father's teachings.[12] One need not trot out a hermeneutic that has inevitably led to interpretive excess to accept that, as John Stuart Mill's views on utilitarianism, learned from his father, changed, he formulated different convictions on India as well.[13] As Lynn Zastoupil compellingly asserts:

> At each step of his intellectual maturation – early training at his father's side, youthful rebellion accompanied by searching out alternative opinions, and mature retreat from the extreme positions of his rebellious phase – Mill took up, or abandoned, administrative ideas that have much in common with the more abstract concepts that he was absorbing or shedding. (1994: 4)

After many years during which scholarship on Mill accorded little significance to his career in imperial administration, a small number of able studies show how central it, in fact, appears to have been to his development as a liberal thinker. But despite calling attention to the importance of Mill's tenure at India House, these studies have focused principally on the discursive rather than the non-discursive, the immaterial (ideas) over the material (the architectural spaces within which and the mechanisms by which ideas were produced). India House, in other words, serves in these studies as a backdrop for the formation of Mill's independent opinions rather than as a constituent part of their production. Thus, while I am indebted to the insights this body of work provides, I argue that the material culture of governmental administration in the Examiner's Office played a role in shaping Mill's initial understanding of liberal thought as private and individuated and his understanding of the expression of thoughtful opinion as a key characteristic of liberal individuality. This chapter also considers how that environment contributed to his turn towards a more collectivist orientation.

Administrative Reform

Aimed from the outset at gaining a foothold in the lucrative spice trade in the East Indies and facing competition from both the Dutch and the Portuguese, the East India Company's founding merchants soon recognised the competitive advantage they could achieve through an exclusive commercial arrangement with mainland India to establish trading posts along its western and eastern coasts. With the patronage of the Mughal emperor Jahangir secured, the company set up a key trading post in Surat by 1612, with many more to follow, and built a considerable number of 'factories', consisting of combined warehouses (for cotton, silks, dyes, saltpetre and tea), office spaces and living accommodations for the senior merchants and their staff. These trading posts were not intended to be permanent settlements; the company acquired the land immediately surrounding the complexes to build up forts largely to protect its merchandise.[14] As the Mughal Empire collapsed in the mid-eighteenth century, however, the company launched an aggressive militaristic expansion inland, seizing territory from both the nawab of Bengal, a regional figure who had briefly taken Calcutta from the company in 1756, and the French, who sought to expand their colonial presence in South Asia. Robert Clive's and Hector Munro's decisive victories, in, respectively, the 1757 Battle of Plassey and the 1764 Battle of Buxar, resulted in the company's annexation of Bengal. Subsequent conflicts expanded the company's dominion throughout much of southern India and around Bombay and Madras. With France's defeat in the Seven Years War and the signing of the Treaty of Paris in 1763, the company found itself the pre-eminent military power in the subcontinent.[15]

Although it was an occupying military force, the company initially ruled Bengal in conformity with the system of dual government Robert Clive established as the first British administrator, relying on the nawab and his officials to administer justice and collect revenue. This proved untenable, however. As David Kopf summarises the problem, 'The local governor or Nawab, who ruled, did so without power, while the Company, which held the power, refused the responsibility of administration' (1969: 14).[16] In 1765 the company took direct control of civil administration, including enforcing payment of compulsory taxes, by maintaining a police force and strengthening the judiciary (Spear 1958: 502–3). Additionally, it established jurisdiction over criminal cases. (As early as 1670, Charles II had vested in the company the authority to levy taxes, administer justice, acquire land and keep a private army.) To solidify its position in South Asia, the company also formed alliances with provincial Indian princes and installed officials at their courts. Under this system of indirect rule, the so-called native states were granted limited internal autonomy while policies related to defence and foreign relations fell within the company's purview.

Some in London feared the company had become dangerously autonomous. Arising 'from very slender beginnings', the company had grown into 'a state of the highest importance', the anonymous author of an article in *The Monthly Review* noted in 1772. 'They are no longer mere traders, and confined in their privileges; they are sovereigns over fertile and populous territories' (Anon. 1772: 236). The author articulated a widespread concern with the company as a vehicle for individual enrichment. A succession of scandals involving company employees dismissed from service in India, having been accused of avaricious conduct and self-aggrandising behaviour, helped engender this view.

Beginning with Pitt's India Act of 1784, the British government implemented a series of measures designed to make the company more responsible to the Crown. The act instituted a Board of Commissioners for the Affairs of India, commonly known as the Board of Control, whose members included the Chancellor of the Exchequer and a secretary of state, to oversee and regulate the company's involvement in political matters (Foster 1917). The company's Court of Directors was, thereafter, accountable to the Board. But a question remained: how should a commercial enterprise govern territories over which it claimed sovereignty? Eric Stokes has argued that colonial rule in India must be understood in differentiated terms. An era of militaristic interventionism, designed to extract and defend the accumulation of wealth, was superseded by a period in which competing strategies were 'consciously directed upon Indian society itself' (Stokes 1959: 27). These strategies varied according to the systems of moral authority – Orientalism and Anglicism – that attempted to exert influence over Indian policy in this period.[17]

In Bengal, even after its annexation, the company maintained a tactical policy of respecting social and religious differences, as well as legal customs and precedents, to ensure uninterrupted trade and full cooperation by the local intermediaries. For example, in assuming responsibility for the administration of justice, the company, while redefining property law in British terms, utilised many aspects of the Indian legal culture. The Persian language was used in the law courts and official correspondence, and Islamic law governed criminal matters (Raman 1994: 741–50). From 1774 to 1785, under Warren

Hastings's administration as Governor-General of Bengal, a position appointed by and responsible to the Court of Directors, deference to local customs continued (J. Bernstein 2000: 89–90; Davies 1935: 433). But Hastings also encouraged cultural intercourse. Before his arrival, company officials, who were mostly ignorant of India's languages and customs, had only limited contact with residents (Spear 1963: 127). Hastings, by contrast, felt it was necessary not simply to respect religious and cultural differences but to understand the culture's history. His 'Orientalist ethic of administration' presupposed that 'one can only govern on the basis of an almost intuitive linguistic sympathy with those who are the objects of government' (Osborne 1994: 298). Thus, East India Company troops participated in celebratory processions for Hindu deities; its offices followed the local calendar, opening on Sundays but closing on Indian holidays (Forbes 1951: 22); and officials were not prohibited, as they were after 1830, from wearing traditional Indian dress at public functions (Tarlo 1996: 36). Hastings offered opportunities for employees to learn South Asian languages and study the subcontinent's sacred and literary texts. By establishing a madrassa, the Mohammedan College in Calcutta, initially at his expense, he sought to educate the indigenous population in the principles of Islamic law and to provide classes in Arabic and Persian. The founding of the madrassa paved the way, ten years later, for the creation of its counterpart, the Sanskrit College in Benares, by Jonathan Duncan, the company's representative there (McCully 1966: 26). These two educational institutions, it was hoped, would produce administrators from the native ranks, both Muslim and Hindu, for the government's judicial and revenue branches.[18]

The impeachment trial of Hastings on charges of official mismanagement and personal corruption, which commenced in Parliament in 1788 and ended with his acquittal in 1795,[19] provided Anglicists with ample opportunity to press their case for a different approach. Charles Cornwallis, Hastings's successor as Governor-General (1786–93), sought ways to eradicate Indian customs and beliefs. He was encouraged by Charles Grant, then an influential member of the Board of Trade, which managed the company's commercial interests from Calcutta. Grant argued for cultural and linguistic intervention into Indian society instead of sensitivity towards it.

Throughout his administration, Cornwallis introduced a series of reforms designed 'to make everything as English as possible in a country which resembles England in nothing', as Thomas Munro quipped years later, while serving as governor of Madras (Munro 1987: 241).

In the judicial sphere, as I have noted, criminal cases were brought under the company's purview, and, while Hindu and Islamic law were still administered, the Muslim criminal code was sheared of facets perceived to be unacceptably inhumane. Cornwallis's most significant reform was an agreement between the company and the zamindars, the revenue collectors responsible for collecting taxes from the peasants.[20] Grant, who drafted the dispatch from the Court of Directors establishing the policy of permanent settlement, held that India's great stability before the conquest of Bengal by the Persians had been secured by its system of fixed land tenures. 'The great evil was annual leases', Ainslie Embree writes, summarising Grant's thinking and quoting from a parliamentary debate, 'for these meant insecurity of tenure and the arbitrary fixing of rents according to what the tax collectors thought the peasants could pay, with the result that industry was "wholly discouraged, for it was taxed in proportion to its exertion"' (1962: 114). Under the Permanent Settlement Act of 1793, zamindars were recognised not merely as tax collectors but as owners of the land under their jurisdiction, provided they paid the company a fixed portion of their revenues. This system, which spread beyond Bengal to all of northern India, was designed to spur economic growth by introducing the concept of property rights and establishing a large class of landowners on the English model.

Beyond these judicial and economic reforms, Grant advocated evangelisation of the subcontinent. Social reforms alone, he believed, could not exterminate the 'internal principles of depravity' so characteristic of Indian cultures (Grant [1797]: 47). Only Christianity would facilitate an effective break with these principles, and English-language instruction would render Indians far more amenable to the teachings of the Good Book (171). Through a shared 'identity of sentiments and principles', Grant rhapsodised, the hearts of the British and the Indians would be cemented together (204).

Given the slowness of correspondence between India and London, it was unfeasible for the members of the Court of Directors to involve themselves in every decision taken by Hastings, Cornwallis and others on the ground. Instead, detailed reports of their actions were sent to London; these reports were reviewed and commented on; and, with remarks attached to the original submission, one copy was filed at India House and another returned to the sender.[21] On this archive – which documented the reasons for all policy decisions as well as the strategies for their implementation, refinement or curtailment – rested the company's governmental authority. Mindful of its voluminous correspondence, the Court of Directors was concerned that its continuous changes of membership would cause a lack of institutional memory and continuity of policy. Thus, the directors determined on both ethical and practical grounds that a 'better arrangement and a more strict inspection' of these reports necessitated hiring an 'able person' whose responsibility would be 'to inspect, examine and make the necessary References to and Observations on the important Branches of the Indian correspondence'.[22] The position of examiner of Indian correspondence and records was established soon thereafter.

Breaking with the company's policy of internal promotion based on longevity, the directors appointed Samuel Wilks, an outsider. He was hired largely because, as noted by the Committee of Correspondence, a standing committee appointed by the Court of Directors to consider all letters and reports sent to the Court and to serve 'as a central problem-scanning body in the whole decision system' (Chaudhuri 1978: 29), the directors had 'received a very favourable account of . . . [his] Abilities, Experience, and good Character' as an individual engaged in respectable 'Public Business'.[23] If good government in India required an effective and efficient system of document filing and retrieval in London, it depended even more on the expertise of the person charged with examining those communications. Focus, thoughtfulness and discernment were all implied criteria. Technical competence, no matter how finely honed, was insufficient. To use the system effectively, the examiner, besides having legible penmanship, mastery of grammar and organisational abilities, was required to demonstrate ethical competence: distinctive perceptual abilities, interpretive capacity and independent discretionary judgement. Yet, lacking a system to nurture ethical competence, the directors were unable to judge accurately whether Wilks, or anyone for that matter, was right for the job. In any case they found him unable to keep up with the workload. In January 1770, a few months after he was hired, the company appointed one of his sons, Thomas, assistant examiner;[24] two other sons soon joined the office as clerks. In May 1770 the company also hired George Oldmixon as the 'Compiler and Writer of the Company's Foreign Correspondence with their Settlements in the East Indies', leaving Wilks the sole responsibility of examination (Moir 1986: 124). Despite this reorganisation, a year later the Committee of Correspondence recorded exasperation with the 'confused and disorderly state' of the records 'to which frequent recourse is necessary to be had'. This disarray had led to numerous 'inconveniences, difficulties and loss of time'.[25]

Even after Parliament passed the Regulating Act of 1773, which enhanced continuity by stipulating staggered four-year terms for the directors, the Court of Directors found the examiner's role crucial to steady Indian administration. By 1776 the examiner, initially a functionary within the Secretary's Office, which received all correspondence and distributed it among the various departments, was head of his own office. In 1782, with Wilks's health in decline, the directors incorporated the compiler's responsibilities into those of the examiner and appointed Samuel Johnson – no relation to Boswell's idol – to the position in an interim capacity. This was an unusual step. Although Wilks had been brought in from the outside, the company's hiring and promotion practices were otherwise fundamentally unaltered. Throughout its existence, it was a great resource for middle-class patronage, often infused with nepotism, as the appointment of Wilks's sons indicates. Employees were typically appointed to routine clerical positions; promotion was strictly determined by departmental seniority. Thus, the Wilks brothers had every expectation that, with their father incapacitated, Thomas, having worked as assistant examiner for more than a decade, would ascend to the position. By choosing Johnson instead, the directors affirmed that ability trumped departmental longevity.[26] Unlike Samuel Wilks, Johnson, formerly employed in the Secretary's Office, was a company insider with known capacities. But he had no previous connection with the office of which he became the interim head. In 1785 his position was made permanent. Under his stewardship, the office entered a period of stability that lasted nearly two decades.

By the turn of the century the directors were relying almost solely on the examiner of Indian correspondence to draft, utilising background provided by his assistants, all political, revenue, military, judicial and public dispatches. In 1804 the Committee of Correspondence recognised the examiner's workload was 'too bulky' for any one person to manage.[27] Steps were taken to relieve the examiner of his onerous burden, including reassigning military correspondence outside the office and creating several new positions to assist him, to be staffed from within the office based on longevity (Moir 1979: 26–7). By 1809, however, the Committee of Correspondence was urging the directors to look outside India House immediately for 'Men of matured knowledge and talents' who 'with expedition, intelligence and Ability' could assist in corresponding with India.[28] Candidates with refined perceptual capacities of concentration, scrupulous attention to detail and careful reading had to be identified. Such capacities were not necessarily cultivated through copying, précis-writing, document filing and retrieval and other routine clerical duties. The directors hired three assistant secretaries from the outside, including

William McCulloch, who would assume the office's top spot on Johnson's death in 1817.[29] In 1819, with three positions as assistant to the examiner vacant, the directors again took the extraordinary step of filling them with external appointees. James Mill was hired to oversee revenue matters;[30] Edward Strachey to manage judicial affairs;[31] and the poet and satirical novelist Thomas Love Peacock, who would succeed James Mill as examiner (1836–56), to hold a miscellaneous portfolio of responsibilities (Moir 1990: xii).[32]

By recruiting individuals from outside the company known for their intellectual capabilities, the directors solidified distinctions among employees.[33] 'From being a very small department, staffed mainly by Company clerks trained only in the rudiments of writing and accounts', Martin Moir relates, the Examiner's Office 'developed into an advanced semi-élite organisation manned by some of the leading British intellectuals' (1979: 25). In March 1825 the directors formalised the distinction between types of labour by establishing within the Examiner's Office a Correspondence Branch that rigorously cordoned off individuated, mental labour (conceptualisation, formulation and articulation of authoritative policy statements) from the mechanical tasks performed by ordinary clerks (Moir 1990: xiv–xv; Moir 1979: 36).

With these changes, the Examiner's Office came to occupy a large portion of the building's second floor (Figure 1.2).[34] Relatively little is known about the upper floors, where most work was done. But the public areas were frequently described in print, even including the dimensions of various rooms. Remarking on 'the grandeur of the house within', one account of the old India House of 1729, which was incorporated into the remodelled and extended structure completed in 1800, notes that 'the public hall and the committee room [are] scarce inferior to anything of the like nature in the City' (Gonzales 1888: 38). The old India House nonetheless lacked what David Hughson – the pseudonymous author of several topographical sketches of London during the first two decades of the nineteenth century – deemed the degree of 'grandeur' one necessarily associates with 'the opulent corporation to which it belonged' (1805: 158). The greater the responsibilities assumed by the company, the greater the grandeur its headquarters required. The interior of the new India House, a 'vast edifice' (Hughson 1817: 6), consisted of 'a great number of apartments and offices, several of the former being of large dimensions and noble architecture' (Lewis 1831: 131). The public rooms were 'considerably decorated' (Britton et al. 1838: 37) and 'embellished either with emblematical designs and paintings illustrative of commerce, statues and portraits of distinguished individuals who have

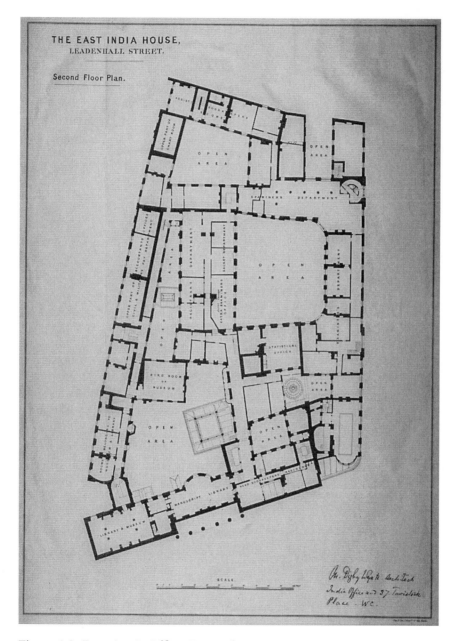

Figure 1.2 Examiner's Office, East India House, c.1850s.
Source: London Metropolitan Archives, City of London.

been connected with the company, or with India generally, views of Indian scenery, or architectural ornaments' (Lewis 1831: 131). The General Court Room, where regular directors' and quarterly proprietors' meetings were held, was 'splendidly ornamented by gilding and by large looking-glasses' (Knight 1843: 61). It was 'extremely' bright during the day (Allen and Wright 1839: 701), illuminated by 'windows near the ceiling' (Knight 1843: 61). The room featured massive Corinthian pilasters and carved mahogany furniture decorated by Doric and Ionic capitals and the company's lion, holding a crown. A particularly striking element was the chimney-piece and overmantel: a large bas-relief frieze in white marble designed by the Flemish sculptor John Michael Rysbrack for the old India House. It depicted Britannia seated on a globe by the seashore, looking towards the East as Asia, Africa and India pay their respects, with the latter offering a box of jewels. Six oil paintings, hanging from the cornice, illustrated the company's main factories in Bombay, Calcutta, Cape Town, Madras, St Helena and Tellicherry. Although these canvases, produced by British artists, served as a visual reminder of the company's extensive overseas territories, Indian export wares were rigorously excluded from display except within the museum space set aside for that purpose.

Studies of India House, although limited in number, are enormously helpful in disclosing the company's internal operations and employees' day-to-day work experience. Yet none include floor plans or precise details of spatial arrangements.[35] I was able to obtain the floor plans, which shed some light on how offices were configured, but these architectural renderings provide scant information about the space as workers inhabited it. It is impossible to glean through first-hand experience any insight, however tenuous, into the space the Examiner's Office occupied, because India House was demolished in 1861. Thus, for many years I have made my way to the British Library, St Pancras, to consult the East India Company's vast administrative archive.

The company records, visitors' accounts and illustrations housed at the British Library and the floor plans at the London Metropolitan Archives, when juxtaposed with recollections of employees from other departments, give some sense of the working environment of the Examiner's Office. In the decades following the establishment of the Correspondence Branch in 1825, the office was allocated additional space. But, throughout, it chiefly comprised a messengers' anteroom, a long clerks' room, private offices for the examiner and the assistant examiners and a meeting space for the Secret Committee, which I will discuss shortly. Overall, the upper floors, including the area assigned to the Examiner's Office, have been described as 'gloomy and dingy" (Philips 1940a: 1). Company records suggest this applied mainly to workspaces inhabited by clerical staff. There were ongoing complaints about the dimly lit clerks' room, where Mill started his career; at one point a skylight was contemplated (Anon. 1857).

The recollections of Charles Lamb, an employee for several decades in the Accountant's Office, provide a striking contrast with accounts documenting the publicly visible interior spaces of the building. He refers to the 'labyrinthine passages, and light-excluding, pent-up offices, where candles for one half the year supplied the place of the sun's light' (1875: 166). The large rooms where the accounting clerks toiled were, instead of being spacious, generally partitioned into 'compounds' (compartments). The main function of these compounds, each of which included six clerks screened off by seven-foot-high partitions, was the coordination of the workflow among the 'collection of simples' (qtd in Lamb 1876: 261 n. 1). Clerical staffers sat close together on high stools, perched over shared slanted wooden desks fitted with heavy inkwells. 'Oh, how I remember our legs wedged into those uncomfortable sloping desks, where we sat elbowing each other', Lamb recalls (1870: 345). The arrangement of staff within compounds had other benefits besides coordinating their work, at least as far as the directors were concerned, including the ability to expand or eliminate compounds without making structural changes and to heat the architectural space by one large fire. The clerks evidently failed to see the method of heating as an unqualified benefit. Low-level employees often complained of the 'sickly and stuffy' atmosphere of rooms that lacked ventilation (McKechnie 1946: 227).

The long clerks' room in the Examiner's Office – accessible through a swing door, upholstered in baize for soundproofing, at the end of the messengers' anteroom – appears to have been arranged along the same lines as other comparably sized divisions such as the Accountant's Office. Grouped into compounds, the clerks would have had an experience similar to Lamb's. Because the directors required complete copies of all documents to which draft dispatches referred, the 'simples' in the Examiner's Office performed the labour of abstracting, indexing and reproducing facsimiles from the vast archive. When clerks gathered around the fireplace at the far end of the room, as they were frequently seen to do, it was as much for the physical relief of standing as for warmth. The fireplace may also have been attractive because of the light it cast. The 'screened boxes' separating the compounds were positioned near the windows, which would have provided some natural light. However, during winter months, daylight was limited to as few as five hours a day, and on grey, dreary days at any time of the year natural light would have been minimal. Also, the screens would have blocked light from the rest of the room, including the 'matted passage' that ran along its length (Bain 1969: 64).

The Correspondence Branch, consisting of the assistant examiners and their assistants, was accessible from the clerks' room through another baize swing door. Occupying cellular offices, the assistant examiners would have appeared to the ordinary clerical staff, from whom they were physically and auditorily separated, as emblems of individual studiousness. Their offices were lofty, with woodwork, carpeting that provided sound absorption and colour, and, in contrast to the long clerks' room, good lighting (Anon. 1857). Adjacent to the private offices of the examiner and the assistant examiners was one of the most important architectural spaces in the building: the meeting room of the Secret Committee. Essentially an executive body made up of the company's chairman and deputy chairman, who were elected by their fellow directors, and a senior member of the Court of Directors, the Secret Committee dealt with urgent and politically sensitive matters.[36] The examiner of Indian correspondence served as the committee's secretary, and those with access to confidential materials relating to its work were required to sign oaths of secrecy (Philips 1940c: 702). Leading to a well-lit meeting room, which overlooked a courtyard, was a green baize door, which was latched open when the committee was not using the room.

From the late eighteenth century green baize doors were a standard feature of upper-class houses. They minimised noise emanating from the kitchen, scullery and related service areas. The use of green baize in the Examiner's Office to divide the meeting room from the rest of the office, while preventing discussions from being overheard, also marked its importance. It is not surprising that the East India Company's headquarters borrowed features from manor houses. It was, in fact, a house, incorporating the pre-existing building from 1729 as its main hall and western wing. Because the concept of purpose-built facilities was still in its earliest stages, the structure replicated the interior of a home: until the early 1800s, 'the commercial office function as we know it today was accommodated generally within other structural elements of the city' (Cowan and Fine 1969: 26).[37] India House also reproduced the class relations of an upper-class home (upstairs/downstairs), but with a difference: since clerks were mostly from middle- and upper-class families (Foster 1924: 235), distinctions among company employees in the eighteenth century indicated the extent of their social capital and, in the Examiner's Office after the establishment of the Correspondence Branch in 1825, their cultural capital. The perquisites for those with sufficient cultural capital were enhanced domestic-like conditions. John Stuart Mill not only obtained a cellular office furnished according to his tastes, where he received guests and worked on non-company-related writings and correspondence, but had a daily cooked breakfast of tea, buttered bread and a boiled egg delivered on his arrival at ten (Bain 1969: 64).

The various changes I have been documenting – introducing quasi-meritocratic criteria for staffing positions ('intelligence', 'ability'); spatially dividing intellectual and clerical labour; and establishing a separate office for the examiner within a 'domestic' environment – can be seen as attempts to stimulate, as a form of cultural capital, the privately conceived and individuated opinion of the examiner and the assistant examiners. We are not accustomed to thinking about policy documents as expressions of individual opinion. Bureaucratic writing, as Patrick Joyce characterises it, depends heavily on 'the extinction of the individual personality' (2010: 109). While it may be true, regarding the heyday of civil service administration, that 'the agency of the bureaucrat' is not evinced by official documents (Joyce 2010: 109), this would be an entirely misleading characterisation of John Stuart Mill's tenure at India House. When the examiner was an official within the Secretary's Office, regarded as 'a separate and distinct Officer', in the words of the Court of Directors, his independence was tempered by 'such Directions as shall be given him from time to time by the Secretary'.[38] But later the directors depended almost solely on the judgement of the examiner and, by extension, his assistants. They saw his considered and expert opinion on political, judicial, educational and taxation matters as an important ethical component of Indian governance. Through an exhaustive scrutiny of correspondence, the examiner's duty, responsibility and obligation was to form ideas about governing India which would then, through his dispatches, be expressed as thoughtful opinion. The examiner, as Samuel Johnson testified in 1813 before a select committee appointed by the Court of Proprietors, was granted significant discretionary autonomy to 'originate': 'It is possible that, on some particular and important points, I may receive some directions from the Chairs [chair and deputy chair of the Court of Directors]; but that seldom happens' (East India Company 1814: 47). Robert Hudson, then an assistant examiner, described the process of preparing a dispatch in similar terms. 'The officers under my direction collect the various matters and paragraphs relating to the dispatch', he explained. 'The Examiner forms the paragraphs of the dispatch; but it is not unfrequent that the Directors frame paragraphs themselves, though the general practice . . . is for the Examiner to prepare them in the first instance' (East India Company 1814: 64).[39]

When James Mill assumed increasingly significant responsibilities in the Examiner's Office, the intellectual influence he brought to the company was widely acknowledged. 'I am going to British India, but I shall not be Governor-General', William Bentinck told Mill before setting sail for the subcontinent to take up that position, which he assumed in 1828 and held until 1835. 'It is you that will be Governor-General' (qtd in Bentinck 1977: xv). In his *Autobiography* John Stuart Mill recalls that his father's 'real opinions on Indian subjects' largely carried the day; his draft dispatches as both assistant examiner and examiner made it through the approval process 'without having their force much weakened' (1981: 30). That John Stuart Mill saw his drafts of company dispatches as expressions of his privately conceived opinion is suggested by the detailed record of them he kept.[40] He understood them not as bureaucratic documents but as contributions to the expert study and governance of India. 'I have indeed written no small number of pages on subjects of great importance viz. the "affairs of the Guicowar" and the "disputes between the Rao of Cutch and certain Wagur chiefs"', he proclaimed in an 1840 letter to an acquaintance, 'with one considerable advantage over the more speculative topics which I have sometimes written about, that I can foresee much more exactly the effects with which my lucubrations will be attended' (1991: 54).

A Matter of Opinion

As I have noted, James Mill was hired as assistant to the examiner shortly after publishing *The History of British India*. Informed by a historicist methodology, Mill's monumental work sought 'to ascertain the true state' of India in 'the scale of civilization' (J. Mill 1840: II, 152).[41] One of Mill's aims in penning 'a *judging* history' (I, xv) was to refute the belief, shaped by influential Orientalist scholarship, that under Hinduism India had achieved an advanced society the Muslims had decimated.[42] In his judgement the 'Mohammedans' had attained a higher state of civilisation in general. Following earlier incursions from the north, including a succession of Muslim conquerors beginning with Mahmud of Ghazni, the Mughal Empire established itself in India as a 'native' rather than a 'foreign' government (II, 485), bringing about an advance in civilisation. The Muslims did not have castes or a ruling class; their form of government was better because it was not afflicted by the exercise of priestly power; they possessed better manners and a more advanced system of law; and their religion, which acknowledged one God, was indisputably superior (II, 486–516). Mill contended that they were also more advanced in moral character, fine arts and literature, including historiography (II, 518–22). Orientalist scholarship, he held, romanticised Indian history and culture; it was thereby complicit in enslaving the Hindus, who were afflicted by despotism and priestcraft, by failing to shine the light of reason on ignorance and superstition.

In his view Hindu India, with its corrupt and inefficient governing caste, defective code of laws, religious tyranny and general air of ignorance, lacked all the distinguishing characteristics of civilisation. Hinduism was 'the most enormous and tormenting superstition that ever harassed and degraded any portion of mankind', preventing Indian society from advancement (II, 187). India was an archaic space whose inhabitants lived in asynchronous time: 'in beholding the Hindus of the present day, we are beholding the Hindus of many ages past; and are carried back, as it were, into the deepest recesses of antiquity' (II, 214). Attempts to strengthen and preserve existing institutions and customs, which reflected a primitive developmental stage, were therefore misguided. 'If they have conceived the Hindus to be a people of high civilization, while they have in reality made but a few of the earliest steps in the progress to civilization', he claimed, 'it is impossible that in many of the measures pursued for the government of that people, the mark aimed at should not have been wrong' (II, 153).

Mill's argument should not be seen as a narrowly focused racial interpretation of cross-cultural difference. Instead, he contended that human nature was universal but had developed unevenly through time and in different nations (Majeed 1992: 138). Thus, both Britons and Indians were, initially, 'rude'; however, in line with the Scottish historicism to which he subscribed for a time, Mill maintained that Britain had passed through distinct economic stages (hunting, herding, farming and commerce) that corresponded with more advanced civilisational phases.

For him the task of the British was to accomplish what the Muslims had not. More interventionist than the Orientalists, the Anglicists were closer to his thinking, but he was critical of many of their policies as well. For example, Cornwallis's attempt to concentrate wealth in the hands of a few through the Permanent Settlement of 1793, Mill complained, had been flawed. It had reproduced in India the great divide in Britain between the people, the benefits of whose labour needed to be secured by a more equitable economic scheme, and a rapacious aristocracy with its 'sinister interests'.[43] Mill may have had greater sympathy with the Anglicists than the Orientalists, but his *History of British India* outlined an approach differentiated from both.[44] Because he considered representative government entirely unsuited to an immature population, he prescribed legal, political and economic reforms to unleash the spirit of economic self-interest and self-help. These reforms would spur colonised subjects to better their material condition by, for example, protecting the right of property for those who cultivated land rather than a minority of elites; creating an impartial judicial system; and establishing a modest scheme of land taxation. Under a regime of progressive colonial despotism, corporeal life would be secured by outlawing superstitious rites such as sati and infanticide and implementing a set of laws to maintain public order. Mental life would be elevated through the promotion of useful knowledge.[45] These were the keys, he believed, to propelling Indian society out of its stagnant condition.

It was likely not despite but because of James Mill's censure of past East India Company practices that the directors selected him for a key position in the Examiner's Office. With the company's commercial operations waning, the directors surely saw him as someone who could help identify and elaborate the appropriate stylisation for ruling the subcontinent. In his *History* Mill, an advocate of free trade, had argued that Britannia's responsibility to secure the progressive improvement of her colonial subjects was irreconcilable with maximising profit.[46] The 1813 Charter Act, which stripped the corporation of its export monopoly in Indian trade and clarified the state's role as proprietor and the company's as manager of South Asian territories,[47] also called for social reforms. Conceptualising and implementing them required someone of Mill's calibre. But the act, by opening the country to Christian missionaries and setting aside significant funds for Indian education, seemed to direct the company towards the Anglicist solutions of which many directors had long been wary. Mill's criticism of both the Anglicist and the Orientalist approaches would have suggested to them the possibility of an alternative.

From his perspective as a proponent of utilitarianism who acknowledged British rule in India could not be undone, Mill was predisposed to accept the offer of a key managerial appointment in the Office of the Examiner of Indian Correspondence. 'Because utilitarian ethics aim at maximizing the sum total of happiness, there is a strong current in the theory which exalts good management as the greatest of skills', writes Alan Ryan. 'Maximizing happiness is a task which calls for organization and methodical administration . . .' (1972: 42–3). Mill would have seen a post in the East India Company as affording an opportunity to realise in India some of the reforms – legal, political, social and ecclesiastical – he hoped would one day transform England. Indeed, styling themselves as Radicals, Jeremy Bentham and James Mill, who were the architects of classical utilitarianism in the nineteenth century, John Stuart Mill and a number of their associates endeavoured but ultimately failed to constitute a political party that would pursue these aims at home.

The friendship between Mill and Bentham, begun in 1808, greatly benefitted both. Mill, who championed representative government, which he judged would minimise the predominating influence of any one class, drew Bentham into social and political affairs and facilitated his conversion to democracy. Bentham led Mill, who already held some degree of belief in associationist psychology, far more deeply into the theory, which he in turn helped to elaborate, and increasingly away from his historicist predilections.

Although an extensive account of utilitarianism and associationism cannot be offered here, I want to explicate some of the more salient points of these bodies of thought as they bear on Indian policy and John Stuart Mill. For Bentham and James Mill, humans were intrinsically predisposed to maximise their pleasure and minimise their pain. The only way to secure the greatest happiness for the greatest number was to remove external barriers to the pursuit of happiness while ensuring social and political institutions were reconstituted so as to foster social feeling, thereby moderating the selfish propensities of individuals. Utilitarians saw the House of Commons and the House of Lords, the ancient universities, the two political parties (Whigs and Tories) and the law courts as obstructing the maximisation of happiness.[48] But these were not the worst. As Leslie Stephen would later recall, 'The Utilitarians saw in the established church the most palpable illustration of a "sinister interest"' (1950: 478). The Church of England, they believed, was the pre-eminent means by which the aristocracy's power and privileges, their 'sinister interests' as a class, were maintained at the expense of the general welfare.

As a psychological theory, associationism appealed to utilitarians. It provided an account of mental life consistent with their presumptions about human motivations. It was also ballast for their arguments for social and political reform. In his *Analysis of the Phenomena of the Human Mind*, published in 1829 but expressing long-held beliefs, James Mill asserts that human character is formed by and sustained through embodied experience (1878: 127). Sensory data and perceptual stimuli experienced in childhood form rudimentary ideas or images – mental impressions – that serve as components of an individual's cognitive architecture. In maturity, the mind automatically organises these impressions into 'trains', sequences of ideas, according to the principle of contiguity (proximity in time and space) rather than, as earlier associationists had concluded, resemblance and causation (103–11). An association is stronger or weaker depending on the vividness of its impression and the frequency of the sensation: a child, for example, learns to call a particular woman 'mamma' because the word is uttered repeatedly when that woman is in sight (82–9).[49] Thus, complex ideas are founded on simple ideas generated by sensations, and abstract concepts are based on the averages of recurrence. Because associationism theorised the self as a product of its environment, it merged easily with the utilitarian aim of maximising happiness and welfare by changing the various social, economic and legal circumstances in which people lead their lives. The key to change is fostering appropriate associations through which enhancing social good correlates with pleasure and obstructing good with pain. Practices of thought, sentiment and belief are, therefore, the consequences of social change rather than its engines.

Once James Mill began working in the Examiner's Office, he focused on transforming India's environment so new associations could be formed. To assist him in this effort, which he pursued vigorously after being appointed to the second highest position in the Examiner's Office in April 1823, he secured for his son, a month later, a three-year unsalaried clerkship. Although nominally a clerk, John Stuart was tasked with the weighty responsibility of drafting dispatches on political affairs and educational policy under his father's supervision. The company had only just begun implementing a decade-old directive from Parliament concerning improvement of Indian education in the three presidencies: Bengal, Madras and Bombay. The 1813 charter renewal required the Governor-General to fund programmes for 'the revival and improvement of literature, and the encouragement of the learned natives of India, and for the introduction and promotion of a knowledge of the sciences among the inhabitants of the British territories in India' ('53 GEORGII III' 1841: 172). The ten members of the General Committee of Public Instruction, established in 1823 and charged with expending these funds, were predominantly Orientalists, including Holt Mackenzie, Henry Prinsep and Horace Hayman Wilson, who was for a time the committee's president.[50] The Orientalist members understood their mandate to include revitalising indigenous classical – Sanskritic and Arabic – learning. The vernaculars of India were considered suitable only for everyday use because they were too impoverished to convey European literary or scientific knowledge easily. Sanskrit or Arabic terminology and synonyms needed to be incorporated into the dialects. This additive policy, known as engraftment, aimed to raise from among the native population a cadre of highly educated intermediaries. The creation of an educated class, it was hoped, would in turn bring greater numbers of natives into the fold of Western civilisation. Members of the Committee of Public Instruction floated proposals to expand both the number of colleges that might invigorate the study of the Sanskritic literary tradition among the Brahman caste and the number of Arabic schools for the Muslim population.

James Mill was sceptical of this policy of engraftment and the financial support provided to Hindu seminaries and Islamic madrassas. In a February 1824 dispatch to Bengal, he argued that a premise on which these institutions were founded – making 'a favourable impression, by our encouragement of their literature, upon the minds of the natives' – was 'erroneous'.[51] Educational policy needed to have 'useful learning' alone as its end (J. Mill 1824: 1073). While he acknowledged the possibility of useful learning through Arabic and Sanskrit, he thought that founding institutions expressly to promote the study of Hindu and Islamic literature fell markedly short of the utility principle. Since 'Hindoo learning, or Mahomedan learning' were of little use, providing such instruction would simply compel the teaching of 'a great deal of what was frivolous, not a little of what was purely mischievous, and a small remainder indeed in which utility was in any way concerned' (1073). Mill's shrill critique of Hinduism in *The History of British India* indicates that he would have been disinclined to support a system that relied for the transmission of Western knowledge on what he perceived as a despotic priestcraft. Instead, Mill increasingly focused his energies on penning drafts on economic and legal reforms he considered essential to engendering a new social environment in India. He left the drafting of political and educational dispatches to his son, who by 1825 assumed almost sole responsibility for their preparation.

Initially, John Stuart Mill's dispatches recapitulated and extended his father's opinions. In a March 1825 dispatch to the presidency of Bengal, for example, he reaffirmed, 'There is nothing . . . which we regard as of greater importance than the diffusion of English language, and of European Arts and Sciences, among the Natives of

India' (JSM 1825: 167–8).[52] He also praised the financial support the presidency provided for construction of a permanent facility to house Hindu College, an educational institution originally called the Mahabidyala that indigenous intellectuals had established with the aim of providing English-language instruction and propagating Western art and literature.[53] In the same dispatch he lauded the presidency's having further strengthened the college by endowing it with a professorship in natural philosophy (170–1). These steps, Mill concluded, would generate 'a very efficient stimulus to the cultivation of the English language, and of useful knowledge in general among the natives' (172–3).

As I mentioned earlier in this chapter, several scholars have noted that Mill diverged from his father's views on matters of Indian policy around the time of his mental crisis, which began, as he recounts in his *Autobiography*, 'in the autumn of 1826' (1981: 138). I want to rehearse briefly the implications of a psychologically inflected argument before shifting to more empirically tenable ground. In the years immediately preceding his crisis, the deterministic strain of associationism had weighed heavily on him. Mill must have been profoundly affected by Samuel Taylor Coleridge's *Biographia Literaria*, published in 1817, which vociferously condemned associationism as 'the despotism of outward impressions' for characterising the mind as created passively and constructionally (Coleridge 1983: 111). While pondering these criticisms, Mill was reading portions of his father's *Analysis of the Phenomena of the Human Mind*, which unfolded in manuscript form over many years, beginning in 1822. He also read the work of Robert Owen, initially a follower of Bentham. Mill found Owen's arguments particularly unsettling. Owen posited that character is entirely the product of social circumstances; therefore, individuals cannot be held accountable for either their actions or the desires motivating them. To engender civic-minded, sociable beings, Owen favoured total control of their environments during childhood (Owen 1970: 99–108). As Mill recalls in his *Autobiography*, he recognised much of his own upbringing in this approach and began to despair. 'I felt as if I was scientifically proved to be the helpless slave of antecedent circumstances', he lamented, 'as if my character and that of all others had been formed for us by agencies beyond our control, and was wholly out of our own power' (1981: 176–7). In time, however, Mill rejected this premise as faulty. If desires, beliefs and actions are causally determined by prior ideas and experiences, they are not properly the subject's own. Thus:

I pondered painfully on the subject, till gradually I saw . . . that though our character is formed by circumstances, our own desires can do much to shape those circumstances; and that what is really inspiriting and ennobling in the doctrine of freewill, is the conviction that we have real power over the formation of our own character; that our will, by influencing some of our circumstances, can modify our future habits or capabilities of willing. (JSM 1981: 177)

Here, then, was a way of escaping the bleak implications of associationist thought that, in seeming to render moot the concepts of both human freedom and moral responsibility, had burdened him. Our volitions and actions may well depend on antecedent circumstances, he decided, but we have the capacity to develop our own desires and, in doing so, to reconstruct our character through self-improvement: 'We are exactly as capable of making our own character, *if we will*, as others are of making it for us' (JSM 1974: VIII, 840). If utilitarians were to focus solely on realising 'outward changes', they would fail to appreciate that the larger part of social improvement depended on individuals cultivating their 'inward nature' (JSM 1981: 185). In his view imaginative literature, which Bentham and his father had dismissed, could play a leading role in developing one's inward nature. He resolved to give 'its proper place, among the prime necessities of human well-being, to the internal culture of the individual' (147).

Coleridge, whom Mill met occasionally and whose writings he studied intensively, affected him in several ways.[54] First, through reading the German Romanticists and idealists who had informed Coleridge's thinking, he was introduced to the importance of individuality. Second, through Coleridge's notion of an intellectual clerisy that would supplant the clergy in morally and intellectually guiding others and in safeguarding and expanding the essential values and learnings of a society, Mill derived his belief that some minds were superior to others. Third, Coleridge awakened in him a vital appreciation of history he found absent in the work of his father and Bentham (JSM 1985b: 120, 132). While attending classes at the University of Göttingen in 1799, Coleridge had become deeply influenced by German historical criticism. He read notes of lectures given by the theologian Johann Gottfried Eichhorn, who viewed the stories of creation not as literal truths but as myths that reflected a historically specific mentality (Coleridge 1983: 207). From Eichhorn and others Coleridge concluded that the assumption that scripture is the infallible word of God was no longer tenable. As Mill later characterised it in his essay 'Coleridge', 'the Germano-Coleridgian school' supplants '*bibliolatry*', referring to Coleridge's term, and 'slavery to the letter' with historical understanding (1985b: 138, 144).

Raised an atheist by his father, Mill, unlike many of his contemporaries, was not unsettled by these views. Instead, he was interested in Coleridge's attempt to understand how a 'doctrine had been believed by thoughtful men, and received by whole nations or generations of mankind' (JSM 1985b: 120). In other words, through Coleridge, Mill came to recognise that the utilitarian tendency to ascribe responsibility for 'the long duration of a belief' to sinister interest – whether 'of aristocracies, or priests, or lawyers, or some other species of impostors' (120) – was inadequate. One had to study the past impartially, reserving judgement, at least at the outset, in order to understand why people over many generations hold fast to a particular belief. This, in turn, had important implications for reform. If history was, as John Robson summarises Mill's emerging view, 'a record of the various and continuous means by which institutions have been moulded by man to satisfy his needs' (1968: 71), then reforms must necessarily be modified according to local circumstances.

Once he reached these conclusions, Mill would have undoubtedly altered his approach to reforming India. But a review of his dispatches suggests he was, in fact, diverging from his father's opinions even before the mental crisis. For example, in a December 1826 Public Department dispatch to the presidency of Bengal (which, given the length of time required to research and draft it, would have been many months in the making, probably starting well before the onset of his crisis in 'the autumn of 1826'),[55] Mill asserts the necessity 'of securing to the people of India the free and unmolested exercise and enjoyment of their own religion' (1826: 450–1). He does so even though the company's long-standing policy of religious non-interference was one of James Mill's numerous targets for reform. Although the elder Mill did not share in the Christian missionary fervour of most Anglicists, he held, as I have noted, that Hinduism and, to a lesser extent, Islam had contributed to India's stagnation.

Shifting from psychological interpretations, I wish to suggest another explanation for John Stuart Mill's divergence from his father's views during this period: that the quasi-meritocratic system of employee advancement the directors implemented when they split the Examiner's Office into separate divisions in 1825, establishing a Correspondence Branch, played a role in drawing out and rewarding subjective individuation and ideation. By promoting the younger Mill, the company directors sought to give 'expression to the new principles' of merit (Moir 1990: xv). In a whimsical essay written after the dissolution of the East India Company in 1858, J. W. Kaye, who served directly under John Stuart Mill between 1856 and 1858, put the distinction the directors attempted to introduce this way: staff members were deemed either 'good heads' or, evoking the habitual and repetitious nature of clerical work, 'good hands' (1860: 117). If 'good hands' did not 'grow into good heads' through internal promotion, Kaye wrote, summing up the policy introduced in the Examiner's Office and later extended throughout the company, the directors would conduct external searches (117).[56] Positions within the Correspondence Branch were filled based on discipline, hard work and talent: 'mere length of service in the absence of the necessary qualifications' would not be considered (Moir 1990: xv).

In early 1825, after John Stuart Mill had served as an unsalaried junior clerk for nearly two years, the Court of Directors recognised his 'acquirements' by assigning him a clerical position within the Correspondence Branch, which had just been constituted, and awarding him a £100 gratuity.[57] After completing his three-year probationary period a year later, in May 1826, Mill was appointed eleventh clerk of the Correspondence Branch, formalising the arrangement of his having special responsibility for dispatches on political affairs and educational policy, at an annual salary of £100.[58] Within three months of Mill's December 1826 dispatch, in which he had differed from his father's views, the directors awarded him a special gratuity of £200 in recognition of the 'zeal and assiduity' with which he performed his duties.[59]

Mill's ascent through the company's hierarchy corresponded to his physical relocation from oppressive compounds and conjoint space to a cellular office with optimal conditions for drafting dispatches. In February 1828 he was appointed fourth assistant to the examiner with a base salary of £310.[60] He was again awarded a gratuity of £200. It was likely on this promotion that Mill moved to one of the spacious and private cellular offices. While he does not refer in his published writings or letters to his new surroundings, the impact must have been profound. For the first time he was not expected to share a workspace: either at home, where he had been, evocatively, 'an habitual inmate' of his father's study (JSM 1981: 55), or at India House. As a senior administrator, he experienced a degree of physical freedom in his work impossible for staff at lower levels. Unlike the clerks who sat at sloping desks, experiencing the extreme discomfort described by Charles Lamb, Mill was unconstrained by the need to sit constantly. George Birdwood, who, late in the century, collected the reminiscences of East India Company pensioners in connection with his work to preserve old records, maintained he had been told that 'even when in conversation with others, [Mill] would seem to have been pre-occupied with his own thoughts, all the time moving restlessly to and fro, "like a hyena" . . .' (1890: 47).

The philosopher and psychologist Alexander Bain, who knew Mill well for three decades, has described Mill's office (1969: 64–5). Approximately thirty by eighteen feet, it was illuminated by 'three large windows'. Much of the room, largely 'free from furniture', served as Mill's 'promenade': 'While reading he was generally always on foot', walking back and forth across the carpeted floor (Bain 1969: 65).[61] When writing, Mill worked, either on his feet or resting on a high stool, at a standing desk situated between the fireplace and a window at one end of the room (Bain 1969: 65). On occasion, he is alleged to have engaged in an odd ritual. 'When particularly inspired, before sitting down to his desk, he used not only to strip himself of his coat and waistcoat, but of his trousers', according to an account related to Birdwood, 'and so set to work, alternately striding up and down the room, and writing at great speed' (1890: 48). Mill was clearly lost in his own thought.

The refinement in Mill's understanding of how truth is produced can be traced to this period of increased physical and psychological freedom. As the 'habitual inmate' of his father's study, he had been expected to ascertain the truth of a given argument through a process of verbal disputation. So committed had he been to this conviction that in 1825 he founded the London Debating Society. Yet just a year after being promoted to the position of fourth assistant, and likely having taken possession of his cellular office, Mill withdrew from the society. 'I have a great dislike to controversy', he wrote a friend in 1830, 'and am persuaded that discussion, as discussion, seldom did any good' (1963a: 45). By 1833 Mill was insisting to Thomas Carlyle that 'Truth' is rarely the product 'of what the "free discussion" men, call the "collision of opinions"'; instead, it 'is *sown* and germinates in the mind itself, and is not to be struck *out* suddenly like a fire from a flint by knocking another hard body against it' (153). He concluded that truth emerged less through the verbal clash of different opinions than through inward deliberation on them.

Mill's new understanding of thought processes as dialogic had implications for his thinking about governance as well. 'The *post* of a good and wise legislator is his own study: it is there that all good laws are made, all improvements in human affairs really elaborated', Mill wrote in an 1834 essay. 'To look at the present practice, one would imagine that the government of a great nation was performed by talking and hearing talk. It is performed by thinking' (1982: 159). From the serene seclusion of his office and on company stationery, Mill would write *Principles of Political Economy*, which he published in 1848, arguing that 'a world from which solitude is extirpated, is a very poor ideal' (1965: 756). Privacy and isolation, because they cultivate one's 'inward nature', have both individual and collective utility: 'Solitude, in the sense of being often alone, is essential to any depth of meditation or of character' (756). As he had learned from Coleridge, superior minds, when they are able to meditate deeply on the profound issues of the moment, may in turn influence the direction of a particular course of events.

While Mill was moving towards these conclusions about truth as the mental reconciliation, in solitude, of opposing views, he was drifting further from his father's opinions on the cultural differences between India and the West. Mill's deep appreciation for classical languages and civilisation, firmly established in early childhood through his acquisition of Greek and Latin, increased during his tenure at India House. His friend Bain, citing in particular Mill's two trips to Greece, which 'he traversed . . . from end to end', called him 'a Greece-intoxicated man' (1969: 94). Between 1834 and 1835 Mill published a series of annotated translations of four dialogues by Plato, whose 'almost boundless reputation' did not, in his view, reflect either wide reading or deep understanding of Plato's writings (1978c: 39). A decade later, describing the Greeks as 'the most remarkable people who have yet existed', Mill observed that 'they alone among nations, so far as is known to us, emerged from barbarism by their own efforts' (1978a: 273). Within the ancient world, he noted some years later, the Greeks were unique in possessing a 'spring of unborrowed progress', which European countries inherited (1978b: 313).[62] The notion of a distinction between stationary Hindus and progressive Europeans, inherited from his father, was reinforced daily in his administrative work. For John Stuart Mill, Hindus were 'that curious people, who reproduce in so many respects the mental characteristics of the infancy of the human race' (1978a: 290). Nevertheless, he was a more reflective and subtle thinker than his father on matters of cultural difference. At times tolerant and respectful, Mill even envisioned reciprocity: 'whatever promotes friendly intercourse between these two varieties of mankind [Eastern and Western peoples]', he wrote to the French Hellenist Gustave d'Eichthal in 1837, '& whatever teaches them to know & to like one another' has the effect of producing a laudatory cultural hybridity. 'I quite agree with you that an infusion of the Oriental character into that of the nations of northern Europe would form a combination very much better than either separately' (1963a: 329).

Similarly, Mill diverged increasingly from his father's views on educational policy, inclining towards the policy of engraftment. Whereas James Mill considered the Indian middle and upper classes parasitic, his son came to see them as important allies. Indian elites, motivated by an 'improved spirit . . . imbibed from the influence of European ideas and sentiments', would yield teachers, writers or translators, John Stuart Mill stated in an 1830 dispatch to Bengal, and 'contribute in an eminent degree to the more general extension among their countrymen of a portion of the acquirements which they have themselves gained' (1830: 400, 399). He noted in the same document that printed material in indigenous languages was an essential part of a 'more complete education' (398). He also cautioned officials against concluding, in view of the evident interest in learning English, that 'the medium of books and oral instruction in their own languages' was unnecessary 'to spread useful knowledge among the natives' (397–8). That same year, 1830, Mill had been reading Coleridge's *On the Constitution of the Church and State*, Lynn Zastoupil notes (1994: 42–6). Thus, the echo of Coleridge in Mill's defence of the Indian lettered classes is unmistakable. But Coleridge is unlikely to have been the only source: as I have suggested, Mill was coevally developing a practical understanding – in Pierre Bourdieu's sense of the term as knowledge derived from daily, mundane practice (1980: 52–79) – of rank and apportionment founded on intellect and merit. Pacing back and forth in the spacious, airy office to which he had been promoted, Mill was coming to believe in a set of cognitive techniques, cultivated and encouraged by the company's quasi-meritocratic system, that he later codified as the process by which liberalised ideas could be produced, felt and rendered.

'Inward Domain'

While Mill was ascending the ranks of the Examiner's Office at the East India Company, he was also developing a name for himself as a speculative writer whose views increasingly garnered public acclaim. In 1830 he was elected to London's exclusive Athenaeum Club, which admitted 'individuals known for their scientific or literary attainments' (Athenaeum Club 1882). Yet he made little use of the club. Few published or private accounts refer to his presence there;

he mentioned it only occasionally in his letters, once noting he was 'not often at the Athenaeum without some special cause' (1963b: 578); and he eventually resigned, seeing little value in continuing to pay the annual dues.

Nevertheless, because Athenaeum membership was predicated on individual accomplishment in the arts and sciences, rather than on wealth or social position alone, being added to its rolls served as an index of social nobility. By the 1830s it had become the leading club for men of letters, who constituted a new kind of aristocracy – the term 'meritocracy' not yet having been coined – based on talent, accomplishment and imagination. Despite Mill's not availing himself of the benefits of membership, his election to the Athenaeum served to reinforce the understanding of rank and apportionment he was learning on the job at the East India Company.

In fact, intellect and merit were central to Mill's best-known work of speculative writing. He began to pen *On Liberty* from his cellular office at India House in 1854 and finished much of it before his retirement in 1858.[63] The book reflects two aspects of his experience at India House with which I will deal in turn: the necessity of liberty of thought and, as I will elaborate in the next section, of discussion, which he had once deprecated only to embrace and advocate.

Mental autonomy, which Mill's working environment nurtured, is central to his argument for individual freedom. In *On Liberty* he provides an account of liberal individuality as the expression of privately conceived and individuated opinion. Mill believed he and his contemporaries lived in an era of transition in which a perplexing assortment of philosophies and theories vied with one another. German biblical criticism, in particular, was undermining long-held beliefs. Thus, Mill exhorts his readers not to accept the views of others as the premise of one's own life, because doing so gravely compromises one's capacity for self-formation. Linking character to individuality, he remarks:

> A person whose desires and impulses are his own – are the expression of his own nature, as it has been developed and modified by his own culture – is said to have a character. One whose desires and impulses are not his own, has no character, no more than a steam-engine has a character. (1977d: 264)

He uses the term 'character' to designate a specific moral achievement. Lauren Goodlad turns to the second edition of the *Oxford English Dictionary* to explain Mill's intended meaning: 'moral qualities strongly developed or strikingly displayed; distinct or distinguished character; *character worth speaking of* (2008: 14). So central did character become to Mill's theory of social change that in *Considerations on Representative Government* he observes, perhaps in a gibe at the utilitarianism of his father and Bentham, that 'moral convictions', not 'any change in the distribution of material interests', had brought about the end of slavery (1977b: 382).

Character, in Mill's view, depends on the interior space of individuated privacy. He contends in *On Liberty* that 'the free development of individuality' (1977d: 261) is founded on three types of liberty: 'human liberty', which he glosses as an 'inward domain of consciousness' where 'absolute freedom of opinion and sentiment on all subjects' resides; 'liberty of tastes and pursuits', defined as 'framing the plan of our life to suit our own character; of doing as we like, subject to such consequences as may follow'; and liberty of individuals 'to unite, for any purpose not involving harm to others' (225–6). Only under such conditions of liberty can liberal individuality be realised. In Mill's description a person who builds an 'inward domain of consciousness' also recognises that truth often emerges from deliberating, within that inward domain, a range of differing opinions.

Through his work at India House, Mill developed an objectivising stance that, he believed, facilitated dispassionate assessment of distinct claims. Accordingly, one weighs diverse points of view before coming to one's own conclusions. 'Ninety-nine in a hundred of what are called educated men' never test the veracity of their beliefs, Mill writes in *On Liberty* (1977d: 245). As a result:

> Their conclusion may be true, but it might be false for anything they know: they have never thrown themselves into the mental position of those who think differently from them, and considered what such persons may have to say; and consequently they do not, in any proper sense of the word, know the doctrine which they themselves profess. [This kind of testing was so] essential . . . that if opponents of all important truths do not exist, it is indispensable to imagine them, and supply them with the strongest arguments which the most skilful devil's advocate can conjure up. (245)

One who evinces a serenely detached relation even to one's own convictions, let alone those of others, is not a partisan but a 'calmer and more disinterested bystander' on whom 'this collision of opinions works its salutary effect' (257). Through the autonomous thought and choice on which deliberate decisions depend, one is freed from received opinion as well as from associationist conceptions of mind and Evangelicalism's cramped mentality. By reasserting individuality through 'the trial of new and original experiments in living', one confronts the tyranny of convention and groupthink, with their inordinate pressures to conform (281). Mill concludes that society needs enticements to individuality, including meritocratic systems (as they would be called a century later).

On Liberty contains Mill's most explicit articulation of liberal individuality. His spatial metaphorisation of consciousness as proprietary – as a state in which 'liberty of thought and feeling' (JSM 1977d: 225) can be experienced and which is obtainable through mental liberalisation – parallels, by interiorising, his occupational ascent. Indeed, the seeds of *On Liberty* were planted in his mind when he wrote two far earlier texts: a speculative essay titled 'Civilization' and a controversial, cancelled dispatch titled 'Recent Changes in Native Education', which extended some of the ideas in the essay. He composed them within six months of each other in 1836, the year of his promotion to one of the highest positions in the Examiner's Office and also the year of his father's death. James Mill was ill and largely absent from India House throughout the first half of 1836, preceding his death in late June. Consequently, John Stuart was able to free himself increasingly from his father's shadow.[64] 'Civilization' and 'Recent Changes in Native Education' represented the most decisive break yet with his father's views and sectarian tendencies.

Published in *The London and Westminster Review* in April 1836, 'Civilization' begins by considering the effects 'in modern Europe, and especially in Great Britain' of an expanding franchise and of the emergence of a fully commercialised society (JSM 1977a: 120–1). As the 'general arrangements of society' become more advanced, individuals no longer need to rely solely on themselves for survival, protection and prosperity (129). This passing of power 'from individuals to masses' contributes to 'greater and greater insignificance' accorded to 'the weight and importance of an individual' (126). As a result, 'the individual is lost and becomes impotent in the crowd, and . . . individual character itself becomes relaxed and enervated' (136). Because progress is not an intrinsic feature of society, Mill warns, societies need to enable 'greater and more perfect combination among individuals' and to develop 'national institutions of education, and forms of polity, calculated to invigorate the individual character' (136). Aligning character with the capacity to form and express individual opinion, Mill argues that the universities have failed as generative sites of intellect. In a trenchant critique of the educational approach taken at the major universities, which, like his father, he sees as representative of the sinister interest of the Anglican Church, Mill anticipates the views he expresses several months later in his 'Recent Changes' dispatch. Using a term of John Locke's, he reasons that the effect of sectarian 'principling' of students in religion, morality, politics and philosophy – and especially the requirement that at graduation students subscribe to the thirty-nine articles, the doctrinal tenets of the Church of England – is the opposite of cultivating intellect (141). Making graduation conditional on the acceptance of 'a particular set of opinions' (141) engenders what he would call in *On Liberty* 'dull and torpid assent' rather than 'living belief' (JSM 1977d: 248, 247). In 'Civilization' he recommends a meritocratic system that incentivises the assiduous formulation of individual opinion (JSM 1977a: 147). Rejecting the passive cultivation of the intellect that subscribing to the thirty-nine articles requires, he claims that students, and by implication everyone, should be allowed to 'choose doctrines for themselves' (146).

For Mill this point was more than theoretical. In February 1836 the directors promoted him to second assistant to the examiner. By July he held the position of first assistant with a salary of £1,200 per annum.[65] While ascending the ladder at India House, he was learning to believe in his own views. Meritocratic systems, he was also concluding, made possible this 'living belief': a deeply felt conviction animating one's whole being.

He articulated similar conclusions in 'Recent Changes in Native Education', which communicated displeasure with Governor-General William Bentinck's decision, actualised in the 1835 English Education Act, to support only English-language instruction in Bengal. Thomas Babington Macaulay's infamous memorandum or 'minute' on Indian education had provided the rationale for Bentinck's decision. Given economic restraints, Macaulay, who had taken up a position in Bengal as a member of the newly established supreme council for India, opined that English-language instruction was the most effective medium through which 'a class of persons, Indian in blood and colour, but English in taste, in opinions, in morals, and in intellect' could be produced (Macaulay 1935: 359). The English language, Macaulay supposed, had brought together the peoples of the United Kingdom. India's mix of religious and linguistic differences warranted a similar coagulant. With Macaulay's argument providing an intellectual rationale, Bentinck adopted a series of measures designed to promote European literature and scientific texts among Indians.[66] These included making English the official language of government;

ending stipendiary positions for students studying Sanskrit and Arabic; cutting off endowments for schools of Indian classical learning; and excluding the Sanskrit College and the Calcutta Madrassa from the list of institutions where the English language might be studied. Bentinck's decision proved to be extraordinarily unpopular and led to unrest in Muslim and Hindu communities alike. Believing the act portended the dissolution of the Calcutta Madrassa, more than 8,000 signatories petitioned the new Governor-General, George Eden, Lord Auckland, to reverse this policy ('Humble petition of the Moosliman inhabitants' 1836). Seventy students of the Sanskrit College submitted a similar petition to the Governor-General ('Humble petition of the students' 1836).

With educational matters falling under his purview, Mill prepared a response to the new policy on behalf of the directors. In 'Recent Changes' he expressed 'serious apprehension and regret' over the adoption of a system 'in opposition to our recorded opinions' and over the abrupt reversal of a 'course of measures' that reflected 'thoughtfulness, sobriety, and deliberate wisdom'.[67] Drawing a contrast between thought and whim, Mill remonstrated: 'Those who change their opinions hastily, are those who form them hastily, and without due consideration.' The dispatch accords with Hindu and Muslim arguments made against the policy as well as with an article by Horace Hayman Wilson, who had been for many years the leading advocate of Orientalism on the Committee of Public Instruction.[68] Without mincing words, 'Recent Changes' declared it 'altogether chimerical to expect that the main portion of the mental cultivation of a people can ever take place through the medium of a foreign language'. Western knowledge could be effectively imparted only through the vernaculars, which, in turn, needed to be enriched by Sanskrit and Arabic.

This much he shared with his father. Behind the insistence on English-language instruction, the elder Mill believed, was unreflective patriotism, not utility – the proper criterion for determining the linguistic mode of instruction (Stokes 1959: 57). But James Mill had also dismissed formal education as a vehicle for reform. By contrast, John Stuart Mill concluded in 'Recent Changes', if not earlier, that developing moral faculties and nourishing the mind were the means by which human improvement (in India or elsewhere) could be secured.[69] He contended that the only individuals in India keenly interested in English-language classes were those eager for employment. Once they acquired the necessary level of proficiency to perform the tasks associated with their actual or aspirational positions, they sought no additional education. One need look no further than the company's native employees, who possessed 'English for all the demands of their daily duties, [but] who have no taste for our literature, no participation in our sentiments, no impression of our principles.' Mill asserted that they, 'in all essential respects of character, are upon a level with the rest of their countrymen'. However, traditional forms of learning encouraged, rather than the pursuit of a pay cheque, the cultivation of the intellect: 'a disinterested love of knowledge or intelligent wish for information'. The indigenous population, whose religious beliefs led them to reverence a learned class, would regard with alarm any steps that would seem to portend its 'degradation and extinction'. For their part, in Mill's view, the lettered class, on whom the British government depended for the effective dissemination of Western ideas, would grow disaffected and perhaps resentful of British rule.

The decision to suspend instruction or publication of materials in non-English languages threatened, as Mill saw it, to undo all his efforts to instil the progressive principle in a supposedly recalcitrant society. Mill regarded as entirely erroneous the assumption that Indians were 'indifferent to their national learning', which had motivated Bentinck to act (JSM 1836). Macaulay had cited, on the one hand, the necessity of stipends to entice individuals to study Sanskrit and Arabic and, on the other hand, the eagerness with which students pursued classes in English. Mill retorted that the maintenance of a traditional learned class, whose members took up the laborious task of linguistic and literary study, had been common in Europe for centuries. Stipendiary support for indigenous intellectuals should be seen as the modern equivalent of this system. While financial aid in an impoverished country was necessary, such stipends could serve as enticements to excellence: 'merit and talent' would thereby be encouraged (JSM 1836).

We do not know how James Mill might have responded to his son's rebuke of Macaulay's minute.[70] But John Cam Hobhouse, the powerful president of the Board of Control, reacted to the draft dispatch, which he was responsible for approving, with shock and dismay.[71] Severely inclined towards anglicising the subcontinent, Hobhouse had a long association with and deep respect for James Mill and had once considered himself a Radical.[72] On 12 December 1836 he sent a letter, enclosing a marked copy of the dispatch, to J. R. Carnac, chairman of the Court of Directors. Hobhouse lamented the dispatch's 'manifest partiality', 'inconclusive' reasoning, and misstatement of facts; having come 'to a conclusion entirely different from the writer', he advised that no 'opinion as to the past occurrences in reference to the Education question' should be relayed (J. Hobhouse 1836).[73] Carnac, who along with his deputy had approved the submission, deferred to Hobhouse and, with 'regret', withdrew the dispatch. 'The draft was chiefly prepared by Mr John Mill, who was not likely to have any extravagant prepossessions in favor of ancient oriental literature', Carnac noted in reply to Hobhouse, 'and I venture to think that it entertains a fair, able, and statesmanlike view of the question' (Carnac 1836). Mill's relationship to his opinion mattered as much to Carnac as the opinion itself. With Mill's utilitarian upbringing, he was not inclined to support Orientalist views on educational policy, Carnac implied. Therefore, the dispatch manifested a disinterested relation even to Mill's own predispositions and evinced broadmindedness that encompassed a reflexive critique of the author's beliefs.

Indignant that his judgement had not prevailed, Mill vented his frustration to his friend Henry Taylor, a dramatist and Colonial Office official:

> I . . . send you a draft of a despatch to India, prepared by myself, on one of his [Macaulay's] measures. The authorities at this house went entirely with me, but Hobhouse would not: the thing dropped . . . In any case you will sympathize in the annoyance of one having for years, (contrary to the instincts of his own nature, which are all for *rapid* change) assisted in nurturing & raising up a system of cautious & deliberate measures for a great public end, & having been rewarded with a success quite beyond expectation, finds them upset in a week by a coxcombical dilettante litterateur who never did a thing for a practical object in his life. (1972b: 1969–70)

Indicating the importance of individual opinion within the administrative culture of India House, the directors, despite being accountable to Hobhouse, did not instruct Mill to write at variance with his beliefs. Instead, they acceded to Hobhouse's instruction to Carnac that 'a short acknowledgement' of Bentinck's decision, without opinion, be transmitted to India.

Although Mill would wait twenty years for his next and final promotion, to the position of examiner of Indian correspondence, he was throughout this period the company's indispensable intellectual authority on Indian affairs. In 1854 the directors unanimously singled Mill out for 'some special mark of consideration'. Acknowledging his 'eminent merits and services' and their gratitude for 'the admirable manner in which . . . [he] conducts his important duties', they awarded him 'a special and personal addition of two hundred pounds (£200) per annum . . . to his salary, the same to commence from midsummer last'.[74] Two years later, he was appointed examiner. In his *Autobiography* Mill looked back on his career, noting that, whereas his drafts 'required at first much revision from my immediate superiors', he quickly became so well versed in the matters under his purview that, 'by my father's instructions and the general growth of my own powers', he was 'qualified to be, and practically was, the chief conductor of the correspondence with India in one of the leading departments, that of the Native States' (1981: 84–5). By 1840, regardless of his title, it was Mill, the diarist Caroline Fox observed, who 'arrange[d] the government of the native states' (1883: 129). J. W. Kaye, ventriloquising the company as a personification, 'John Company', noted, 'We were reasonably proud of Mr. James Mill; but as years advanced we took a still greater pride in his son, who was brought up amongst us' (1860: 118). The writer Justin McCarthy remarked that both Mills were 'among the ablest civil servants the East India Company ever had' (1880: 89).[75] Like his father, John Stuart showed that effective imperial administration rested on the schematising capacities of the mind (arranging, in Fox's apposite phrasing, the government of India). But he also evinced a particular stylisation of authority, stimulated and shaped by the system of professional ascent he pioneered, which linked analytical reasoning and ethical commitment to opinion formation.

Deliberative Decisions

Over the course of his career, Mill began his service in an outer circle of clerical labour, tasked with fetching and transmitting data. He then moved to a middle circle, working at shared desks, where that data was organised and digested, and subsequently to an inner circle of senior administrators, who took the organised data and, by reflecting on it and applying their experience and knowledge, produced the opinions on which company decisions rested. Once he was ensconced in the inner circle, Mill reached his thoughtful decisions by internalising the 'collision of opinions' from which, in its interpersonal form, he had earlier retreated (JSM 1963a: 153). Instead of engaging primarily in verbal disputation, he weighed the different perspectives on a given issue voiced in the paperwork on file:

> If the local officer and the Government differ in opinion, or if the opinions of the different members of the Government differ from one another, the reasons on both sides, and the discussions that take place, are put in writing . . . (JSM 1990: 33)

Thus, before reaching decisions, Mill contemplated, on the one hand, the actions of company officials in India and, on the other, the views of the directors and the Board of Control.

For many years, while conducting research for this chapter, I was narrowly centred on the processes of individuation the meritocratic system encouraged. This fit with my knowledge of Mill's simultaneous re-education through the likes of Coleridge and accorded with my understanding of *On Liberty*, shaped as it then was by decades of scholarship that sees Mill as an inheritor of Lockean possessive individualism. In other words, while poring over archival materials, I tended to see confirmation of my initial hypothesis: that the non-discursive and material elements of Mill's experience at India House influenced his conception of individuality as much as the intellectual ideas to which he was exposed while working in his office on either official correspondence or speculative essays. In essence, I fell victim to what Arlette Farge calls the 'blinding symbiosis with the object of study' to which archival scholars are prone: the 'imperceptible, yet very real, way in which a historian is only drawn to things that will reinforce the working hypotheses she has settled on' (2013: 71). But my view of Mill muted other equally strong intellectual influences evident in *On Liberty*, especially strands of civic republicanism that emphasise cultivating civic virtue, propagating a collectivist ideal, safeguarding the common good and catalysing a public sphere of debate.

Indeed, in *On Liberty*, Mill attempts to marry an individualism born of German Romanticism with the republican notion of active civic engagement.[76] But here, too, India House provided not just a setting in which he wrestled with these ideas but an environment that facilitated practical understanding of them. What I did not see initially was that, over time, Mill had occasion at India House to develop and refine his view that opinion formation, analytical reasoning and ethical commitment were bound together. As he became one of the company's most trusted servants, he assumed responsibility for formulating opinions and persuading others – at India House, in Parliament and on the subcontinent – of their efficacy. This led him to moderate the emphasis he sometimes placed on inward deliberation. Whereas Mill's experience of drafting 'Recent Changes' underscored for him the importance of formulating and articulating an opinion, his increasing role in policy debates facilitated his embrace of discussion as part of that process. Reflecting on the lessons he derived from internal negotiations over Indian policy, Mill noted in his *Autobiography*:

> The occupation [his 'official position'] accustomed me to see and hear the difficulties of every course, and the means of obviating them, stated

and discussed deliberately . . . above all it was valuable to me by making me, in this portion of my activity, merely one wheel in a machine, the whole of which had to work together . . . I was thus in a good position for finding out by practice the mode of putting a thought which gives it easiest admittance into minds not prepared for it by habit; while I became practically conversant with the difficulties of moving bodies of men, the necessities of compromise, the art of sacrificing the non-essential to preserve the essential . . . I have found, through life, these acquisitions to be of the greatest possible importance for personal happiness, and they are also a very necessary condition for enabling any one, either as theorist or as practical man, to effect the greatest amount of good compatible with his opportunities. (1981: 88)

In other words Mill had to experiment with different ways of articulating ideas that went against the company's prevailing attitudes and practices. He learned how to influence large groups in order to make his ideas prevail and how to sacrifice what he considered important to achieve a more crucial goal. The process of composing letters of instruction and guidance to the governors of India is one of many instances in which individuals, as Mill writes in another context, 'learn a practical lesson of submitting themselves to guidance, and subduing themselves to act as interdependent parts of a complex whole' (1977a: 124).

Discussion, which is central to his defence of liberal individuality, also became a cornerstone of his defence of imperial, not to mention national, governance. In his testimony in 1852 before a select committee established in advance of debate in the House of Lords over the renewal of the company's charter, Mill expressed strong opposition to the idea of assigning sole responsibility for governing to a Secretary of State for India. He told the members of the committee:

I should think it would be the most complete despotism that could possibly exist in a country like this; because there would be no provision for any discussion or deliberation, except that which might take place between the Secretary of State and his subordinates in office, whose advice and opinion he would not be bound to listen to; and who, even if he were, would not be responsible for the advice or opinion that they might give. (1990: 50)

As a Member of Parliament, he continued to press this point more than a decade after the company's dissolution and the appointment of the first Secretary of State for India. In a parliamentary speech he argued that governing India 'should not rely solely upon the policy of one man': 'the deliberative was quite as extensive as the executive work, and even more important' (1988: 233). He observed in his *Considerations on Representative Government*, published in 1861, that a cabinet member would be too enmeshed in British politics and would hold the ministry for too short a period 'to acquire an intelligent interest in so complicated a subject' (1977b: 573). He would likely put politics ahead of principle, making decisions with his electorate in mind. Thus, the administration of India would be subject to public opinion and to various pressure groups, including the press.

Underlying the debate throughout the 1850s over revocation of the company's charter was the implicit suggestion that no special proficiency was needed for South Asian administration. Mill categorically rejected this notion in his 1852 testimony:

India is a peculiar country; the state of society and civilization, the character and habits of the people, and the private and public rights established among them, are totally different from those which are known or recognised in this country; in fact the study of India must be as much a profession in itself as law or medicine. (1990: 49)

Territorial governance should therefore be assigned to 'those who possess the requisite knowledge, and whose examination is much more effectual than any examination that can be exercised by persons less acquainted with the subject'. Those possessing such knowledge, he concluded, bear 'the feeling of responsibility' much more strongly than those lacking 'requisite knowledge' (54). Mill was certainly thinking of men such as himself.

When charter renewal was again debated in 1853, Mill, whose views on the proper management of India were firm, was the company's public face. In part because of his strong defence of the company, in 1856 the directors named him examiner, with an annual salary of £2,000, which placed him firmly within the top half-per-cent income bracket in Britain.[77] When the Palmerston ministry signalled in the aftermath of the Indian Rebellion a year later its plan to bring India under the Crown's direct purview, Mill vociferously defended in public discussion the company's role as a territorial administrator.[78] On Parliament's passage in 1858 of the Government of India Act, which abolished the East India Company and replaced it and the Board of Control with an Office of the Secretary of State for India, Mill announced his decision to retire. He ruled out serving in an office whose creation he opposed and refused to consider appointment to the newly established Council of India. In short, Mill chose to live his belief, on a generous pension of £1,500 a year. He must certainly have thought of his decision as an experiment in living, the terminology he uses in *On Liberty* – 'new and original experiments in living' – to capture the process of realising individuality through autonomous thinking and choice (1977d: 281).

Mill's experiences at India House, especially during the last years when he represented the company externally, likely led to his decision to stand, in the absence of a Radical party, as a Liberal candidate for Parliament in 1865. He had come to recognise while advocating for the company's continued existence that 'the great security for good government' rested on public discussion (JSM 1990: 49). Thus, having left the company, Mill turned to writing about and publicly debating issues of individuality and governance. For many who, like Mill, subscribed to tenets of civic republicanism, 'reading and writing were tangible . . . modes of political action' (Kuduk Weiner 2005: 9). During his brief stint as a Member of Parliament (he was defeated in the general election of 1868), Mill devoted himself to provoking debate on unpopular topics, including women's suffrage, and vigorously defended his views.

Public and Private

Mill's shift towards deliberation had important implications for his understanding of public and private subjectivity. Daniel Malachuk – singling out the passage from Mill's *Autobiography*, quoted earlier, in which Mill elaborates on what he learned at India House – notes that 'Mill found . . . political and moral goods yielded by the instrument of professional life' (1981: 100). Mill's reflections are similar to those in *Considerations on Representative Government* and elsewhere in which he discusses cultivating fellow feeling and awareness that, through debate and compromise, one is part of a larger community. His gradual turn towards collectivism, born partly through the practical understanding he obtained at India House, resonated with the views of varied French and Scottish writers as well as the German Romanticists in the 1830s and 1840s, all espousers of civic republicanism or thinkers otherwise indebted to it, whom he studied during those decades. These sources alerted him to the pitfalls of atomised and privatised individualism and moderated whatever libertarian leanings he possessed.

But Mill alludes in this passage from his *Autobiography* to more than the 'political and moral goods' Malachuk highlights. Mill also attributes much of his 'personal happiness' to the acquisition of certain professional skills. If one can extend 'personal' to include the private, non-professional sphere, he would seem to be referring to close interpersonal relations. Well into adulthood, Mill lived at his parents' home. While his father was alive, it was not an environment, as he recalls in his *Autobiography*, conducive to self-formation. India House, which, once he obtained a cellular office, came to function as a second home, was such a place. With an individual fireplace and an area to welcome guests, his office had an undeniably domestic quality. Mill frequently used it to socialise with friends and acquaintances (Foster 1924: 217–18). After visiting India House with a group of friends in 1840, Caroline Fox, whose friendship with Mill's family had begun a few months earlier in Cornwall, remarked on the 'comfort' of the room (1883: 129). Harriet Taylor, who married Mill in 1851, may also have spent time there. At least one of her essays, a short fragment on Christianity and ethics, was penned on India House stationery (H. Mill 1998: 162).

India House, then, functioned as both a private and a public space for Mill. This had implications for his thinking regarding the separation between those spheres. Indeed, Mill criticised that divide in *The Subjection of Women*, his essay of 1869, when he asserted the incongruity between public justice and private oppression. For him, marriage was, ideally, liberalism's principal social relationship, conjoining equal, autonomous adults. His contemporary, the liberal historian and journalist Goldwin Smith, wittily declared that for Mill marriage was 'a union of two philosophers in search of truth' (1874: 140). In any case Mill extolled marriage as 'the only school of genuine moral sentiment' (1984: 293). In so doing, he used a public rather than a private analogy, likening marriage to an educational institution. His advocacy for reforming marriage extended both to its public character, as an institution based on a contract, and its private nature, as a relationship between women and men.

So conducive to private thought and reflection was Mill's office, with its many amenities to support reading and writing, that he allowed his membership in the Athenaeum Club to lapse. Although he lost the use of the India House office on his retirement, his pattern of working from a private office remained unchanged.[79] In 1866, less than a year after Mill was elected Member of Parliament for Westminster, the educationalist J. P. Kay-Shuttleworth offered to put his name forward for admission to the Athenaeum. 'I was formerly a member of the Athenaeum', Mill wrote in reply, 'but finding that I made no use of the privilege I resigned; and I am still inclined to see whether I sustain any real inconvenience from not being a member of any club' (JSM 1899: 160).

Many of Mill's friends and acquaintances, lacking workspaces conducive to ideation and composition like his India House office, found club membership a significant boon in their lives. In the eighteenth century, although clubhouses and coffee houses were domestic in character, customers and subscribers did not typically consider them a home. They were markedly someone else's place, belonging to proprietors who often occupied quarters on the premises. In contrast, Athenaeum members inhabited the club and availed themselves of its amenities 'with the same freedom as in their own houses', the police magistrate and author Thomas Walker, an early member, averred (1835: 253). A gentleman's club, a mid-nineteenth century article in *The Builder* contended, was 'as much the private property of its members as any ordinary dwelling-house is the property of the man who built it' (qtd in Timbs 1866: 252). The scientist Thomas Huxley, who was elected to the Athenaeum in 1858, reportedly thought of it as a 'second home' (Jensen 1991: 147).

In 1867, eight years after *On Liberty* was published and one year after Mill declined having his name proposed for Athenaeum membership, Matthew Arnold sat down at his familiar desk at the Athenaeum to write the essays that would constitute *Culture and Anarchy*. One of the targets he had in mind to oppose was Mill. Arnold took a barely concealed swipe at *On Liberty*, which he, perhaps purposefully, misread; he inveighed against its supposed mantra, devoting a chapter to 'Doing as One Likes' (1965a: 115–36). In *St. Paul and Protestantism* Arnold singled out Mill by name as having spawned a 'somewhat degenerated and inadequate form of Hellenism' (1968d: 126), the term with which Arnold himself is most closely associated and which he defines as 'intelligence driving at . . . ideas' (1965a: 163). Sharing the view of his utilitarian forebears that the Church of England was a particularly demonstrable example of a sinister interest, Mill had, in Arnold's phraseology, dismissed the church as 'the dominant sect' in religion, thereby emboldening other sects, 'in whom there appears scarcely anything that is truly sound or Hellenic at all', to call for universal disestablishment (MA 1968d: 126). Although Arnold acknowledged that the church in his time furthered 'the prejudices of rank and property, instead of contending with them', he allowed that historically it had played an important role by preserving social continuity (1972b: 74); promoting goodness and establishing standards of morality; and encouraging appreciation for beauty and grandeur.

Without an authority to which all were subject, society, in his view, would devolve into hedonism (explored in poems such as 'The New Sirens').

Arnold's dispute with Mill was less about religion than about modes of seeing. He thought Mill, despite his incomparable education, remained blinkered to certain aspects of the historic church because he examined the institution only close at hand. It is to the ways in which Arnold's embodied experiences shaped his perceptual ideals that I now turn.

Notes

1. The humourist James Smith, writing as a foreign visitor to London, shared his impressions in 1808: 'I was lately much struck, in my rambles through the city, with a magnificent Grecian building . . . [It] forcibly strikes the eye of a stranger . . .' (1808: 213).
2. Craven House, the company's first headquarters, instantiated its commercial interests abroad. On purchasing from the Earl of Craven in 1709 a half-timbered Elizabethan mansion, which it had rented for £100 annually since 1648, the traders sought to lend dignity to the company's activities by commissioning a large painting depicting vessels returning from the East for the external entrance façade. In 1726 the company tasked Theodore Jacobsen, a merchant and amateur architect, to design a building in then fashionable Palladian style. Its façade, featuring a balustrade supported by six Doric pilasters, was intended to convey to shareholders solidity of purpose, thereby inspiring confidence that their interests were being faithfully served. Erected over a three-year period on the foundation of Craven House, the stone structure articulated through its spare form the relatively harmonious and stable period of commercial expansion company officials believed themselves to be entering. On the history of the company's headquarters, see Foster 1924.
3. 'Although generally so decorated by the Greeks, there is hardly an instance of it among ourselves', one architectural assessment averred ('Civil architecture' 1837: 219).
4. Bacon's design was reportedly criticised, in part, because the allegorical figures were deemed insufficiently distinct for the meaning to be clear (Britton et al. 1838: 36–7).
5. Although Mill did not receive a salary during his three years as a junior clerk, he was awarded a small gratuity annually.
6. I am borrowing the concept of ethical competence from Thomas Osborne's pellucid, and differently focused, study of bureaucracy as a vocation (1994).

7. For an exposition of the directors' responsibilities and details on their annual election, see Parkinson 1937: 11–28.
8. Although I have consulted original materials in the British Library's India Office Records, all scholars interested in these issues will be grateful for the painstaking groundwork of Zastoupil and Moir in publishing *The Great Indian Education Debate: Documents Relating to the Orientalist-Anglicist Controversy, 1781–1843* (1999).
9. This is one of several points of agreement between the two movements.
10. On the Orientalist's gaze, see Said's classic account (1978). On the missionary's, see Nielssen et al. 2011.
11. The most compelling account is advanced by Zastoupil 1994: 26–31.
12. For readings of James and John Stuart Mill's relationship in Oedipal terms, see Levi 1945 and Mazlish 1975, especially pp. 15–43.
13. Himmelfarb provides an incisive critique of psychohistory (2004: 112–25), though, in *On Liberty and Liberalism* (1974), she uses the concept of the Oedipal struggle in a restrained way.
14. On the company's early years, see Chaudhuri 1978, St John 2012 and Parkinson 1937: 29–120.
15. The only remaining challenge to the company's ascendency came from the state of Mysore, whose rulers, Haidar Ali and his son Tipu Sultan, had their own expansionist ambitions. Tipu Sultan was defeated in the final battle of the Anglo-Mysore Wars (1767–99).
16. See also Gleig 1841: 214.
17. See Boman-Behram 1943, especially pp. 12–64 and 542–57. However, Viswanathan cautions that differences between Anglicists and Orientalists have been too often emphasised at the expense of their similarities (1989: 29–30).
18. The literature on this period of British rule in India is vast. See, in particular, Davies 1935: 340–1; Franklin 2011: 13–14; Majeed 1992: 12–16; Kopf 1969: 31–42; and McCully 1966: 20–7.
19. The trial has been widely recounted. See, for example, J. Bernstein 2000: 203–64 and Davies 1935: 373–418. For contextualisation of the Hastings trial within the 'scandal of empire', see Dirks 2006, especially pp. 18–25, 87–131.
20. Aspinall provides a full discussion of these elements of the so-called Cornwallis code (1931: 86–98).
21. For an overview of the process, see JSM 1990: 33. See also A. Ryan 1972: 40.
22. Court of Directors (1599–1858), Minutes, 1 November 1769, B/85, fol. 284.
23. Committee of Correspondence (1719–1834), Report, 1 November 1769, IOR/D/26, fol. 34.
24. Ibid., 25 January 1770, IOR/D/26, fol. 125.
25. Ibid., 26 March 1771, IOR/D/26, fols 343–4.
26. See Foster 1919: iii; Moir 1986: 124–5.

27. Committee of Correspondence (1719–1834), Report, 6 April 1804, IOR/D/44, fol. 239.
28. Ibid., 24 February 1809, IOR/D/50, fol. 321.
29. Mason et al. [1817]: xiii; Philips 1940a: 18.
30. On James Mill's employment at India House, see Bain 1882; Forbes 1951; Stokes 1959.
31. Strachey's appointment as an external hire is not as clear-cut as the others. He had been employed by the company in India from 1793 to 1815, including as judge of the provincial court of appeal at Dacca, which qualified him to oversee judicial affairs. He was not an employee when he was appointed in 1819, however, nor had he ever worked at India House.
32. A separate portfolio for infrastructure (public works) was added in 1856. For a useful summary of the responsibilities in each administrative area, see Moir 1986, especially pp. 126–7.
33. Many of the company's proprietors were aghast at the decision to break with policy and hire from outside India House. Although most clerks were never promoted, by not hiring from the outside the company had at least held open that possibility. The only 'consolation' for clerks who 'pass with fortitude so great a proportion of their lives on such narrow stipends', one participant in an 1807 debate over staffing policy argued, 'was the assurance which they had the right to indulge in from the unbroken history of the Company for near three centuries, that they should in time arrive at or near the top of their respective offices' (qtd in Moir 1979: 29). The debate continued through the appointment of Mill, Strachey and Peacock.
34. I use British terminology here in referencing the third storey above the street.
35. On the history of the company's headquarters, see Foster 1924; on the company's administrative structure, see Bowen 2006; on the centrality of the Examiner's Office, see Moir 1979 and 1986.
36. The Secret Committee, established by Pitt's India Act of 1784, provided the British government and the company with the means of transmitting confidential communications to India. But it has a much longer history, originating in the need for swift executive action in response to threats to the company's trading ships and routes. See Philips 1940b and 1940c.
37. Until the late eighteenth century, for example, notaries and lawyers most often worked out of their living rooms (Pélegrin-Genel 1996: 26); larger businesses, including banks, might operate from the ground floor or mezzanine of large homes. This common practice reflected the relative lack of importance given to specially designed office space before 1800.
38. Court of Directors (1599–1858), Minutes, 1 November 1769, B/85, fol. 284.

39. See also Bowen's discussion of the examiner's independent thought and judgement during the office's early period (2006: 191–2).
40. Mill's list is reproduced in his *Bibliography* (1945) and in Robson et al. (1990). Several scholars have claimed Mill's dispatches cannot be considered straightforward expressions of his opinion. R. J. Moore, for example, asserts that Mill's 'authentic voice' in the dispatches is 'stifled and sometimes strangled' (1983: 519). This assumes that Mill was frequently directed to write dispatches that did not reflect his beliefs. There is little evidence for this assertion. Mill did not include in his list any dispatches significantly altered by others in the approval process.
41. In Mill's scale of civilisations, which hierarchised societies by the extent to which they reflected the principle of utility, India had always been populated by a 'rude' people. 'Exactly in proportion as *Utility* is the object of every pursuit, may we regard a nation as civilized', James Mill opined. 'Exactly in proportion as its ingenuity is wasted on contemptible or mischievous objects, though it may be, in itself, an ingenuity of no ordinary kind, the nation may safely be denominated barbarous' (J. Mill 1840: II, 150).
42. James Mill's vociferous disagreement with the Orientalists, particularly William Jones, is discussed in Kopf 1969: 236–52.
43. 'Sinister interests' is a phrase favoured by both James Mill and Bentham, with whom it originated. According to Bentham, 'Interest, when acting in such a direction and with such effect as to give birth to falsehood, may be termed *sinister* interest' (1838–43: VII, 385).
44. On the need to separate the utilitarian approach from the Anglicist, with which it is often linked, see Majeed 1992 and Osborne 1994. As Majeed elaborates elsewhere, the idiom with which Mill attempted to formulate his ideas for reform, in contrast to the Anglicists' ideas, was secular (2005).
45. Metcalf provides an elaboration of these points (1994: 3–45).
46. 'The mercantile interest', Alexander Bain notes in summarising James Mill's view, 'could not see . . . [as the utilitarian reformer could] the very stagnant condition of the native population in India . . .' (1882: 348).
47. The new act settled the debate over whether the company could claim as private property the land it had acquired and the taxes it levied as income.
48. James Mill's essays in *Political Writings*, originally published between 1819 and 1823, address these issues. See J. Mill 1992, especially pp. 1–194. Bentham memorably described the difference between political parties, in regard to 'the People's interests', as merely a 'semblance': 'All parties are, in fact, at all times resolvable into two: that which is in possession, and that which is in expectancy, of the sweets of government' (1838–43: X, 81). On James Mill's antipathy towards both Whigs and Tories, see Hamburger 1963: 33–47 and Mill's February 1818 letter

to Thomas Thomson, in which he commented 'though I am any thing in the world rather than a Whig, I am quite as far from being a Tory' (qtd in Bain 1882: 167).

49. James Mill gives the example of 'learning to play on a musical instrument' to illustrate 'the effect of repetition in strengthening associations'. He explains that, note by note, 'at first, the learner . . . has each time to look out with care for the key or the string which he is to touch, and the finger he is to touch it with'. The student overcomes mistakes only through repeated effort. 'As the repetition goes on, the sight of the note, or even the idea of the note, becomes associated with the place of the key or the string; and that of the key or the string with the proper finger', he continues. 'The association for a time is imperfect, but at last becomes so strong, that it is performed with the greatest rapidity, without an effort, and almost without consciousness' (1878: 89).

50. The General Committee of Public Instruction's letter of appointment is reproduced in H. Sharp 1920: 54–7.

51. James Mill's authorship of these early dispatches on education is discussed by Stokes 1959: 324 n. D.

52. Correspondence regarding company administration and related matters generated by the Examiner's Office was divided among a number of departments, including a Revenue Department and a Public and Judicial Department.

53. For an overview of the early years of Hindu College, see McCully 1966: 20–7.

54. To one correspondent Mill writes in 1834, shortly before Coleridge's death: 'Few persons have exercised more influence over my thoughts and character than Coleridge has; not much by personal knowledge of him, though I have seen and conversed with him several times, but by his works . . .' (1963a: 221).

55. On the composition process, see Moir 1999.

56. An analogical relation of head and hand legitimates a hierarchical arrangement even as it celebrates the possibility of an individual's progression from one form of employment to another. For a thorough exploration of how the head-and-hand analogy functioned in the industrial area, see Shapin and Barnes 1976.

57. Court of Directors (1599–1858), Minutes, 2 March 1825, B/177, fols 666–7.

58. Committee of Correspondence (1719–1834), Report, 31 May 1826, IOR/D/74, fols 77–8.

59. Ibid., 23 March 1827, IOR/D/75, fol. 362.

60. Ibid., 19 February 1828, IOR/D/77, fols 293–4.

61. See Finance and Home Committee 1849 and Finance and Home Committee 1851 for minuted discussions of Mill's carpet.

62. Only the 'European family of nations', Mill believed, possessed 'any capability of spontaneous improvement' (JSM 1977c: 197).

63. Mill gave much credit for *On Liberty* to his wife, Harriet Taylor (JSM 1981: 258–9). The initial essay on which it was based was completed in 1854. In collaboration with Taylor, Mill wrote much of the longer work between 1856 and October 1858, when he resigned from the company. While scholars have disputed the extent of her role, I suggest only that Mill's embodied experience at India House contributed to its production.

64. James Mill's death was a severe blow from which his son never quite recovered. 'I had now to try what it might be possible for me to accomplish without him', John Stuart Mill recalled (1981: 214). Yet, he acknowledged, 'Deprived of my father's aid, I was also exempted from the restraints and retinences by which that aid had been purchased' (1981: 216). Noting his involvement with *The London and Westminster Review*, for which he served as editor and subsequently proprietor from 1836 to 1840, he observed that 'the Review was the instrument on which I built my chief hopes of establishing a useful influence over the liberal and democratic section of the public mind' (1981: 214–15). With this increased independence he made the review the voice for an inclusive philosophical radicalism that went beyond his father's thinking, with its indebtedness to Bentham.

65. Court of Directors (1599–1858), Minutes, 27 July 1836, B/192, fols 443–4.

66. 'Macaulay's minute', Gauri Viswanathan argues, 'paved the way for the transition from religious to secular motives in English education' (1989: 145).

67. See JSM 1836. All quotations from 'Recent Changes' in this and the subsequent paragraphs are from the unpaginated original in the India Office Records. It is also available in Zastoupil and Moir 1999: 225–43.

68. See 'Humble petition of the Moosliman inhabitants' 1836, especially pp. 13–14, 17–18, and 'Humble petition of the students' 1836. Sirkin and Sirkin first identified tangible evidence of Mill's indebtedness to Wilson: a January 1836 letter to him in which Mill acknowledges the 'pleasure' derived from Wilson's arguments against Bentinck's decision that had been published in *The Asiatic Journal* (Sirkin and Sirkin 1974: 4). Mill drafted his response to Bentinck only a few months later, touching on many of the same points. See Wilson 1836.

69. He continued to espouse this view in later writings, including *Utilitarianism* (1985c: 221) and *Considerations on Representative Government* (1977b: 400, 404, 407, 436).

70. Some scholars contend that Macaulay's position closely approximated James Mill's. Duncan Forbes, for example, refers to the minute as 'James Mill's philosophy expressed in Macaulayese' (1951: 23). But this view lacks nuance. Closer to my position, Zastoupil and Moir see evidence of potential agreement and disagreement between father and son on several key points in the dispatch (1999: 49–51).

71. Although the company was required to submit all incoming correspondence and drafts of outgoing dispatches to the Board of Control for review and approval, the Board vested its president with significant authority. Its powers were strengthened by the Charter Act of 1833, with which the British government asserted full authority over the East India Company. On the review process, see Philips 1940a: 10–11. (The Board of Control could also correspond directly with the leading administrative bodies in India, on matters of war and negotiation, through the Secret Committee of the Court of Directors.)

72. On the connection between James Mill and Hobhouse, see W. Thomas 1979: 95.

73. Zegger discusses this episode in the context of Hobhouse's presidency of the Board of Control (1973: 247–66).

74. Court of Directors (1599–1858), Minutes, 30 August 1854, B/228, fols 928–9.

75. Mill was indeed what we now call 'a Company man' (Peers 1999: 203).

76. On this point, see Kahan 2001: 102–3; Goodlad 2008.

77. See Court of Directors (1599–1858), Minutes, 28 March 1856, B/231, fol. 1307. Harold Perkin, using R. D. Baxter's 1868 publication *National Income*, suggests that in 1867 .41 per cent of all individuals in Britain had an annual income of £1,000–5,000 and only .07 per cent greater than £5,000 (1969: 420). In Zuzanna Shonfield's estimation of the late 1870s, 'Somewhere between £1,000 and £2,000 a year lay the line between middle-class comfort and gentlemanly ease for a professional man with a wife and three adult children to his charge' (1987: 134). Thus, if £2,000, supporting five adults, allowed gentlemanly ease later in the century, Mill's financial position in 1856 was strong.

78. Eileen Sullivan discusses 'Mill's theory of empire' (1983: 599), which he worked out, in part, by depending on the company's continued rule of the subcontinent.

79. During much of his retirement, spanning the last fifteen years of his life, Mill worked from his house in Avignon, France.

Chapter 2

Matthew Arnold's Beatitude

From the Athenaeum Club's founding in 1824, membership was highly prized. Unlike the eighteenth-century aristocratic clubs on St James's Street in central London, including Boodle's, White's and Brooks's, the Athenaeum admitted members, drawn from the old and new professions, who were select if no longer principally titled. Candidates were nominated by individual members and elected by the full membership under a system of blackballing common to other clubs.[1] But eligibility for election to the Athenaeum differed: 'individuals known for their scientific or literary attainments, artists of eminence in any class of the Fine Arts, and noblemen and gentlemen distinguished as liberal patrons of Science, Literature or the Arts' were admitted either by the club as a whole or, in extraordinary circumstances, by committee (Athenaeum Club 1882). In addition, a provision known as Rule II enabled the club's administrative committee to grant invitations to individuals deemed to have distinguished themselves in these fields.

Just a few years before the club was founded, establishing quasi-meritocratic criteria for membership would not have been an obvious choice. The Welsh Grenadier Guards officer and man-about-town Rees Gronow recalled that clubs in the early nineteenth century were made up of titled and landed members 'almost without exception' (1862: 76). The emphasis on achievement in electing individuals to club membership reflected widespread social changes. In the 1810s and early 1820s the East India Company, as I discussed in Chapter 1, was slowly and haltingly introducing meritocratic criteria for recruitment and promotion in the Examiner's Office. At Oxford and Cambridge students were being reimagined as individuated subjects with measurable mental abilities. Cambridge led the way with the Senate House examination, later known as the Mathematical Tripos, which had assumed its basic shape in 1753, more than seventy years before the Athenaeum established its membership criteria. Publication of a list of successful candidates, in order of merit, began several decades later.[2] The formal system of university examination – initially oral but, partly for logistical reasons, soon written – instituted at Oxford in 1800 meant that candidates, regardless of social status, faced the prospect of failure for the first time. Moreover, undergraduates from upper-class families were no longer able 'to take honorary MA degrees at the conclusion of their residence' (Curthoys 1997: 343). The principle of merit was supplanting privilege. 'Examinations', Christopher Stray argues, 'symbolized the power of individual achievement rather than group inheritance' (1998: 52). So, too, did election to the Athenaeum: early club members included sons of carpenters, gardeners, schoolmasters and butlers (Athenaeum Club 1830).

Like most new members, Matthew Arnold considered his election epochal.[3] For almost seven years following his marriage to Frances Lucy ('Flu') Wightman in 1851, the couple lived in temporary accommodations. Throughout much of this period Arnold found his concentration stymied. He longed for a place where, after discharging his many responsibilities as an inspector of schools, he could engage in quiet literary study and composition. After more than four years he settled on the Athenaeum Club as a possible solution. While election to club membership was outside one's control, connections often enabled an application to be considered far earlier than it might have been otherwise. On the basis of his already distinctive literary credentials, Arnold had no qualms about encouraging William Forster, his brother-in-law, to help expedite his application to the Athenaeum (MA 1996: 326). Less than two months later, on 11 February 1856, Arnold was confirmed as candidate 2772 (Athenaeum Club 1850–8). He began using the club every weekday afternoon whenever he was in London, maintaining this regimen even after he and Flu established a home in 1858. For the remaining thirty years of his life the Athenaeum was not only an environment where, as he repeatedly told others, 'so much of my work is done', but in fact 'the only place' where he could accomplish 'any real work' (1998: 97, 54).[4]

At his preferred desk in the south library on the upper floor, Arnold, as a new member, would read a book from the Athenaeum's enviable collection, take up his pen at a solitary desk or enjoy quiet contemplation while looking out on the world, removed from the clamour of the streets below.[5] The club served as Arnold's 'refuge' from unwanted contact, according to an obituary: to avoid giving out his 'private address', he 'professed to have no home except the Athenaeum Club' ('Matthew Arnold' 1888: 242).[6] As he wrote to his sister Jane Forster (using his nickname for her, 'K') in March 1856, he found the club 'a place at which I enjoy something resembling beatitude' (1996: 336).

What might it mean to feel a special blessedness, akin to the favour of God, in a resolutely secular environment? Historians of Western religion have tended to focus on the set of teachings, creeds and doctrines learned from scripture, whether read in individual or familial privacy or interpreted through clerical intermediaries, and then professed through speech. In other words, rather than investigating beliefs as 'what people do, how they do it, where, and when', these historians have been long been preoccupied, according to the religious scholar David Morgan, with 'the why, which is the traditional framing of the contents of belief' (2010b: xiv). The philosopher Charles Sanders Peirce proposes an alternative: 'The essence of belief is the establishment of a habit' (1992: 129). In his terms, belief governs how one is disposed to act in daily life. In glossing this assertion, Morgan argues that Peirce, by linking belief to action, also makes it possible for us to understand belief as the 'condensation' or 'sedimentation' of somatic and material practice (2010a: 1–12). Belief may produce a habit, but conversely a habit may engender belief. The architectural spaces one regularly inhabits, therefore, are not just the backdrop for belief. They may also be, in a way, belief itself.[7]

By the age of twenty-two Arnold, raised an Anglican, no longer believed Christ's divinity as proven by prophecy and miracle and had grave doubts about the immortality of the soul. He wrestled with this crisis of faith until, at the Athenaeum, he underwent conversion to a wholehearted belief in culture: the pursuit of 'sweetness', 'light' and 'perfection' (MA 1965a: 99, 91) that results in 'acquainting ourselves with the best that has been known and said in the world, and thus with the history of the human spirit' (MA 1968b: 151). In a set of essays largely written at the Athenaeum for *The Cornhill Magazine* in 1867–8 and published in 1869 as *Culture and Anarchy*, he described culture as 'the disinterested and active use of reading, reflection, and observation . . . in the endeavour to know the best that can be known' and as an aspirational process that bears the promise of 'the harmonious perfection of our whole being' (1965a: 204, 244). Arnold professed, 'I am, above all, a believer in culture' (1965a: 88). He was well aware of the religious implications of his language. Both religion and culture, he claimed, locate 'human perfection in an *internal* condition, in the growth and predominance of our humanity proper, as distinguished from our animality' (1965a: 94). But whereas religion, 'the greatest and most important of the efforts by which the human race has manifested its impulse to perfect itself', emphasises morality, culture extends its reach to include '*all* the voices of human experience', including 'art, science, poetry, philosophy, history, as well as of religion' (1965a: 93). So committed a believer had Arnold become that in 1882 Thomas Huxley referred to him as 'our chief apostle of culture' (1882: 14). Arnold embraced the appellation.

Despite Arnold's doubts about religion, he was reluctant to give up on the national church altogether. 'At the present moment two things about the Christian religion must surely be clear to anybody with eyes in his head', he bluntly asserted in later life. 'One is, that men cannot do without it; the other, that they cannot do with it as it is' (1971a: 378). In 1869 Arnold proffered a robust defence of 'establishments', including the church and the ancient universities: providing individuals with 'a sense of a historical life of the human spirit, outside and beyond our own fancies and feelings', establishments 'tend to suggest new sides and sympathies in us to cultivate' (1965h: 243–4). He contended:

> The great works by which, not only in literature, art, and science generally, but in religion itself, the human spirit has manifested its approaches to totality and to a full, harmonious perfection, and by which it stimulates and helps forward the world's general perfection come, not from Nonconformists, but from men who either belong to Establishments or have been trained in them. (1965h: 237)

Religious nonconformists, busy inventing new forms of faith and fighting for legitimacy, lacked the 'leisure and calm' of those within the established religion 'to steady our view of religion itself' (MA 1965h: 244).

Arnold thought religious nonconformists, by elevating moral discipline above other concerns, prevented realisation of humanity's full potential. They held 'a limited conception of human nature, the notion of a one thing needful, a one side in us to be made uppermost, the disregard of a full and harmonious development of ourselves' (MA 1965a: 181). To Arnold no 'one thing needful' would free individuals from the duty of developing 'all sides of our humanity' (MA 1965h: 235). Instead of nurturing an ideal of human life 'completing itself on all sides', dissenting Christian sects encouraged 'a life of jealousy of the Establishment, disputes, tea-meetings, openings of chapels, sermons' (MA 1965a: 103). But establishments, he insisted, were 'a help towards culture and harmonious perfection'

(MA 1965h: 239). They enabled individuals to cultivate their aesthetic sensibilities and capacity for measured reflection. He never relinquished the hope, expressed in 1870 in *St. Paul and Protestantism*, that a national church might facilitate a 'joint life' by opening its doors to Anglican, Catholic and Dissenter (1968d: 105).

Although the Athenaeum was not an establishment according to Arnold's definition, it was similar in many ways. This chapter explicates the material environment, as Arnold knew it, of the clubhouse, informed by German Hellenic ideals, to show that many of his key ideas were shaped by his embodied experience of its architecture, interior and milieu. In particular, 'On the modern element in literature', his inaugural lecture as Professor of Poetry at Oxford University in 1857, and the series of periodical essays, begun a decade later with his last lecture as Professor of Poetry, that became *Culture and Anarchy* articulate the premises on which Arnold's social thought rests. These premises are that modern eras distinguish themselves by the extent to which disinterestedness at the level of the individual functions as a perceptual ideal; that achievement of this vantage point requires the harmonious development of human nature (socially, politically, religiously and morally); and that, through being developed on all sides, which is the effect of culture, one can obtain intellectual deliverance.

Writing on the upper floor of the Athenaeum, Arnold expounded on culture as something for which individuals should strive. He figured culture as an extension of the concept in German Hellenism of *Bildung*, the indefinite and extended process of self-cultivation towards realisation of a whole self. Arnold held that culture consisted 'not in resting and being, but in growing and becoming' (1965a: 130). By the time he wrote *Culture and Anarchy*, he had concluded that the temperate, equipoised and transcendent 'best self' (1965a: 162) could be educed only by culture. As one contemplates 'the best that has been thought and known', culture works its salvific effects (MA 1965a: 113). Thus, the concept of self-development, and of individuality as its promised culmination, was for Arnold a rich resource to repel the anarchic forces of class competition, the homogenising effects of mass opinion.

Because Arnold wrote at the Athenaeum for more than three decades, his prose works and his collections of poetry from this period can all be examined in relation to the club. There he engaged in the experience he prescribed to others. His 'untransformed self' (MA 1965a: 135) was disassembled through the daily study of 'the best that has been known and said in the world'. In her study of Victorian clubland Barbara Black argues, 'Club life at the Athenaeum was the embodiment of Arnoldian culture' (2012: 62). But this retrospective characterisation fails to account for the Athenaeum having existed for more than thirty years before Arnold became a member. A more accurate proposition is that Arnold derived his ideas about culture, at least in part, from his association with the club. Through the effort of disassembling his old self, Arnold aimed to reconstitute himself as a classless alien, a notion he developed from the biblical concept of a remnant. Aliens were, he believed, 'mainly led, not by their class spirit but by a general *humane* spirit, by the love of human perfection' (MA 1965a: 146). To the readers of *Culture and Anarchy* he confessed, 'I myself am properly a Philistine' – a member of the middle class, in the sense he uses here – but one who had 'broken with the ideas and the tea-meetings of my own class' while not thereby having 'been brought much the nearer to the ideas and works of the Barbarians [the aristocracy] or of the Populace [the working class]' (1965a: 144). He did not expatiate on the process by which he was able to leave his philistinism behind and become an alien. Nonetheless, for reasons this chapter will elaborate, the Athenaeum surely played a causal, and until now undocumented, role.

'Impious Uproar'

In the fall of 1848, when he set out for Switzerland on holiday, Arnold had been working in London for just over a year as private secretary to the influential Whig politician Lord Lansdowne, President of the Privy Council and head of the Committee of the Council on Education. Thun, his destination in the Bernese Alps, offered relief from the bombardment of sensory stimuli in London to which he was unaccustomed, having grown up in Laleham and Rugby with brief stints in the Lake District and several years in Oxford as an undergraduate (1841–4) and a fellow of Oriel College. The trip was, equally, a restful interval after an eventful year. Revolutions had swept through Europe, plunging the Continent into political chaos, while Chartist protests across England had caused considerable instability. In March, Arnold had mingled among the 'great mob' of Chartists that assembled in Trafalgar Square. He sympathised in general with their economic distress (MA 1996: 91). The incongruity of desperate and dissatisfied workers, whose plight originated in the industrial regions, protesting in the West End, the centre of conspicuous consumption, impressed itself upon him. As he travelled through the French countryside en route to Switzerland, he thought about 'the armies of the homeless and the unfed', as he later put it in 'To a Republican Friend', a poem addressed to fellow poet Arthur Hugh Clough (1965n: 102).

Arnold returned to Thun a year later, seeking a respite from inner and outer turmoil. As he exclaimed in an 1849 letter to Clough, a friend since their student years at Rugby:

> These are damned times – everything is against one – the height to which knowledge is come, the spread of luxury, our physical enervation, the absence of great *natures*, the unavoidable contact with millions of small ones, newspapers, cities, light profligate friends, moral desperadoes like [Thomas] Carlyle, our own selves, and the sickening consciousness of our difficulties . . . (1996: 156)

Although he enumerated a variety of stressors, it is hard not to see industrialisation and urbanisation as commonalities. Until his election to the Athenaeum, where he sought refuge from the 'impious uproar' of London's streets (MA 1965d: 256), Arnold feared that the city – with its clanging bells, rattling carriages, beseeching cries from hawkers, barking dogs and peripatetic musicians – would leave him 'shatter-brained' (MA 1996: 348).[8]

Moreover, the urban environment intensified his feelings of spatial and social fragmentation. Religious sectarianism was particularly palpable in the metropolis. Not only did the city seem to magnify the inharmonious relationship between God and humankind wrought by materialism, but the proliferation of Dissenting houses of worship, which Arnold believed were established solely for the purpose of promoting particularistic views, chipped away at national unity. The most strident disputes among rival Christian sects, whose members lived in close proximity to one another, took place in cities (McLeod 1995).

Social classes, themselves intensely divided, were spatially stratified. The West End, where Arnold lived and until 1851 also worked, was an upper-class enclave. During the day he was firmly ensconced in Mayfair, tending to Lansdowne's private secretarial needs at his Berkeley Square residence, convenient for Parliament, or attending social functions at his request. At night, throughout 1849–50, Arnold attended splendid balls and soirees with his new friend Wyndham Slade, a graduate of Balliol, Arnold's college at Oxford, who was well connected in fashionable London society. (He would meet Flu at one of these parties.) Arnold rented rooms from Slade at 101 Mount Street, about a half-mile from Lansdowne House.[9]

But Arnold's perspective broadened when, in 1851, Lansdowne arranged for his appointment as one of Her Majesty's Inspectors of Schools. Elementary schools established to educate the poor were run by religious institutions and financially supported by a mix of private philanthropy, fees paid by parents and government grants. At the time of Arnold's appointment, there were only twenty inspectors for some 4,000 schools receiving grants, all subject to annual inspection (M. Black 1987: 15); only three inspectors had responsibility for schools not run by either the Roman Catholic Church or the Church of England (Machann 1998: 28). The inspector's position was, therefore, highly demanding. As Park Honan notes, in a typical year early in his career Arnold 'examined 173 "elementary schools" and 117 "institutions," 368 pupil-teachers and 97 certified teachers, as well as 20,000 pupils' (1981: 262). The job was onerous and physically demanding. To arrive at the start of a school day, Arnold needed to awaken no later than six. His responsibilities took him well beyond the affluent confines of Mayfair and Belgravia, necessitating travel to the Continent as well as to, among other areas in England and Wales, London's poor East End. As his paired sonnets 'West London' and 'East London', written in 1863 but published in 1867, suggest, he was deeply affected by the economic divide.[10] He frequently set out from his home in one of Europe's wealthiest areas to inspect schools in the region east of the Tower of London, down both sides of the River Thames, containing some of Europe's worst slums.

Such high levels of poverty contributed, Arnold felt, to low levels of social cohesion. Print publications, which flourished in the city and throughout the British Isles, exacerbated incohesion. With each story referring only to itself, daily newspapers parcelled out information and statistics in de-contextualised ways that made it difficult to assimilate data.[11] The print explosion of which newspapers were a part led to 'overfeeding' (MA 1965j: 278)[12] and, to stay with the metaphor, indigestion: 'Why the devil do I read about Ld. Grey's sending convicts to the Cape, & excite myself thereby, when I can thereby produce no possible good', he groused to Clough after reading an item about the colonial secretary's plan to distribute prisoners among British settlements (1996: 156–7). Besides feeling helpless, Arnold often found himself depressed by the ignorance displayed in discussions in newspapers: 'one is so struck with the fact of the utter insensibility one may say of people to the number of ideas & schemes now ventilated on the Continent', he complained to his sister Jane in March 1848, 'not because they have judged them or seen beyond them, but, from sheer habitual want of wide reading

& thinking' (1996: 98). When not dejected by the provincialism of newspapers, he was disheartened by the state of world affairs they reported. 'The newspaper makes one melancholy', he lamented to Flu in 1855, referring to news of the Crimean War (1996: 311). He found reading reviews and quarterlies equally stressful. An exception was France's *Revue des deux mondes*, each issue of which brought him mental relief: in 1864 he described it as 'an organ . . . having for its main function to understand and utter the best that is known and thought' (1962c: 270). But the English reviews all pressed their factional interests. *The Edinburgh Review* aligned with the Whigs; *The Quarterly Review* with the Tories; *The North British Review* propagated the opinions of 'political Dissenters'; and *The Dublin Review* tilted heavily towards Catholicism (1962c: 270–1).[13]

In the early 1860s Arnold singled out *The Times* for particular umbrage. He held that it was the premier 'organ of the common, satisfied, well-to-do Englishman' (1962c: 270–1). In London's teeming streets Arnold daily encountered philistine men of business, each carrying a copy under his arm. *The Times* only confirmed, in Arnold's view, the feelings of the middle class that, having become prosperous, they had reached the pinnacle of civilisation. The disposable income of this self-confidently ambitious bourgeoisie fuelled the production of a startling array of luxurious goods: the middle class looked up to the aristocracy and set about aping its lifestyle, Arnold observed in his essay 'Equality' (1972c: 301). Social pretensions and a wide variety of misperceptions followed.

Although Arnold was alienated by middle-class materialism, he was also increasingly repelled by the denunciatory, anti-materialistic polemic of writers like Carlyle who, he believed, peddled dangerous nostrums. Instead of Carlylean heroes, Arnold thought, the age needed 'great *natures*'. He was, as Basil Willey points out, thinking of 'leading men . . . [who] were . . . conscious of a destiny and a duty, whose fulfilment, whether conceived as an obligation to God or to one's fellow-creatures, would make life significant and satisfying' (1949: 52). Arnold did not see the likelihood of 'leading men' arising from the ranks of his associates. In London he experienced a quantitatively high degree of social interaction but a qualitatively low degree of social connection. With greater social interaction came increased occasions to experience a range of unsettling feelings: disappointment, jealousy, confusion. Writing to Clough in 1849, Arnold dismissed his 'light profligate friends', finding that the lifestyles of those with whom he came into frequent contact centred on amusements. His education at Oxford and his employment as Lansdowne's personal secretary had placed him within the orbit of young aristo-crats; he found their dignity and nobility of manner admirable but their minds vacuous.

In sum, metropolitan life exhausted Arnold. The pace was hectic: 'Too fast we live, too much are tried' (MA 1965k: 133). The sensory demands were unceasing. Modern man, Arnold noted to himself, was 'overexcited', 'over-stimulated' and 'nervous' (MA 1989: 199). Arnold's experience of London's geographic and economic divides as a school inspector, his navigation of its social scene and his encounter with heightened sectarianism and crass materialism led him in *Culture and Anarchy* to condemn the city for 'its unutterable external hideousness' and its deep 'internal canker of *publicè egestas, privatim opulentia* [public poverty, private opulence]' (1965a: 103–4).

Arnold contrasted London's repulsiveness with 'the beauty and sweetness of that beautiful place': Oxford (1965a: 106). After settling in London, he made repeated visits to Oxford, especially after being appointed Professor of Poetry, a chiefly honorary posi-tion he held for two five-year terms, from 1857 to 1867. When he could not visit, he turned, as Mill had during his mental crisis, to the 'soothing voice' of William Wordsworth, whose poetry, if not about Oxford, nevertheless captures the pleasures of the English countryside (MA 1965e: 228).

In 1798 the speaker of Wordsworth's 'Lines Composed above Tintern Abbey' imagines that by contemplating nature he can expe-rience, 'in lonely rooms, and 'mid the din / Of towns and cities' (1892: 6), the state Arnold describes as 'Wordsworth's sweet calm' (1965k: 133). The speaker in 'Tintern Abbey' recounts how, in con-tradistinction to his embodied experience of the landscape in his youth, he now cultivates, in his mature years, a disembodied rela-tion to the natural world:

> the breath of this corporeal frame
> And even the motion of our human blood
> Almost suspended, we are laid asleep
> In body, and become a living soul:
> While with an eye made quiet by the power
> Of harmony, and the deep power of joy,
> We see into the life of things. (Wordsworth 1892: 7–8)

In this dreamlike state, the speaker is released from 'the dreary inter-course of daily life', temporarily divested of corporeality itself, and experiences 'tranquil restoration' of his 'purer mind' (1892: 12, 7, 7).

He achieves an unadulterated form of subjective vision unimpaired by the body's other distal and proximal senses. With his penetrating eye, 'made quiet by the power / Of harmony, and the deep power of joy', the speaker looks through the material conditions of objects to discern their essence. In so doing, 'the weary weight / Of all this unintelligible world / Is lightened' (1892: 7).

Yet by mid-century, Arnold averred, times had changed. People were 'too harassed, to attain / Wordsworth's sweet calm'; equally impossible of attainment was 'Goethe's wide / And luminous view' (MA 1965k: 133). In Arnold's 'Resignation: To Fausta', published in 1849 as part of *The Strayed Reveller, and Other Poems*, the speaker lauds the ideal poet, 'whose mighty heart' possesses 'a quicker pulse', but 'Subdues that energy to scan / Not his own course, but that of man' (MA 1965i: 89). Having ascended a hilltop to view life in its true perspective, the poet 'surveys' the scene before him (MA 1965i: 91). From this 'high station', he 'sees the gentle stir of birth / When morning purifies the earth'; recognises the peculiar call and response of the natural world ('The cuckoo, loud on some high lawn, / Is answered from the depth of dawn'); and yearns to be part of it (MA 1965i: 90, 91). He 'looks down' on 'a populous town', making distinctions among 'each happy group', 'Each with some errand of its own' (MA 1965i: 90, 91). Although he feels connected to the townspeople (he 'does not say: *I am alone*'), he discerns that life is an 'unreal show': 'passionate hopes', amusement, even love are 'transient' (MA 1965i: 91, 93). Feeling estranged from 'general Life', from 'The Life of plants, and stones, and rain', he yearns to relinquish 'His sad lucidity of soul' by becoming one with 'That general Life, which does not cease, / Whose secret is not joy, but peace' (MA 1965i: 92, 91). The 'general Life' is an existence free equally of 'passionate hopes' and intense disappointments. This life, which the poet 'craves' (MA 1965i: 92), is essentially divested of consciousness itself: 'sheer existential subsistence, expressed most clearly in the least complex phenomena', as Alan Grob glosses the poet's desire (2002: 78).

However, with the declaratory phrase ('Enough, we live!') that begins the poem's final stanza (MA 1965i: 94), the speaker rejects the subjective indulgence of the ideal poet. When the speaker looks out from a vantage point similar to the poet's, he admits to seeing a startlingly different scene:

> the mute turf we tread,
> The solemn hills around us spread,
> This stream which falls incessantly,

The strange-scrawled rocks, the lonely sky,
If I might lend their life a voice,
Seem to bear rather than rejoice. (MA 1965i: 94)

The field is silent, and the hills are grave. The speaker hears one continual and unremitting sound: the endless, grating cascade of water. The rocks appear to have been formed in a hurried and careless way; they are unusual, odd, thus illegible. The sky seems disconnected from the plain, not part of one continuous whole. The speaker must 'lend' his voice to the natural objects which surround him, instead of to Wordsworth's responsive topography, to reach the conclusion that they speak not of joy but of endurance.[14]

Arnold's sister Jane found his poems during this period 'very beautiful' and likely to 'attract a great deal of attention'. But she concluded that they were unlikely to 'take lasting possession of the heart', as she baldly asserted to their brother Tom in 1848, before publication of *The Strayed Reveller*, because 'Matt's philosophy holds out no help in the deep questions which are stirring in every heart' (J. Arnold 1996: 123). Whereas for his generation Wordsworth had 'led men back to nature', she felt Arnold did not offer assistance, although he had the power to do so. For those with 'spiritual, social, or political' struggles and in need of 'some Mighty Helper', he 'tells them of a dumb inalterable order of the universe . . . [that] will seem too unreal & far too hopeless for them to listen to' (J. Arnold 1996: 123–4).

By the early 1850s Arnold had come to agree. Endurance seemed an inadequate philosophy by which to live. For this reason, in 1853 Arnold suppressed his dramatic poem 'Empedocles on Etna', published just a year earlier. He believed it fell into a 'class of situations' in which 'everything [is] to be endured, nothing to be done' (MA 1960c: 3). Like the ideal poet in 'Resignation', Empedocles has attained the wide view; as Arnold himself analysed the character, 'He sees things as they are – the world as it is – God as he is: in their stern simplicity' (qtd in Allott 1965: 148). But unlike the serenity of Apollo, to whom the closing lines of the poem are sung and whose inward placidity is mirrored by the calm exterior of cliff and sea, Empedocles' inner tumult finds its counterpart in his volcanic surroundings. For him 'sad lucidity of soul' is exacerbated by feelings of estrangement from humanity, which the ideal poet of 'Resignation' shares. The resolution for Empedocles, with whom Arnold had identified aspects of himself at the time of writing, is suicide.

Arnold's increasing dissatisfaction with stoical melancholy was partly tied to his urban experience. Stoicism is more easily obtained when one can keep at bay non-visual sensory data. In Arnold's 1852 'Lines Written in Kensington Gardens', the speaker, accepting the conditions of modernity, asks only for a reprieve: the experience of peaceful solitude 'amid the city's jar' (1965d: 257).[15] Four years later, Arnold found this reprieve in the Athenaeum, which functioned as a material analogue to the poem's 'lone, open glade', where 'Screened by deep boughs on either hand', the speaker experiences 'peace for ever new' (MA 1965d: 255, 256).

Latter-Day Athenians

Arnold does not write at length about the Athenaeum. Yet over three decades he penned hundreds of letters from the club. Correspondence is a source of historical evidence and experience. The existence of letters written on Athenaeum Club stationary constitutes one type of evidence, showing that he used the club often and spent time there corresponding with others. The contents of his letters are another type of evidence. However, even if a letter supplies evidence of what is in the writer's mind, or what the writer purports to have in mind, that evidence is not determinative. Arnold commented at one stage about not having any peace at the Athenaeum because he knew too many members. In December 1866, a decade after his election to membership, he grumbled in a letter to his mother that 'this club is getting to be no working place for me, I know too many men', and a month later he told her, 'I get so much interrupted here, from knowing so many people, that I shall be obliged to give up working here and take to the British Museum' (1998: 97, 106). But he continued writing letters from the club and mentioning it in letters written elsewhere. Although he often discussed interactions with club members, he also referred to work he did there. It remained 'the only place' where, in perfect tranquillity, he believed himself able to accomplish 'any real work'. For example, by 2 March 1867, he seems to have surmounted whatever difficulties he had been experiencing, noting to his mother that 'to come in at three in the afternoon at home and work for three or four hours I find the hardest thing in the world, though I can do it here' (1998: 119). Nine years later, he wrote to his sister Frances, whom he called 'Fan', that he 'had to hurry back to the Athenaeum' to undertake important work on *Literature and Dogma* (2000: 332). Determinative evidence is, therefore, not what Arnold said, first one thing and then (mostly) another, but evidence of his actions, culled from a variety of sources.

The Athenaeum, which he referred to in letters in one decade as 'delightful' and, in another, as that 'happy place' (1998: 54; 2001: 74), solved a vexing problem with which he had been grappling: separating his home life from his life as a writer. The Arnolds lived a nomadic existence for nearly the first seven years of their marriage, often staying with Flu's parents in Eaton Place. During this period, he expressed perturbation over 'the everlasting going in and coming out' of his in-laws' home (MA 1996: 348). Later, as a frequent visitor, he continued criticising its distractions. 'I am writing after dinner in Eaton Place', he wrote his mother in March 1861, 'amidst the noise of talking, which rather interrupts me' (MA 1997: 67). To Arnold, instead of helping to preserve one from the noise of the metropolis, 'where everybody chatters', the home was frequently an extension of it (1997: 100).

He had not always held this view. In his poem 'Dover Beach', which he likely wrote on his honeymoon in 1851, several years before becoming an Athenaeum member, the speaker stages the cultivation of a self who uses love as the means by which one forms knowledge of and engages with the consciousnesses of others. Reflecting on the 'confused alarms of struggle and flight', symptomatic of a disjointed culture weighted down by class divisions and religious uncertainty, in which 'ignorant armies clash by night', the speaker turns away from the convulsing social order and towards the salvific effects of reciprocal intimacy: 'Ah, love, let us be true / To one another!' (MA 1965b: 243, 242). But Arnold looked beyond the idealisation of a self nourished and maintained by the nuclearity of a family when his experience of home impinged on his intellectual and literary productivity. Just as he broadened the definition of domesticity to include the club, which became a quasi-residence to him, he broadened the notion of sacredness, which at mid-century was used to embroider domesticity, to include the Athenaeum.

Before considering some of the ways in which the Athenaeum shaped Arnold's thinking, I need to provide an overview of the club's founding and the development of its classical ethos. Soon after Lord Elgin's pilfered antiquities from the Parthenon arrived on English shores in the first decade of the nineteenth century, the writer and politician John Wilson Croker, the moving force behind the club's founding, viewed them at a makeshift museum in Piccadilly. Inspirited by these and other remnants of Greek civilisation's material culture, he became a leading advocate of utilising Greek Revival architecture to distinguish the British Regency from the French Empire. For much of the eighteenth century Britons of the literate classes had seen their political and cultural inheritance as Roman rather than Greek.[16] Yet, when Napoleon set out to transform Paris into a modern-day Rome during his rule as emperor,[17] the British literati found Athens an attractive alternative. It could be all things to all people and was, for differing reasons, embraced by Tory, Whig and Radical alike.[18] Athens was seen by Radicals as having achieved unprecedented political freedom; by Whigs as a society in which commerce and industry flourished; and by Tories as the pinnacle of culture, providing a legacy of refined beauty and simplicity.

In 1816 Croker was instrumental in persuading his parliamentary colleagues to purchase the Parthenon sculptures, which would play a prominent role in the city's transformation. London, and especially its West End, assumed its modern appearance between 1813 and 1838, when a major project of urban beautification and transformation refashioned the city in the image of Periclean Athens.[19] John Nash, architect of the Office of Woods and Forests, drew up the plans and oversaw the project. The centrepiece of this effort was a processional route connecting Regent's Park in the north with St James's Park in the south. A parliamentary bill authorising expenditures for what would become known as Regent's Park and Regent Street was debated in June 1813 and passed the following month.[20]

Regent Street divided London along a north–south axis. It consolidated the upper classes to its west and artisans, shopkeepers and the destitute to its east.[21] When George IV resolved to reconstruct Buckingham House as the monarchy's official seat, he decided to demolish his town residence, Carlton House, in St James's district – for which Lower Regent Street and Waterloo Place, an oblong space that crosses Pall Mall, had been conceived as providing a respectable forecourt. In 1825 the Commissioners of Woods, Forests and Land Revenues awarded the Athenaeum a plot on Pall Mall at the western corner of Waterloo Place, on land where Carlton House had stood, as the site of its permanent clubhouse.

When the club's founding members chose its name, derived from Athena, the Greek goddess of wisdom, craft and war (who nevertheless prefers peaceful resolutions to conflict),[22] they sought to distinguish between Britain's war of necessity, as they perceived it to have been, and France's war of choice, which had ended just a decade earlier. But the selection was significant for another reason as well. Founded at the height of a period of rancour and asperity between Whigs and Tories, the club was to be an institutional meeting-ground for members of different parties, who were expected to moderate their expressions of political disagreement (Brightfield 1940: 161). Croker, a staunch Tory, issued two of his first three invitations to join the club to Whigs: Lord Lansdowne, to whom Arnold would become private secretary in 1847, and the author Thomas Moore.[23] The founders did much to encourage conciliating tendencies,[24] including extending an invitation as part of the club's first cohort to James Mill, who had recently begun to pillory the aristocracy for its 'sinister interests'. Soon thereafter the Athenaeum was born.

But setting aside partisan and religious differences was more than a conscious choice the members made. It was an ideal stimulated, encouraged and amplified by the club's architectural design and layout. Having successfully persuaded the founders to settle on its name, Croker arranged for Decimus Burton – a rising young architect who, along with his father, was a founding member – to design their clubhouse. Burton, like Croker, had been awed by the so-called Elgin Marbles, which he had first encountered on display at the British Museum in 1817.[25] In his design for the Athenaeum, Burton incorporated strong Greek elements to express the club's purpose as an institution for literary and scientific study. Along with Croker, he persuaded the administrative committee to add, at considerable expense, a bas-relief frieze to the building's exterior as a way of visually enunciating the institution's purpose as a meeting place for learned minds:

> The committee had no hesitation in selecting the Panathenaic procession which formed the frieze of the Parthenon, as the most appropriate, as well as the most beautiful specimen of sculpture which could be adopted. To an edifice which borrows its name from Athens, intended for the reception of a Society professedly connected with Literature and the Fine Arts, they flatter themselves that this celebrated production of Athenian taste, restored, as it is here, to a degree of perfection in which it had never been seen in modern times, would not be considered inappropriate.[26]

Croker commissioned the sculptor John Henning and his son, John Junior, collaborators with Burton on the Ionic Screen at Hyde Park, to undertake the work. Based on drawings and models of the Parthenon sculptures that the senior Henning had completed in 1811, the frieze is 260 feet long, carved in Bath stone. It incorporates scenes from three sides of the Athenian original. Just as the Parthenon memorialised the Battle of Marathon, in which the Athenians bested the Persians, so too did the Henning frieze commemorate England's triumph over Napoleon in 1815 at the Battle of Waterloo.[27]

The clubhouse, therefore, functioned as an icon (Figure 2.1). It stood for the original Greek institution, dedicated to the goddess Athena, in which orators, poets, students and philosophers assembled, and it invited members to think of themselves as latter-day Athenians. To the passer-by, the club's external design enunciated its links to Athens and the ancient universities, especially Oxford, where the course of classical studies known as Literae Humaniores (or Greats) was central to the undergraduate experience.[28] Throughout the century most club members were graduates of the ancient universities, with more from Oxford than Cambridge (Waugh 1900: 46). Arnold himself had received a second-class honours degree in Literae Humaniores in 1844. One commentator captures the intention of the club's architect:

> The Athenaeum is altogether one of the best examples in London of characterisation in architecture ... so clearly does the design express a certain reserved and distinguished air of art and *literae humaniores*, which is enhanced by the classical allusions of the Parthenon frieze, the tripods, and the statue of Athene [above the entrance portico]. (R. Jones 1905: 155, 157)

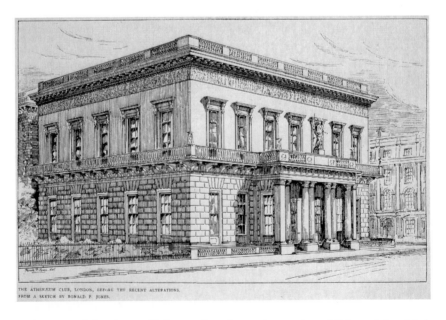

THE ATHENÆUM CLUB, LONDON, BEFORE THE RECENT ALTERATIONS.
FROM A SKETCH BY RONALD P. JONES.

Figure 2.1 Athenaeum Club exterior view prior to the addition of the third storey in 1898.

Source: *The Architectural Review* (September 1913): 154.

The statue of Athena, situated between three fluted columns on each side, condenses the building's iconographical components into a sign. Adorned by a Corinthian helmet, Athena extends 'her prone hand as if welcoming worshippers into her temple', the Athenaeum's historian F. R. Cowell lovingly notes (1975: 18). Designed by Edward Hodges Baily to replicate Athena of Velletri, the statue signifies, as the goddess does more generally, 'the potential our species has to create an ideal state, to banish barbarism, and to ensure that the physical and spiritual resources of humans have optimum encouragement for development and expression' (Hall 1997: 2). It reminds onlookers that only through cultivating wisdom and justice can 'humankind's aspiration to be superior to other animals' be fulfilled (Hall 1997: 2).

Saturated with symbolism, the clubhouse is nevertheless more than a material expression of discourse. As a physical structure, it provides 'structuring templates' for human action.[29] Some of these effects were intentional. While working on the Hyde Park Screen, Burton had developed a keen interest in the Greek concept of the *propylaeum*: a gateway into a sacred precinct. In 1823 he was tasked with designing a befitting western entrance to London at Hyde Park Corner. His triple archway is connected by Ionic columns; along the attic is the sculpted frieze by Henning Junior that would be adapted for the Athenaeum. A number of architectural historians have drawn parallels between Burton's triumphal gateway and the Arch of Titus in Rome, with which he would have been familiar.[30] Burton's contemporaries heralded the monumental entrance as a modern propylaeum, although some critics judged that it fell short.[31]

Burton never visited Greece, but he had access to a wealth of sketches, veduta paintings (detailed, realistic depictions of cities or towns) and architecture books on acropolises. Since the formation in 1734 of the Dilettanti Society, which aimed to direct the English public's taste towards classical civilisation, architects and draughtsmen had worked painstakingly to document Athenian temples and antiquities.[32] The Propylaea of the Acropolis in Athens, with a six-columned Doric façade, was a monumental gateway through which one passed to enter the consecrated sanctuary dedicated to Athena. The participants of the Panathenaic procession would make their way up the hill; pause to admire the Propylaea's magnificence or the equally impressive views of the town below; and then, when it was their turn, ascend the ramp or stairs, passing into the religious citadel through the central gate. The Propylaea made it possible for worshippers to prepare themselves mentally for their experience by screening out the secular world.[33]

Because the effect of propylaea is to establish a definitive distinction between the inside of a sanctuary and the fractious world outside, architects have often drawn on the concept in designing doorways.[34] Burton clearly had propylaea in mind when designing the Athenaeum entrance. Members, then as now, ascend a short flight of steps from Waterloo Place, pass Doric columns on either side, proceed under the entrance portico, push open a pair of double swing doors and enter the vestibule. Containing a cloakroom and a visitors' waiting area, the Athenaeum vestibule is a space of transition. Le Corbusier in his analysis of Roman architecture describes the vestibule as a feature that 'frees your mind from the street' (1931: 183). A nineteenth-century member entering the vestibule did not simply remove his coat. He was expected to shed temporarily his vested interests and partisan leanings. Francis Gledstanes Waugh, whose membership overlapped with Arnold's in later years, explicitly celebrated the vestibule's liberating effect when proclaiming that, on entering the club, one was freed from 'the shibboleth of party' (1900: 40). His comment registers the impact of architectural features that were intentionally tutelary.

By Arnold's time the result of electing individuals on the basis of merit, without regard to political party or religious belief, had become pronounced. Men who were opposed philosophically, politically and religiously gathered together, if they wished, each Monday evening in the coffee-room on the ground floor for a formal *conversazione* on topical issues. Many exchanged 'pleasant fragmentary talk' in the entrance hall (Figure 2.2): 'always a busy spot', Waugh recalls, because its capaciousness facilitated spontaneous socialising (1900: 14). After ascending the branching staircase – adorned with richly detailed balusters and illuminated, until a third storey was added in 1898, by a large octagonal skylight – they often sat at shared worktables in the library, separated only by blotters and inkwells, rather than at individual desks. Thus, within the confines of the club walls, Arnold would have glimpsed the possibility of individuals rising above sectarianism and political divisiveness to experience the ethos of Literae Humaniores.

Beauty, Sweetness and Light

Ostensibly, the Athenaeum might seem to have been less potent in shaping Arnold's life than Oxford, the city and the university, to both of which he had a lifelong attachment. Although he was an active club member for more than three decades, his relationship with

Figure 2.2 Athenaeum Club entrance hall. Artist: George B. Moore.
Engraver: William Radclyffe.
Source: London Metropolitan Archives, City of London.

Oxford was more extensive and varied. He spent formative years
at the university as a student, arriving at the age of eighteen as the
recipient of a coveted Open Scholarship at Balliol College, which
offered the opportunity for two out of thirty-three students from
public schools to gain admittance on the basis of having passed a
stringent exam.[35] Later he held Oxford's influential Professorship of
Poetry for ten years. His election to the Athenaeum occurred when he
was thirty-three, already an accomplished writer. Struck by Oxford's
physical beauty, Arnold extolled 'that sweet City with her dreaming
spires' in his poem 'Thyrsis', first published in 1866: 'Lovely all times
she lies, lovely to-night!' (1965m: 499).[36] He was never moved to
write poetry about the Athenaeum, however, although he referred to
it repeatedly and fondly in his letters. Oxford was, he recounted late
in life in a letter to his daughter Lucy Charlotte, 'still, on the whole,
the place in the world to which I am most attached' (MA 2002: 63).
Moreover, while libraries were a chief feature of both the club and
the university, they were hardly comparable. The Athenaeum's collection, impressive by the standards of private libraries in London
in the mid-nineteenth century, could not compete with the Bodleian,
one of the finest libraries in the world.

Yet Arnold's letters contain scant references to the Bodleian. With few exceptions, such as when he briefly contemplated applying for a position there in late 1881 and early 1882, none are significant.[37] Given Arnold's remarkably unremarkable academic career – in which he achieved only a second-class degree, an unprecedentedly mediocre, even scandalous, result at Balliol (Honan 1981: 46) – one might conclude that he seldom used the Bodleian. This is true, but not because of indifference: undergraduates were excluded before 1856. As a fellow at Oriel College from 1845 to 1852, Arnold had library access. He wrote about using it once during this period,[38] when the number of readers on any given day might have been no more than ten (Philip 1997: 585). But, despite its extensive holdings, the Bodleian was not an idyllic place to work.

The German philologist Friedrich Max Müller, who moved to Oxford in 1848, needed to study materials in Duke Humfrey's Library, at the time the Bodleian's only reading room. His initial view that it was 'a perfect paradise for a student' changed with the onset of a particularly harsh winter: 'I had to sit there every day . . . shivering and shaking, and almost unable to hold my pen' (1901: 258). Müller's miserable experience, which occurred three years after installation of a steam-heating system that 'made no contribution to human comfort' (Philip 1997: 586), indicates how intolerable conditions often were. After witnessing a librarian's suffering, Müller recounted, a Russian scholar who undertook research at the Bodleian had sent him 'a splendid fur' (1901: 258).

In addition to its cold temperature during winter, the library was dark. External readers like me who, in order to gain admission, have engaged in the ritual of declaring aloud 'I hereby undertake . . . not to bring into the Library or kindle therein any fire or flame', may smile at the antiquatedness of this procedure. But for much of the nineteenth century this policy meant that the building could neither be heated nor fitted with gaslights. Thus, access was limited to daylight hours. When Arnold became a fellow at Oriel, the library was open just seven hours a day in summer and five in winter (Philip 1997: 585). The Radcliffe Camera, originally not part of the Bodleian, was lit by gas; however, it became a reading room only in 1861. Arnold could certainly have used the library as Professor of Poetry from 1857 to 1867, but it is not clear that he would have wished to. During this period many griped about its severe understaffing, insufficient cataloguing and cramped accommodations.

By contrast, the Athenaeum stayed open past midnight; employed a librarian who worked closely with members; and, as I will discuss shortly, provided spacious accommodations. Before 1886, when the clubhouse was fitted with electric generators, its interior spaces were well lit by lamp oil and gas.[39] The library was heated by coal fires until a steam boiler was installed in 1869.[40] In a letter to his mother, written from the club on a blustery March day in 1867, Arnold notes that 'the fires and the arm chairs of the Athenaeum are very comfortable' (1998: 118). He took pleasure in the open – rather than, at the Bodleian, closed – stacks. As he wrote to Jane in 1856, 'It is really as good as having the books of one's own – one can use them at a club in such perfect quiet and comfort' (1996: 330). Late one night in 1867, having gone to the Athenaeum to cast his vote for a friend seeking membership, Arnold penned a quick letter to his brother Thomas, encouraging him to apply. 'To me the club is a Paradise', he declared, just a few months after complaining that he knew too many members to get much work done, 'for the goodness of its library and the librarian' (1998: 121). By capitalising 'paradise', Arnold appropriates a religious concept to characterise his secular experience of the library as an idyllic place containing everything he might have wished.

In many ways the Athenaeum offered Arnold something even Oxford did not. The venerable university had, he averred, taught the many generations who studied there that beauty and sweetness were fundamental elements of human perfection. But, as he told the audience at his last lecture as Professor of Poetry in 1867, Oxford needed to strive more for light. 'The pursuit of perfection is the pursuit of sweetness and light. Oxford has worked with all the bent of her nature for sweetness, for beauty', he proclaimed in the lecture, reprinted as 'Culture and its enemies' in *The Cornhill*. 'Light, too, is a necessary character of perfection; Oxford must not suffer herself to forget that!' (1867: 52).

While Arnold was an undergraduate, the university was plunged into internecine conflicts over criticisms of the Anglican Church's shortcomings by John Henry Newman, the prominent theologian – vicar of the University Church of St Mary the Virgin for many years before converting to Roman Catholicism in 1845 – and other members of the Oxford Movement. During much of Arnold's tenure as Professor of Poetry, Oxford was, as I consider more fully in the next chapter, a battleground in the struggle between science and religion, intellect and faith. In times of conflict, light is obscured. 'The world [. . .]', as Arnold writes in 'Dover Beach',

> Hath really neither joy, nor love, nor light,
> Nor certitude, nor peace, nor help for pain;
> And we are here as on a darkling plain
> Swept with confused alarms of struggle and flight,
> Where ignorant armies clash by night. (1965b: 242–3)

Thus, the placidity of the university town Arnold's phraseology evoked ('the beauty and sweetness of that beautiful place') was not the entirety of his experience. Oxford nevertheless represented to him 'the truth that beauty and sweetness are essential characters of a complete human perfection' (MA 1965a: 106). It was at the Athenaeum, however, that Arnold found beauty, sweetness and light in a more perfect equilibrium.

When Arnold refers to the Athenaeum in his letters, he discusses the drawing room and the adjacent libraries on the upper floor rather than the rooms on the entrance level. Turning to the recollections of a contemporary of Arnold's, we get a sense of why members were drawn to the upper floor. The Oxford scholar and official Mark Pattison, who was elected a decade after Arnold, seems to have felt, on entering the grand entrance hall, an irresistible upward pull. Years later, in declining health, he lamented to a friend: 'I feel I shall never ascend the staircase of the Athenaeum again' (Pattison 1884).[41] In the entrance hall his eyes would have been immediately drawn to a plaster cast of *Apollo Belvedere*, embedded within a niche just before the imposing staircase branches into two flights. Rather than flooding the hall with light, the skylight above the staircase created a beacon-like effect: Apollo, the god of light, beckoned members upward to the library, the locus of intellectual work (Figure 2.3).

When the Athenaeum was built, its staircase, like those in other buildings, required natural light during the day. A large octagonal skylight illuminated both the entrance hall and the staircase. Beginning in the 1750s, octagonal skylights, formerly rare, were increasingly featured in wealthy homes and occasionally in public buildings. Still, most architects in the 1820s continued to solve the lighting problem by placing windows alongside or atop a staircase.[42] The functions of the Athenaeum skylight exceeded its practical use. Like doorways, staircases, especially when evocatively lit, entice.[43] These and other architectural elements combine to make a sequence of meaningful spatial experiences (Unwin 2007: 72). Although the experience of climbing the stairway changed when a third storey was added in 1898, eliminating the skylight, by then electricity compensated for any loss.

What would it have meant to Arnold to pass the *Apollo Belvedere* on a daily basis as he made his way to the library? Donated by Burton on the club's opening, the cast was copied from the marble statue located in the Cortile del Belvedere in the Vatican, itself derived from the Hellenistic original. After its discovery in the early modern period, but before its relocation to the Vatican, the

Figure 2.3 Athenaeum Club staircase.
Source: © Country Life Picture Library.

sculpture was popularised by a print made by the Italian engraver Marcantonio. Even though the mythological episode it evoked remained unclear, the statue was taken as a model of unparalleled stylistic precision. By the early nineteenth century reproductions proliferated throughout Europe.[44] Copies of the *Apollo Belvedere* were seen as incontrovertibly superior to the original. John Wilson Croker thought the perfection of reproductions consisted less in their beauty than in their 'expression of real moral character and feeling': these statues conveyed 'consistency of character, mingled grace and dignity, which pervade the whole from the forehead to the foot' (Croker 1816: 545). At mid-century many still numbered the *Apollo Belvedere* 'among the half dozen greatest works of art in the world' (Haskell and Penny 1981: 150). Croker, who focused on emotional countenance rather than sculptural form, might nevertheless have inclined towards Johann Winckelmann's assessment, if for reasons differing from the eighteenth-century Swiss-German art historian's. 'Of all the works of antiquity, the statue of Apollo is the highest ideal of art', Winckelmann declared, 'for in it there is nothing mortal, nothing presupposing human wretchedness [. . .] I forget everything else when I behold this miraculous work of art' (qtd in Günther 2010: 55). By claiming his attention, the Apollo allowed Winckelmann to bracket momentarily whatever cares or concerns pressed upon him. In this respect forgetting is not ancillary to thoughtfulness but a constitutive component.

Because no reference to the statue has been found among Arnold's letters, one can only speculate about his response to it. It seems unlikely that he would have forgotten 'everything else' while approaching the *Apollo*, although he might have embraced aspects of Winckelmann's assessment.[45] But he could hardly have failed to be struck by the statue's commanding presence. Having concluded that the purpose of poetry is to engender pleasure, not morbidity, Arnold found increasing personal significance in Apollo as a model of serenity, an alternative to 'a continuous state of mental distress' (MA 1960c: 2), which had beset Empedocles, and as a better subject for poetry. A few years earlier, when Arnold suppressed 'Empedocles on Etna', he had not yet achieved the mental harmony and order Apollo represented. But at the Athenaeum Arnold immersed himself in the works of classical Greek authors and found his answers there, as I will shortly discuss. He came to see Apollo, who directed the Muses, as 'the great awakener and sustainer of genius and intellect' (1965f: 270). In *Culture and Anarchy* Arnold insisted on an analogical link between Apollo and culture. Just as the Tarquins had brought 'the worship of Apollo, the god of light, healing, and reconciliation', to the Roman people, enabling them to leave behind 'Latin and Sabine religious ideas', so culture, operating 'in a similar way', prevented one from becoming narrowly focused on a single idea – 'the one thing needful' of religious nonconformists – or a single school of thought (MA 1965a: 110, 181). Arnold, like the historian Ernst Curtius, attributed to the Apollonian instinct 'every prophecy resulting from a state of illumination and elevation of the human soul' (MA 1965f: 270).[46]

But even if the Athenaeum's *Apollo* was simply a fixture he passed on the staircase, its presence would have helped him disengage from the world outside the club's doors. Objects that elicit one's attention often have subtle effects. Mihaly Csikszentmihalyi and Eugene Rochberg-Halton argue that domestic objects selected and displayed by their owners establish at varying levels of consciousness 'a structured and structuring process of attention' (1981: 185). On the one hand, individuals decorate their homes with objects of aesthetic, emotional or intellectual significance. Thus, intimate objects may be clustered in the bedroom and items demarcating social status exhibited in the public areas. Because human beings are incapable of attending to all things equally, such decorative schemes create an 'organized pattern of attention' that channels and directs mindfulness (Csikszentmihalyi and Rochberg-Halton 1981: 185). On the other hand, through the routinised inhabitation of domestic space, the number of objects that attract conscious attention is curtailed:

> The total context of artifacts in a household acts as a constant sign of familiarity, telling us who we and our kindred are, what we have done or plan to do, and in this way reduces the amount of information we have to pay attention to in order to act with ease. (Csikszentmihalyi and Rochberg-Halton 1981: 185)

While a few objects stand out, the rest play more diffuse roles in engendering overall ambience.

Csikszentmihalyi and Rochberg-Halton do not discuss the 'surrogate home', which many Victorian gentlemen, including Arnold, considered their clubs to be.[47] Even though clubs were not personalised domestic spaces, an 'organized pattern of attention' was possible. In an individual's choice to affiliate with a particular club, the décor is likely to have played a role, making it feel like home. In the individual's interactions with objects within the club, as more generally, it would have been true that, as Csikszentmihalyi and Rochberg-Halton contend, 'most of our interactions . . . consist of habitual patterns of attention' (1981: 184). Habitual patterns, like routines of everyday life more generally, stimulate and maintain attention because they '"relieve" the individual of constant uncertainty or doubts' (Lüdtke 1995: 5), thereby enabling focus. Or, as David

Morgan claims, repetitive actions and tasks 'free up' one's mental energies 'for those experiences that are more demanding, absorbing, sensuously rewarding, or critical' (1998: 14). Arnold's routine experience of the Athenaeum's entrance and ground floor, then, would have relieved him of life's provocations so that, in the upper-floor drawing room and library, he could 'endeavour to know the best that can be known' through focused attention on surveying great works of literature. His use of the term 'sweetness and light', which he popularised although it originated with Jonathan Swift,[48] captures the vividness of the strikingly lit grand staircase leading to the upper floor, where one might pursue perfection.[49]

The Library

The upper floor's dominating feature is the library. By Arnold's time it comprised three rooms: the larger south library, 30 by 43 feet, at one end of the drawing room, and the smaller, interconnected west and north libraries at the other end. Each provided a mix of shared worktables and separate niches offering more privacy. But the south library was most impressive, as it remains today. Lit by large vertical windows, it contains floor-to-ceiling stacks and a cast-iron staircase enabling access to the shelves. One observer remarked of the upper floor, 'If a friend shows you over the establishment, you will notice that the stillness which reigns throughout all the rooms is broken by nothing save the crisp sound of paper, or the swift scratching of pens' (Hay 1870: 212).

The club's library symbolised the ethos of Literae Humaniores, encouraging members to transcend differences. Some scholars have seen libraries as a material instantiation of Arnold's ideas of light and culture.[50] But one might as easily posit that Arnold elucidated his ideas of light and culture from a library, which shaped his thought in distinct ways. From the opening of its permanent clubhouse, the Athenaeum held some 4,000 volumes, arguably constituting the most significant private collection of books in London. Within a year the club committee had established an acquisitions policy. The principal aim was to provide robust coverage of the humanities with solid and respectable holdings in belles-lettres. Standard works of reference; scholarly studies in humanistic disciplines (ranging from classics to literature, and from aesthetics to theology); memoir and biography; and history (from military to ecclesiastical, and European to British) were all favoured, as were major contributions to, among other fields, science and medicine, politics, economics and law. Although many titles were in English, works in Greek, Latin and French were well represented. The library also acquired series that would have been prohibitively expensive for individuals to own. Finally, to supplement its holdings, the club made available a number of new books borrowed each month from a circulating library (Cowell 1975: 66–7). By 1844 the library had 20,300 volumes. When Arnold was elected in 1856, the figure had climbed to well over 31,000 (Cowell 1975: 20).[51] By the end of the century, the Athenaeum was widely acknowledged to have 'the finest and most important club library in the world' (Waugh 1893: 309).

The writings of eighteenth-century German Hellenists were favoured by many of the club's founders. *Kultur*, as well as the related notions of *Bildung* (self-cultivation) and *Vielseitigkeit* (many-sidedness), informed aspects of the club's construction and design as well as its members' daily activities. This was particularly true of the library. The historiographer John Hill Burton's dictum on reading, F. R. Cowell suggests, proved apposite to the Athenaeum's efforts to establish a pre-eminent collection. Cowell quotes Burton as asserting, 'Either the possession of, or, in some other shape, access to a far larger collection of books than can be read through in a lifetime, is in fact an absolute condition of intellectual culture and expansion' (Cowell 1975: 65).[52] Implicitly underwriting this aphorism is the concept of self-cultivation, which the club library, with vast holdings far in excess of what an individual can read, indicates. As early as 1835 the German historian Friedrich von Raumer recognised a link between cultivated individuality and London clubs, including the Athenaeum. Recording his impressions of the three clubs to which he had been introduced, Raumer evoked the classical ideal of the whole man, whose intellectual, emotional, moral and physical capacities are all equally developed. The Athenaeum, he enthused, provided 'all possible provision for body and mind' (Raumer 1836: 59). If he had read Raumer's account, Arnold would certainly have agreed: 'I . . . could not have got to a place more perfectly to my mind', he rhapsodised to his brother William (Willy) in an 1856 letter (1996: 331).

The principle of many-sidedness governed the club's policy on periodicals as well as books. The Athenaeum encouraged the non-sectarian spirit on which it had been founded by subscribing to all the political periodicals, thereby placing within the member's reach a broad range of opinions. With current issues of periodicals available for perusal in the drawing room and older issues in the stacks, the member could, should he wish, avail himself of all perspectives on an issue. Additionally, the club subscribed to all the London newspapers (morning, evening and Sunday editions) and several provincial, American and French newspapers. A considerable number of specialised English-language journals, covering topics from anthropology to economics, as well as European periodicals, were also received (Cowell 1975: 74–7). Thus, the library provided an institutional context for eliciting in users what David Wayne Thomas would call regulative rather than substantive liberality: a reflective disposition to consider a range of views on public and private matters (2004: 10).

The upper floor demonstrated one definition of 'athenaeum' as, according to the *Oxford English Dictionary*, 'a building or institution in which books, periodicals, and newspapers are provided for use; a literary club-room, reading-room, library'. Less than a week after his membership was confirmed, Arnold wrote to his sister Jane, saying, 'I am elected at the Athenaeum . . . and look forward with rapture to the use of that library in London' (1996: 330). With its obvious connotations of mental ecstasy, 'rapture' also implies the religious experience of having one's mind elevated by the grace of God over distinctly human concerns.[53] Raised aloft, one is released from the shackles of subjective vision.

Arnold surely sensed that in the library he was freed from the pervasive spirit of national insularity and the parochial mind-set of the middle classes (whose sensibilities had largely been shaped by their Bible reading and nothing more), which he continually excoriated in his writings. Indeed, it was widely claimed, as one member put it, that one could escape the 'suburban Philistine' by retreating to the Athenaeum ('A returned empty' 1900: 31). There Arnold seems to have felt liberated, if only temporarily, from an environment pervaded by practical philistinism and religious sectarianism, both of which impeded cultivation of wholeness.

The Drawing Room

As the chairman of the Athenaeum's general committee noted soon after the club occupied the building, the drawing room is 'a light and commodious gallery for the library'.[54] Chroniclers of club life and architectural critics throughout the century agreed, hailing it as 'splendid', 'one of the most beautiful rooms, of its class, anywhere to be seen', and 'one of the finest rooms in London'.[55] Occupying the building's entire east side, the drawing room measures 100 feet long,

30 feet wide and 27 feet high. Its spaciousness is thrown into relief, however, by its tripartite division, an effect Decimus Burton obtained through use of pairs of pilasters and scagliola columns to separate the compartments; by its Grecian style of decoration, which dictates relatively plain interior surfaces and sparing use of ornament; and by the seven large windows overlooking Waterloo Place and two equally large windows, separated by white-marble chimney pieces and large mirrors, in each end wall, north and south. In Arnold's day, while the ceilings of the north and south compartments were flat, the middle ceiling was saucer domed.

The drawing room, as Arnold inhabited it, has long since been substantially modified. When electricity was introduced in 1886, perceptions of colour changed, and Burton's original interior was deemed too muted. In the 1890s a redecorative scheme was undertaken by the artists Edward Poynter and Lawrence Alma-Tadema and the civil engineer Arthur Lucas. Alma-Tadema painted the dome and beams in an aluminium tone[56] and hung green brocade on the walls to draw out the yellow marble of the scagliola columns more effectively. In 1927 the ribbed saucer dome on pendentives in the middle compartment of the drawing room was flattened to make further space available for the additional floor added in 1898. Modest changes were made throughout the twentieth century. In the 1980s a Redecoration Advisory Group oversaw restoration of the drawing room 'to something like its original appearance': the walls were swathed in leaf green; the ceilings painted in white (later beige); and a red patterned carpet, intended to evoke the early nineteenth century, laid (Boucher 2001: 68–9). But, whatever feeling of reversion the décor now engenders, the drawing room is not as Arnold experienced it.

Images of the room, including Burton's designs, engravings and paintings, enable one to reconstruct its original appearance. These images are not unproblematic. The club maintains a folio of drawing-room designs and watercolours, but no designs were implemented exactly as proposed. In 1836 James Holland depicted the drawing room in an oil painting (Figure 2.4). Widely reproduced in studies of the club as a straightforward rendering, Holland's painting does not, in fact, faithfully represent the drawing room's size and scale. When I visited the club in 2008, having already studied the painting and subsequent efforts to renovate and restore the room, I carried a set of expectations. But the drawing room seemed considerably smaller than the painting led me to imagine. The ceilings, although I had accounted for the elimination of the saucer dome, were lower; the

Figure 2.4 *The Athenaeum: The Drawing Room* by James Holland.
Engraver: William Taylor.

Source: London Metropolitan Archives, City of London.

walls closer together; and the length of the room, while arresting, did
not make the objects on either side seem as far away as Holland had
portrayed them. Instead of providing simple visual documentation,
the painting communicates information about how individuals felt
about a room that was, by London standards at the time, remarkably large.

Although Holland's *The Drawing Room* is inhabited, it captures
the quality of expansive tranquillity for which the upper floor of
the Athenaeum became known. Arnold's letters suggest that he, like
Holland, partook of this feeling. 'I am sitting now, at ½ past 12 in
the day, writing at a window in the great Drawing Room', Arnold
recounts to his brother Willy in March 1856, 'with only two other
people in the room – every side of this magnificent room covered
with books and the room opening into others also full of books'
(1996: 331). Repeating 'room' four times within one sentence,
Arnold's prose reproduces what he perceives as the 'great' drawing
room's capaciousness even as it celebrates temporary withdrawal
into a sparsely inhabited space that serves as an environment for

thinking about the world: as he notes appreciatively, there are 'only two other people in the room'.

Because Holland's and Arnold's perceptions of space inevitably differ from mine, even by visiting the Athenaeum I cannot feel or experience what Arnold's generation would have felt and experienced. Early twentieth-century photographs more closely approximate my perceptions of the drawing room but are also misleading. Unlike Holland's painting, they rarely include club members. In the early twentieth century the drawing room was documented without occupants (Figure 2.5). The biases of architectural and design history, which tend to favour creators rather than users, likely account for the absence of members in photographs accompanying write-ups about the club in fine-art and architecture magazines.

Attempting to experience the view from the club windows is similarly problematic. On the evening when I gazed out one of the great vertical windows on the upper floor, as Arnold might have, I could identify little he would have seen except for the former United Service Club across Waterloo Place. When Arnold first looked at

Figure 2.5 Athenaeum Club drawing room.
Source: © Country Life Picture Library.

the neighbouring club, as designed by John Nash, it was noticeably different from his own clubhouse. This had not been the original intention. The clubs were to be uniform.[57] By the time Arnold
wrote *Culture and Anarchy*, however, he would have seen a near
mirror reflection of the Athenaeum. In the 1850s the United Service,
whose members were senior army and navy officers, commissioned
Burton to reface and redecorate their clubhouse. He made a number
of structural changes, including relocating the main entrance, and
added noteworthy embellishments. The most striking is a frieze on
the northern façade in which military horsemen are participating
in the Panathenaic procession. The result, completed in 1859, was
increased likeness between the club designs.[58] These architectural
details remain, although the United Service building now houses the
Institute of Directors, serving as a gathering place for business leaders, entrepreneurs and corporate directors.

   I do not know whether, as he looked out the window while writing *Culture and Anarchy*, Arnold thought about the symmetry of the
Athenaeum and the United Service clubs – one standing for mental
life, the other for regimented conduct – and the balance achieved in
their visual design, when he asserted: 'man's two great natural forces,
Hebraism and Hellenism, will no longer be dissociated and rival, but
will be a joint force of right thinking and strong doing to carry him
on towards perfection' (MA 1965a: 226). As is well known, Arnold
concluded that many problems besetting his age originated in the dis-
equilibrium between these balancing 'forces'. Arnold used 'Hebraism'
to designate the Judeo-Christian concern with duty, work and conduct
that had reached its apogee in contemporaneous religious nonconformity and dissent. Hebraism, he said, was an 'energy driving at practice'
(163). 'Hellenism' indicated practices of cognitive detachment aimed
at objectifying the social world in order to understand it better and
ultimately transform it (163). The ethical thrust of Hellenism was 'to
leave the world better and happier than we found it' (91). Whereas the
German writer Heinrich Heine, from whom Arnold derived his notion
of the Hellenic and Hebraic,[59] saw only continuous battling between
these two forces, Arnold argued in *Culture and Anarchy* for establishing equilibrium between them: 'the true and smooth order of humanity's development is not reached' by either Hebraism or Hellenism alone
but through their fusion, a 'mutual understanding and balance' (177).
Both Hebraism and Hellenism had perfection as their aim. But while
Hebraism stressed commitment to individual discipline, to instrumental thinking and thus to largely mechanical action, Hellenism encouraged the pursuit of perfection through disinterested study.

Although Arnold hoped a proper balance between these two forces might one day be realised, he advocated meanwhile for greater Hellenising. He thought Hebraism had become far too dominant. Critical of his contemporaries, who possessed social ideas founded on insufficient light, Arnold asserted the importance of cultivating a state, devoid of activity, where the 'the free play of the mind' (MA 1962c: 268) and a 'fresh stream' of critical thought might enable an individual to solve social problems more efficaciously and to discern 'some lasting truth to minister to the diseased spirit of his time' (MA 1965a: 235, 199). The Athenaeum's upper floor, housing the greatest private library in London, provided an atmosphere conducive to cultivating such a state.

In fact, the Athenaeum drawing room might be thought of as a physical correlate to the capaciousness of the Greek mind. This capaciousness, which Arnold proffered as an alternative to the cramped, austere models of human perfection propagated by politics, religion, class and even city life, stemmed from a commitment to the harmonious development of the various sides of human nature. London's claustrophobic conditions, which he explored in his poetry, engendered narrowing of the human mind: 'For most men in a brazen prison live, / . . . / Their lives to some unmeaning taskwork give, / Dreaming of nought beyond their prison-wall' (MA 1965l: 269). Thus, I mean 'physical correlate' in two senses: the nineteenth-century users of the Athenaeum's upper floor experienced it as impressively spacious, and the books and periodicals in the library, if one availed oneself of them, facilitated an expansive worldview.

Raised Aloft

After becoming a member of the Athenaeum, Arnold underwent a pivotal transformation: from poet to essayist. His *Poems, Second Series* had been published in December 1854, slightly more than a year before his election to the club. For roughly his first eighteen months of membership, Arnold devoted himself to preparing, not publishing. He began spending many weekday afternoons between two and six in the library, engaged in preparatory reading for his long-planned poem on the Roman poet and philosopher Lucretius and his verse drama *Merope*. 'What I learn in studying Sophocles for my present purpose is, or seems to me, wonderful: so far exceeding all that one would learn in years' reading of him without such a purpose', he exclaimed to his sister Jane. 'And what a man! What works!' (MA 1996: 364).

In May 1857 Arnold's election as Professor of Poetry at Oxford added a new focus to his literary endeavours. The position, which required delivering several lectures annually, functioned as a further spur to reading widely, facilitating his turn towards criticism. Having ensconced himself among books for months at that 'dear old place', the Athenaeum (MA 1998: 374), Arnold emerged to deliver his inaugural lecture, 'On the modern element in literature', in November 1857.[60] Briefly, Arnold argued that in Periclean Athens 'human nature developed in a number of directions, politically, socially, religiously, morally' and thereby achieved 'its completest and most harmonious development in all these directions' (1960a: 28). Because Greek poets were fully developed, they obtained 'that noble serenity which always accompanies true insight'. Thus, Arnold remarked, 'I have ventured to say of Sophocles, that he "saw life steadily, and saw it whole"' (1960a: 28). Indeed, whenever he discussed classical literature, Arnold celebrated the jubilant 'lucidity of mind' and 'clear view' of the ancient Greeks in contrast with the 'sad lucidity of soul' of the contemporary poet (MA 1960b: 141; MA 1965i: 92), including himself. As the terms 'point of view', 'clear view' and 'lucidity' imply, Arnold, while writing from the Athenaeum's upper floor, was developing a visual idiom that continued to dominate his discussion of intellectual deliverance in the years to come.

In the essays that constitute *Culture and Anarchy*, which he began writing in the library ten years after his inaugural lecture, Arnold elaborates, through a grammar of visual distance, on his perceptual ideals, with their promise of overcoming the limitations of the subjective view. As his contemporaries understood, the notion of critical distance is only intelligible through invocations of seeing, often from an explicitly aerial viewpoint.[61] In *Culture and Anarchy* obtaining 'intellectual vision', bound up with achieving 'excellence', is likened to attaining a perch on 'high and steep rocks' that 'can only be reached by those who sweat blood to reach her' (1965a: 152). Arnold asks readers to 'see . . . how indispensable to that human perfection which we seek is . . . establishment of our best self' (162) – a perspective that, in transcending the bounded view of one's 'ordinary self', characterised by class envy, habitual intractability and insistent individualism, recognises general rather than class interest. He insists: 'To get rid of one's ignorance, to see things as they are, and by seeing them as they are to see them in their beauty, is the simple and attractive ideal which Hellenism holds out before human nature' (167). Therefore, he urges his contemporaries to Hellenise, to think more critically in order to 'see things as they really are' (178, 252), 'by keeping aloof from what is called "the practical view of things"' (1962c: 270). All these statements depend on the larger conceptual metaphor of intellectual activity as a form of seeing. That is to say, although his use of 'vision' and 'to see' is identical with 'understanding' and 'to understand', the ontological metaphors undergirding what might otherwise be dismissed as a literal expression are alive: conceptualising the mind as a structure or edifice in which individuality is located and from which thinking, troped as a form of seeing, occurs.[62]

A frame of mind and a perceptual ideal based on disinterestedness – described in *Culture and Anarchy* as 'see[ing] things as they really are'; in 'On translating Homer' as 'see[ing] the object as in itself it really is' (1960b: 140); and in 'The function of criticism' as 'keeping aloof from what is called "the practical view of things"' – are, indeed, the conceptual analogues to the tranquillity, privileged views and relative privacy of the Athenaeum's upper-floor windows.[63] By examining Arnold's conceptual vocabulary in the context of its material referent, one sees that his notion of critical distance derives force and coherence from the particular vantage point he enjoyed while gazing at the world from the upper floor.

When writing letters, Arnold often sat at a solitary desk in the drawing room beside one of the large vertical windows. Shortly after his election to the club, Arnold shared with his brother Willy his impressions of the room. He commented particularly on the view:

> I look out upon the façade of the Senior United and the open place in front between that club and ours, and on the roofs and colonnade of the old Italian opera–and the Park below the Duke of York's column is full of people . . . (1996: 331)

His gaze travelled from the opposing club, the United Service, to the Doric colonnades of Her Majesty's Theatre, formerly called the Italian Opera House; to the Duke of York's column, a monument to state power and military aptitude, between the east and west wings of Carlton House Terrace. In looking at the United Service Club, Arnold would have perceived its association with discipline, uniformity and rigid order.

What Arnold saw from the Athenaeum's upper floor was not a panorama. But the great vertical windows' perceptual framing of scenes, which enabled viewing foreground, middle ground and horizon, freed him as an observer 'from the occlusions of a narrowed and partial experience of the world' and, given the club's many amenities that sustained quiet reflection, also 'from an experience of the world as *material*.[64] Released from the close press of the everyday, Arnold again took up the notion of the wide view, which he seemed partially to abandon in 'Resignation' and 'Empedocles on Etna' because of the sense of estrangement from humanity it provoked. In these poems the wide view is linked to 'sad lucidity of soul'. In work written at the Athenaeum, however, he argued that the wide view engenders calm equipoise, instead of subjective indulgence, and enables one to move beyond the personal.

Thus, by metaphorising intellectual activity as a form of vision, Arnold relied on a spatial orientation that resonated evocatively with his aloof vantage point at the windows of the drawing room and the library. For many members, the West End defined London, with the Athenaeum at the intersection of its social and intellectual life. To look out its windows was to watch 'the stupendous tide of life that is ever moving past in that wonderful city' (Fields 1872: 35). The windows were unusually tall and rectangular, extending almost from floor to cornice, and made of novel material: plate glass. In 'On translating Homer' and 'On the modern element in literature', both written at the Athenaeum, Arnold lauds Greek 'lucidity of mind' and capacity for clear thinking, which resonates with the translucency of plate glass that enables proper vision (1960b: 141).[65] The nineteenth-century architect Aston Webb boasted of plate glass's 'perfection in manufacture': 'we can see objects through it without distortion or obstruction of any kind' (1878: 221). Unlike sheet glass, which was prone to visual fluctuations that magnified or diminished objects, depending on the part of the glass through which one was looking, or crown glass, which might contain noticeable small bubbles or striations, plate glass was remarkably free of flaws and seemed entirely translucent. As the distinguished metallurgist Walter Rosenhain noted early in the twentieth century, 'no kind of glass is perfectly transparent', but 'the slight tinge of colour' in plate glass, at its best, 'has no deleterious effect whatever, the majority of persons being entirely unconscious of its presence' (1908: 32, 34). According with human physiognomy and fitted with translucent glass, the Athenaeum's windows invited silent rumination on the world they enframed.

Deliverance and Deliverers

As a student at Oxford, Arnold had found his belief in the atonement and Jesus Christ's physical resurrection no longer tenable. He had already been exposed to German historical and biblical scholarship at home. His father, the educational reformer and Broad Church proponent Thomas Arnold, accepted that some statements in the Bible needed to be understood metaphorically rather than literally.[66] But Arnold's occasional use of religious terminology to describe his feelings about the club ('beatitude', 'Paradise', 'rapture') suggests a kind of certitude. At the Athenaeum, where some reported experiencing feelings of reverence, Arnold gained a new belief: 'I am, above all, a believer in culture' (MA 1965a: 88).

Silence augmented the impression the drawing room and library made on Arnold and sacralised the time he spent there. To be sure, the club provided both spaces where spontaneous exchanges might occur and formal occasions for conversation and debate. But, more than any other club at mid-century, it offered solitude over convivial chatter. Noted for its hushed, studious atmosphere, the Athenaeum was, as the Tory Rudyard Kipling, evoking the breadth and beauty of the drawing room and its sparse occupancy, once quipped, 'till one got to know it . . . rather like a cathedral between services' (1990: 84). Kipling's description identifies more than absence of sound. Silence creates the conditions for awe and enchantment.[67]

Like Kipling, Arnold inclined towards cathedrals, which many Tories saw as essential to the Anglican Church. His intellectual engagement with Tory ideas dated from his undergraduate days at Oxford, then a bastion of political and intellectual Toryism, where he was first exposed to conservative thought. His father had railed against 'the wickedness of Toryism' (T. Arnold 1845: 359), but Matthew Arnold, as a result of his time at Balliol, became more receptive to ideas associated with a party for which he would never vote.[68] His friend group at Oxford exposed him to a range of views: from the republican sentiments of Arthur Hugh Clough, his most intimate confidant, to the conservatism of their mutual friend James Anthony Froude, the Tory historian. Neither aligned with Arnold's temper. On the formation of the Liberal Party, Arnold was predisposed to support it. Yet, concerned that the party's reform efforts lacked sufficient light, he sought distance, proclaiming himself 'a Liberal of the future rather than a Liberal of the present' (1973a: 138).

At Oxford, John Henry Newman exerted great influence on Arnold although the two did not meet then. Arnold's inclination, shaped by his father's sensibility, was for less mysticism and dogma in the Anglican Church, whereas Newman moved from criticising the Anglican Church to adopting Roman Catholicism. Arnold, therefore, dismissed as 'impossible' the 'solution' Newman had embraced for the doubts and difficulties which beset men's minds to-day' (MA 1975a: 165).

But his exposure to Newman's ideas was formative. Several decades later Arnold declared to Newman that 'nothing can ever do away the effect you have produced upon me, for it consists in a general disposition of mind rather than in a particular set of ideas' (2000: 71).[69] This disposition of mind, which he began to work out as early as 1864, several years before writing *Culture and Anarchy*, sought to balance 'the thinking-power' and 'the religious sense' (MA 1962e: 231).

As a religiously evocative site of ideation, the Athenaeum provided Arnold a milieu in which such balance was keenly felt. Additionally, it was a place where Tory and Liberal, Anglican and Dissenter, intermingled. The church's founding purpose, Arnold contended, was to be a big tent that welcomed and tolerated diverse beliefs (MA 1972e: 95). Unlike Dissenting sects, the established church did not exist to promote 'special opinions', such as Eucharistic prayer or baptism, but to advance 'goodness' (MA 1968c: 85; MA 1972b: 67). Doctrinal variety within the church was conducive to moderation and unity, and these conditions were, in turn, necessary for complete development of the self:

> Instead of battling for his own private forms for expressing the inexpressible and defining the undefinable, a man takes those which have commended themselves most to the religious life of his nation; and while he may be sure that within those forms the religious side of his own nature may find its satisfaction, he has leisure and composure to satisfy other sides of his nature as well. (MA 1965a: 239)

Despite the church's abandonment of inclusiveness, Arnold believed that those raised within it, an experience of which Mill, for example, knew nothing, still gained perspectival breadth: 'a sense of a historical life of the human spirit, outside and beyond our own fancies and feelings' (MA 1965a: 243).

If Christianity were to survive, he thought, it needed to be established on non-theological grounds, with individual righteousness, not fallible stories or purported miracles, as its basis (MA 1968a: 257). Tradition and ritual would persist, but as religion's 'poetry' (MA 1973b: 161). Although some of Arnold's contemporaries attempted to align his thought with German higher criticism, he saw himself as advocating his father's Broad Church or Liberal Anglicanism (Collini 2008: 101). Unable to embrace fully the paths staked out by either Newman or German biblical criticism, torn between the republican opinions of Clough and his own conservative political tendencies, in short, overwhelmed by 'the multitude of voices counselling different things', Arnold sought to cultivate at the Athenaeum Club a disinterested intelligence, founded on studying the ancient world, that distanced one from the controversies of modern life and therefore placed one 'under the empire of facts' (MA 1960c: 8, 13). Thus, instead of turning to the established church for 'help out of our present difficulties' (an unstable society riven by conflict and division), Arnold looked to culture, which he saw as offering society much that the established church no longer did (MA 1965a: 233).

Arnold's use of the term 'beatitude' in regard to his pursuit of culture within the Athenaeum evokes a state of ultimate felicity; it also calls to mind those individuals who, when God's reign is established, experience deliverance. For Arnold 'intellectual deliverance', which he felt he had obtained within the sanctified realm of the club, was a pressing need for society:

> The demand arises, because our present age has around it a copious and complex present, and behind it a copious and complex past; it arises, because the present age exhibits to the individual man who contemplates it the spectacle of a vast multitude of facts awaiting and inviting his comprehension. The deliverance consists in man's comprehension of this present and past. It begins when our mind begins to enter into possession of the general ideas which are the law of this vast multitude of facts. (1960a: 20)

In this effort, which Arnold defines by drawing on the visual metaphor of a 'spectacle', 'the literature of ancient Greece is, even for modern times, a mighty agent of intellectual deliverance; even for modern times, therefore, an object of indestructible interest' (1960a: 20). The consummate achievement of this state, when intellectual deliverance becomes 'perfect', occurs 'when we have acquired that harmonious acquiescence of mind which we feel in contemplating a grand spectacle that is intelligible to us', Arnold asserts, 'when we have lost that impatient irritation of mind which we feel in presence of an immense, moving, confused spectacle which, while it perpetually excites our curiosity, perpetually baffles our comprehension' (20). Contemporary verse should help readers comprehend the spectacle of the age, thus serving as an agent of intellectual deliverance. But, he posits, the modern poet is like Lucretius: insufficiently developed on all sides, 'overstrained, gloom-weighted, morbid' and therefore 'no adequate interpreter' (34).

Obtaining a vantage point from which one 'saw life steadily, and saw it whole', Arnold thought, was necessary in order to achieve intellectual deliverance in the nineteenth century.

Much like the Greek mind, a harmoniously developed nature enables one to grasp 'the general ideas' underlying the bewildering 'multitude of facts' competing for attention. Having understood these general ideas, one is then able to impart them to others: 'he who communicates that point of view to his age, he who interprets to it that spectacle, is one of his age's intellectual deliverers' (MA 1960a: 20).

Accordingly, Arnold turned from poetry to interpretive criticism, which he defined as the disinterested 'endeavour, in all branches of knowledge, – theology, philosophy, history, art, science, – to see the object as in itself it really is' (1960b: 140). By producing a climate of 'fresh' and 'intelligent' ideas, criticism lays the groundwork for truly valuable poetry (MA 1962c: 263). As Arnold developed this notion of the interpreter as an intellectual deliverer, he began simultaneously to see the need for a learned class. The first obligation of a member of this class was to purify one's own vision before undertaking to educate others.

In 1860 Arnold was earnestly contemplating the form a democratic society might take. Having accepted the inevitability of universal suffrage, he, like Mill, was anxious about the mediocrity and conformity an enlarged franchise portended. Also, like Mill, he came to favour a strong meritocracy that would preserve qualitative distinctions among members of a democratising society.[70] Those who had obtained greater self-development and mental liberalisation should serve as guides for those who had not. Writing to Harriet Martineau, he baldly stated:

> I have never read of any democracy which truly succeeded except by entering into that alliance with the best intelligence and virtue within itself, and submitting to that guidance from it, which aristocratic and oligarchic governments manage to get on without. (1997: 15)

In an essay published in 1861 and republished as 'Democracy' in 1879, Arnold, while accepting that the aristocracy was no longer capable of providing intellectual and moral leadership, fretted about 'the dangers which come from the multitude being in power, with no adequate ideal to elevate or guide the multitude' (1962b: 18). He insisted in an 1863 essay that 'freedom of inquiry' must be vested in 'the whole body of men of letters or science' (1962a: 51). Eleven years later he argued that guidance on social, political and religious matters should come from 'a disinterested literary class – a class of non-political writers, having no organised and embodied set of supporters to please, simply setting themselves to observe and report faithfully' (1971b: 92).

Arnold saw the possibility of such faithful reporters emerging from any class. He termed them 'aliens'. Having 'a curiosity about their best self' (MA 1965a: 145), they laboured to shed the narrow prejudices, motivations and conditions of the class of their birth. This enabled them, in a formulation I quoted earlier, to be 'mainly led, not by their class spirit, but by a general *humane* spirit, by the love of human perfection'. Ideally, an education in the classics (Literae Humaniores at Oxford, and Classical Tripos at Cambridge), which many club members shared, would produce this spirit. Although the Athenaeum may not have pointed the way towards a world without a socio-economic hierarchy, it would have nevertheless suggested to Arnold the possibility of living without the stifling conformity of class interests. Aliens – the remnant, as he sometimes called them – were seekers of wisdom who divested themselves of the pernicious characteristics of their originating classes (MA 1975b). Club members, each time they were welcomed into their temple by Athena's outstretched hand, would have been reminded, and perhaps gently admonished, to divest themselves of partisan leanings and vested interests and evince allegiance to their respective fields of knowledge.

Arnold first broached the concept of the 'best self' in *Culture and Anarchy*, returning to it nearly a decade later in 'Bishop Butler and the zeit-geist'. In this lesser-known essay Arnold contends that 'as man advances in his development, he becomes aware of two lives, one permanent and impersonal, the other transient and bound to our contracted self' (1972a: 44). These two selves, existing simultaneously, compete and conflict with each another. In becoming one's impersonal best self, the 'instinct' for life, which had waxed and waned in Arnold's poetry, is 'truly served and the desire [for happiness] truly satisfied' (42). One who leads this 'higher and impersonal life' is 'thus no longer living to himself', Arnold concludes, 'but *living*, as St. Paul says, *to God*' (62) – God being a term he glosses elsewhere as 'a deeply moved way of saying *conduct* or *righteousness*' (1968a: 193).

Arnold's division of the self into two entities has much in common with Adam Smith's conception of the self-governing individual. In *The Theory of Moral Sentiments* of 1759, Smith asserts that we derive our sense of 'personal beauty and deformity' from praise or censure by others rather than from any sense within ourselves (1767: 200). If our appearance is either admired or criticised, we scrutinise ourselves in front of the mirror as if 'with the eyes of other people' and attempt to understand what they see

(200). Moving from appearance to decorum, Smith observes that a similar dynamic is at work, in which the eyes of another are integrated into the self:

> We suppose ourselves the spectators of our own behaviour, and endeavour to imagine what effect it would, in this light, produce upon us. This is the only looking glass by which we can, in some measure, with the eyes of others, scrutinize the propriety of our own conduct. (201)

Split into two, the individual is both 'the examiner and judge' of one's own behaviour, from a perspective outside the self, and 'the agent' whose actions deserve either applause or disapproval (202).

Similarly, Arnold maintains that the best self possesses eyes with which to evaluate the 'transient' and 'contracted' self (1972a: 44). Instead of championing Wordsworthian disembodiment from the natural world, Arnold extols re-embodiment of a higher self with the ability to see through objective eyes the ordinary self that needs 'correcting' and ultimately 'dominating' (44). Because he is committed to living an impersonal life in a bodily way, he seeks to specify ways by which the higher self might distinguish itself to others. He finds his answer in the vestigial remains, the conduct and manners, of an aristocratic culture in which he otherwise lacks faith.

'Behaviour is not intelligible, does not account for itself to the mind and show the reason for its existing, unless it is beautiful', Arnold notes (1965a: 184). Aristocratic behaviour was intelligible to Arnold. Although the Athenaeum was decidedly not an aristocratic club, as evidenced by the active membership of vociferous critics of landed interests, from James Mill to Thomas Huxley, aristocratic manners and bearing were widely diffused there. 'The atmosphere of dignity which pervades the interior is almost funereal', a visitor observed (Hay 1870: 212). Arnold concluded that members of the aristocracy, despite lacking light, discerned the essential truth of 'sweetness' as a law of life, as evidenced by their 'distinguished manners and dignity', their 'high spirit, choice manners, and distinguished bearing' (MA 1965a: 125, 141). Although aristocrats had achieved a 'noble way of thinking and behaving', the aristocracy had not produced best selves (MA 1962b: 6). No class had. But, for all their deficiencies, aristocrats had come nearest the mark. Best selves, Arnold thought, were most likely to emerge from among aliens, those who had achieved perspectival breadth. Through their labour, culture would be diffused throughout society.

The Athenaeum Writ Large

For Arnold, the counterpart of the individual best self was the state: the 'organ of our collective best self, of our national right reason' (1965a: 136). In tandem with aliens, who, ideally, represented the best self, the state would work to diffuse sweetness and light. The reshaping of London's urban landscape, of which the Athenaeum was a part, besides being an expression of English supremacy and self-confidence, was a reassertion of state authority. Above all, the metropolitan improvement works in the early nineteenth century reflected an effort to redefine the individual's relationship to a constitutional monarchy. 'Unlike the Rue de Rivoli in Paris, to which it was often compared, Regent Street is not a grand axis of absolute authority, rather it is a routeway between the heart of the city and open country', Denis Cosgrove reminds us, 'which deploys a linked series of crescents and squares to follow a compromise path, unified by the white-painted stucco of its classical architecture: a tribute to constitutionalism' (1985: 217). Through direct citations of Hellenistic architecture, erected as expressions of civic pride and reverence for a putatively more democratic governmental structure than Napoleon's, the West End became a monument to the triumph of Anglo-Saxon constitutionalism over feudal authority.

Had Burton's and the Hennings' edifices, with their friezes and statues symbolising military prowess and architectural styles evoking order and unity, played a role in shaping Arnold's belief that, like culture, the state was a key resource in staving off anarchy? When Arnold strolled through the West End in the 1850s and 1860s, he would have recognised the spirit of interconnection among the various civic buildings and private clubhouses constructed as part of early-century Greek Revivalism and contrasted this with the Gothic eclecticism that was increasingly taking hold. As he approached the Athenaeum's entrance portico or, once upstairs, gazed out the window from his favourite spot in the drawing room, Arnold would have seen, as his letters attest, the Duke of York Column, towering over Carlton House Terrace. Hyde Park's monumental entrance, the Revivalist architecture of the 1810s and 1820s, the Duke of York Column: all were representations of political authority intended to underscore the importance of a constitutional monarchy.[71] They evoked a 'sense of shared community and belonging', previously manufactured almost solely by municipal ritual and royal pageantry (D. Arnold 2000: 79).

For Matthew Arnold, strong assertions of state power, in part through close association with establishments, could counter the religious sectarianism and political factionalism that fomented anarchy. 'We want an authority', he writes, against the backdrop of popular protestation, 'and we find nothing but jealous classes, checks, and a dead-lock; culture suggests the idea of *the State*' (1965a: 135). As an impersonal entity transcending class, the state emblematises the concept of a whole community. But Arnold finds English political culture fracturing because of class competition:

> Our leading class is an aristocracy, and no aristocracy likes the notion of a State-authority greater than itself, with a stringent administrative machinery superseding the decorative inutilities of lord-lieutenancy, deputy-lieutenancy, and the *posse comitatus*, which are all in its own hands. Our middle class, the great representative of trade and Dissent, with its maxims of every man for himself in business, every man for himself in religion, dreads a powerful administration which might somehow interfere with it; and besides, it has its own decorative inutilities of vestry-manship and guardianship, which are to this class what lord-lieutenancy and the county magistracy are to the aristocratic class . . . (117–18)

The aristocracy and the middle class, each ruling over a political domain with distinct offices and titles, attempted to make government a reflection of their self-interests. This, for Arnold, was a way of seeing the object as it really was not.

As culture helps educe the individual best self and the state represents the collective best self, the state should be seen as the instantiation of 'the very self which culture, or the study of perfection, seeks to develop in us; at the expense of our old untransformed self' (MA 1965a: 134–5). If the state were perceived this way, then those elected to office would, instead of advocating for their vested interests, take advantage of the 'almost boundless means of information' available and commit themselves more fully to 'the enlargement of mind which the habit of dealing with great affairs tends to produce' (MA 1962b: 27). For their part, those not elected would still identify with the state, as the 'organ of our collective best self, of our national right reason', and therefore consider themselves connected to it.

Because Arnold thought culture would perish in a fully democratised society if the state did not insist on preserving it, he forswore identification with his originating class and declared allegiance to the state: 'Thus, in our eyes, the very framework and exterior order of the State, whoever may administer the State, is sacred . . .' (1965a: 223).

Although the Athenaeum and the state were dissimilar, he connected them by a common vocabulary; in both, in contrast with religion, he saw the possibility of salvation and rebirth. The state would secure a harmonious, tranquil world akin to the Athenaeum Club writ large. Indeed, his ultimate hope, expressed through an evocatively spatial idiom, was that 'all men [may] live in an atmosphere of sweetness and light, where they may use ideas, . . . nourished, and not bound by them' (113).

By championing the power of the state, Arnold understood himself to be rebuking Mill, who was so wary of the predominating influence of political, civil or religious institutions. This has led a number of scholars to see Arnold aligned with 'social stasis' and 'conformity' (Knights 1978: 123; Rothblatt 1968: 129), problems Mill perceived as besetting his age, for which plurality of living was the answer. But even as Mill encouraged eccentricity as a means of opposing the tyranny of conformity, he always assumed that at a more advanced stage of humanity the necessity for different 'experiments in living' would recede (JSM 1977d: 281). Freedom would become conjoined with predictability. The resultant society would be, as Arnold also hoped, harmonious and tranquil. Perhaps conscious that more united than divided them, a greatly perplexed Mill wondered to one correspondent why Arnold persisted in 'enumerating me among the enemies of culture' (JSM 1972a: 1324).

Although both Mill and Arnold worked in quasi-domestic environments, their experiences took their thought about the public and private facets of the self in different directions. Promoted to a cellular office, Mill came to value strongly both the private self, constituted by 'liberty of thought and feeling' (JSM 1977d: 225), and the public self who engaged in vigorous debate. Arnold's routine inhabitation of a club that shielded him from the turmoil of the world led him to complicate the terms 'public' and 'private'. In his estimation, the public self was, in fact, 'personal', with class and religious-based affiliations that led it to be 'separate' and 'at war'. Only through the cultivation of an 'impersonal', private best self could peace and tranquillity be achieved (MA 1965a: 134).

Among those with whom Arnold frequently interacted at the Athenaeum was John Morley, one of Britain's premier journalists and politicians. As editor of *The Fortnightly Review* (1867–82), which had been modelled on the *Revue des deux mondes* because of Arnold's praise for that periodical, Morley published several pieces by the poet-cum-social critic. As John Stuart Mill's leading disciple, Morley was impatient with aspects of Arnold's thought. In 1871, in a letter to his friend Frederic Harrison, Morley alluded dismissively to Arnold: 'I don't mean you are to write nonsensical flummery about sweetness and light' (qtd in Hirst 1927: I, 192). Yet, although Morley believed himself and Arnold to be 'of a very different school', he recognised that they 'had common enemies to encounter' (Morley 1917: 128).

For his part Arnold never singled out Morley, as he did Mill, as an enemy of culture. Moreover, he commented to his mother that Morley 'has certainly learnt something from me, and knows it' (2000: 23). Morley thought Arnold had rather underestimated his impact on him. Writing near the end of life, Morley observes of Arnold: 'He says in a private letter to somebody that I owed him more than I thought. This was not so, for I owed him much, and from Oxford days I well knew it' (1917: 128). In 1883 he proclaimed Arnold to be 'among the foremost poets of his period' and 'the 'most distinguished' figure in the literature of the age and country to which he belongs' (1883: 87–8). In 1886, when Morley and his family moved to a newly constructed property in South Kensington, he drew on the writings of both Mill and Arnold in an effort, as the next chapter will document, to recreate the architectural spaces of the home with the aim of living, as Arnold had counselled, 'united, impersonal, at harmony' (MA 1965a: 134).

Notes

1. Once a week, between February and May, Athenaeum members cast their votes in favour of or against nominees by placing white or black wooden balls in bins marked 'aye' or 'no'. The original number of black balls for denying admission, one in ten, was later changed to one in fifteen. See J. Crook 2001: 19.

2. On systems of examination at the ancient universities, see Gascoigne 1989; Curthoys 1997; and Stray 1998. On examinations and the production of individuality, see Meadmore 1993.

3. See, for example, comments by Henry Crabb Robinson (1870: 8), Edward Wilmot Blyden (Lynch 1970: 182) and Joseph Conrad (2002: 193, 197). Membership was greatly prized even if the club was not a primary haunt. Anthony Trollope recounts in his autobiography never having been more surprised than when the 'honour' of membership in the Athenaeum was conferred on him through Rule II (1999: 160). Nevertheless, he preferred the Garrick Club.

4. See also MA 2001: 118. Matthew and Flu Arnold had a large family, with six children born between 1852 and 1866, in whose upbringing he was closely involved.

5. After about a decade of membership, Arnold began working more frequently in the smaller north library, which he preferred because it was not gaslit (MA 1998: 106).
6. Amy Milne-Smith notes, 'It was natural for men to use their club, rather than their home, as a base. Many clubmen used their club as their primary address, taking advantage of club stationery and postal services' (2011: 118).
7. 'Religion happens not *in* spaces and performances as indifferent containers', Morgan asserts, 'but *as* them' (2010a: 8).
8. For a substantive discussion of Arnold's poetic response to the urban experience, see Thesing 1982: 64–76.
9. After his marriage to Flu and the arrival of three children in close succession, but before his election to membership at the Athenaeum, Arnold sometimes escaped the distractions at home by working at his old apartment in Mount Street, which Slade made available to him from eleven to five on weekend days (MA 1996: 348).
10. Little critical attention has been given to these poems. An exception is Wolfreys 1994: 49–52.
11. A point later made by the Frankfurt School theorist Walter Benjamin (2003: 315).
12. In his poem 'The Second Best' Arnold uses the term in reference to books.
13. Although Arnold found most English newspapers and periodicals distressing, he experienced mental relief with each issue of the *Revue des deux mondes*, which he described in 1864 as 'an organ . . . having for its main function to understand and utter the best that is known and thought' (1962c: 270).
14. On the 'designification of nature' in Arnold's poetry, see Lorsch 1983: 31–50 and J. Miller 2000: 212–69.
15. As Alan Roper helpfully points out, Arnold 'wishes to translate the peace he finds in a glade *surrounded* by the city's jar into a peace when he is *included* in the city's jar' (1969: 52).
16. See Ayres 1997 for a discussion of Rome as a political model for eighteenth-century Britain.
17. Rowell 2012 provides an overview of the reinvention of Paris as a new Rome.
18. See Turner 1981: 1–14; Stray 2007b:103–4 and 1998: 18–19; and Jenkyns 1980: 13–14.
19. This project was a mode of 'associationism' in which architects selected a historical style that most closely approximated the values they sought to instantiate (Hersey 1972: 2, 7–10). Between 1825 and 1838 a number of cultural and educational institutions were erected to remake West London into Periclean Athens. Among them were the British Museum, designed by Robert Smirke in the Grecian style with striking Ionic porticoes, and University College and the National Gallery, both designed by

William Wilkins, who had studied and documented Greek architectural remains. Reshaping the urban landscape according to the stylistic ideals of Greek antiquity functioned as a declaration to the wider world of English supremacy and self-confidence (Olsen 1986: 12).

20. The New Street Act of 1813 (53 Geo III c121) and the New Street Act of 1826 (7 Geo IV c77) authorised the two main stages of the project.

21. Constructing Regent Street in a simple north-to-south line would have taken it through seedy Soho. Instead, as Nash explained in his proposal, 'the new street should cross the eastern entrance to all the streets occupied by the higher classes and to leave out to the east all the bad streets' (qtd in Summerson 1980: 124). Nash's plan explicitly called for 'a boundary and complete separation between the streets and squares occupied by the nobility and gentry, and the narrow streets and meaner houses occupied by mechanics and the trading part of the community' ('Mr. Nash's report' 1813: 30). Dana Arnold therefore notes, 'The open agenda behind Regent Street to create a class divide through London shows the fissure between the rich west and poor east' (2005: 7).

22. See Waugh's discussion of the name selection (1900: 3).

23. See Croker 1884: 256–7 and T. Moore 1984: 692.

24. On the Athenaeum as a venue for assuaging political differences, see Thomson 2001: 3. Nevertheless, tensions occasionally flared up between members of opposing political beliefs; see W. Thomas 2000.

25. H. Ward summarises the importance of the Elgin Marbles to Burton's vision (1926: 35).

26. Athenaeum Club (1825–31), Report of the Committee, 11 May 1829.

27. On the relationship between Henning frieze and the Parthenon, see I. Jenkins 1994 and 1992: 19.

28. Cambridge established Classical Tripos in 1822, with the first examination occurring in 1824, whereas an examination in Literae Humaniores was established at Oxford in 1800 and first held in 1801 (Stray 2007a: 3–5).

29. I am borrowing Bruno Latour's phrase (2005: 196).

30. Dana Arnold cautions that this link is far from 'obvious' (2005: 139).

31. 'New Grand Entrance' 1827 provides one such critique.

32. For a history of the Dilettanti Society, see Cust 1898, especially pp. 68–106, and Gaunt 1952, especially p. 14.

33. On propylaea as spaces of transition, see Hopper 1971 and Rhodes 1995.

34. On the relationship of propylaea to doorways, see Unwin 2007: 68–72.

35. See Curgenven, who outlines the 'unusually fierce' nature of the several-day exam process (1946: 54).

36. Arnold worked on the poem for a year: January 1865 to January 1866 (DeLaura 1969a: 192).

37. For a discussion of this point, see my forthcoming 'Matthew Arnold: Sir Thomas Bodley's librarian?'

38. In his essay 'George Sand', Arnold recalls having used 'Cassini's great map at the Bodleian Library' (an eighteenth-century portfolio of maps of France) in 1846, looking for the town of Toulx-Sainte-Croix, which Sand describes at some length in her novel *Jeanne* (1972d: 217).
39. In 1896 the clubhouse was connected to mains laid by the St James's and Pall Mall Electricity Company (Cowell 1975: 25). Electricity was, at this point, a limited and privileged amenity.
40. Cowell 1975: 21–38 provides an overview of the club's technological amenities.
41. H. S. Jones discusses Pattison's attachment to the Athenaeum (2007: 149, 164).
42. Campbell discusses the history of illuminating stairways with windows (2014: 105, 109–15).
43. On illumination as a form of enticement, see Tutton 2014.
44. The statue is discussed by, among others, Günther 2010 and Haskell and Penny 1981: 148–9.
45. Arnold's knowledge of Goethe, Lessing and Schiller is more commonly discussed than his knowledge of Winckelmann. But, as Richard Unger suggests, 'a heretofore unnoticed affinity of thought' between Winckelmann and Arnold is possible (1978: 208).
46. Arnold uses but does not cite Curtius's words here.
47. The term 'surrogate home' is Milne-Smith's (2011: 109).
48. The term 'light' also had biblical resonance. It appears among Bible phrases Arnold jotted down repeatedly in his notebooks, including 'in thy light shall we see light' from Ps. 36: 9 and, from Eccles. 11: 7, 'Truly the light is sweet' (MA 1952: 72, 366).
49. The association of light and ideas with elevation is part of the experiential grounding of orientational metaphors. 'These spatial orientations', Lakoff and Johnson argue, 'arise from the fact that we have bodies of the sort we have and that they function as they do in our physical environment' – hence the often-moralised distinctions between high and low, up and down and so on (2003: 14).
50. On this point, see Augst 2007.
51. See also Athenaeum Club 1853: 100.
52. Cowell slightly misquotes John Hill Burton's 'The book-hunter again', which reads, 'possession, or in some other shape the access to a far larger collection of books than can be read through in a lifetime' (1861: 59).
53. In the context of theology, 'rapture' also means, according to the *Oxford English Dictionary*, 'the transport of believers to heaven at the Second Coming of Christ', but that definition would not have resonated with Arnold.
54. See Athenaeum Club (1825–31), Report of the Committee, 9 May 1831. For a discussion of the club's drawing room, see also G. Williams 1990, especially pp. 37–60; Thornton 1984: 142; Waugh 1893: 309.

55. 'Athenaeum Club House' 1830; Obituary notice 1883: ix; Nevill and Jerningham 1909: 211.
56. See Ramsey's discussion of the ceiling (1913: 57).
57. The Commissioners of Woods and Forests, through John Nash as their architect, wrote the Athenaeum initially to say that the east and north fronts of their clubhouse must correspond with the west and north fronts of the United Service. However, confusion ensued, partly because of Nash's dual role and propensity to act without consultation. In any case, because the frontages differed in size, complete uniformity was impossible. Both Nash and Burton altered their first designs, although an affinity between them remained. See Athenaeum Club 1828; Athenaeum Club (1825–31), Report of the Committee, 9 May and 11 May 1825; 'Pall Mall' 1960.
58. The relationship between the United Service and the Athenaeum in Arnold's time was more than architectural: a reciprocal arrangement was established in 1865, enabling members of one to visit the other when theirs was closed for cleaning or repairs (H. Ward 1926: 68–9). Arnold regularly exercised this option in the 1870s.
59. Arnold wrote both a poem and an essay on Heine. In the essay Arnold says, 'He has excellently pointed out how in the sixteenth century there was a double renascence, – a Hellenic renascence and a Hebrew renascence, – and how both have been great powers ever since' (1962d: 127).
60. Arnold was the first holder of the chair to deliver his lectures in English rather than Latin, necessitating a different approach to their preparation. He would have had to consider making his arguments more relatable, more contemporary, more engaging, more convincing because his listeners would be processing ideas expressed in their native language.
61. The cartoonist Frederick Waddy depicted Arnold as a trapeze artist swinging from poetry to philosophy (1873: 136). A more accurate depiction, albeit lacking in amusement, might have been of Arnold at one of the drawing room's eleven vertical windows. The critic and novelist Arthur Quiller-Couch seemed to recognise as much when, in 1893, alluding to Arnold's famous praise of Sophocles, he rebuked literary critics for assuming that 'only through the plate-glass windows of the Athenaeum Club is it possible to see life steadily, and see it whole' (1893: 357).
62. On the relationship between conceptual metaphors and idioms, see Gibbs 1994: 157–61.
63. A trace of this material origin can be gleaned from G. K. Chesterton's loving appraisal of Arnold's legacy. For Chesterton, Arnold's chief insight is that the English soul, likened to a window, was 'opaque with its own purple'. Hence, it functioned as a gorgeous mirror with no 'opening on the world without'. Culture, however, enabled one to 'wash' the window 'and then forget it' (1906: ix). In this conceit, the window does not reveal the soul; rather, it enables the cleansed soul's outward vision.

64. I am borrowing Barrell's differently focused terminology from his account of eighteenth-century landscape painting (1992: 42). Isobel Armstrong compellingly argues that 'what matters is how the *window* makes you see, not only how you *see* through it' (2008: 115).

65. There is, of course, a long history of thinking about vision in philosophical texts, having nothing to do with windows or plate glass, with which Arnold would have been familiar. Nevertheless, plate glass provided a meaningful nuance in so far as it enabled Arnold to gain 'practical understanding' – the term used by Pierre Bourdieu in reference to knowledge derived from daily, mundane practice (1980: 52–79).

66. For excellent discussions of German higher criticism and its impact on Thomas Arnold, see apRoberts 1983: 56–79 and Zemka 1997: 68–99.

67. An illustration in *Punch* in 1858 defined an imaginary conversation as 'anybody speaking to anybody at the Athenaeum' ('Imaginary conversation' 1858). The poet and politician Richard Monckton Milnes, writing in 1873, complained that members of the club 'live together, without encounter, and little recognition' (qtd in T. Reid 1891: 284).

68. Late in life, Arnold declared to his sister Frances that, although he hoped Lord Salisbury's Conservative majority would be returned to Parliament ('the Liberals being so unripe'), 'I should never myself vote for a Tory' (2002: 94).

69. Arnold confessed subsequently that even some of his fundamental ideas had been shaped by Newman. He was one of the few from whom Arnold was 'conscious of having *learnt* . . . habits, methods, ruling ideas', Arnold wrote Newman (2000:123). These ideas included what Arnold would term 'disinterestedness', which is rooted in Newman's notion of knowledge for its own sake; cultivation of an urbane rather than a provincial style; and abhorrence of middle-class philistinism and resistance to liberalism. DeLaura 1965 provides a thorough analysis of Arnold's lifelong engagement with Newman's thought.

70. This is unsurprising, because both men had been recognised for their individual aptitudes, Mill at India House and Arnold, first at Balliol as the recipient of a merit scholarship and then at the Athenaeum. The systems of promotion at India House and of election at the Athenaeum uncoupled birth and inheritance from rewards and opportunities. The Athenaeum's discourse of merit obviously differed from the East India Company's in several crucial respects, not least that it was associational while the company's was occupational. But, as a technology of individuation, merit-based systems of promotion and election produce similar results.

71. For a consideration of monuments to military prowess and state authority, see D. Arnold 2005: 79–81, 123–86.

Chapter 3

John Morley's Impersonal Domesticity

When John and Rose Morley began house-hunting in late December 1885, the couple had intended to secure accommodation close to Westminster.[1] As Member of Parliament for Newcastle upon Tyne, Morley – who had ventured into politics with the by-election of 1883, having distinguished himself as a journalist and editor – found the daily commute from Wimbledon, where the couple had been residing, increasingly onerous. After viewing a number of houses that were centrally located but incommodious and lacking in amenities, however, Morley lamented to his sister, Grace, that the experience was 'very doleful'.[2] The Morleys settled instead on a suburban property. Morley wrote to Grace in April 1886 to share the news:

> The scene of our future glories is to be at Elm Park Gardens – a great pack of dwellings in S. Kensington, about six minutes' walk from Gloucester Road station, and on the Fulham Road, almost close to the Brompton hospital. There is an immense large garden belonging to all the houses collectively, and the rooms are wonderfully light and bright. The house has never been inhabited, and we have the privilege of choosing our own papers, paint, tiles, etc., etc. – which we like very much. Also we are well pleased to go into a place which has not the heart-sickening smell of old London houses. The servants will have very fair quarters indeed – and on the whole, considering the awful dog-holes of London, we are more than satisfied. The rent is more than I like, but we shall cut down at some other end . . . We shall migrate as soon as the painters will let us – probably in about a month's time. It is very handsome and mighty genteel, and you will not be at all ashamed to come to see us. (qtd in Hirst 1927: II, 277)[3]

With its excellent transportation links, South Kensington offered spacious, newly constructed houses with modern amenities and rents lower than in central London.[4] In writing about his new residence, Morley does not boast about the location. Rather, he refers to the property's newness and spaciousness and the freedom to express individual preferences in decoration. As this chapter will explore, Morley's enthusiasm for these three characteristics, coming from a second-generation liberal whose views took shape against the backdrop of scientific developments that catalysed materialist and determinist understandings of the self, has broad and significant implications.

Published interviews and biographical vignettes that describe Morley's two Elm Park Gardens residences – no. 95 (1886–96) and no. 57 (1896–1903) – frequently juxtapose the acute particularity of his domestic interiors with the indistinguishability of their Queen Anne exteriors (Figure 3.1). 'Because the external structure of the houses built during the building booms of the Victorian period were often uniform in external appearance, as is the case today,' Mike Hepworth points out, 'it was the home within which gave these homes their individual character and which encouraged an increasing fascination of outsiders (newspaper reporters, novelists, gossips) with the lives of those inside' (1999: 18).[5] Although biographical profiles of all kinds proliferated in print, the 'at home' feature was particularly successful because it tapped into an emergent belief that domestic

Figure 3.1 Elm Park Gardens, December 1944.
Source: BB45/00150 © Historic England Archive.

interiors reflected the personality, and hence the individuality, of their occupants (Cohen 2006: 123).

Morley was the subject of numerous 'at home' portraits, beginning in the mid-1880s. 'A broad, quiet street', with its 'prospect of a hundred similar houses, four storeys high, with steps leading to a portico and three front windows', the French critic and Anglophile Augustin Filon remarks in the opening paragraphs of his lengthy character sketch of Morley, published in the *Revue des deux mondes* (Filon 1891: 155).[6] While Filon thought Elm Park Gardens evinced a high degree of stylistic uniformity (each house 'differs in no way from its neighbours'), the interior of no. 95 seemed singularly different (155).

From the 1860s the Victorian middle class began practising dense massing of furniture and knick-knacks. This process accelerated, Deborah Cohen has argued, towards the close of the century, with the home becoming the staging ground for a new concept of personality; instead of being associated with honesty and sincerity, personality was about performance and display (2006: xi–xiii). Through tasteful and adept, or even incongruous, choices and the presentation of sentimental memorabilia, bibelots and goods acquired in travels abroad, individuals could establish a meaningful and intelligible relation to the home as a representation of their interiority (Cohen 2006: 136–44). But this was not what Filon encountered:

> On the first floor,[7] you are left alone in a drawing room that reinforces the impression [of this house as a place for quiet contemplation]. Bookshelves take up an entire wall. No knick-knacks, no bright colours, not a trace of affectation or exoticism. The furniture is vaguely modern, without an exact date and without a distinguishing style. There is a severity half-way between banality and elegance in a harmony of subtle and pale tones. The master of the house must like whiteness, not the glaring, aggressive whiteness that affronts the eye, but the discreet, slightly grey whiteness that rests and caresses the sight. (1891: 155–6)

If the concept of personality enabled homeowners to revel in decorative eclecticism, based on individual whimsy rather than slavish adherence to design rules, here was a domestic environment that presented an enigma. Excess and clutter, including objects that symbolised emotional attachments and the exotic knick-knacks popular among much of the middle class, were nowhere to be found.

Filon's 1891 essay was picked up by the English press and disseminated in summary form. Subsequently, he published *Profils anglais*, a widely reviewed collection of essays on leading English political figures, which included a slightly revised version of the Morley essay.[8] Although Filon was particularly influential and widely read, others commented on Morley's home. *The Windsor Magazine* included two paragraphs as part of its 'Houses of celebrated people' series (Bell 1895: 335). More ephemeral publications, such as *The Star, The Penny Illustrated Paper and Illustrated Times* and *Moonshine*, provided brief observations of the 'wholly unpretentious outside' of Morley's Elm Park Gardens home and the omnipresence of books within ('Mr. John Morley's London home' 1892).[9] In 1903 *The Pall Mall Magazine* published a vignette by Harold Begbie, who subsequently included it in a book of profiles of notable men (Begbie 1905). Years later *The Graphic* provided an intimate glimpse, with photographs by the commercial photographer Alfred Abraham, of Rose and John in retirement at Flowermead, the home on Princes Road in Putney to which they had moved in 1903 ('A great English man' 1917).[10]

Biographical pieces on Morley are remarkably consistent in depicting his domestic environments as sparsely furnished and, for an upper-middle-class home, atypically decorated.[11] In 1892 a journalist visited no. 95 and pronounced that 'simplicity is the note within' ('Mr. John Morley's London home' 1892: 157). Seven years later, an anonymous parliamentary colleague who met with Morley at no. 57, built according to the same floor plan as no. 95, described it as 'his roomy but simple house' (Anon. 1899: 874). These minimalist interiors were always attributed to Morley, who, for reasons I will soon elaborate, was responsible for decorating the couple's homes. The accounts leave one with the impression that, by controlling the selection and quantity of furnishings, as well as their colour, which, together with the unadorned walls, effected a soothing whiteness, Morley was able to create a disparate, serene environment.

Frequently described but never examined in depth, Morley's residential interiors reflect a strong sense of order, unity and freedom from distraction. Conspicuously absent was the dense massing of textiles, bric-a-brac and furniture characteristic of the bourgeois home in that era. His interiors fostered cultivation of detachment and impersonality.[12] Morley, whose intellectual mentor was John Stuart Mill, might be expected to have realised Mill's notion of the ideal home as a site of deliberation between autonomous adults who, as spouses, have achieved friendship of the 'highest order' (JSM 1984: 411). But Morley's liberalism was inflected by his religious upbringing and his experience of institutionalised homosocial relations – at boarding schools and Oxford, as a member of the Athenaeum Club (where he was elected in 1874) and of Parliament, and as a cabinet minister in several Liberal governments – in ways that complicate our understanding of his indebtedness to Mill. In the spaces of the home, Morley engaged in a strenuous practice that I call 'impersonal domesticity', which Mill might term an experiment in living. However, in attempting to live as a free subject, emancipated from the narrow interests of class, from the feminine influence ascribed to the home and even from the constraints of physical proximity, Morley continued to rely on class- and gender-based prerogatives he otherwise disavowed.

'A Large and Serene Internal Activity'

In her influential *Household Gods: The British and Their Possessions*, Cohen argues that changing theological views in the nineteenth century, from emphasis on the atoning death of Christ to an incarnationalist view of creation and sanctification, enabled the increasingly prosperous middle class to celebrate the acquisition, distribution and display of material goods (2006). Christ began to be seen less as a saviour than as a perfect exemplar. 'A worldly Christian compassion, inspired by the life of Jesus', Boyd Hilton writes, 'had alleviated such stark evangelical doctrines as those of eternal and vicarious punishment' (1988: 5). The doctrine of incarnation, which began to pervade Anglican and Nonconformist theology, was seen by many as liberating and ennobling.

In Cohen's account the doctrine of atonement had facilitated rejection of worldly goods. The incarnationalist doctrine, widely embraced beginning in mid-century and positing human beings and their possessions as repositories of the divine, undergirded the emergent self-confidence and optimism of the British middle classes. This doctrine enabled them to reconcile religious morality with what the earlier Evangelical culture had often opposed: material prosperity (Cohen 2006: 3). Thus, the quintessential Victorian drawing room came into its own in the 1860s and 1870s as a monument to self-expression.

The simple décor of Morley's residences indicates that he largely eschewed the late nineteenth-century turn towards demonstrating material abundance. Yet it would be inaccurate to conclude that Morley's homes simply reflected the residual traces of austerity and abstemiousness associated with the age of atonement. Unfolding alongside and informed by the design reform efforts late in the century, such as aestheticism, Morley's impersonal domesticity necessitated the transmogrification of these and other Evangelical principles.

Before elaborating on the elements that make up this experiment in living, I need to begin by considering Morley's religious upbringing. These biographical details are important to my argument for two reasons. First, Morley's early religious convictions and subsequent loss of faith are essential to his contributions to philosophical thought. In emphasising the religious aspect of Morley's childhood and youth, I am not thereby claiming, as a psychological reading might, that the singularity of his experience is what matters in understanding his work. Rather, Morley could generalise in his writings from the occurrences in his own life precisely because these experiences were widely shared (Hamer 1968: 2). The liberalising individuals of mid-century had been raised in similarly devout homes; at university, they found their convictions becoming unsettled; and, if they renounced their faith, often their families rejected them.[13] Loss of faith produced, in turn, collective longing for some synthesis or system to replace Christianity.

Second, as I have already suggested, Morley did not so much abandon as transform the practices of Protestant Dissent with which he and many contemporaries were raised. At the centre of Evangelical theology was Christ's atoning death on the cross. Through abiding and demonstrable faith in this sacrificial propitiation, an individual, tainted at birth by original sin, could be forgiven. The individual conscience, which served as the instrument by which salvation was achieved, held one to account for any lapses. One's conscience also remained ever attuned to the signs of God's infinite blessings. An individual needed to engage in prayer, biblical study and self-examination, commonly through writing diaries and spiritual account books, in order to recognise susceptibility to worldliness. The home as the site for Dissenting Christianity's most significant devotional practices inevitably became paramount because, within its discrete spaces, Evangelicals could employ their privileged tools of introspection and self-scrutiny in an effort to discern deviations from the strictest principles of conduct.[14] Indeed, with its emphasis on personal transformation and individual salvation rather than communal religious expression, Evangelicalism was principally a domestic religion.

For Morley, the home became a site for achieving, instead of God's saving grace, an agnostic ethic of belief. In the domestic setting he cultivated impersonality evinced through disinterestedness. He substituted for religious faith a no less fervently held devotion to opinion, produced through the mental techniques of abstraction, reasoning and induction.[15] In Morley's daily practice, liberalism was a religion of the home no less than Evangelicalism had been in his earlier years.

His upbringing had been profoundly shaped by the Evangelical revival, which invested new power in the godly household as a protection and defence against worldliness. Both his parents were raised Methodists. His mother, Priscilla Mary, was, in Grace's words, an ardent 'John Wesleyan' throughout her life (qtd in Hirst 1927: I, 7). His father, Jonathan, converted to Anglicanism as an adult, but Methodism left its stamp. In response to the perceived excesses and smug satisfaction of the eighteenth century, Evangelical clergymen exhorted believers to abstain from the pleasures of this world to attain the eternal bliss of the next. 'He who lays greatest restraint on his passions and appetites, and contemns upon principle, every merely sensual gratification', the Reverend John Styles, a Congregationalist, sermonised, 'increases, in a wonderful degree, his powers of intellectual enjoyment, and opens to himself boundless resources of spiritual delight. His happiness is seated in the mind; it is pure and refined; it is the happiness of angels' (1815: 26). To stimulate 'intellectual enjoyment' within the home, daily life was highly regulated, requiring prayer, biblical study and introspection. Decoration, which was to be minimal, reflected an emphasis on self-denial through restricted practices of consumption. With the exception of religious verse and hymnody, the arts, having no relevance to atonement, were highly discouraged. Their sensuousness could stimulate worldly appetites.

Serious Christianity pervaded both the domestic interiors and the wider environment in which Morley spent his childhood. Thrift and abstemiousness were widely practised in Lancashire, the county of Morley's birth, by the many current and former Methodists who settled there. Blackburn, where Jonathan Morley, a surgeon, established his practice, was markedly puritan (Phillips 1982: 128–32). Even after John Morley renounced Christianity, he continued to endorse Lancashire's puritan values, but for their social rather than religious signification:

> Although the theology of a town like Blackburn is of a narrow, unhistoric, and rancorous kind, yet one must give even this dull and cramped Evangelicalism its due, and admit that the churches and chapels have done a good service, through their Sunday Schools and otherwise, in impressing a kind of moral organization on the mass of barbarism which surged chaotically into the factory towns. (Morley 1878: 5)[16]

Regardless of Evangelicalism's deficiencies, which Morley rendered through spatial metaphors ('narrow', 'cramped'), its chief attraction for him was its privileging of ethos. Although 'Lancashire theology does not make a man love his neighbour', yet 'its external system promotes cleanliness, truth-telling, and chastity', Morley insisted (5).

Morley's abiding interest in the characterological dimension of belief began at Hoole's Academy in Blackburn, where he was enrolled at the age of eight or nine. He recalled being nursed there on the 'unadulterated milk of the Independent word' even as he was trained in the 'general habits' the pupils were expected to adopt, modelled with 'severe exactitude' by the proprietor and headmaster (1917: 6). William Hoole, an influential alderman and strict Congregationalist, ensured his pupils memorised lines of scripture daily and attended services at the Independent chapel twice each Sunday.[17] This rigorous training, Morley believed, 'perhaps accounted for the nonconformist affinities . . . of days to come' (6). It also prepared him, more immediately, for University College School – a non-religiously affiliated educational institution in London – and subsequently for Cheltenham College, at which he remained for just under two years. From there Morley secured in 1856 a scholarship to Lincoln College, Oxford, where he intended to take holy orders and become an Evangelical clergyman.

In the late 1850s the struggle between the opposing forces of science and religion, intellect and faith, was on full display at Oxford.[18] Morley was quickly exposed to 'the great controversy' then waging between Mill, with his theory of empirical rationality, and William Hamilton, a leading advocate of intuitionism (Morley 1917: 8, 12). According to Hamilton, the intuitive faculty enabled one to perceive in the physical world an underlying spiritual reality and to discern, independent of observation or experience, right from wrong.[19] Mill found such arguments specious, entirely lacking in rational or objective foundation, and contended in his *System of Logic* that empirical principles offered the best solution to pressing scientific, social and political problems.

At Oxford in 1858 Morley attended Henry Longueville Mansel's Bampton Lectures on religious thought and its limits. These lectures were, as Morley recalls somewhat snarkily, the 'official reply, if reply it was', to the debate between Mill and Hamilton (1917: 8).[20] One of the editors of Hamilton's works, Mansel expounded on the intuitionist view. Morley also rarely missed Samuel Wilberforce's sermons at the University Church of St Mary the Virgin. As Bishop of Oxford from 1845 to 1869, Wilberforce was a vociferous opponent of the church's critics, persistently arguing that 'irreverence and doubt' should be an individual's 'greatest fear' (qtd in Meacham 1970: 229). One biographer summarises Wilberforce's position thus: 'In an age that pressed desperately for answers to all sorts of questions, Wilberforce believed they were better left unasked' (Meacham 1970: 228). Despite the growing doubt he experienced during his Oxford years, Morley continued to harbour great affection for Wilberforce: 'he had a glorious voice, unquestioning faith, full and ready knowledge of apt texts of the Bible, and a deep earnest desire to reach the hearts of congregations who were just as earnest in response' (Morley 1917: 9).

A little more than a decade earlier, John Henry Newman had profoundly influenced the minds of students, including Matthew Arnold, who had come under his sway. But Newman's 'star' had set, while John Stuart Mill's 'sun . . . had risen' (Morley 1901: 115). If Mill was not a religious figure, he certainly foretold the coming of a new faith.[21] As early as 1831, he had been proclaiming, 'Mankind have outgrown old institutions and old doctrines, and have not yet acquired new ones' (JSM 1986a: 230). He and his contemporaries were living in a 'transitional period' characterised by 'weak convictions, paralysed intellects, and growing laxity of principle' (JSM 1981: 247).[22] Such a stage of uncertainty was a painful but natural part of the 'renovation' in thought necessary for 'the evolution of some faith, whether religious or merely human', in which all can 'believe' (247). If Wilberforce's sermons discouraged subjecting religious belief to critical analysis, Mill's *A System of Logic*, published in 1843 and required for students studying classics for decades to come, exerted a corrosive effect on the Christian theology, especially in its examination of miracles, to which many undergraduates subscribed (Capaldi 2004: 186). At Oxford, Morley was known to carry around a volume of Mill's writings and to have virtually memorised *On Liberty*, Mill's encomium to the liberating practices of free thought and individuality, published during Morley's final term (Hirst 1927: I, 22). It was becoming clear to Morley, then, that the tenets of revealed religion were susceptible to critical reflection. They had lost their utility. On one side of the debate between intuitionism and rationalism, it increasingly seemed to Morley, were 'people of common, plain intelligence', possessing unbelievable, dogmatic notions produced by facile practices of thought (Morley 1917: 12). On the other side stood individuals of considerable learning, whose meticulous and diligent engagement with Anglican orthodoxy showed – by demonstrating the liberating power of critical thinking to demystify and dismantle 'traditional thought, devotion, [and] dogma' (13) – that belief in religion was untenable without, in Mill's words, 'modifications amounting to an essential change of its character' (JSM 1981: 247). Such strikingly opposed views inevitably resulted in discord: 'Loud became the din of internecine war', writes Morley of this 'agitated' period at Oxford (1917: 13).

While Morley was beginning to think critically about aspects of theology he had previously accepted as articles of faith, he was also finding himself susceptible to arguments in favour of beauty. Years later, as editor of *The Fortnightly Review* (1867–82), he published contributions by several aesthetes, some of whom were likely among his acquaintances at Oxford (Hirst 1927: I, 28). Algernon Swinburne was, along with Morley, a member of the Oxford Union Debating Society. Less than a year after Morley matriculated as an undergraduate, William Morris, Dante Gabriel Rossetti and other members of the Pre-Raphaelite Brotherhood began experimenting in surface decoration by painting figure scenes from Arthurian legends on the Oxford Union walls and ceiling. The intense perceptual experience engendered by the bold colours with which they worked – dark reds, rich greens, gold – may have forced Morley to call into question the principles of self-denial and vigilance against worldliness on which the decoration of his childhood home was based. His comments in defence of Paterian aestheticism nearly two decades later suggests as much: 'The prodigious block of our philistinism needs to have wedges driven in at many points' (1873: 476–7).

In John Wesley's former lodgings at Lincoln College, where Morley resided for a period, he found his religious convictions had waned. The irony was not lost on him.[23] Jonathan Morley, on learning his son was unwilling to enter the church, refused to continue providing financial support. Morley had been planning to stay at Oxford for a fourth year to read Greats but was forced to terminate his studies. He accepted a 'Pass' degree in Classical Moderations in 1859 and then moved to London to make a living (Hirst 1927: I, 17, 33).

As the prevailing religious concern with the soul and its relationship to the body began to ebb, many of the leading figures in Morley's post-Oxford intellectual circle were helping to make the concept of environment central to British thought. At Oxford, Morley was introduced by his friend James Cotter Morison to the positivist teachings of Auguste Comte. These did not, initially, resonate with him (Morley 1917: 6). Soon after arriving in London, however, Morley contributed to *The Leader*, a newspaper with which George Henry Lewes, a principal disseminator of positivist philosophy in England, was also associated.[24] Morley became friends with Lewes and George Eliot (Marian Evans), regularly sharing meals with the couple. Through his friendship with them as well as with the philosopher and historian Frederic Harrison, Morley found himself greatly attracted to Comte's view of intellectual, political and social evolution from primitivism to enlightenment. Bereft of the religious convictions that had once guided him, Morley found solace in the notion that the dark era of doubt and confusion in which he lived, the age of transition Mill had identified, was part of an ordered movement leading towards the dawn of a new age based on 'positive' scientific principles.

A principal contention of Comte's was that the physical and social milieu profoundly affected one's consciousness and rational agency. Comte was not much interested in individual psychology, however. Lewes sought to remedy this omission by developing a theory of physiological psychology based on positivistic principles. In his influential study *Problems of Life and Mind*, Lewes contended that one's perceptual and cognitive processes were inextricable from one's milieu (1879: I, 71). Human sense perception was moulded by the wider medium (society) in which one lived. Because this medium was the product of historical development and change, understanding individual psychology required taking into consideration society's entire evolution.

One of Morley's other chief interlocutors during this period was Herbert Spencer, who moved in the same circles. Spencer was developing an immense speculative cosmology that combined Jean-Baptiste Lamarck's notion of heritable traits with Darwinian evolutionary theory. The development and evolution of the species, Spencer argued, were dependent on reciprocity between self and milieu or, in his phraseology, *'the continuous adjustment of internal relations to external relations'* (1910: 99). Although Spencer abhorred any suggestion that his thought was comparable to Comte's, it clearly bore many similarities to positivism.[25] In their different ways, Spencer and Lewes vociferously repudiated the notion of a spiritual essence transcending the corporeal frame and undermined the view that a given environment is simply the background against which human agency is exercised.

Ultimately, Morley sided with Mill, whom he had long admired and with whom he had begun a friendship in 1867. Comte's so-called absolute method, no less than Spencer's synthetic philosophy, Morley felt, inhibited the free play of the mind – a notion he had embraced despite his differences with Matthew Arnold, which I have discussed in Chapter 2. The sectarian tendencies of the positivist London group, too, inhibited Morley's 'formal union with this new church' (Morley 1917: 69). Moreover, with his commitment to ratiocination firmly intact, Morley was never entirely persuaded by Lewes's attempts to establish a somatic basis for consciousness. He did not deny embodied experience shaped one's character. However, as a firm proponent of Mill's dictum 'mind over matter', Morley believed that character, if it was a relation of inner essence to outer environment, emerged first as the self's 'creature' and then as its 'master' (Morley 1923b: 98).

In *On Compromise*, his 1874 treatise on political ethics, Morley outlines the process of self-development by which the self-governing individual, formed in private, becomes recognisable as a citizen in the public sphere. In so doing, Morley mobilises an architectural metaphor by likening those who possess obsolete beliefs to those who dwell in an unstable tower. The social and epistemological changes of the time are equated with earthquakes rattling the tower's foundation and missiles flying past its spire. For the occupants, he writes, 'all is doubt, hesitation, and shivering expectancy' (1901: 37). Wavering beliefs lead to inconsistent principles and frail convictions: all signs of a disjointed, fragmentary personality (31). As a figure for one's frame of mind, the tower, cramped and narrow, also evokes Morley's characterisation of the Evangelical creed. When he turns to a description of the mind engaged in a liberalising process, he relies further on architectonic language. Those who possess sound convictions arrived at through abstraction, reasoning and induction – which is to say, thinking reflexively rather than responding impulsively to pressing contemporary events – experience 'a large and serene internal activity' (Morley 1867e: 170). Because these beliefs can withstand critical scrutiny and do not change to meet the necessity of any particular exigency, they eradicate 'paralysing dubieties' and leave an individual 'in full possession' of oneself 'by furnishing an unshaken and inexpugnable base for action and thought' (Morley 1871a: 230–1). The phraseology here may not appear to be intentionally figurative. But, etymologically, an 'inexpugnable base' contains architectural associations, while 'a large and serene internal activity', like his characterisation of Evangelicalism as 'narrow' and 'cramped', is in some sense spatial.[26] In so far as metaphorical dwelling places (such as towers, houses and rooms) became more frequently used in the latter half of the century to express the experience of human interiority within a body, Morley's thinking here draws on the habitable interior as a topos.[27] He portrays reasoned opinion as that which makes the individual whole, thwarting any 'paralysing dubieties' and ensuring mental repose. This resonates in some ways with the non-denominational but evangelically inspired idealisation of the Victorian home as, in John Ruskin's words, a 'place of Peace; the shelter, not only from all injury, but from all terror, doubt, and division', and a bulwark against the 'inconsistently-minded' outside world (1905: 122). Morley's reference to furnishing a base also, at the very least, alludes to, if not directly indexes, a building's foundation.

Morley likens mental liberalisation to dismantling one edifice, the materials of which derive from 'the old faith' (Morley 1901: 152), and constructing a new one. The individual who engages in this process is akin to a 'prudent architect, who, when obliged to destroy a building, and knowing how its parts are united together, sets about its demolition in such a way as to prevent its fall from being dangerous' (58). After tearing down the outmoded structure, the liberalising individual begins 'building up a state of mind', gathering 'material' from 'the purified and sublimated ideas' of Christianity as an antiquated system of belief, a process which thereby preserves continuity between present and past (152, 155). With the figure of the prudent architect, Morley attempts to show – no doubt recalling the rift with his father, which never healed – how commitment to nonconformity, or dissent from popular belief, need not cause estrangement from others. An individual's dissenting opinion, far from being associated with profligacy, can coordinate and direct one's conduct. Insisting that 'disbelief' need not be 'thrust' upon others 'in gross and irreverent forms' (164), Morley's account takes up Evangelicalism's privileging of ethos and transforms it into a moralised and moralising opinion.[28]

For Morley, political individuality is substantially dependent on the patient and patiently ordered construction of this cognitive architecture, characterised by capaciousness and serenity and fortified against incursions from the outside world. Self-governing individuals possess a character that is 'as little as possible broken, incoherent, and fragmentary' (Morley 1901: 120). They enjoy integrity and serenity, 'a large and serene internal activity' that rests on reasoned, consistent opinions.[29] Instead of thrusting opinions on others, individuals live them; as a result, 'independent convictions inspire the intellectual self-respect and strenuous self-possession which the clamour of majorities and the silent yet ever-pressing force of the *status quo* are equally powerless to shake' (120). The liberalising individual's principal social obligation, Morley had learned from Mill, is to be true to one's convictions. Individual opinion, confidently held, leads slowly, carefully to social and political change.[30]

Written as a defence of *On Liberty* against the explicit criticism of James Fitzjames Stephen and the implicit criticism of Arnold's *Culture and Anarchy*, *On Compromise* utilises the idiom of architecture – as

Mill's evocative phrasing, the necessary 'renovation' in thought, did – to conceptualise the liberalising self. Informed by new theories about perceptual experience, however, Morley was already beginning to draw connections between states of mind and spatial environments that were not merely figurative. In Elm Park Gardens and Flowermead, Morley's ideas found their symbolic form. It is no coincidence that Morley analogised the process of liberalising the mind to tearing down old buildings for new. Each architectural style, instead of emerging anew, evolves from preceding styles. It draws mostly on the same construction materials, perhaps differently conjoined, and incorporates or juxtaposes in new or unexpected ways the insignia and decorative details of the past. The term 'Queen Anne Revival', used to describe the domestic architecture of which Elm Park Gardens was a part, emphasises restoration and renewal. This continuity between present and past is the equivalent of what Morley imagines as the outcome of mental liberalisation. But suburban residences offered Morley something more than a spatial analogue, contrasted with the cramped narrowness of the Evangelical mind, to the 'large and serene' cognitive edifice he designates as the very condition of liberal individuality. These architectural spaces and settings actualised a set of distinctive perceptual and cognitive practices.

'The Place Is Quiet and Sheltered'

By the time that Morley began making significant contributions to philosophical thought, the concern with the barely perceptible, often unregistered, effects of spatial experience had become widely popularised. Acceptance of this notion was evident in psychology, architecture, education, literature and decorative advice. In 1879 William Young called attention to the 'power' domestic architecture exerts over one's moral and physical constitution. This was especially so, he argued, in the British Isles, 'where we spend so much of our life indoors'; thus, 'the kind of houses we live in have a by no means insignificant effect upon us' (1879: 1). Young maintained:

> If the important fact that the house a man lives in has a great influence on his health, both of body and mind, were more generally known, the object of making our houses more healthy and beautiful would be regarded as a study worthy of the attention of the public. (1879: preface, n.p.)

Social reformers, who departed from the more deterministic accounts of subjectivity that held sway earlier in the century, were particularly emphatic. If the human organism was influenced by its surroundings, then tackling problems like slum housing could change the character of the residents. By the early 1870s decorating manuals insisted that the home's interior spaces shaped one's character. Beauty, the writer and illustrator Mary Eliza Haweis observed, was becoming widely recognised as 'a refining influence' (1881: 2) – hence, the need for instruction in purchasing and displaying domestic goods. Haweis, a painter's daughter and a minister's spouse, played a crucial role in realigning art, long suspected of whetting the sensual appetite, with morality (Cohen 2006: 63). The assumption that environment mattered was so widespread by the late 1880s that the writer and domestic advisor Jane Panton, also a painter's daughter, admonished her readers, in a vein more practical than religious, that they should always 'remember this axiom':

> Let sunshine and brightness and cheerfulness be found . . . in every . . . room and place in the house; for we are insensibly and immensely influenced by our surroundings, and we should always make the best of our lives and belongings in every way we possibly can. (1889: 98)

Combining idealism and practicality, the pleasures of the countryside with the conveniences and amenities of the metropolis, the suburban home represented for many Londoners 'the apotheosis of the Englishman's castle' (Dyos 1961: 22).[31] To Morley, Elm Park Gardens, with its 'immense large garden belonging to all the houses collectively', offered the good life, in contrast to 'the awful dog-holes of London'. The anti-urban rhetoric of Evangelicals and the promotional language of speculative developers alike imbued suburbs with Romanticism.[32] The housing complexes near the Royal Albert Hall, including De Vere Gardens, where Robert Browning would for a time reside, were particularly attractive because their strategic position near Kensington Gardens and Hyde Park facilitated ease of travel to the clubs of St James's and the West End theatres. Elm Park Gardens was located about a mile south of the Royal Albert Hall – 'a long way off', one of Morley's colleagues sniffed (Harcourt 2006: 144), although Morley did not hold that view.

Terraced houses were not favoured in suburbs, which were attractive precisely because they offered the possibility of living in a low-density, verdant environment. By the closing decades of the century the wealthier members of the middle class held increasingly negative perceptions of terraces. One commentator on English residential districts, deriding the English penchant for bestowing stylish names on modest brick terraces, scoffed: 'The word "Mansion" has long ceased to convey the idea of a mansion, and when "Gardens" are referred to, few people expect to see a garden' (Perks 1905: 204). Detached villas or semi-detached houses were prized. Detached suburban villas or semi-detached houses promised, instead of the fluidity and permeability of urban life, achievement of an ideal domestic space – private, self-contained, interiorised – on the periphery of an easily accessible metropolis. Morley was greatly attracted to the domestic ideal of the detached home: 'I like the civilized fashion of one's own house best', he wrote to Grace in August 1886, during a six-week stay at a free-standing house in Surrey.[33]

But the speculative builder Alexander Thorn proved adept at marketing Elm Park Gardens to a class wary of terraces.[34] Constructed between 1878 and 1885, Elm Park Gardens was designed by George Godwin, a leading architect, the editor of the influential *Builder* magazine and a vociferous housing reformer. Along with his brother Henry, he was converting late nineteenth-century Brompton and South Kensington into elite suburbs (A. King 1976: 35).[35] Queen Anne, although applied in constructing buildings ranging from schools to pubs, was principally the domestic architecture of the new West London suburbs of Chelsea, Holland Park and South Kensington.

Opposing domestic to urban space, Thorn's advertisements attempted to allay concerns about the property's similarity to a block of city apartments by emphasising the size of the units (calling them 'Modern Mansions') and their intended use by single families and individuals: 'Red-brick HOUSES of the Queen Anne type', according to a frequent notice in newspapers. In contrast to the growing but unpopular architectural form of flats, with a common entrance from the street, a shared hallway leading to individual living spaces and incomplete mitigation of the sounds and smells of others, these houses were spatially enclosed.[36]

Because Elm Park Gardens was constructed on a vast expanse of previously undeveloped land, Godwin, who worked closely with Thorn on its design, was not constrained by surrounding properties. As a result, the residences were generously sized and incorporated many amenities not yet added to extant houses in central London. 'If anyone wishes to see how the British metropolis is pushing out into the country', the *Birmingham Daily Post* noted in 1877, 'he need only take the underground railway and alight at the South Kensington or West Brompton stations. Here he will see acres occupied by palatial residences.' The residences at Elm Park Gardens, in particular, were being 'hired or bought as fast as they can be built' ('Private correspondence' 1877).

The estate was built in a slightly skewed U shape with five principal buildings facing a street that opened onto Fulham Road at both ends.[37] The centre of the U contained a large communal garden, as Morley noted in describing the property to Grace. The two buildings erected on the north-eastern and south-western sides of the garden were made of red gault brick and featured gable roofs, a number of wood-framed sash windows, wrought-iron railings and terracotta panelling. A single building, also in red gault brick, was erected at the bottom of the U; its houses faced the garden just across the road. This building and the two abutting the garden were more exclusive than the two on the outer periphery. Thorn erected a sixth building, again according to Godwin's specifications: a small detached house in the centre of the garden, fronting Fulham Road. Park House, later called Elm Park House, was built in Gothic style but utilised the same brick as the three more exclusive terraces.

Elm Park Gardens was the only private estate at the time in South Kensington and nearby Chelsea in which the principal houses flanked a large open ground (Chelsea Society 1962: 17). The garden's large cedar, elm and mulberry trees acted as a luxuriant screen that maintained the privacy of the adjacent buildings. 'The place is quiet and sheltered', Morley rhapsodised.[38] Intended to be used solely by residents, the garden was a space of symbolic inwardness.[39]

With minor variations, the layout of Elm Park Gardens residences was fairly typical of the urban terraced house. Each had a basement, four floors and an attic.[40] Two rooms were on the ground floor, the dining room and the morning room, and another two, the boudoir and the drawing room, on the first floor. But whereas the basic plan of the urban terraced house provided for two bedrooms on each of two additional floors, the houses at Elm Park Gardens had no less than five bedrooms and two dressing rooms on the second and third floors, with an additional two bedrooms in the servants' quarters in the attic.[41] 'The very fair [working] quarters', as Morley called them, were located in the basement: a large servants' hall, butler's pantry, kitchen and scullery, in addition to coal and wine cellars. Godwin, who advocated utilising advanced sanitary technologies in new buildings, ensured that each house was fitted with excellent drainage and ventilation as well as four toilets: one in the basement for the servants, one close to the morning room on the ground floor, one as part of a full bathroom on the second floor and one on the third floor.[42] The interiors, in other words, were distinctly modern with considerable aeration, adequate plumbing and, from the mid-1890s, electric light.[43]

For Morley, as he remarks in his April 1886 letter to Grace, one of the most attractive features of no. 95 was that it had never been occupied. It was not tainted by what Harold Begbie, a younger contemporary of Morley's, called 'a smell of Time – the smell of the Past' (1909: 97). The couple could express their individual feelings and desires without having to contend with the design preferences of previous residents. In contrast to closely shaded middle-class homes, with their windows covered by both translucent muslin and more colourful and elaborate fabric, often resulting in a musty, acrid and heavy atmosphere, no. 95 boasted rooms that were 'wonderfully light and bright', as Morley enthusiastically reported to Grace. Despite Morley's preference for detached houses, the spaciousness of the individual units, their layout around a garden, which obscured the view of other buildings, and their newness all contributed to his feeling of having realised the ideal of a private, self-contained and interiorised domestic environment.

'Domestic Gods'

The Morleys resided at no. 95 for a decade (1886–96) and at no. 57 for only a slightly shorter period (1896–1903). The difference between the two was largely positional because all the Elm Park Gardens residences were built according to the same floor plan. Whereas the former was situated between other houses, the latter was a corner unit with additional windows. Although no. 57 had previously been occupied, Morley was able to decorate it anew.[44] As a result, the residences were strikingly similar. Overall, Morley's diaries and letters are frustratingly silent on decorative choices. However, by turning to other sources, including a few extant photographs, his periodical essays in *The Saturday Review* and *The Fortnightly Review* and recollections of visits to the Morleys' homes, we can begin to reconstruct these domestic environments.

From his review of Walter Pater's *Studies in the History of the Renaissance*, published in *The Fortnightly Review* during Morley's tenure as editor, one can infer certain ideas of his about home decoration:

A great many people in all times, perhaps the most, give a practical answer to the question [of what will give their lives significance] by ignoring it, and living unaccented lives of dulness and frivolity. A great many others find an answer in devotion to divine mysteries, which round the purpose of their lives and light the weariness of mechanical days. The writer of the essays before us [Pater] answers it as we have seen, and there is now a numerous sect among cultivated people who accept his answer and act upon it. So far as we know, there never was seen before in this country so distinct an attempt to bring the aesthetical element closely and vividly round daily life. (1873: 475)

Morley concludes that Pater, in enunciating the dictum 'art for art's sake', makes visible how outmoded the old theologies have become. Although Pater 'has no design of interfering with the minor or major morals of the world, but only of dealing with what we may perhaps call the accentuating portion of life', his aestheticism nevertheless provides a noble counterpoint to middle-class philistinism (475). The Aesthetic Movement represents 'a craving for the infusion of something harmonious and beautiful about the bare lines of daily living' (476). After all, philistinism and Evangelicalism both discouraged appreciation of sensory experience. Thus, aestheticism is clearly valuable because it makes plain that there is more to life than politics or material gain – interests to which, as Matthew Arnold had complained, so many of Morley's contemporaries turned in the absence of strong religious convictions.

But aestheticism was also in danger of becoming a substitute belief:

It has an exaggerated side. Dutch farmhouses are systematically swept by brokers, that the vulgarity of ormolu may be replaced by delft, and nankin, and magic bits of oriental blue and white. There is an orthodoxy in wall-papers, and you may commit the unpardonable sin in discordant window-curtains. Members of the sect are as solicitous about the right in tables and the correct in legs of chairs, as members of another sect are careful about the cut of chasuble or dalmatica [clerical vestments]. Bric-a-brac rises to the level of religions, and the whirligig of time is bringing us back to fetishism and the worship of little domestic gods, not seldom bleak and uncouth. (Morley 1873: 475)

In its quest to make primary what Morley calls the 'secondary adjuncts of grace and dignity' (1865f: 15), aestheticism engendered a return to primitive fetishism: home decoration as no longer a representation of meaning but, as the phrase 'domestic gods' suggests, meaning itself. Hence, for all its good, aestheticism contributed to society's devolution into an incapacity for abstraction.

Implicit in Morley's comments is that, while domestic environments may be outward manifestations of inner preferences and beliefs, they also profoundly affect one's frame of mind and the mental techniques that produce ideas. Thus, it stands to reason, a home's interior spaces can be decorated and inhabited in ways that nurture an optimal liberal life. Although contemporary critics tend to see individual expression in Victorian domestic interiors as an activity that primarily occupied women,[45] Morley took responsibility in decorating his residences. One might argue that, at least initially, this occurred as much out of necessity as of interest. Beginning in 1873, Rose was frequently unwell. The couple relocated twice for her health, moving from Surrey, where they lived from 1870 to 1873, to Tunbridge Wells (1873–5) and then to Brighton (1875–9) in search of, respectively, medicinal spring waters and therapeutic sea breezes.[46] In 1879 they moved to Wimbledon, where they resided when he was elected to Parliament, before settling in Elm Park Gardens and subsequently at Flowermead. But even when Rose's health was good, Morley demonstrated keen interest in the domestic environment (Hirst 1927: I, 193). He had learned in his childhood and youth that the home was central to obtaining an ideal life: the strong rhetorical framing in theological treatises of the domestic sphere as a fortress for spiritual well-being helped engender in many Evangelicals a great 'love of domesticity' (Clive 1975: 39). Even as Morley shed his religious beliefs, he continued to derive most of his pleasures, as well as his sense of moral direction and integrity, from the interiors and rituals of the home through his practice of impersonal domesticity. He did not 'divert himself after the fashion of most of us', according to a friend who had worked with him; he was completely uninterested in sport, for example, although he relished 'long walks across the hills' (Stead 1890: 427). These were not signs of vestigial puritanism, however. 'He delighted in good living' (Staebler 1943: 32); was 'passionately fond' of music (Stead 1890: 427); surrounded himself with books; enjoyed early evening dining, complemented by select wines chosen from his cellar and erudite conversation; and took an interest in the decorative principles of the Aesthetic Movement while freely adapting them to his surroundings.

Towards Whiteness

While waiting to be received by Morley in the drawing room at no. 95, Augustin Filon, as I noted at the outset of this chapter, was struck by the absence of decorative objects. No room in a typical middle-class residence was more subject to decorative display than the drawing room, which held both practical and symbolic importance. It was a place to exhibit the family's latest treasure: 'a Persian tile, an Algerian flower-pot, an old Flemish cup, a piece of Nankin blue, an Icelandic spoon, a Japanese cabinet, a Chinese fan', writes Lucy Orrinsmith, a leading Victorian authority on interior design (1878: 133). Through the heterogeneity and multiplicity of objects on display, a middle-class family asserted its status, educated its visitors about the world and told others who they were. Meanwhile, the medley of objects also told the owners themselves who they were (Tristram 1989: 260). Handcrafted articles symbolised a family's ability to purchase items that were not mass produced; heirlooms asserted familial lineage; photographs and drawings represented countries visited, childhood experiences or the family's originary moments (a wedding, a birth). 'At no period before or since have movable objects played so vital a part in deciding the character of an interior as they did in mid-Victorian Europe', Denys Hinton notes (1967: 180). Not unlike a museum, the typical middle-class drawing room was the principal location of collection and exhibition, a site, at least according to its critics then as now, of excessive ornamentation and sentimentality.

Practices of accumulation and display within a domestic environment are not, of course, limited to either the nineteenth century or the middle class. Noblemen in Renaissance Europe assembled geological artefacts and botanical specimens in chambers or cabinets used for collections of curiosities (*wunderkammern*), and aristocrats more generally have long acquired objects of art, great and small, to exhibit in splendorous settings. But the late-Victorian proliferation of objects in the middle-class drawing room, while indebted to these earlier forms, differed in at least two ways. First, whereas cabinets of curiosities were linked to men, the highly ornamented drawing room, with its appeals to sensual pleasure and its complex accounts of social standing, was seen as a quintessentially female space. Second, the literature on interior decoration, instead of simply adapting aristocratic models of splendour and elegance, championed homely comforts. 'The excessive ornamentation of nearly every article used in the Victorian home', John Gloag remarks, 'made even the spacious rooms of large houses seem overcrowded, and in small rooms the effect was overwhelming: yet this excess of ornament, this restless conflict of motifs, helped to create an atmosphere of solid, unshakable comfort' (1962: 137). Collected and displayed in the middle-class drawing room, the family's treasures – whether souvenirs, novelties, handcrafted articles, photographs or drawings – were not part of a sumptuous display of wealth. Rather, they reflected a new desire for cosy living, the distinctive middle-class mode of inhabiting domestic space through individual expression.[47] Although the trend of cosy living did not begin with them, the upper classes embraced it; their homes, too, might contain bibelots and ormolu.

The absence of bric-a-brac in Morley's home was perhaps all the more pronounced because the interior was, according to written accounts, painted in large swaths of white. The vast majority of middle- and upper-class homes eschewed the colour (Muthesius 2009: 127). The aristocratically inclined Mary Eliza Haweis summed up the necessity for a dark-coloured wall: it 'is easier to cover than a light one, enlarges the apparent size of the room, and is more becoming to the human face' (1889: 30). Concluding that 'a light wall looks aggressively bare', she denounced white walls in particular: 'They greatly diminish the size of the room, as a white ceiling diminishes its height' (1889: 30; 1881: 217). White walls, Haweis insisted, 'cast an unpleasant glare on all polished surfaces, [and] ruin pictures'; in contrast, 'a dark wall adds size, because the eye cannot exactly measure the distance at which the wall stands' (1881: 217). Advisors with a more middle-class sensibility encouraged naturalistic representations, which were favoured well into the twentieth century. Benefitting from an ample disposable income and technological developments that made mass production of wallpaper possible from the 1840s onward, middle-class families aimed to produce a sense of envelopment in decorating their walls. In the mid-Victorian period the flora and fauna that adorned wallpaper in sitting and dining rooms were often realistic. In the century's closing decades these representations became much more stylised. By the 1880s damask designs were particularly vivacious, largely owing to the invention of aniline dyes, which made colours far richer, even garish. Frequently made of embossed imitation leather, wallpapers might include flowers or animals in high relief. More often than not, then, wall treatments served as the visual effects of membership in a distinct class: solid colours for the upper class, patterns for the middle class.

Morley desired to break free from these designations, and his partiality for white was noticeable indeed. Filon, who had ample time to observe Morley's surroundings, describes an evident love not for 'the glaring, aggressive whiteness that affronts the eye, but the discreet, slightly grey whiteness that rests and caresses the sight'. It was a white, Filon says, 'that perhaps, to the thinker, has the symbolic charm of a synthesis of colours' (1891: 156) – a tantalising phrase by which he intends, presumably, to draw a connection between a peculiar shade and the comprehensive new creed Morley sought to establish. Warren Staebler, paraphrasing Filon's description, asserted that 'the tranquillity, the cool quietness, the immaculateness, the restful, discreet whiteness' that characterised Morley's decorative schemes at Elm Park Gardens 'remained distinctions of his household to the end', at Flowermead (1943: 187). While assembling various written accounts of Morley's interiors, I recalled Le Corbusier's remark that civilisation is the abandonment of decoration, with its 'caresses of the senses', in favour of the visual harmony of proportion, which whiteness facilitates (qtd in Wigley 2001: 3). For many months during my research, it seemed to me that one might even characterise Morley's domestic environments as proto-modernist. Two kinds of textual evidence supported this initial hypothesis: frequent references to Morley's obvious partiality for whiteness and insistence by those who had been there that no. 95, without the characteristic signs of accumulation and display, was distinctively minimalist ('simplicity is the note within').[48]

When I finally located a photograph of Morley in his library at no. 95, I found myself unable to reconcile these textual accounts with the clear visual evidence (Figure 3.2). His interior did not bear any

Figure 3.2 John Morley in his library at no. 95 Elm Park Gardens.
Source: *The Review of Reviews* (November 1890): 423.

relationship to, say, modernism's white geometrical houses. At least nine portraits of various sizes are above the mantel of the fireplace, which is draped in fabric and adorned with a few mementos. When reading Filon's description of the total effect of Morley's decorative interior as 'a harmony of subtle and pale tones' (1891: 155), I had not conjured either an armchair of dark wood, perhaps mahogany, upholstered in damask, or an ornate and rather regally gilded wooden chair, upholstered in velvet. Finally, instead of painted white walls, there is floral wallpaper. Besides the fireplace and the fixed bookcase frame, where is the white that so many biographical sketches single out as a remarkable aspect of Morley's domestic interiors? Where is the absence of bric-a-brac?

A photograph of Morley's library at Flowermead was only slightly less unsettling (Figure 3.3). On the one hand, white is unmistakably dominant. The walls, barrel-vaulted ceiling and fixed bookcase frames all painted white. On the other hand, my definition of decorative 'simplicity' and 'severity' had left me unprepared for the Turkey carpets, naturalistic chintz slipcovers, ebonised Aesthetic Movement tables, ornate vases and potted plants. I had not reckoned with the clustered furnishings in the centre of the room that seem to serve a wholly ornamental purpose: the velvet upholstered chair on which rests a portrait of a figure whom I cannot quite make out but who is

Figure 3.3 John Morley's library at Flowermead.
Source: *The Graphic* (November 1917): 149.

recognisably male; the newspaper and magazine stand, which is not close to any sitting area; and the elaborate, likely hand-carved, trestle table on which rests a flowerpot and a few journals.

I was fully aware of the interpretative problems photographs pose as historical evidence, especially in their presumed mimetic accuracy. But, given the descriptions of Morley's residences, I had assumed that photographs, if and when I located them, would corroborate my initial findings. These photographs presented me, instead, with rooms that seemed neither distinctive nor particular to Morley but were entirely representative of the movement in the 1880s and 1890s away from the decorative incongruities of mid-century and towards more aesthetic environments. Helena Michie and Robyn Warhol have written about the impulses and fantasies that motivate archival work undertaken by literary scholars. I recognised myself in their description of the scholar whose intuition leads to scouring the historical record in search of something that makes a biographical subject 'individual, something like a character' (Michie and Warhol 2015: 40). This was perhaps what I was after: elements of a domestic life that made Morley different, even unique, his experiment in living constituting a form of resistance to the tyranny of custom and conformity.

But a disciplinary difference in perspective was not, in the end, the problem. After all, Staebler, a twentieth-century historian whose work on Morley omits the illustrated articles I consulted, repeatedly references 'the tranquillity, the cool quietness, the immaculateness, the restful, discreet whiteness' of Elm Park Gardens, based solely on Filon's account (1943: 187). The discrepancy between written records and visual imagery – each set of evidence producing seemingly contradictory and certainly partial knowledge – may well be an admonition to those whose epistemological desires include recovering the individual experiences of domestic interiors. It is also, I have concluded, a function of historical distance. Because my modern eyes were unable to discern the minimalism for which Morley's interiors were widely known, I could see only evidential inconsistency in the two sets of records. But Morley's contemporaries apparently did not have similar difficulty. To them, his interiors were noticeably different. In an effort to see Morley as exceptional, I had mistakenly reasoned that this difference would be in kind rather than in degree.

Complicating my initial hypothesis that Morley's mental hygiene, or agnostic free thought, found expression in the architectural spaces of the home, the photograph of his library at no. 95 revealed, as I have noted, that it was not entirely or even predominantly white. It was, however, pale in hue. The walls were papered in a subdued floral pattern, containing white accents that harmonised with the fireplace, bookcase frame, frieze and ceiling as well as the patterned damask of his upholstered armchair. In the late nineteenth century, during the heyday of exuberant wallpapers, often printed on Lincrusta, a subdued floral pattern was a marked departure from prevalent trends in decoration.[49] Susan Weber Soros, in her study of the influential architect and designer E. W. Godwin, a leader in reforming interior design, notes, 'Strongly colored, boldly patterned wallpapers were the most common form of wall decoration at this time. Godwin, however, endorsed plain-colored walls or simple wallpapers' (1999: 187). Soros quotes Godwin as saying his preferences were 'carried out with a leaning, perhaps in excess, towards lightness, and a simplicity almost amounting to severity' (187). Filon's use of the term 'severity' to describe the library, which he sees as somewhere 'between banality and elegance in a harmony of subtle and pale tones', precisely registers this sense of difference.

The effect of severity is achieved in part by Morley's use of white as an accent colour. At the time, even for accenting, white was a bold choice. Gas lighting left a filthy residue, as Morley himself was aware: shortly after the move to no. 95, he urged Grace to 'see our white paint' as soon as possible.[50] Because gas lighting also cast a yellow pall over the interior spaces of the home, browns and reds were considered appropriate. Thus, the decision to use white is notable. When the future statesman and twentieth-century liberal political thinker Herbert Samuel was an undergraduate, he met with Morley at no. 95 and, like Filon, was struck by the play of white: Morley, Samuel would recount years later, 'received me in his library – a bright room with large windows, lined with books in white-painted book-cases' (1951: 13).

While Morley's library at no. 95 did contain some knick-knacks, a profusion of exotica is entirely absent from the photograph. A bust, possibly of William Ewart Gladstone, flowers in a small vase and a paperweight share space on the mantelpiece with a candlestick that, without electric lighting, may have served a practical as much as an ornamental purpose. What appear at first to be family memory objects turn out to be reminders of the entwined nature of literature and liberal politics: framed portraits of Mill, the poet and novelist George Meredith, whose philosophical fiction narrativises liberal self-possession, and Liberal politicians (Gladstone, the Earl of Rosebery and Henry Campbell-Bannerman).

Morley's library at Flowermead was evidently responsive to aestheticism but not reducible to a direct instantiation of that movement's aims, as the absence of, say, peacock feathers or Japanese fans suggests. White was much more prevalent than at no. 95. Jane Panton, who championed hygienic decorative schemes, rather surprisingly admitted her partiality for white: 'Perhaps the very prettiest library I have ever seen', she informed her undoubtedly sceptical readers, 'is one in London . . . enamelled white – doors, cupboards, bookshelves, overmantel, indeed everything . . .' (1889: 94). To Panton, a library should have a character of 'sobriety', not frivolity; it should be furnished for 'study', not 'flirtation', for 'proper, severe application to one's books', not 'sweet sleep' (94). The white library in London was striking because the colour complemented the important activity the owner pursued in that room: 'some of the most serious work of the nation [is] done between its four walls', and such intellectual labour 'requires absolute peace and solitude' (94, 95). Inveighing against 'the orthodox dark green and carved oak', Panton implies that white is the *sine qua non* of intellectual nonconformity (95).

The white library was notable precisely because it was so uncommon. Even Panton confesses: 'Now this white idea for a library in London – dirty, smoky London – does seem absurd and a trifle frivolous, but the effect thereof is perfect . . .' (1889: 95). Although white may have seemed hygienic, rarely was it so. 'Replacement of browns and reds by white in interior decoration from the end of the nineteenth century at least in part reflected a wish to see greater cleanliness in the home', Adrian Forty explains, 'but . . . does not indicate that life was objectively any cleaner' (1992: 159). Few families were in the privileged position of being able to create and maintain such 'perfect', bright and clean interiors. No. 57, a corner unit, had numerous windows; it was also fitted for electricity. As Morley himself noted to Grace in February 1896, after a round of house-hunting, 'It looks as if we should stick to E. P. Gardens, but migrate to another house at the bottom of this side – about the same accommodations, in fact just the same – but a good deal brighter, and with electric light.'[51]

By emphasising white, therefore, some written accounts of no. 57 may reflect the visitor's perceptual experience: the sharp glare of electricity registering chromatically as bluish rather than yellow, and the various shades of Morley's walls and furnishings appearing especially crisp, lacking the grey filmy traces of soot left by gas lighting.[52] Visitors accustomed to the yellowish hue of gas lighting would have had an unwonted perceptual experience of the library at Flowermead, with its white walls and two chandeliers, each with six electrical bulbs.

Rather than introducing a radical difference in interior decoration, the practice of impersonal domesticity, I concluded after seeing the photographs, produced modest reconfigurations. At Flowermead, naturalistic patterns persist: slipcovers on chairs feature sheaves of wheat, a motif frequently utilised by designers associated with the Aesthetic and Arts and Crafts Movements. Morley seems to have heeded the call, as much aesthetic as hygienic, for wooden floors complemented by oriental or Turkey carpets, which could be regularly shaken or beaten, rather than fitted carpeting with bold and vivid designs that imitated Eastern patterns. The use of hygienic decorative principles espoused by some of the leading advisors of the day is visible, too, in Morley's treatment of the fireplace. The mantel at Flowermead is draped, as at no. 95, with a solid fabric. These simple fabrics could be easily and routinely cleaned, unlike the 'elaborate flutings and flounces of muslin and general awfulnesses' Panton abhorred (1889: 66).

Just above the fireplace, liberalism's practical and theoretical sides find expression in the dominating portraits of Gladstone and Mill. Between them is a painting by Jean-François Millet depicting, in its figure of a woodcutter, male industriousness. Along the crown moulding, Morley hung Giovanni Battista Piranesi's etchings of Roman scenes, including the arches of Titus, Septimius Severus and Constantine.[53] These artworks had personal or symbolic significance for Morley. Millet's painting may have evoked memories of the axe-wielding Gladstone felling trees. Another painting directly above the fireplace, depicting waves crashing on the rocks, represented, in Morley's words, 'the life political' (qtd in Begbie 1905: 134). To modern eyes, the library may appear rather fully furnished, but a Victorian visitor would have gained the overwhelming impression of a vast expanse.

The interiors at Elm Park Gardens and Flowermead reflected Morley's ongoing effort to free himself from the limiting designations of family, clan and class. The orthodox carved oak and dark green of the gentleman's library; the yellow and crimson damask and the velvet-covered walls of an aristocratic estate; the dense massing of furniture and the display of bric-a-brac, whether judiciously chosen or indiscriminately acquired, were all to be avoided because they signified and displayed attachment to a particular class status and, consequently, inhibited free thought. Cognitive liberalisation, as Morley intended to practise it, required that he form opinions disinterestedly, impersonally, individually: 'Truth is the single object', he insisted (1901: 147).

This aim, it seems, required facilitating abstraction from quotidian personal interests within the spaces of the home. Meanwhile, by surrounding himself with decorative artefacts representing liberalism's philosophical and political sides, Morley attempted to domesticate impersonal practices that might be seen today as alienating and isolating. Rather than anticipating the stark-white, stripped-down interiors of Modernism, therefore, Morley's residences attempted to make the states of abstraction and detachment, which some may find sterile and disembodied, part of a meaningfully lived experience.[54]

Yet this rather visionary experiment in living relies on specific class-based prerogatives, even if Morley intended to forswear obvious class markers such as preferred wall treatments. In order to maintain the pale hues of no. 95, for example, servants would have scrubbed the rooms to mitigate the effects of gas lighting. When the Morleys moved to no. 57 in 1896, electricity was still an exclusive amenity. By 1911 there were only 122,000 customers throughout London and its suburbs (London County Council 1912: 483). Although the artefacts and portraits with which Morley decorated the home, which housemaids regularly dusted, were not reminders of familial interest, they nevertheless reflected his status as a member of London's political elite.

Body, Privacy, Space

Morley's practice of impersonal domesticity, with the aim of achieving disinterested thought, necessarily existed in tension with the emotional intimacy and inter-familial attentiveness many Victorians had long celebrated as the foundation of home life. Within the domestic sphere one's actions were liable to be motivated by spontaneous feeling and unreflective attachments that inhibited detachment. Indeed, Arnold saw the home as a less than ideal environment for the free play of mind. Mill thought of the home in far different terms: it was potentially a place where spouses – as independent, self-governing friends – worked together in a spirit of equality and cooperation.

In his attempt to live impersonally, Morley accepted certain aspects of his mentor's argument in *The Subjection of Women*.[55] Taking his cue from Mill, Morley sought, through the spatial arrangements of the home, to create an environment that nurtured the individuality of its residents. In *On Compromise*, published in 1874, Morley argues that 'the painful element in companionship is not difference of opinion, but discord of temperament' (1901: 184). Husbands and wives need not hold the same beliefs; instead, 'each of them should hold his and her own convictions in a high and worthy spirit' (184). He gives the example of religious belief:

> It is certainly not less possible to disbelieve religiously than to believe religiously. This accord of mind, this emulation in freedom and loftiness of soul, this kindred sense of the awful depth of the enigma which the one believes to be answered, and the other suspects to be for ever unanswerable – here, and not in a degrading and hypocritical conformity, is the true gratification of those spiritual sensibilities which are alleged to be so much higher in women than in men. (184)

Were women to 'insist on more than this kind of harmony', Morley affirms, 'their system of divinity is little better than a special manifestation of shrewishness' (185). If a husband 'suppresses' his beliefs, capitulating to a wife who insists on harmony of belief rather than of aim, he is guilty of 'weakness of will and principle' (185). As did Mill, Morley believed that accepting the views of others as the premise of one's own life fatally compromised one's capacity for self-formation.

But these ideas about living in harmony of aim, formulated after he read *The Subjection of Women*, existed in tension with his previous notions about women, the vestigial remains of which are evoked by his reference to 'shrewishness'. In his early essays Morley expresses less faith than Mill in women's mental capacities. 'As a rule', women are 'not thoughtful readers' and are 'so intensely practical, in the narrowest, and often the worst, sense of the term, as to look with habitual distrust upon those general ideas which it is the chief business of literature to sow' (Morley 1867c: 175). The mind of a wife and mother is not 'roomy enough to contain at once a vigorous taste for books and a just interest in the various duties of her position', a condition in which men played a role by encouraging their wives to devote themselves 'not to books, but to their children' (175). A man may discover on marriage that his wife is not the 'high-souled sympathetic woman' she seemed, having instead 'a confirmed habit of looking at things in a narrow, fractious, half-hearted way' (Morley 1867d: 47). The traces of such views may have contributed to his separating the masculine and feminine spaces of the home in ways that reflected lingering attachment to masculine amity and difficulty in relinquishing the intimacy, security and enjoyment of homosocial settings.

With a total of five bedrooms and two dressing rooms on the third and fourth floors, both houses at Elm Park Gardens were, by any measure, remarkably spacious. But, at least for the decade they spent at no. 95, the Morleys did not live alone, with just their staff in attendance. When the couple met, Rose already had two children, Florence and John Ayling, who had been born out of wedlock. In 1877 Morley adopted his eight-year-old nephew, Guy, whose parents, Morley's brother William and his wife, Maria, had died in India several years earlier. After returning from boarding school in Bristol, Guy took up residence at Elm Park Gardens for a few years. Grace, too, moved into no. 95 for a period. Even after obtaining her own accommodations, she made frequent, extended visits.[56]

How were the issues of body, privacy and space negotiated within the Morleys' homes? A floor plan of no. 95 annotated in Morley's hand, fortuitously included among his collected papers, provides some guidance (Morley n.d.; Figure 3.4). Both houses included two dressing-rooms. Thus they met Victorian architect Robert Kerr's definition of a gentleman's residence: at least one bedroom with an attached dressing-room should be found in 'every instance of what we might call a Gentleman's House, however small', with 'more of these as the size of the house increases' (1871: 137–8). Grace, according to Morley's notation, used a bedroom with an attached dressing-room on the third floor. Florence, who probably shared the dressing-room with Grace, had her own room across the hall, and Morley allocates another bedroom on that floor to Guy and John. The three live-in servants would have been assigned the attic rooms. John and Rose,

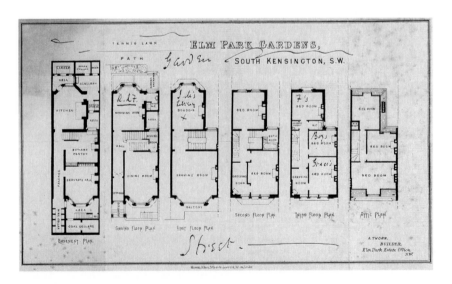

Figure 3.4 No. 95 Elm Park Gardens floor plan. The Bodleian Libraries, The University of Oxford. MS. Eng. C. 7090, fol. 4

while they would have shared the other dressing-room, may have occupied separate bedrooms on the second floor.

There were, for Morley, philosophical reasons for such an arrangement for him and Rose. In an early essay, written before his marriage and before being deeply influenced by *The Subjection of Women*, he rejected the notion that one's wife is 'the most desirable companion he [a husband] could have at all times and under every circumstance'. He asserted, 'Nobody wants to have his wife in his chambers or at his counting-house' (1865b: 116). Although Morley's views may have evolved over time, the floor plan suggests the possibility that such a separation extended to their bedchambers. Despite being generously sized, the houses at Elm Park Gardens could not accommodate every family member in a separate room. With five bedrooms and six family members in residence, it would have been necessary for two people to share a room. According to Morley's annotated floor plan, Guy and John did so. The three bedrooms on the fourth floor are clearly assigned, but the two bedrooms on the third floor are not. If he and Rose did sleep apart, Morley probably would have stayed in the bedroom overlooking the communal park, accessing the dressing room from the hallway. She probably would have taken the larger bedroom, entering the dressing room directly from the bedroom.[57]

Intimacy between women and men, for which the shared bedroom is a symbol, is a vexing problem for Morley's version of liberal individualism. On the one hand, a world without feeling is an unliveable one. On the other hand, 'a great many clever and likeable men seem to demand a certain amount of solitude' (Morley 1865b: 121).[58] By possibly arranging for separate bedrooms and, as I will shortly consider, separate workspaces on separate floors, Morley minimised bodily proximity between Rose and himself, facilitating privacy while also ensuring that distractions and aggravations would not frequently disrupt the 'large and serene internal activity' he attempted to cultivate.

For him, romantic or familial love is a key step in the challenging journey every liberalising individual must undertake. 'When he is in love', Morley wrote of courtship while in his late twenties, 'a man may think as a child and speak as a child; but, if he is to go on growing, he must put away childish things' (1865c: 107). Because tenderness and love are the foundations of the family as a communal or corporate unit, they are not themselves the destination. Instead, one must transcend those feelings, without relinquishing them, to embrace higher-order abstractions. 'If he is a genuine lover of truth, if he is inspired by the divine passion for seeing things as they are', Morley avows, with a nod to Arnold, 'and a divine abhorrence of holding ideas which do not conform to the facts, he will be wholly independent of the approval or assent of the persons around him' (1901: 201). But this independence must be tempered: 'When he proceeds to apply his beliefs in the practical conduct of life, the position is different. There are now good reasons why his attitude should be in some ways less inflexible' (201).

The frequent descriptions of Morley as an ascetic, as well as erroneous press reports that he was single, indicate that many who saw his commitment to truth and independence were unaware of the flexible, practical aspects of his private life, about which he was extremely reticent. His devotion to ideas was often registered as an impoverished substitute for familial relations or romantic love. On Morley's death, one writer proclaimed that Morley 'lived and died a bachelor, and I cannot imagine from his writings at least that he ever commanded from anybody passionate affection' (Abbott 1923: 173). Others made similar observations.[59]

In Morley's view, the relationship that best matched a lived commitment to higher-order abstractions is friendship. While Mill saw friendship as the basis of marriage in its highest form, Morley began his adult life believing that 'it is only a small and lucky minority who find in their wives anything at all resembling the ideal of friendship' (Morley 1865b: 115). Marriage brought together two people whose camaraderie, if it developed, was born of daily routines more than of intellectual affinity. A wife may be 'a sufficiently agreeable companion', he acknowledged, 'provided she has sense enough to throw the children's boots, and coughs, and teeth off her mind' (116). But most women, he found, were unable to formulate thoughtful opinions: 'tenderness and love are very excellent things, but many husbands would be delighted if the wives of their bosoms were rather more like old college friends than they are, and if their tenderness were solidified by rather more judgment' (115). Although Morley may have moderated his views later, especially in light of Mill's influence, his relative silence on these subjects after the 1860s makes it difficult to assess changes in his thinking. Looking back at his life in his *Recollections*, published in 1917, Morley mentions Rose only occasionally – she appears as 'my wife' or 'R.' – but freely discusses homosocial relationships. He notes that throughout life he formed deep friendships with 'men vastly my superiors', including Mill and Gladstone. Such relationships, he felt, were 'golden boons' (1917: 163). Other bonds, such as his with George Meredith and with

James Cotter Morison, which formed at Oxford, were abiding. Until they broke over the question of Irish home rule, Morley and Joseph Chamberlain 'lived the life of brothers' (163). Morley received his many (male) parliamentary, journalistic and literary friends in the masculine precincts of the drawing room and the library, which he decorated with portraits of friends and reminders of their shared interests. This atmosphere of camaraderie was a way to ensure that free and independent living, untainted by influence, was never experienced as loneliness or isolation.

'The Pure Serene'

The principal location within the home for cultivating a love of truth, Morley believed, was the study or library, which functioned for him as the generative site of critical reason. By the time he moved his books to his 400-square-foot library at Flowermead, Morley owned more than 11,000. His tranquil domesticity was founded, in part, on their possession. Books were, Morley once confessed, his 'genial, instructive, fortifying comrades' (qtd in Staebler 1943: 187). Biographical sketches made frequent reference to Morley's collection. 'Mr. Morley's study, which is upstairs, is simply packed with books', reads a brief sketch of no. 95 published in *The Star*, a London daily newspaper, and subsequently republished in a popular Liberal-leaning weekly. 'Perhaps it is as true to-day as it was long ago', the journalist concludes, 'that Mr. Morley is never more happy than among his books' ('Mr. John Morley's London home' 1892). If the library was a place of retirement for Morley, retirement was decidedly not spent in idleness and complacency. Instead of being a restful withdrawal from political activity, his seclusion in the library is framed as a 'change of employment', Gladstone's vaunted definition of 'recreation' (Bailey 1978: 67). Morley understood, and the biographical sketches of him in the popular illustrated press helped to confirm, that the scholarly activities he undertook within his library were a form of strenuous labour of public benefit.

The floor plan for the Elm Park Gardens residences did not designate any room as a library. George Godwin's architectural rendering provides for a morning room on the ground floor, which he likely intended for the use of women and children; a dining room, often considered a masculine space, on the same floor; and a drawing room and a boudoir, principally feminine, if not female, spaces, on the first floor.[60] By using the French term rather than 'sitting room', its English equivalent, Godwin's plan evokes the word's etymological association with feeling – from *bouder* (to sulk or pout). While the boudoir was a place of female withdrawal, the drawing room, as Thad Logan describes it, was far more complex. It was simultaneously 'an inner sanctum . . . set aside for the private life of the family members', usually under the decorative sway of the household mistress, and, in what may seem like an extraordinary contradiction, also the most public space in one's ostensibly private home, a place to greet or entertain guests (Logan 2001: 27). Godwin's design reflected widely held assumptions about the sexual geography of the home: certain rooms were to be more masculine or feminine than others.[61]

By placing an *X* just below the word 'boudoir' on his copy of the floor plan, scrawling 'J. M.'s library' just above it and designating the morning room for use by Rose and Florence, Morley makes a subtle change that might be seen as an attempt to allocate female conviviality and occupations to the ground floor, where the morning room was located in both no. 95 and no. 57, and male studiousness to the next floor (Morley n.d.). While the morning room in a Victorian home was to be utilised chiefly by women, it was not strictly a place for retreat or receiving formal calls. Instead, it was to be used by the lady of the house to coordinate household activities and to oversee the work of domestic servants. It was most often considered a practical workspace: the female equivalent of a library.[62] The library, according to Kerr, is 'primarily a sort of Morning-room for gentlemen' (1871: 116). Rather than reorganising the spaces within the home to separate perceived frivolity from sobriety, Morley establishes complementary, though unequal, work spaces. In so doing he negates a space synonymous with femininity – annexing the drawing room, which will function instead as an antechamber to his library, and eliminating the boudoir – to privilege (masculine) intellect.[63]

Yet I think it would be a mistake to see Morley's home as a site of contest between male and female. The larger point, it seems to me, is that individuals in the house are allowed to live according to their own definitions of the good life. By spending large portions of their time on separate floors, Morley and Rose could, as Morley once theorised, 'pursue pleasure after their respective tastes' (1865b: 116).[64] In so far as Morley's spatial arrangements, drawing on but also creatively adapting prevalent notions of sexual geography, attempted to facilitate necessary propinquity while lessening the disruptions of chance encounters, impersonal domesticity shares modernism's emphasis on functionality, regularity and predictability. But it does not simply prefigure it: Morley's use of the architectural spaces of his homes, which took advantage of the architectural trend towards differentiation and specialisation (to each room its purpose), reflects transmogrification of the Evangelical desire for solitariness wherein the deepest personal experiences of truth occur.[65]

To discern truth from falsehood, Morley had concluded during his university days, one must extricate oneself from the clamour of competing theories. In his essay on Paterian aestheticism, Morley remarks:

> The speculative distractions of the epoch are noisy and multitudinous, and the first effort of the serious spirit must be to disengage itself from the futile hubbub which is sedulously maintained by the bodies of rival partisans in philosophy and philosophical theology. This effort after detachment naturally takes the form of criticism of the past, the only way in which a man can take part in the discussion and propagation of ideas, while yet standing in some sort aloof from the agitation of the present. (1873: 470)

The 'internecine war' at Oxford, which he characterises as 'loud', and the general air of intellectual discordance were anathema to him (1917: 13). 'Truth', the reconciliation of opposing views, 'is quiet', he famously contends (1987: 49).

Although Morley's remark about the 'futile hubbub' refers to the clamour of contemporaneous religious debate rather than to disturbing sounds within a spatial environment, he nevertheless sought to cultivate, within the home, an environment conducive to discovering truth in a quiet way. When Filon visited Morley, he noted the unusual quiet, as if the sabbatical principle of avoiding idle conversation had been extended to each day of the week:

> A parlour maid greets you, wearing the traditional bonnet and printed cotton dress if it is morning, or black merino wool if it is after three o'clock. You have an appointment: you are introduced without unnecessary words . . . the house is silent . . . (1891: 155)

Escorted by the parlour maid to the drawing room, across the hall from Morley's library, Filon immediately experienced 'a feeling of contemplation' while waiting to be received (155). Absent were the recognisably domestic sounds that made a middle-class house a home: the chords of a piano (although the Morleys owned one) or ladies talking in the morning room. The relative quiet in which the domestic inhabitants went about their business was a constituent element of Morley's aesthetic of serenity.

On the garden side of the house, away from the street, Morley's library was a place for quiet reflection. No less than the private rooms of an Evangelical home dedicated to contemplation and conversion, the library was, for Morley, a sanctified space wherein he expected the experience of truth to occur. When Morley readied himself to read and write, the process by which truth could be apprehended, he engaged in a particular ritual, which he recounted to the Clerk to the Privy Council and literary figure Arthur Helps: 'Like Buffon, I insist upon shaving and clean linen before sitting down to composition' (qtd in Helps 1917: 294). The eighteenth-century French naturalist Georges-Louis Leclerc, comte de Buffon asserts in his famous lecture on style: 'Writing well is thinking, feeling and expressing well; it is having at the same time wit, soul and taste . . . The style is the man himself.'[66] But to take Morley at his word that these preparatory activities were like Buffon's would be to miss their religious overtones: in the biblical phrase 'in fine linen, clean and white' (Rev. 19:8), 'linen' signifies righteousness, the adjectives purity.

Cleansed of impurities and dressed in clean linen, Morley would enter his library, which was decorated on hygienic principles that complemented the mental hygiene for which he strove. He diligently filed his many papers into the drawers of his two desks (Robertson Scott 1952: 24). Discernible in the photograph of Flowermead, these desks – the first in the foreground, right, and the second in the background, left – appear to have separated, following Gladstone's practice, Morley's literary and political work.[67] The distinction between politics and literature, though, is less neat than this arrangement might imply. In the realms of both literature and politics, Morley wrestled with a choice between directly intervening in the contemporary issues of the moment, which his work as a journalist, Member of Parliament, cabinet official and, from 1908, a peer often required, and indirectly intervening through writing biography (mainly historical biography). As one who continually sought to ensure that his mind was thinking reflexively rather than responding impulsively to the concerns of the present, Morley was most comfortable when he withdrew from the 'futile hubbub' and turned his mind to 'criticism of the past'. W. T. Stead, Morley's deputy editor at *The Pall Mall Gazette*, recognised this when remarking, in assessing Morley as a journalist, that he 'had no eye for news' and 'was totally devoid of the journalistic instinct', adding that 'to him a newspaper was simply a pulpit from which he could preach' (1890: 430–1). Morley's more effective means of moralising was through biography, which he either wrote or edited at his literary desk.

Morley sought to discern truth through studying historical personages and, by writing about them, to relay that truth to readers. He authored numerous historical biographies. As general editor between 1878 and 1892, and again from 1902 to 1919, he also oversaw the publication of Macmillan's English Men of Letters series, profiles of individuals through which one was meant to glimpse the underlying impersonal historical forces that moved them. As I noted in the introduction, Morley vigorously disagreed with the still-influential eighteenth-century approaches to life writing. The essayist Samuel Johnson thought that only by leading readers 'into domestick privacies, and display[ing] the minute details of daily life, where exterior appendages are cast aside', was character best discerned (Boswell 1826: 6). Morley felt otherwise: assessing the truthfulness of a published opinion in no way required knowledge of the writer's conduct (Morley 1865a). Therefore, Morley's biographies, as well as those he solicited as editor, were, for all their contextualisation, intended to illuminate universal rather than ephemeral concerns. They were to avoid what he derisively termed 'domesticities' or ordinary, insignificant details (qtd in Hamer 1968: 45).

By concentrating on individuals through whom larger historical forces moved, Morley differed somewhat from Mill. In *A System of Logic*, written after his ascent to the upper echelons of East India House management, Mill argued that 'eminent men do not merely see the coming light from the hill-top, they mount on the hill-top and evoke it' (1974: VIII, 938). In accord with this line of thinking, which resonated to a limited extent with Thomas Carlyle's notion of the hero, Mill insisted that 'had there been no Socrates, no Plato, and no Aristotle, there would have been no philosophy for the next two thousand years, nor in all probability then' (VIII, 938). But Morley understood historical writing, and biography as a subgenre, slightly differently:

> History has strictly only to do with individual men as the originals, the furtherers, the opponents, or the representatives of some of those thousand diverse forces which, uniting in one vast sweep, bear along the successive generations of men as upon the broad wings of sea-winds to new and more fertile shores. (1867b: 63)

Although Morley insisted one could discern the progress of truth through history by studying a wide variety of literary genres, he privileged historical over imaginative writing. Knowing about the past, he affirmed, lent 'stability and substance to character' (1887: 43). Through his Men of Letters series, Morley trained a popular readership, too 'busy' and 'preoccupied' by the concerns of daily life to spend much time acquiring 'knowledge' or engaging in 'reflection' (Morley 1917: 92), to understand what he considered the proper methods of studying history.

A number of volumes in the series suggest that fiction and poetry are deficient when their subject is a historical event or personage. Thus, the volume on Charles Dickens, written by A. W. Ward, declares *A Tale of Two Cities* 'an extraordinary *tour de force*' but 'not [a] perfectly constructed novel' (1882: 157, 155), with at least one 'historically questionable' character portrayal (157). G. K. Chesterton, in his estimation of Robert Browning for the series, notes a similar lack of discipline. Browning's love of historical detail creates a 'turbulent democracy of things', with 'sometimes no background and no middle distance in his mind' (Chesterton 1903: 166). Morley shared James Cotter Morison's view that to effect a fair representation of history the writer must ensure that 'the whole temper of his mind and feelings is in a state of balanced equipoise' (Morison 1878: 238).

By maintaining his 'large and serene internal activity', Morley approached writing history as he attempted to live his life. In the quietude of his domestic library, he sought first to think. He practised 'the all-important habit of taking care that . . . [the] mind works at ideas instead of allowing it to absorb their pale shadows' (Morley 1866a: 273). The mind at work is precisely what a photograph of Morley at Flowermead attempts to capture (Figure 3.3). Reclining in a chair to the right of the fireplace, Morley is enveloped in streams of light. Early photographic experts frequently advised that windows be screened 'to yield pleasant portraits in home situations' ('Lessons' 1901: 613).[68] In this photo the natural light flooding the room is not a lapse by the photographer. Rather, light, a frequent symbol of knowledge in representational imagery, is harnessed to depict Morley as a man of thought, diffusing, as Morley himself would write of Burke, 'that clear, undisturbed light which we are accustomed to find in men who have trained themselves to balance ideas, to weigh mutually opposed speculations' (1867b: 25). Morley is shown engaged in the process of achieving 'a state of slow but never-staying fermentation, in which everything that enters the mind is transformed and assimilated' (Morley 1867e: 169–70).

'Coherency of Character'

Once he resolved to write, Morley approached composition as he did interior decoration. One might imagine that Morley has such consistency in mind when he asserts, through an aesthetic idiom, that 'coherency of character and conduct' is one aim of 'the great art of living' (1901: 67). Noting that 'the flash and the glitter' of Carlyle, Macaulay and Ruskin, 'three great giants of prose writing', has had its day, Morley maintains that 'a quieter style' is beginning to take hold (Morley 1887: 12–13). This style, 'the steadfast use of a language in which truth can be told . . . without trick, without affectation, without mannerisms', is the natural outcome of measured reflection (13). His parliamentary colleague, whom I quoted earlier, agreed. After referring to the simplicity of the home at Elm Park Gardens, he declared that Morley's prose is 'contemptuous of glitter': 'the style is not only the man, but the revelation of the man' (Anon. 1899: 879).[69]

Other contemporaries used the idioms of decoration and space when referring to Morley's writings or personality, evoking, intentionally or not, widely understood features of his homes. They lauded Morley's lack of interest in 'mere rhetorical ornament'; his embodiment of 'the splendid austerity of truth'; and the development of 'a style which, with all its severity, often rises into lofty eloquence'.[70] Many readers of these portraits shared Morley's confidence in the possibility of an achieved coherence. The principles of orderliness and minimalism governing his decorative choices are shown also to inflect his writings and persona, revealing coherence of character across the public/private divide. For a time this consistency among person, place and idea (printed word) counted as integrity in the increasing intimisation of the public sphere, in which politics is reduced to the spectacle of public figures leading private lives.[71] Until Morley was unseated in the 1895 general election, the largely working-class electorate in Newcastle referred to him simply as 'Honest John'. In the opinion of one contemporary, 'Honest John' did not, as the concept of personality emerging at the end of the nineteenth century seemed to require, engage in 'pushing himself to the center of the stage': 'Lord Morley's is not a personality that flaunts its virtues or affects a theatrical pose' (Ford 1908: 212–13). But this claim, it seems to me, like Cohen's more recent assertion that 'unlike character, which was silent, personality was constantly on display', severely underestimates how much character was dependent for its confirmation on public staging (2006: 125). The seeming congruence between Morley and his domestic environments at Elm Park Gardens and Flowermead helped fashion the popular perception that – as one columnist proclaimed, perhaps unintentionally echoing Morley's assumptions about character as the self's 'creature' and then as its 'master' – 'he was always master of himself' (W. Ryan 1923: 94).

Morley's interiors are evidence that he accepted what the espousers of the new concept of personality had vociferously contended: the fundamentally reciprocal relationship between the self and its environments. He would not, however, have shared the writer Hallie Miles's view that 'everything in a human dwelling is bathed in personality', that each object has 'a voice' that bespeaks the 'individuality of the person to whom the room belongs' (Miles 1911: 231). Through practising impersonal domesticity, one was no longer to be hindered by mere individuality. Robert Browning, the subject of my next chapter, would have disagreed with Miles as well, but for entirely different reasons. To him, as G. K. Chesterton recognised, each object had a voice of its own.

Notes

1. Between 29 and 31 December 1885 Morley notes daily in his diary that he and Rose looked at houses (Morley 1882–92: MS. Eng. d. 3440).
2. Morley 1874–1918: 31 December 1885, MS. Eng. e. 3433.
3. Although indexed, the original letter is not in the file of correspondence with Grace in the Morley Papers at the Bodleian Library. Just one day after Morley characterised the house-hunting experience as 'very doleful', he noted in his diary that they had inspected Elm Park Gardens (Morley 1882–92: 1 January 1886, MS. Eng. d. 3441). Between excised pages and long periods in which Morley failed to record his activities, it remains unclear why, after visiting Elm Park Gardens on 1 January 1886, they did not move until April. If they continued house-hunting after their initial visit to Elm Park Gardens, Morley does not mention it.
4. On the development of London's 'railway suburbs', see Kellett 1969: 365–82; Barker and Robbins 2007: 198–240; and Waller 1983: 145–59.
5. Influenced by seventeenth- and early eighteenth-century vernacular architecture, Queen Anne, which gained popularity in the 1870s, was initially hailed as symbolising receptivity to socially efficacious ideas and eagerness to dwell in beauty. Some saw it as a response to Matthew Arnold's call for more sweetness and light to counter middle-class philistinism (Girouard 1977: 3–4). Queen Anne architecture was not intended to be uniform. One claim made on its behalf was that 'it gives more variety and character to city houses than was possessed by houses of the old style, that stood along the streets like regiments of drilled soldiers' (*Carpentry and Building* 1885). Whereas John Nash's terraces earlier in the century were intended to appear as singular compositions, late-Victorian terraced houses sought to emphasise the separateness of each residence. 'Less monumentality and more cosiness, less classicism and more individuality' were the primary aims (Dohme 1888:

28; translation mine). Nevertheless, observers increasingly viewed this style as contributing to the uniformity of residential streets.

6. The translation of Filon's essay is mine.

7. Filon is using British terminology in referring to one level above the ground floor.

8. For examples of how the English press reviewed Filon's article and book, see 'Echoes' 1891: 12; Greville 1893: 346; 'A French view' 1891: 1–2; 'John Morley as others see him' 1891.

9. This brief sketch of no. 95 was originally published in *The Star*. See also 'Ollendorfiana' 1892.

10. Although Morley often referred to Flowermead's location as Wimbledon Park, it stood just over the Wandsworth boundary in Putney. The house appears in the 1881 census index but not on the 1869 Ordnance Survey map; hence, it was built between these dates. In street directories Morley is listed at the property first in 1904 and last in 1923, the year he and Rose died. His move to Flowermead is often given as 1904; however, he began sending letters on Flowermead stationery in midsummer 1903. See his letters to Francis Wrigley Hirst in the Hirst Papers at the Bodleian Library, Oxford.

11. Morley was also featured in so-called gallery portraits, a form of biographical sketch focusing on the subject's life and works instead of the home. See, for example, Banfield 1884: 25–6; *Cassell's Universal Portrait Gallery* 1895: 172–3; *Cabinet Portrait Gallery* 1890: 81–3; and Hansard [1912?]: 25–32.

12. Although Judith Neiswander and I start from a similar premise, linking liberalism to home decoration, she pursues a different angle. While contemporary critics have tended to see individual expression in residential interiors as primarily an activity by women, who were frequently charged with furnishing and maintaining the home, Neiswander contends that decoration was, in fact, 'once part of a broader conversation', which she associates with British liberalism, 'about optimal ways of living, both within the family and within the culture as a whole' (2008: 9). In her view the increasingly widespread belief, emergent in the 1870s, that domestic interiors should mirror the unique characteristics of their inhabitants reflected the popularisation of John Stuart Mill's support for 'the trial of new and original experiments in living' (JSM 1977d: 281). Neiswander focuses almost exclusively on a few phrases of Mill's, which she sees as authorising the expression of individuality in choosing domestic goods and furnishings.

13. 'In the Victorian period', Walter Houghton writes, 'a great many thoughtful people shared the same fate': intellectual and social isolation (1957: 81).

14. See I. Bradley 1976: 179; Tosh 1999a: 36; and Rosman 2011: 97–118.

15. See Hadley 2010: 147; Willey 1956: 248–301; and B. Russell 2009: 441. For considerations of other ways in which practices of Protestant

Dissent saturated political liberalism, see Parry 1986; Biagini 1992: 15–17; Brent 1987.

16. On Evangelicalism's role in establishing and spreading Sunday schools, see Laqueur 1979: 21–36, 73–7, 124–5, 225–9.
17. Hirst 1927: I, 9; Phillips 1982: 115, 129–30.
18. At Oxford, Morley came to recognise that he was living in 'the age of science, new knowledge, searching criticism, followed by multiplied doubts and shaken beliefs' (Morley 1917: 100).
19. See JSM 1979: 16, 170.
20. On Mansel's Bampton Lectures, see Sampson 1959. For a discussion of Mansel's points of disagreement with Mill, see Lightman 1987: 34–5, 49, 104–5.
21. Thus, when Morley claims he discovered in Mill's writings 'that sense of truth having many mansions', the religious – and spatial – phraseology is undoubtedly intentional (1904b: 131).
22. 'Though the Victorians never ceased to look forward to a new period of firm convictions and established beliefs', Houghton notes, 'they had to live in the meantime between two worlds, one dead or dying, one struggling but powerless to be born, in an age of doubt' (1957: 9–10). On this age of transition, see also Culler 1985.
23. I have, necessarily, truncated the account of Morley's waning religious belief. He experienced many other blows to his faith, including from the first stirrings of Darwinism during his crucial final year at Oxford. On Morley's time at Oxford, see Hirst 1927: I, 15–32; Morley 1917: 7–13.
24. Hirst 1927: I, 40–1; and Staebler 1943: 40–1. For background on the London positivist set and their beliefs, see Postlethwaite 1984: 39–52.
25. Ever the eccentric, Spencer refused to read any books (Morley 1917: 111), which left him vulnerable to charges of plagiarism when he did not acknowledge similarities between his work and others'.
26. The *Oxford English Dictionary* dates one of the literal meanings of 'inexpugnable' (a fortress that cannot be conquered) to 1490. 'Base' has been part of an architectural idiom since the 1300s.
27. See, for example, Charles Rice, who argues that bourgeois interiority and domestic interiors emerge coevally (2007: 2–3).
28. As Stefan Collini states, Victorian intellectuals linked morality to thought; they believed that with the decline of orthodox Christianity there still were correct ways to solve problems (1991: 75). Elaine Hadley claims that 'mid-Victorian political liberalism was . . . stoked by particular – and clearly still influential – practices of moralized cognition' (2010: 9). For liberal thinkers such as Morley, who fashioned a morality of knowledge and its expression through opinion, the principles of earnestness and sincerity were the characterological manifestations of rigorously formed and faithfully held belief.
29. The self-governing individual also possesses 'an intelligent set of convictions upon the problems that vex and harass society' and is in the

'habit of expressing it and supporting it in season and out of season' (Morley 1866b: 382). See also Hamer 1968: 23.

30. 'Every considerable advance in material civilization', Mill argues in *A System of Logic*, 'has been preceded by an advance in knowledge: and when any great social change has come to pass . . . it has had for its precursor a great change in the opinions and modes of thinking of society' (1974: VIII, 927).

31. See also Muthesius 1982 and Marcus 1999: 89–127.

32. See Leonore Davidoff and Catherine Hall on the anti-urban strand in Evangelical thought (1987: 157–8, 162–7, 357–69).

33. Morley 1874–1918: 9 August 1886, MS. Eng. e. 3433.

34. Peter and Alexander Thorn undertook several residential construction projects in South Kensington. Their most important commission, however, was Blackfriars Bridge. Elm Park Gardens, one of Alexander's first solo ventures after a period of insolvency following his brother's death, was successful. Several other properties were not. In late 1886, after the Morleys rented their house, his firm collapsed under the weight of its debt. See 'Failure' 1886; 'Princes Gate' 2000.

35. Elm Park Gardens was sanctioned as a new road in 1875. Building leases were granted to Alexander Thorn beginning in 1878 (Croot 2004: 74). Thorn constructed the terraces in stages: although the first houses were available in the late 1870s and promptly purchased or rented, the development was not finished until the mid-1880s.

36. Flats were so undesirable that, according to Stefan Muthesius's estimate, they made up only about 3 per cent of all dwellings in England and Wales by 1911 (1982: 1).

37. I discuss the development as it existed when built. Much of Elm Park Gardens remains, although conversion into flats began during World War Two. Extensions into the garden have been added to some houses, and modern apartment blocks have replaced a number of others.

38. Morley 1874–1918: 7 May 1886, MS. Eng. e. 3433.

39. Davidoff and Hall discuss privacy as a characteristic of middle-class home life and the role played by garden spaces in securing such privacy (1987: 361–2, 370–5). Tyack documents the enclosure of the garden square in 'smarter' districts for the residents' exclusive use (1992: 87).

40. In my discussion of Morley's residences at Elm Park Gardens, I adhere to the British floor-numbering system as represented by the floor plan.

41. For a consideration of standard floor plans, see Muthesius 1982: 79–100.

42. Harold Dyos argues that part of the lure of the suburb for London's wealthier residents was that it offered 'a personal solution to a collective sanitary problem' (1961: 23). On Godwin's role in helping to realise this solution, see Thorne 1987.

43. The laying of electrical distributing mains on the property began in the early 1890s ('Chelsea electric lighting' 1890: 272).

44. The previous occupant of no. 57 was Major W. E. Chapman, a patron of the arts and subscriber to the London Library (R. Harrison 1888: xiii).

45. On the impossibility of female self-expression within the confines of domestic ideology, see Calder 1977. For an account more open to the possibility of female agency and pleasure in decorating, see Logan 2001.

46. For a study of the environmental amenities of seaside towns, see Hassan 2003: 31–107. On Rose's declining health and the couple's moves, which Morley loathed, see Hirst 1927: I, 231, 238; II, 8. Morley's aversion to moving predated her illness; in 1871 he commented on having 'just passed through the horror and anguish of flitting' (qtd in Hirst 1927: I, 194).

47. As Neiswander argues, 'the appearance of the home would be generated from within the middle class itself and would no longer be a diluted and inferior imitation of upper-class magnificence' (2008: 80).

48. If visitors were left with the impression that Morley was frugal, he would not have been displeased. His reclamation from puritanism of the principle of thrift emphasised its positive value. Prudence, 'the wise and careful outlay of money', not penuriousness, was the aim (Morley 1865e: 79). Because thrift necessarily restrained one's whims and impulses, providing delayed rather instant gratification, Morley saw its practice as an outward manifestation of a liberal mind. But self-control was not the same as self-denial: 'The proposition that all pleasant things are right is untrue, but it is certainly not so radically untrue as the more popular proposition that most pleasant things are wrong' (Morley 1867a: 8–9). Consistent refusal of pleasure, out of an erroneous belief that refusing would save one's soul, checked 'all blitheness and freedom of spirit' (9).

49. On the changing colours and patterns of wallpaper, see Barrett and Phillips 1987: 106–11.

50. Morley 1874–1918: 7 May 1886, MS. Eng. e. 3433.

51. Morley 1874–1918: 10 February 1896, MS. Eng. e. 3435.

52. For a compelling discussion of the changing technologies of illumination in the period, see Otter 2008: 173–213.

53. On the citation of classical civilisation through art and sculpture in the gentleman's library, see Whinney 1992: 149 and Windscheffel 2008: 104.

54. In this respect, I share Amanda Anderson's concern with, although perhaps to a lesser extent her optimism about, the liberal cultivation of detachment as a structure of feeling (2001: 178).

55. Morley read *The Subjection of Women* on its publication in 1869 and recommended it to his friend George Meredith, who 'had more experience than Mill of some types of women and the particular arts, "feline chiefly," to which some have recourse to make their way in the world' (Morley 1917: 47).

56. The 1891 census records the residents of no. 95, in addition to John and Rose Morley, as Grace Morley, Florence Ayling and three female servants.

57. 'A lady's [dressing] room' requires 'a door of direct *intercommunication* with the Bedroom', Kerr advises, 'whereas in a gentleman's room it is allowable to have no more than the one outer door, provided this opens close to the door of the Bedroom and within a private Lobby' (1871: 136). The dressing rooms in no. 95 and no. 57 had doors that opened from both the hallway and the adjacent bedroom.

58. In the passage from which this quote is taken, Morley refers specifically to difficulties encountered when travelling with friends. However, the statement may also be understood in a general sense.

59. See the debate on this point in *The Spectator* (Janus 1952: 525; H. Harrison 1952: 570). Morley's relationship with Rose was problematic. It appears that they lived together before marrying. If so, he initially followed his heart (and likely his body) rather than his head. Because their union originated in scandal, Rose was not wholly acceptable socially. This, along with her frail health, helps explain their low profile as a couple even after he rose to prominence. Some felt Morley's decision to enter into a relationship with an 'unsuitable' woman, tainted by scandal, cost him the chance to serve as prime minister. It is possible that Morley's impersonal domesticity was a way to (over)compensate for choices he made earlier in life.

60. In Kerr's influential formulation, the ideal dining room, 'somewhat massive and simple', reflected 'masculine importance', while the drawing room in its 'cheerfulness' and 'elegance' was to be 'entirely *ladylike*' (1871: 94, 107). Kerr notes that in some houses the term 'boudoir' is inaccurately used in reference to a morning room (1871: 114–15). Because the houses at Elm Park Gardens contained both, that is not so here.

61. On the sexual geography of the home, see Logan 2001: 31; Chase and Levenson 2000: 163; and Girouard 1978: 298.

62. See Panton's characterisation of the morning room (1888: 69–77) and Flanders's extensive discussion (2004: 292–323).

63. Jill Casid explores the role the boudoir played not only as a rival to the male library but as a crucial element in fashioning separate spheres. She considers how, in eighteenth-century France, the boudoir, as a place of feminine authority and display, was the counterpart to men's salons (2003: 91–114).

64. These arrangements also had implications for the children residing in the household, which I discuss in *A Microhistory of Victorian Liberal Parenting: John Morley's 'Discrete Indifference'* (forthcoming, Palgrave).

65. On differentiation and specialisation, see Muthesius 1982: 45.

66. Buffon (1992): 28, 30; translation mine.

67. On Gladstone's separation of his literary and political work by using two desks, see Windscheffel 2008: 107.
68. 'In making pictures indoors', the American photographer Alexander Black insisted, 'the illumination, instead of being managed by nature, as out-of-doors, must be managed by the photographer' (1887: 725).
69. See also Bowran 1900: 118.
70. Buchanan 1871: 319; Gardiner 1914: 153; *Cassell's Universal Portrait Gallery* 1895: 173.
71. See Rössler 2005, especially pp. 169–92.

Chapter 4

Robert Browning's Domestic Gods

Four volumes consisting of 21,075 lines, twelve books, ten dramatic monologues and two statements by a narrator in service to providing different perspectives on the rape and murder of a young wife by her aristocratic husband in seventeenth-century Rome. When the first volume appeared in 1868, few Victorian readers knew what to make of Robert Browning's *The Ring and the Book*. A contributor to *The Dublin Review* singled out its 'deliberate offenses, as we are compelled to regard them, against rhythm, good taste, and even the English language' (Doherty 1869: 52). By the time the final volume was published the following year, some critics were objecting to the work's length. An essay on modern English poets in *The Quarterly Review* complained: 'It is a weariness to the flesh to read so many arguments pro and con . . . on a critical case with so many ignoble elements in it . . .' (Mozley 1869: 347).

In the March 1869 issue of *The Fortnightly Review*, John Morley, then editor of the journal, defended the poem against those who 'pronounced [it] . . . sordid, unlovely, morally sterile': 'in its perfection and integrity, [it] fully satisfies the conditions of artistic triumph' (1869: 331, 336). Readers had become 'so debilitated by pastorals, by graceful presentation of the Arthurian legend for drawing-rooms, by idylls, not robust and Theocritean, but such little pictures as might adorn a ladies' school, by verse directly didactic', Morley scoffs, 'that a rude inburst of air from the outside welter of human realities is apt to spread a shock, which might show in what simpleton's paradise we have been living' (1869: 331). He laments, 'Our public is beginning to measure the right and possible in art, by the superficial probabilities of life and manners within a ten-mile radius of Charing Cross' (331). While he acknowledges the poem's many flaws, he affirms that 'a grievous sterility of thought', so typical of 'contemporary verse', is not among them (341). Morley praises Browning for his poetry's impersonality; his objective approach to assembling the facts of the case; and, in considering all possible perspectives on the issue, his many-sidedness (341). His work, Morley implies, is also 'powerfully efficacious from a moral point of view' inasmuch as 'the exercise of an exalted creative art' stirs in the reader 'active thought and curiosity about many types of character and many changeful issues of conduct and fortune, at once enlarging and elevating the range of his reflections on mankind' (336–7). This exercise has the effect of 'ever kindling his sympathies into the warm and continuous glow which purifies and strengthens nature, and fills men with that love of humanity which is the best inspirer of virtue' (337). Thus, Browning's poem need not present a clear moral for it to be morally inspiring. Within acceptable parameters, Morley insists, 'whatever stimulates the fancy, expands the imagination, enlivens meditation upon the great human drama, is essentially moral' (337). In his eyes Browning is, in current phraseology, a 'public moralist', a description Stefan Collini applies to intellectuals in Victorian and early twentieth-century Britain who saw 'failings of character as the chief source of civic as well as private woe' (1991: 2).

Modelled on the *Revue des deux mondes*, which brought Matthew Arnold relief from the welter of factional mid-Victorian periodicals and spurred him to expound on the lack of its equivalent in Britain (MA 1962c: 270), *The Fortnightly Review* sought 'to further the cause of Progress by illumination from many minds' ([Lewes] 1865). But, much as the review preferred light to heat, those most closely associated with it, including Lewes and Morley as its first and second editors, recognised a kindred spirit in Browning more than in Arnold. For nearly three decades Browning had demonstrated a keen interest in human character by working with various dramatic forms, including the closet drama, the theatrical play and, most famously, the dramatic monologue (a term Browning never used). Yet it was his depiction of the choices and actions of ten monologists that made *The Ring and the Book* particularly attractive to dominant intellectual figures like Morley and the poet and novelist George Meredith. Browning's 'conceptions of character in active manifestation', as Morley referred to them (1869: 338),[1] resonated with Meredith's novel of radicalism *Vittoria*, serialised in *The Fortnightly* throughout 1866, and Morley's historical biographies, which appeared regularly in its pages.[2]

John Stuart Mill had taught Meredith, Morley and other second-generation Victorian liberals that individual character is revealed through decision-making. 'The human faculties of perception, judgment, discriminative feeling, mental activity, and even moral preference, are exercised only in making a choice', Mill writes in *On Liberty* (1977d: 262). Mill goes on to explain the consequences of allowing social convention to dictate one's decisions: 'He who does anything because it is the custom, makes no choice. He gains no practice either in discerning or in desiring what is best. The mental and moral, like the muscular powers, are improved only by being used' (262). Thus, in choosing, one reveals character; through continually exercising choice, one builds and maintains it. Morley understands Browning's 'conceptions of character in active manifestation' in precisely this way. By speaking of their actions and motivations, Browning's monologists reveal themselves. Although Morley does not say so, Browning implicitly endorses a liberal civil society in which poems, circulating freely among a populace, enable readers to reflect on and debate their contents. Indeed, in one of several asides, the narrator asks the reader, 'What say you to the right or wrong of that' (RB 1985b: 21).

In his review Morley saw *The Ring and the Book* largely through a Millian lens, but Browning's understanding of character and individuality, while remaining within the liberal-intellectual constellation, differed from either Mill's or Morley's. Browning's friend and biographer Alexandra Orr, remarking on the intermingling of his religious belief and political faith observed, 'His politics were, so far as they went, the practical aspect of his religion' (Orr and Kenyon 1908: 354).[3] The clearest articulation of this relationship is the sonnet he contributed to the anthology *Why I Am a Liberal: Being Definitions and Personal Confessions of Faith by the Best Minds of the Liberal Party*, edited and published by Andrew Reid (1885). To the singular question Reid posed, Browning responded:

> 'Why?' Because all I haply can and do,
>> All that I am now, all I hope to be, –
>> Whence comes it save from fortune setting free
> Body and soul the purpose to pursue,
> God traced for both? If fetters, not a few,
> Of prejudice, convention, fall from me,
>> These shall I bid men – each in his degree
>> Also God-guided – bear, and gaily too?
>
> But little do or can the best of us:
>> THAT LITTLE IS ACHIEVED THROUGH LIBERTY.
> Who, then, dares hold – emancipated thus –
>> His fellow shall continue bound? Not I,
> Who live, love, labour freely, nor discuss
>> A brother's right to freedom. That is 'Why.' (2011c)[4]

Drawing on several currents of thought (Romanticism, liberalism, Evangelical Protestantism) with which he was familiar, Browning's apparent intent here is to link character ('All that I am now, all I hope to be') and individuality ('prejudice, convention fall from me') to a divine plan ('the purpose . . . God traced' for body and soul). In John Woolford's gloss of these lines, 'since every man is "God-guided", and because God's purpose differs for every individual case, each man must remain free to realise that purpose in his own way' (1988: 9). Yet chance, which Browning calls 'fortune', greatly determines the outward circumstances that most often inhibit people from realising God's purpose for them: class, religion, national origin, gender, ideologies of individualism and the historical period of one's birth are all determining factors.[5]

Browning's interest in the determinative force of outward circumstances does not, of course, characterise his work as a whole. At the start of his career, Browning was interested in studying consciousness independent of circumstance. Absence of attention to circumstance contributed to John Stuart Mill's stinging critique of Browning's first published work, *Pauline: A Fragment of a Confession*, issued in 1833 when he was just twenty. Mill had determined, on re-educating himself following his mental crisis, that literature played a vital part in developing an individual's 'internal culture' (JSM 1981: 146). He praised Wordsworth's verse, which he found restorative, for its individual though impersonal expressiveness. Wordsworth articulated universal feelings, even if in private soliloquy. By contrast, *Pauline*, which Mill reviewed at the publisher's request, seemed morbidly introspective.[6] Because of the subtitle and his understanding of poetry as a vehicle for self-expression, he assumed that *Pauline*, in which the speaker sketches his trajectory in life, was straightforwardly autobiographical. Thereafter, to make the distinction between poet and speaker much clearer, Browning utilised historical personages for many of his poems, beginning with the German Renaissance alchemist and occultist Paracelsus and the thirteenth-century Italian troubadour Sordello, the subjects of lengthy dramatic monologues bearing their names published in 1835 and 1840.

Browning's fascination with exploring the private recesses of the mind was abiding. He figured the mind as 'the inner chamber of the soul' (RB 1999: 209), where truths and falsehoods struggle for legitimacy. Historical contextualisation came more slowly. It appears in his poetry initially as a means to an end. As he stated in a preface on republishing *Sordello*, 'The historical decoration was purposely of no more importance than a background requires; and my stress lay on the incidents in the development of a soul: little else is worth study' (1863: 2). With *Dramatic Lyrics* of 1842, part of his Bells and Pomegranates series, Browning began working out the 'contextual-ist' approach to human character that was a defining characteristic of his mature work (Gibson 1987: 24). Beginning with his 1855 col-lection, *Men and Women*, Browning depicted historical individuals fully entangled in the social, political and religious particularities of their age. By teasing out the 'intricate connections between the indi-vidual and a historical moment', Mary Ellis Gibson observes, Brown-ing gave his poetry 'its special quality of making the past immediate in the present' (1987: 23). It was this approach that Meredith, and especially Morley, for whom character was a relation of inner essence to outer environment ('innate conditions of temperament' combined with 'fixed limitations of opportunity' [Morley 1923b: 98]), found so attractive.

But Browning was not exclusively focused on a distant past as it illuminated a more progressive present. What interested him were periods of historical transition, including his own. This latter point he learned from Mill, who had declared in a series of essays pub-lished in 1831 that he and his contemporaries were living in an era of transition, following an era of stasis. In these essays Mill attempted to sort through competing ideas, a confusing array of theories and philosophies, to determine which belonged to 'the stationary part of mankind' and which to 'the progressive part' (JSM 1986b: 245). In Mill's view, 'The idea of comparing one's own age with former ages, or with our notion of those which are yet to come, had occurred to philosophers; but it never before was itself the dominant idea of any age' (1986a: 228). Although the implications for the present were mostly far from clear, Browning's contextualist approach implicitly forged such connections.[7]

Yet his interest in transitions from one historical epoch to another differed from Mill's. Browning was well aware of the higher criti-cism of German biblical scholars. Its consequences distressed many of his contemporaries, but, as a man of faith, he believed in the probability of providential history. Periods of historical transition, precisely because they were turning points, might provide a glimpse into God's purpose for humankind. In 'Reverie', one of his last poems, Browning notes the pervasiveness of evil in history. Still, from the perspective of God's purpose, such evil might be nothing more than 'cloud across / Good's orb, no orb itself' (RB 2011b: 79). Holding fast to this view, Browning had little faith in the notion that history unfolded sequentially or in a progressive arc.[8] In *Prince*

Hohenstiel-Schwangau, Saviour of Society, published in 1871, the monologist, a thinly veiled Napoleon III, purports to be a liberal head of state but reveals himself to be an autocrat.[9] As a republican, Browning loathed hereditary rule. As a liberal, he was averse to authoritarianism. Nevertheless, he looked favourably on Napoleon III's involvement in the Risorgimento.[10] After years of ambivalence, Browning finally concluded, as he wrote to a friend in 1869, 'that Napoleon was capable . . . of acting as grossly and abominably as Guido', the murderous count in *The Ring and the Book*, 'and that, on the large scale, he *did* act quite as falsely, as selfishly and cruelly' (1937: 175).

As president of the Second Republic (1848–52) and emperor during the Second Empire (1852–70), Louis-Napoléon sought to refashion Paris, as his uncle had, in the image of Rome. Many first- and second-generation Victorian liberals, including Mill, Arnold and Morley, followed in the trail of the British literate classes, who, early in the nineteenth century, embraced Greece instead of Rome. These liberals found in ancient Greece both secular ideals to replace or supplement those provided by Christianity and an idiom with which to express them. Browning, however, rejected what he deemed the sterility of Greek art, which represents perfection as a certainty rather than an objective, and found his intellectual forebears in Renaissance Italy. A large, diverse swath of British artists and intellectuals, from the liberal Arnold to the much more conservative John Ruskin, saw the Italian Renaissance as an age of moral and cultural decay (DeLaura 1969b: 385). But Browning viewed it as a moment of individual and political aspiration, 'when the new ideas were poised on the cusp of the dying middle age' (Sharrock 1975: 88), with parallels to his own time.

Focusing on this period of transition from medievalism enabled Browning to analyse the tension between individualism, the spark of which had been ignited in the Italian Renaissance, and the social and political conditions that constrained freedom. In 'Fra Lippo Lippi', which he published in *Men and Women*, Browning asks readers to side with individual eccentricity against religious dogmatism. The eponymous fifteenth-century painter is detained by a policeman in Florence's red-light district. His putative immorality, however, is shown as essential to his positive valuation of body and soul as God's creations. This places the speaker at odds with the church, whose representatives brand fleshly art as part of the 'devil's-game' and insist painters depict 'no more of body than shows soul' (RB 1981b: 188, 189). Browning's argument here is both liberal – anticipating Mill's case, just a few years later, for eccentricity as a means of opposing the tyranny of conformity – and religious, in so far as Lippo's naturalistic paintings and the controversy over them capture the transition from medieval to Renaissance perspectives.[11]

As scholars have long noted, Browning derived his understanding of Italian art history from immersing himself in the works of Renaissance historians Giorgio Vasari and Filippo Baldinucci, the Frenchman Alexis-François Rio and the Brownings' friend Anna Jameson,[12] as well as from frequent visits to the Uffizi and Pitti Palace galleries.[13] Yet Dante Gabriel Rossetti was perhaps the first to note an important connection between Browning's collecting and his writing. In an 1856 letter, commenting on one of the poems in *Men and Women*, Rossetti observed: 'What a jolly thing is *Old Pictures at Florence* [*sic*]! It seems all the pictures *desired* by the poet are in his possession *in fact*' (1897: 160). Many Browning poems were informed as much by his expanding art collection, including works he attributed to Domenico Ghirlandaio, Taddeo Gaddi and others, as by his more generalised and more often discussed knowledge of art history. Browning wrote 'Fra Lippo Lippi' shortly after acquiring a painting allegedly by Filippo Lippi, which adorned the walls of Casa Guidi, Robert and Elizabeth Barrett Browning's long-time residence in Florence.[14]

In this chapter I want to return to the phrase 'historical decoration', which Browning used in his 1863 preface to *Sordello*, and consider its implications, as a principle of interior design, for understanding his poems. While Browning was working out the precise level of historical detail to include in his early poems, he was simultaneously developing a belief in the tenuously animate and agential nature of artefacts. This belief would inform his decorative practices during his marriage and continue throughout his life. 'I have no little insight to the feelings of furniture, and treat books and prints with a reasonable consideration', he confessed to Elizabeth Barrett less than two months into their correspondence, in February 1845 (*BC* 1992: 99), the same year he published *Dramatic Romances and Lyrics*. For Browning, furniture, books and prints were not just objects; they were entities with which one entered into a relationship. Although the medium of that relation was predominately sight, Browning did not engage in detached visual contemplation. His 'characteristic', Elizabeth remarked some years later to her sister Arabella (whom she called 'Arabel'), in discussing his poetic composition, is that he '*sees things passionately*' (*BC* 2007: 112). Elizabeth was not writing about Browning's encounter with objects per se. G. K. Chesterton was, however, when he claimed:

> Any room that he was sitting in glared at him with innumerable eyes and mouths gaping with a story . . . If he looked at a porcelain vase or an old hat . . . each began to be bewitched with the spell of a kind of fairyland of philosophers: the vase, like the jar in the *Arabian Nights*, to send up a smoke of thoughts and shapes; the hat to produce souls, as a conjuror's hat produces rabbits . . . (1903: 166)

Elizabeth's observation and Chesterton's remark capture how Browning's sensory experience of the world – principally visual but, as we will see, often linked to smell, taste and touch – and his attentiveness to the emotional sensations engendered within him produced (historical) ideas that, in turn, manifested themselves in poems.

In Florence, Browning became, as he remained, an avid collector of historical materiality.[15] Owing to his political leanings, he was particularly interested in the furnishings, art and religious iconography of the early modern Florentine republic, when the nobility's powers were curtailed and the individual was accorded increased respect, although not yet political freedom. Bestowing intensive perceptual attention on each object he acquired, he was fascinated by the barely perceptible cultural content that only close study of its physical properties might recover. The material object tells a story through colour, texture, odour, size and weight, relaying a set of 'facts' about itself and the world in which it was created. These objects – the historical decoration, as it were, of his living spaces – often stimulated him to write. By 'making the past immediate in the present' (Gibson 1987: 23), they essentially did for Browning what critics frequently suppose his poems do for the reader. J. Hillis Miller, although not acknowledging the impetus of materiality, observes that 'there is something casual or accidental about Browning's poems' because 'he needed to be impelled into speaking by something outside himself' (2000: 129, 128). Reviewing *The Ring and the Book*, Morley singles out for disapprobation 'the many verbal perversities', 'a coarse violence of expression that is nothing short of barbarous', and 'harsh and formless lines, bursts of metrical chaos, from which a writer's dignity and self-respect ought surely to be enough to preserve him' (1869: 334). The materiality that provoked Browning's thought is registered as traces in such moments. As Browning told the French critic Joseph Milsand, a long-time friend, in 1853, while working on *Men and Women*, he wanted his readers to be confronted with more than just speeches and was thus including 'more music & painting than before, so as to get people to hear and see' (*BC* 2010b: 339). His susceptibility to external provocation made Browning unable to share James Cotter Morison's view, which was also Mill's, Arnold's and Morley's practice, that to effect a fair representation of history the writer must ensure 'the whole temper of his mind and feelings is in a state of balanced equipoise' (Morison 1878: 238).

Forms of Engagement

Robert Browning's upbringing, the details of which have been ably documented by biographers, is central to considering his decorative practice and, therefore, the relationship between the historical reality of Casa Guidi's décor and his literary production while living there. His experiences with nature, music, art and reading during childhood and youth actively enhanced his imagination.[16] His creative impulses were generated by 'seeing things passionately', to use Elizabeth's description. For the impulse to be generated, he needed things to see. Of the four influences, music is the least visual. But, as I will shortly elaborate, Browning learned how to see music through its 'grammar': 'I was studying the grammar of music', he reportedly told his acolyte Annie Ireland, 'when most children are learning the multiplication table' (qtd in Griffin and Minchin 1966: 16). According to his personal attendant William Grove, he also attended concerts, where music as embodied performance was both aural and visual, and was an ardent, lifelong concertgoer (2000: 71). By instilling in him an intensely sensory and imaginative alertness, Browning's early milieu provided the foundation for an expansive understanding of objects as more than domestic embellishments.

The limited information available about the Browning family's residences suggests that they were simply but elegantly decorated, exemplifying a moderate austerity befitting independent Dissenting Christians inclined towards Evangelicalism.[17] From 1813 to 1840 the Brownings lived at three addresses on Southampton Street in Camberwell, then a rural suburb south of London, before settling at New Cross, several miles east.[18] Browning's sister, Sarianna, recalled nothing significant about Hanover Cottage, where the family resided longest, other than its being a semi-detached house (Maynard 1977: 33). Cousin Cyrus Mason described Telegraph Cottage, the New Cross home to which the family moved in 1840, as 'genteely dreary' and 'cheerless': 'genteely dull, yet a well appointed comfortable residence, standing secluded in a carefully tended garden' (1983: 80, 114, 96).[19] Mason is generally recognised not to have been an objective observer; thus, his comments may have been coloured by negative feelings about his relatives.

In any case few functional or decorative objects seem either to have stood out or to have merited passing down the generations. This has led at least one biographer to conclude that the Brownings were poor (B. Miller 1953: 20). But as a clerk at the Bank of England, Browning's father was able to provide his children a comfortable upbringing. John Maynard concludes, based on available evidence, that far from being of straitened means, the Brownings were relatively comfortable and, through the father's steady employment, increasingly prosperous (1977: 34). The family homes were likely furnished in a manner that sought, as Iain Finlayson remarks more generally of Browning's parents, to balance 'the mother's religious principles and the father's cultural enlightenment' (2004: 46).[20]

One object that belonged to the poet's father, prominently displayed at the four family residences, signals that, even with their refined appointments, the Browning homes emphasised the religious principle of self-denial: a Bates of Huddersfield bracket clock (*c*.1814), made of rosewood on a brass-mounted base (Figure 4.1). Functional rather than ornately decorative, an object of neither splendour nor elegance, the clock would have held deep symbolic significance for the members of the household. Its modest appearance calls attention to time itself – and, by extension, the limited quantity of time, the uncertainty of days and the importance of the present moment. As a writer in *The Evangelical Magazine*, the leading Nonconformist and best-selling religious periodical of the early nineteenth century, put it: 'all our temporal blessings are delivered out to us "in number, weight, and measure;" and none more sparingly than our *time*; for we never have two moments, much less days, together' ([T. Williams?] 1821: 9). The clock's large white enamel face, which overwhelms the three short, inconspicuous finials, resonates well with the biblical phrase 'teach us to number our days' (Ps. 90:12), exhorting family members to spend every minute preparing their souls for heaven. Accordingly, the Browning family probably rose early, forming the habit in Robert; he dates one of his early letters, written before breakfast in July 1837, 'Saturday Morning. 6 ½' (BC 1985: 255).[21]

The Browning household was certainly serious in tone.[22] Robert's mother provided early biblical training; the family undoubtedly gathered daily for prayers; and their surroundings reflected a touch of austerity, in keeping with the demands of their religion. But, as

Figure 4.1 Bates of Huddersfield bracket clock (*c.*1814)
Source: Armstrong Browning Library of Baylor University, Waco, Texas.

in many Evangelical families, despite famous characterisations of them,[23] the Brownings enabled creation and sanctification, key features of the doctrine of incarnation, to flourish, sometimes contradictorily, alongside the theology of atonement. Another item in the New Cross house indicates that Evangelical self-restraint provides only partial understanding of the family's relationship to domestic objects. According to a story related to one of Browning's biographers, a visitor to the family was struck by Robert's peculiar attachment to one decorative piece:

> The conversation fell on 'Pilgrims Progress', & young Mr. Browning fetched from the library a carved head which he called 'Christian' & stroked affectionately, saying he was 'very fond of old Christian'. (Lemann 1904: 93)[24]

Even though he was certainly aware that the carving was inanimate matter, Browning acted as if the head were the being himself ('old Christian'), rather than just a sign or symbol.

One might simply dismiss this episode as fanciful. To the visitor's mind, though, the incident could not be ascribed to the whimsy of a young published poet. Rather, it provided insight into the family's religious beliefs: 'not orthodox', she demurred (Lemann 1904: 92). In many devout households, imagination was seen as pernicious or at least a waste of time, that most precious and fleeting resource. Thus, Browning's parents – whose son had developed a relationship with a carved head and acted as if Christian's subjective spirit resided within it – seemed 'very liberal', as the visitor characterised their permissiveness towards Robert's imagination (92).

While some level of austerity existed in the household, the Brownings were committed to developing Robert's imaginative thought through nature, music, art and reading even if this conflicted at times with vigilance against worldliness or transcendence of materiality. As a youngster, Browning spent much time in his mother's garden. Untroubled by the anxieties that weighed so heavily on Lucilla of Hannah More's *Coelebs in Search of a Wife*, who guarded against gratuitously indulging in this otherwise most innocent of pleasures by hanging a watch from a tree, Sarah Browning was an ardent gardener. While she tended her roses, her son developed a sense of intimacy and camaraderie with the natural world. 'I have, you are to know, such a love for flowers and leaves', young Browning proclaims to his friend and confidante Fanny Haworth in 1838. When sight or smell could not satiate him, he would 'bite them to bits': 'there will be some sense in that', he quips. 'One flower or weed', he tells Fanny, activates a chain of associations: 'Snowdrops & Tilsit in Prussia go together; Cowslips & Windsor-park, for instance: flowering palm and some place or other in Holland' (*BC* 1986: 66–7).[25] Even thinking of a natural object provoked a memory. Thus, a snowdrop brought to mind the eastern Prussian town he visited on his first trip abroad, when he travelled as far as Saint Petersburg in 1834, and the flowering palm evoked a long stretch of beach in Scheveningen that Browning traversed in Holland in 1836.[26]

At home Browning found himself increasingly absorbed by music. Stuart Isacoff describes Evangelicals as often on guard against the piano's 'inviting tones', which served as 'a perfect conductor for the erotic current that flowed through the arts as the age of Romance took hold' (2011: 51). Music could stimulate the senses, weakening strength of will. Playing music was 'a fashionable accomplishment', which many Evangelicals associated with vanity (Rosman 2011: 98). Precisely for these reasons, Browning's contemporary Marian Evans, the future George Eliot, who grew up in a Low Church household heavily influenced by Midland Dissent, was averse during 'a brief ascetic phase' to music in any form other than hymns (Sousa Correa 2003: 3–4). Sarah Browning had no qualms about music, however; a skilful pianist and 'natural musician', although with 'little training' (Whiting 1911: 6), she played regularly for the family.[27] She probably believed that music, with its capacity to move one's feelings, augmented other forms of worship.[28]

Although pianos were occasionally found in pious homes in the first half of the nineteenth century, they were mostly a luxury enjoyed by aristocratic and upper-middle-class families (Bashford 2009: 32). Musical accomplishment among the well-to-do was gendered. Women generally learned to sing and play the piano. If men were taught instruments at all, they usually played the flute, cello or violin (32).[29] Robert's musical training was atypical, however: he learned to read sheet music and played the piano and other instruments. As he confided to a friend in 1837, in earlier years he had expressed 'real and strong feeling' primarily through music, even while holding 'the notion that "a poet" was the grandest of God's creatures' (*BC* 1985: 264). So consumed by music was he that at one point he apparently contemplated a musical career (Thompson 1889).[30] He remained an avid concertgoer, as I have noted, and also enjoyed the opera (as well as the theatre).[31] Browning became a mature adult in the 1830s and 1840s, when audiences were being taught to listen quietly and attentively to music. Concerts in particular 'promoted the idea that silence and reverential listening were behavioural imperatives for music' (Bashford 2009: 46). Such a practice resonated with the way Browning viewed art. He increasingly immersed himself in the aural and visual presence (in embodied performances) of musical sound, despite his predilection for socialising.

Music demanded intensity of hearing and seeing. Art provoked deeply attentive quietude. The only major public art gallery in London and its surrounds before the mid-nineteenth century was approximately three miles from Browning's childhood homes in Camberwell. The Dulwich Picture Gallery, which opened in 1817, exhibited several hundred Italian, English, Dutch, French and Spanish paintings. Contemporaneously published museum guides denote the extent of its impressive holdings. Browning's father, partial to its many Dutch realist works, took his young son with him to the gallery. Browning mentions some that most appealed to him. Many had biblical themes: a Madonna and Child by the Spanish Baroque painter Bartolomé Esteban Murillo; Guido Reni's *Saint John the Baptist in the Wilderness*; Andrea del Sarto's *Virgin and Child with Saint John*; Arent de Gelder's

Jacob's Dream (which Browning and his contemporaries attributed to Rembrandt); and *The Woman Taken in Adultery* and *Saint Cecilia* by Giovanni Francesco Barbieri (known as Guercino).[32] Others depicted scenes from classical mythology. All, it seems, were from time periods and cultures different from Browning's.[33]

Because his father modelled an anecdotal approach to history, Browning likely gravitated towards paintings that might be seen as condensations of history *in nuce*. Religious art, while its representation content was not historical, also provided a glimpse into how people once lived and worshipped. Historical study was an intellectual pleasure many Evangelicals encouraged. Although the doctrine of atonement looked forward, emphasising a timeless beyond, some thought historical inquiry was the best means of elucidating and verifying biblical teachings. Others recognised the moral utility of studying history. The past when properly studied, could provide important lessons to guide and correct present and future conduct. Evangelicals, however, eschewed imaginative approaches to the past: the Bible was 'a book full of statements' rather than 'a book full of stories' (Rosman 2011: 126). Robert's father took the opposite approach. The elder Robert took especial pleasure in introducing children to the Bible, less as a repository of divine revelation than as a book of wonderful characters and stories, and inciting curiosity about other historical periods and cultures through games and anecdotes.[34] Through him, Browning developed a keen interest in history. John Maynard remarks, 'It would be wrong to suppose that the awareness of the past that he gave his son was either very accurate or insightful. But he did open up a world . . .' (1977: 89). For Maynard, Robert Senior's 'dilettante antiquarianism' was more akin to amassing information than cultivating knowledge (347, 91). Yet he reportedly knew Horace's *Odes* by heart (Griffin and Minchin 1966: 6), which suggests deep literary appreciation rather than mere antiquarianism. Nevertheless, even if Maynard's characterisation is right, the library itself incited learning. In his quest for knowledge, young Browning perused the copiously filled bookshelves, which eventually included thousands of volumes ranging from theological and philological texts to historical tracts to a wide array of classical, English and foreign-language literary works.[35] Furthermore, Browning's uncle Reuben Browning, just nine years older and reputed to be 'an excellent classical scholar', took an interest in his nephew's studies (Griffin and Minchin 1966: 6).

Paintings, like the elder Robert's historical anecdotes, were evocative. As products of the imagination, works of fine art were viewed with ambivalence by Evangelicals. Some, especially those inclined towards utility in valuating paintings, were distrustful. Many worried about art lacking biblical sanction. Others, Doreen Rosman points out, 'rejected them [the fine arts] as they rejected everything that served no immediate religious function' (2011: 109). For young Robert, however, a painting opened not only the representational world depicted on the canvas but also the historical world of its creation. Because a historical painting persisted into the present, the perceptive modern viewer could imaginatively deconstruct that creational world. As his independent interest in art developed, he often visited 'that Gallery I so love and am so grateful to – having been used to go there when a child, far under the age allowed by the regulations' (*BC* 1994: 124).[36] There, Browning explained to Elizabeth in March 1846, he would sit 'before one, some *one* of those pictures I had predetermined to see, – a good hour and then gone away' (124). Instead of indulging in the passing glance or brief contemplation that accompanies unplanned meanderings through a gallery, Robert developed in his youth a rigorous practice of focusing attention on a single painting.

No direct evidence from this period, such as Robert Browning's diaries or letters, of which only a handful dated before 1835 have survived, enables us to know what he thought and felt while contemplating a painting. We can infer much, though, from his recollections to Elizabeth and, as I will discuss later in this chapter, his poems. Browning's description of his intense affection for the Dulwich Picture Gallery ('that Gallery I so love') indicates he did not look at art with a critical eye – that is, aiming to render a considered evaluation. Even if his sole motivation were to study a painting's texture, colour and, given the kinds of works to which he confessed partiality, narrative, one cannot spend an hour or more gazing at a single work without thinking of oneself in some kind of relationship with it. Paintings and other objects of historical materiality enticed Browning to understand not just their representational content but also the period and culture in which they were created.

I have lingered over these biographical details because Browning's experiences in childhood and youth helped shape a peculiar way of perceiving natural objects and artefacts that ran counter to a strain of Evangelicalism that deemed the written word more reliable and authoritative than other means of discerning divine truth. Browning's approach also opposed the suspicion of non-visual modes of perception by emergent liberal thought, rooted in eighteenth-century reason's distrust of sensory experiences other than sight as unreliable means of apprehending objective reality. For Mill, Arnold and Morley, sight was the privileged means of maintaining distance from and objectification of an object of study, thereby enabling rigorous cerebration. By attending to the look of objects, and to what he could hear, feel and even taste, Browning attempted to discern how people interpreted the world around them and how either their creations or the things they prized infused that world with meaning. By studying objects, he attempted to understand the forms of engagement (subliminal, vicarious, intuitive) these items invited or demanded in the past and also in the present.

'Graceful Disorder'

Browning's early experiences had implications for the marital home he and Elizabeth would create. They arrived in Italy in October 1846, soon after their elopement. After a six-month stay in Pisa, they made their way to Florence, where for ninety days they rented furnished rooms on the *piano nobile* of the Palazzo Guidi. Built by Lorenzo Ridolfi and bought by Count Camillo Guidi in 1618, the original structure was a triangle-shaped corner house dating to the fifteenth century. In the late eighteenth century it was combined with an adjoining property and, by the Brownings' time, subdivided into two rental apartments. The lease included access to the Boboli Gardens behind the Palazzo Pitti, the residence of Grand Duke Leopold II. Being close to the gardens was particularly advantageous for Elizabeth, always in frail health, who often sought repose in its shade.

After a stint away from Florence, they returned the following year and, finding no better accommodation than the Palazzo Guidi apartment, signed a twelve-month lease. It provided them with seven rooms – 'three of which are magnificent', Elizabeth told Arabel in May 1848, '& the others excellent' (*BC* 2005: 70). No other property offered such a 'noble suite of rooms' or a comparable amount of space: 'I do wish you could see what rooms we have – what ceilings, what height & breadth', she exclaimed (87, 82). The Brownings continuously renewed the lease for Casa Guidi, as Elizabeth soon began calling it, until her death in 1861.

The couple returned to the Palazzo Guidi with a simple plan. 'After a good deal of thinking then', Elizabeth wrote to Arabel, 'we resolved on taking advantage of the cheapest moment in the cheapest place, to adopt the infinitely cheapest means of life . . . by taking instead of a furnished apartment, an unfurnished one & furnishing it ourselves' (*BC* 2005: 70). Rather than paying a guinea a week for furnished rooms, they secured for twenty-five guineas an annual lease for the same rooms unfurnished. With this 'new scheme', as Elizabeth described it to her sister-in-law, Sarianna, they anticipated subletting the furnished rooms during their frequent absences from Florence, consequently enabling them, despite limited funds, to spend summers in England (81–2). 'When you come to know the cheapness of furniture (especially in this moment) & the comparative dearness of a furnished apartment', she explained to Arabel, 'you will see the case clearly' (70). In what may seem a striking contradiction to their gratitude for the ample space the unfurnished apartment provided – 'to breathe is delightful in this enlarged atmosphere of ours' (71) – Robert set about accumulating vast quantities of decorative objects and heavy, hand-carved furniture.

Unwilling to be dwarfed by their surroundings, the effect produced by the starkly elegant interiors of eighteenth-century aristocratic homes, the Brownings faced the necessity of expending considerable funds to furnish the palazzo. 'If you could see us in these great rooms (they are so immensely high that they look still larger)', Elizabeth wrote to Arabel before they had obtained much furniture, 'you would think it all rather desolate still' (73). That sense of desolation, the feeling that rooms are somehow uninhabited even though their occupants are fully present, reflected a desire for 'density' in their domestic surroundings, as the design historian Peter Thornton, without reference to the Brownings, calls it (1984).[37] This desire became more widely shared by Victorians in the second half of the century. John Gloag remarks:

> The excessive ornamentation of nearly every article used in the Victorian home made even the spacious rooms of large houses seem overcrowded, and in small rooms the effect was overwhelming: yet this excess of ornament, this restless conflict of motifs, helped to create an atmosphere of solid, unshakable comfort. (1962: 137)[38]

Elizabeth even had a term for the density of furnishings to which she aspired; 'graceful disorder' (*BC* 1998: 322). This decorative principle, she believed, would transform 'a mere palace into a home' (M. Ward 1967: 219).

'Graceful disorder' was achieved through a twofold process of acquisition and distribution. Robert accumulated goods such as 'spring-sofas & chairs & mirrors & carved wood & satin curtains', they explained in a joint letter to Anna Jameson (*BC* 2005: 112). Then he and Elizabeth scattered them about. 'It was found the other day that we had eight sofas', Elizabeth recounted to her sister

Henrietta: 'It's a comfort to have sofas everywhere – three spring ones in the drawingroom, a little spring one in the bookroom – a large spring one in my bedroom [. . .] & others of an ordinary fashion sprinkled here & there' (92). She derived particular comfort, she effused to Arabel, from the accretion of enough sofas and armchairs to lounge upon almost anywhere in the house:

> But of all our purchases, I am not at all sure that I dont [*sic*] enjoy the armchairs most, [. . .] particularly one which Robert calls mine, because it's the most luxurious of possible chairs, very low, very languid looking . . . You sink into it as into a nest of air . . . (103)

The salon at Casa Guidi, made famous by a commemorative portrait painted by George Mignaty shortly after Elizabeth's death in June 1861, provides much insight into the Brownings' decorative practice (Figure 4.2). Along the walls, left and right, are large hand-carved mahogany bookcases. An open-fronted one is adjacent to a hand-carved tall-back settee on the left. Another bookcase, which Elizabeth

Figure 4.2 *Salon at Casa Guidi* by George Mignaty. Source: Special Collections Department, F. W. Olin Library, Mills College. Photograph by permission of Larry E. Fink.

lauded as 'beautiful' in an 1850 letter to Arabella (*BC* 2007: 110), was originally owned by a convent and contains a brass-diamond-panelled screen. From the gilded ceiling hangs a Venetian glass chandelier – an early purchase that, as Elizabeth told Arabel, the couple bought for £2 (*BC* 2005: 75). The centre of the drawing room contains various pieces of furniture, captured by Mignaty in their summer placement, including no fewer than six tables. In addition to a mahogany table for Elizabeth, Browning had acquired two companion tables with inlaid ebony and ivory tops and spirally fluted legs; a so-called lady's work-table, made of maple with a striking landscape oil painting decorating the top; and two North Italian tables of walnut, one with ebonised spirally fluted legs and the other with bowed legs. The settee and most of the wooden chairs with white and gold frames spread throughout the room are richly upholstered in crimson velvet, used as an accent. Catholic religious iconography and an impressive Italian mirror adorn the back wall. The couple's political commitments were evinced through their use of colour: green for the walls, crimson for many of the furnishings and drapery, white muslin for the curtains – the tricolour theme of the Risorgimento flag.

The young American journalist Kate Field, who met the Brownings soon after she arrived in Florence in 1859 and became a frequent visitor to Casa Guidi,[39] described the drawing room in a tribute written just after Elizabeth's sudden death:

> The dark shadows and subdued light gave it a dreamy look, which was enhanced by the tapestry-covered walls and the old pictures of saints that looked out sadly from their carved frames of black wood. Large book-cases, constructed of specimens of Florentine carving selected by Mr. Browning, were brimming over with wise-looking books . . . Dante's grave profile, a cast of Keats's face and brow taken after death, a pen-and-ink sketch of Tennyson, the genial face of John Kenyon, Mrs. Browning's good friend and relative, little paintings of the boy Browning, all attracted the eye in turn, and gave rise to a thousand musings. A quaint mirror, easy-chairs and sofas, and a hundred nothings that always add an indescribable charm, were all massed in this room. (Field 1861: 370)

Certainly, by the closing decades of the nineteenth century, filling one's house with things was the norm. But the amassing of furniture and objects we associate with Victorian interiors began only in the 1860s, after Robert had relocated to London. Yet, because Casa Guidi exhibits a predilection for density of furnishings, it has not been easy for critics to distinguish the Brownings' decorative practices there in the

1840s and 1850s from those of the English middle classes, a decade or more later, that the couple seemingly anticipated.

Indeed, some literary critics have likened the modern reader's feeling of being overwhelmed by detail when encountering a Robert Browning poem to the experience of entering the cluttered interiors of Victorian middle-class homes. Daniel Karlin asserts: 'Browning's poetry is as crowded with *things* as a Victorian drawing-room, the furniture is heavy, the gardens profuse and ornate' (2009: xi). Peter Conrad's discussion of Browning's poetry in *The Victorian Treasure-House* is framed by his observation that the period's literature and art 'often seem, like its interiors, containers to be stuffed as full as possible' (1973: 9).[40] The comparison of Browning's poems to an overstuffed drawing room, however, too easily equates with English embourgeoisement. To account for Casa Guidi's interior as 'very English' and baldly 'bourgeois' (Cordery 2009: 86), as some critics do, flattens significant differences between the Brownings' decorative practices and those to which they are frequently compared.[41]

In fact, Browning eschewed many elements of middle-class domesticity, which he explored in poems at several stages of his career. He was often suspicious of those, like the Duke of 'My Last Duchess', who express themselves through the language of ownership. 'Pictor Ignotus', part of his 1845 collection *Dramatic Romances and Lyrics*, reflects on art's ensnarement in the sixteenth-century Italian marketplace at a time when modern consumer culture was forming (RB 1973b). As paintings are bought and sold, they circulate from owner to owner as mere 'garniture and household-stuff', subjected to the 'prate' and 'daily pettiness' of onlookers: 'This I love, or this I hate, / This likes me more, and this affects me less!' (165, 166). Published nearly two decades later, 'A Likeness' restates Browning's concerns with the commodification of art, using three vignettes set in contemporary London. The 1864 poem follows an etched portrait as it migrates from owner to owner. At first the portrait holds a prominent spot in a middle-class family's dining room, where it is displayed as a consumer good: 'a daub John bought at a sale' (RB 1996b: 282). Then, at a bachelor's residence, it becomes 'queen of the place', part of a collection of miscellanea: 'Alone mid the other spoils / Of youth' such as 'masks, gloves and foils', 'pipe-sticks' and a 'little edition of Rabelais' (282). Finally, in the home of a leisured professional, it is regarded as a connoisseur commodity. The speaker of the poem's third section, whose art collection demonstrates his cultivated taste and rarefied knowledge, boasts:

I keep my prints, an imbroglio,
Fifty in one portfolio.
When somebody tries my claret,
We turn round chairs to the fire,
Chirp over days in a garret,
    Chuckle o'er increase of salary,
Taste the good fruits of our leisure,
Talk about pencil and lyre,
    And the National Portrait Gallery:
Then I exhibit my treasure. (283)

Critics often note a strong resemblance between the speaker and Browning himself: 'as if [Browning were] sharing his experience of high society' with his readers (D. Thomas 1983: 215).[42] But the poem's implicit criticism of the speaker, who confines his mezzotint to a portfolio, complicates any straightforward association.

Browning abhorred his father's practice of keeping prints and drawings in jumbled portfolios. Writing to Elizabeth, Browning specifically ascribes an emotional life to things in order to criticise the practices of many collectors, including his father. 'How some people use their pictures . . . is a mystery to me', he claims, 'very revolting all the same: portraits obliged to face each other forever, – prints put together in portfolios . . .' (*BC* 1992: 99). Thus, as Barbara Black perceptively observes, 'The intrigue of "A Likeness" lies in the old question, "if the mute object could talk, what tales would it tell?"'. The 'pathos of the poem' also stems from the portrait's silence: 'how it becomes everything and anything its owners desire, how its owners speak for it' (B. Black 2000: 141).

What if the question, however, is not what an object would say but whether one has the capacity to hear it? Of course, new objects have little to say. One essential difference between Casa Guidi and later English middle-class domestic spaces is that the vast majority of the Brownings' decorative objects and furnishings were not new. Just after signing their lease, the couple purchased from the Palazzo Guidi their first article of furniture, a walnut chest of drawers inlaid with ivory (McAleer 1979: 20, 92). Soon they bought several items – 'the best of our furniture', according to Elizabeth – from the Baron de Poillet, the French chargé d'affaires (*BC* 2005: 107). Among them was an especially striking twelve-drawer Italian escritoire with an ornate, hand-carved floral design, a folding top and a pull-down front.[43] Robert found additional items at second-hand markets. The abundance of chests he acquired, with their many drawers, provided great fodder for Elizabeth: 'Only, you would laugh to hear us correct one another sometimes– "Dear, you get too many drawers, & not enough washing stands. Pray dont [*sic*] let us have any more drawers, when we've nothing more to put into them"', she writes to one correspondent. 'I reproached Robert, you know, with a drawer-plague', she facetiously tells another, 'he was so fond of raining down drawers upon us . . .' (85, 92).

Before the 1870s furnishing one's home with second-hand goods would have seemed extremely undesirable to many in the English middle class.[44] Although, as early as 1854, John Ruskin had inveighed against the 'terrible lustre' and 'fatal newness' of modern furniture (1904: 334), consumers responsive to his message generally sought new wares with an 'antique look' instead of used furnishings (Edwards and Ponsonby 2008: 133).[45] One way to obtain this look was to choose hand-carved items. In the 1870s advisors on household decoration repeatedly emphasised the inferiority of modern furniture decorated entirely by machinery. 'Sculpture – that is, wood-carving decoration in actual tangible relief – has in all times been considered the best kind of decoration', the decorative designer, art critic and academic John Hungerford Pollen opined in a Royal Society of Arts lecture (1885: 988). Against furniture manufactured by machines, then, 'wood sculpture', a term emphasising provenance in art rather than manufacturing, served as a necessary antidote (988). In 'the play of light' on hand-carved furniture and on ornamentation with 'actual tangible relief', Pollen asserted, one found 'completeness . . . habit-ableness, even a sort of companionship' (988).

In this anthropomorphic formulation, furniture made by hand is transformed into a friend, its unique – because mathematically inexact – sculptural relief into a personality. Soon after moving into Casa Guidi, Robert bought a large, eighteenth-century sideboard, decorated 'with groupes of figures at the sides, and old men's heads for handles & locks of gilt bronze', which had come from a convent in Urbino. 'Beautiful it will be, when polished & done up', Elizabeth exclaimed to Arabel soon after its arrival. 'And with it came a seat of carved wood, all in grinning heads & arabesque, for the drawing room' (*BC* 2005: 103–4). Other items were also elaborately carved (Figure 4.3).

The motivation for the Brownings was comfort, as it was for those to whom decorative advisors spoke later in the century. The aim: to transform 'a mere palace into a home'. Within a few months of leasing their residence, Elizabeth could report to Arabella, 'our apartment [is] . . . putting on a most delightful look of comfort' (*BC* 2005: 189). But, unlike those to whom Pollen spoke, Robert derived his pleasure

Figure 4.3 Detail of hand-carved folding chair.
Source: Armstrong Browning Library of Baylor University, Waco, Texas.

from furniture because it was previously owned, not simply because it was hand-carved. To discern this difference, we need to turn to Browning's poems and not just to Elizabeth's letters. Her letters, which document this period so thoroughly, suggest four interrelated explanations for the great pleasure second-hand furnishings brought them (economy, filling, taste and aristocratic aspirations), but none tells the whole story.

One outcome of Italy's growing political instability and economic fragmentation in the 1840s was that household furnishings, including decorative objects, works of art and parlour and bedroom furniture, became surprisingly affordable to holders of foreign currency. Used goods, inexpensive to acquire, were an attractive option. 'Of course you are to understand that our furniture is not *new* – but it is in good taste & characteristic notwithstanding', Elizabeth reassured Arabel; and she remarked to her friend, the writer Mary Russell Mitford, that 'the cheapness of the furniture . . . [is] something quite fabulous, especially at the present crisis' (*BC* 2005: 77, 84). Because most tourists had fled the country following the Palermo uprising in January 1848 and the spread of revolution to other parts of Italy, the Brownings' only competition for the best finds in second-hand markets, as Elizabeth noted to Jameson in May 1850, was from antique dealers (*BC* 2007: 118). Thus, Elizabeth's often-repeated phrase, that sofas could be purchased '"for a song," chairs "for love," and tables for nothing at all' (*BC* 2005: 70), has been cited by biographers as the principal reason for the condensed massing of furniture and objects in Mignaty's painting.[46]

Yet the cost of furnishing Casa Guidi was far greater than the Brownings had anticipated. Even if a handcrafted item was inexpensive, usually it had to be restored to its former glory. Wood needed to be re-polished.[47] Skeleton sofas, and possibly also chairs, required new padding and springs before being reupholstered in 'crimson satin', Elizabeth told Arabella in July 1848 (*BC* 2005: 104). The residence's large and plentiful windows needed treatments: they were draped with crimson curtains crossed with white muslin, which helped mitigate winter drafts and provided summer shading. 'We are somewhat crushed just now with the weight of curtain & chair expences', Elizabeth noted to Arabel some months later (189). Several purchases and at least one trip to England had to be postponed until they were on more solid financial footing.

Consistent with the Evangelical world view of his childhood, Robert was averse to accumulating debt. Living beyond one's means, acquiring material comforts exceeding what one could afford, was castigated by many Evangelicals, Anglican and Dissenter alike, as a form of dishonesty. Robert resolved that their expenses had to be covered by the proceeds of their literary endeavours: as Elizabeth explained to Arabel, 'everything is to be paid for from our regular income, & without getting into debt' (*BC* 2005: 73). Through a seemingly unorthodox approach to economising, which Elizabeth characterised as 'a kind of witchcraft', Robert thought they would save money by spending money, Elizabeth explained in her part of a joint letter to Jameson. How, 'as a consequence of spending so much', they would 'accomplish it all without being ruined in the least & on the contrary . . . have saved money, [which] Robert says [will happen], by the end of the year', she was not entirely sure (112). At 'the end of the year' there was reason to doubt the notion Robert had championed in July. Although the Brownings sought to reduce their expenses, Elizabeth frequently expressed feeling overwhelmed by the costs. 'The curtains have exceeded the estimate in an especial manner', she lamented (189).

Besides the cost of renovations and window treatments, furnishing Casa Guidi had become much more expensive because economy was never the sole consideration. 'We wanted linen & plate, & then our rooms being immense, yearned for more & more filling', she explained to Arabel (*BC* 2005: 70). 'Filling', a term synonymous with bourgeois decorative practice, creates a semiotic economy of goods with no obvious functional or use value. 'This filling in is a matter of ornamentation and presentation in which the interior is both a model and a projection of self-fashioning', Susan Stewart maintains in *On Longing*:

> For the environment to be an extension of the self, it is necessary not to act upon and transform it, but to declare its essential emptiness by filling it. Ornament, décor, and ultimately decorum define the boundaries of private space by emptying that space of any relevance other than that of the subject. (1993: 157)

In the process of manufacturing an authentic existence, the consumer becomes, phantasmally, the producer of objects through their spatial 'arrangement and manipulation' for display (Stewart 1993: 158). To generate a sense of cosy comfort by filling rooms designed for elegant formality was neither easy nor cheap. 'Through the rooms being so large & the windows so many & high', Elizabeth averred to Arabel, 'our apartment has cost us much more in the furnishing than we had any thought of at first' (*BC* 2005: 189).

The couple's decorative practice was intimately bound up with distinct preferences. 'We grew ambitious, & preferred furnishing them [the rooms] after our own taste rather than after our economy', she notes to a friend (*BC* 2005: 87). Although Elizabeth uses the possessive determiner 'our' in reference to the couple's 'taste', elsewhere she draws on the idiom of connoisseurship to characterise Robert's acquisitive eye. After one particularly striking find, she tells Arabella: 'Certainly he may well be pleased, because if the fortune was good, the perceptive faculty in himself was better & more effective' (*BC* 2007: 111).

Browning was not just buying used goods. He scoured second-hand markets in search of antiques and fine artworks. In this sense he was a collector, far different from a bargain hunter or consumer of bric-a-brac and souvenirs. Collectors were not considered consumers at all; they were connoisseurs who possessed, besides cultivated taste, specialised knowledge. Collecting depended less on luck than on the capacity to distinguish between antiques and mere household relics, souvenirs or outright junk. Although Browning could spot valuable art in the marketplace, he was not readily able to identify a painter or school. For attribution, he relied on his friend Seymour Kirkup, an artist residing in Florence. Elizabeth recounts an occasion when Kirkup hurried over to evaluate a purchase and commended Browning on it and on several other pieces:

> After recognizing & praising the Ghirlandaio, he said that Robert had done admirably in respect to the other pictures – that the crucifixion, if not Giotto, was Giottesque, of his time, and an unique specimen or nearly so, being painted upon linen [. . .] it was very valuable, [. . .] and that the Christ with the open gospel, a deep, solemn, moving picture, he believed to be a Cimabue, & worth five hundred guineas. (*BC* 2007: 111)

In addition to discernment, collecting required perseverance and contentment in deferring the ordinary purchase for the sake of the extraordinary. One waited for a serendipitous conjunction: the right opportunity and the unique find. 'Such furniture as comes by slow degrees into them [the palatial rooms] is antique & worthy of the place', Elizabeth affirms in a letter to Mitford (*BC* 2005: 84). In waiting, one exercised self-restraint, even self-denial, for which Robert's early religious training had certainly prepared him.

As an exercise in taste, connoisseurship, Pierre Bourdieu argues, consecrates not only the antique but also the sophisticated individual who is distinguished from others by having such a discerning eye. Acquiring the object becomes a means of social differentiation, symbolising one's transcendence of necessity (Bourdieu 1984: 71). Although some literary critics have followed Elizabeth's lead in characterising Robert as a connoisseur, his poems contain enough criticism of the connoisseur's performance of discriminating tastes and aesthetic judgements to suggest he would have been ambivalent about that ascription. In 'My Last Duchess', the duke's terrifying worldliness and obsession with rank and status is expressed through his status as a connoisseur. The titular monologist of 'The Bishop Orders His Tomb at Saint Praxed's Church' is much more sympathetic but no less worldly in his desire for a sumptuously embellished resting place: 'peach-blossom marble', 'the bas-relief in bronze', 'the Saviour at his sermon on the mount' (*RB* 1973a: 190–1). And, as I have already mentioned, in 'A Likeness' Browning criticises conventional connoisseurship: 'my prints', 'my treasure' (1996b: 283).

Finally, Elizabeth intimates that Casa Guidi was furnished after Robert's aristocratic aspirations. She explains to Henrietta in June 1848 why she has been sleeping on a borrowed bed: 'Robert wants a ducal bed for my room, all gilding & carving' (*BC* 2005: 92). She found the wait for the right objects with which to make the home functional, let alone decorative, exasperating at times: 'We are getting on slowly in the furnishing department', she sighs (92). But Elizabeth continually acceded to Robert's vision of their home. 'About houses, & furniture . . . he is far more particular than I ever was or can be', she admits to Henrietta (64). The heightened interest he took in decorating and furnishing Casa Guidi often led to playful exchanges: 'Sometimes, in joke, I call him an aristocrat [. . .] I cry out "à bas les aristocrats" [sic] – because he really cares a good deal about external things . . .' (64). On this basis, twentieth- and twenty-first-century historians might characterise Robert's pattern of consumption as an extension of aristocratisation, an attempt to reproduce within middle-class settings the splendours and luxuries of an aristocratic lifestyle.[48] Introducing a collection of Browning poems, for example, Daniel Karlin notes: 'It is possible to find him interesting or boring according to the criteria you might apply to visiting stately homes . . .' (2009: xi). But Elizabeth quickly undercuts her point by acknowledging to Henrietta that Robert possesses 'an artist's sense of grace' – 'only that I choose to make fun of it' by calling it aristocratic (*BC* 2005: 64).

As a way of accounting for the profusion of things at Casa Guidi, Elizabeth's musings about economy, filling, taste and aristocratic aspirations each have limited explanatory force. Frustrating the historian's ability to chart Elizabeth's and Robert's individual perspectives on the practice of decoration, Elizabeth wrote prolifically about their efforts to furnish Casa Guidi, but Robert's surviving letters, far fewer in number, indicate he left such discussions to her, sometimes in joint letters he also signed. Thus, our correspondence-based knowledge of Robert's decorative efforts can be gleaned only from her perspective. Her letters make it clear that, although the couple thought of decorating as a shared endeavour, it was really Robert's passion: 'As to the chairs & tables', Elizabeth humorously proclaims to Mitford, 'I yield the more especial interest in them to Robert' (*BC* 2005: 85). Beyond economy, filling, taste and aristocratic aspirations what may have motivated him?

While Robert's letters offer no illumination, we do have a record of what he read and composed during this period. Of his varied readings in art history, Vasari's *Lives of the Most Eminent Painters, Sculptors, and Architects* perhaps sheds the most light on Browning's approach to collecting. It is unclear exactly when he began reading Vasari, but he owned a thirteen-volume edition published between 1846 and 1857.[49] He was reading it between 1848 and 1853, while writing the majority of the poems that would appear in *Men and Women* and while furnishing Casa Guidi.[50] This 'collection of Lyrics', Elizabeth wrote to Arabella in March 1853, would contain 'a good deal of Italian art [..] pictures, music' (*BC* 2010b: 341). To her close friend Julia Martin in April 1853, Elizabeth reported that Robert was 'fond of digging at Vasari . . ., & goes to and from him . . . constantly, making him a "betwixt & between" to other writers' (*BC* 2012: 61). An artist and a passionate collector of Renaissance objects, Vasari provides a sweeping account of the period's art: from its beginnings, dominated by figures such as Cimabue and Giotto, to mid-period, represented by Brunelleschi, Masaccio and others, to its culmination in the work of Michelangelo, Leonardo and Raphael.

Vasari's multivolume work provides the reader with more than biographical sketches and anecdotes about art and artists. It also models a certain approach towards Renaissance objects. His repeated characterisation of their being regarded by their owners as sanctified gave them, as Paula Findlen persuasively argues, 'an added charge that many pagan antiquities did not quite have' (1998: 109). Vasari refers to one painting by Raphael as 'like a relic or sacred thing' (1850–2: III, 8). Of another, he states that it 'is treasured as if it were a relic, for the love which he [the owner] bears to the art, and more especially to Raphael' (I, 38). 'This sheet I now keep as a relic', he says of a drawing by Michelangelo (V, 231). He keeps a piece by Giotto as 'a rare and valuable relic of the master' (I, 113). For Vasari, these 'cultural fragments' were 'wonder-working objects through their ability to restore the mind and the soul in their contemplation' (Findlen 1998: 109). If we think of what Browning was reading and writing as evidence of his investments in collecting and decorating, then we can complicate both Elizabeth's narrative and the prevalent theoretical accounts – distinction, personality, nostalgia for origins – that might explain his practice.[51] Whereas Elizabeth rather apologises for the used furniture in the letter to Arabel I quoted earlier ('Of course you are to understand that our furniture is not *new* – but it is in good taste & characteristic notwithstanding'), Browning found that much of an object's value inhered in its history.

Translation into Song

Before discussing in greater detail some of the objects Robert Browning collected, I want to turn to a painting that the couple discovered soon after their arrival in Italy and to the poem of his, 'The Guardian-Angel: A Picture at Fano', that it inspired. Widely considered insignificant, this poem marks a change in Browning's approach to writing, in which objects serve as the impetus for developing a contextualist approach. 'The Guardian-Angel' is not the first poem he wrote in response to art. When the writer and historian John Forster asked Browning to pen a verse for an exhibition catalogue to accompany Daniel Maclise's painting *The Serenade*, the poet dashed off a stanza solely based on a verbal description. On seeing the painting sometime later, Browning extended the lines. The result was 'In a Gondola', published in *Dramatic Lyrics* of 1842. Nevertheless, 'The Guardian-Angel' is the first poem of those in *Men and Women* to have been written, signalling a new level of engagement with historical materiality that is amply evident in the volume.

Browning seldom said what impelled him to write. 'We are rarely told what he was brooding about at the time, what train of thought, what emotional mood formed the inspiration and background for a particular poem', Richard Altick notes (1951: 250). Nearing the end of his life, while working on a complete edition of his poetry, as I will discuss, Browning apparently contemplated providing such information but, owing to the press of work, ultimately desisted. Thus, we are left to draw conclusions from the poems themselves. As evidence of the experience it narrates, 'The Guardian-Angel' indicates that, while in Italy, Browning began developing a practice of translation: taking an idea generated in his mind by a single historical object, on which he had focused his perceptual attention, and making it the basis of a poem.

In the summer of 1848, while visiting the town of Fano on the Adriatic coast, Robert and Elizabeth encountered *L'angelo custode*, a seventeenth-century painting by Guercino that enchanted them. Although it was new to Robert, he was familiar with Guercino's work from visits to the Dulwich Picture Gallery. The painting depicts a guardian angel with extended wings standing next to a young child who partially kneels on a tomb. The angel helps to clasp the child's hands in prayer as both look heavenward, where three cherubs gaze down on them.

In the following months, Browning composed 'The Guardian-Angel'. Although it is occasioned by a work of art, thereby echoing

Keats's 'Ode on a Grecian Urn' (Martens 2011: 99), the poem offers few reminders of the painting's material presence. Much as his youthful self meditated before a single work of art, Browning patiently gazes at *L'angelo custode* in hopes that the barrier separating him from Guercino's representational world will dissolve and a moment of recognition between himself and the angel will occur:

> Let me sit all the day here, that when eve
>> Shall find performed thy special ministry,
> And time come for departure, thou, suspending
> Thy flight, mayst see another child for tending
>> Another still, to quiet and retrieve. (1996a: 102)

Indicating his proximity to the painting, Browning yearns for the angel to leave the canvas by taking 'one step, no more, / From where thou standest now, to where I gaze' and to envelop him 'With those wings, white above the child who prays / Now on that tomb' (102). Browning asks that the angel, instead of facilitating an ascent to heaven, repeat the spiritually pedagogic activity the scene depicts: 'And wilt thou bend me low / Like him [the child], and lay, like his, my hands together, / And lift them up to pray' (102).

Like the young child, who is taught to seek heavenly assistance, Browning, hoping to become reacquainted with his own latent spiritual capacities, asks to relearn how to pray. One consequence of being mature in years is the overdevelopment of his powers of cogitation. This has led to a skewed perception of the world and his place within it. The speaker, therefore, asks that the angel apply his 'healing hands' to the speaker's own eyes:

> I would rest
>> My head beneath thine, while thy healing hands
> Close-covered both my eyes beside thy breast,
>> Pressing the brain, which too much thought expands,
> Back to its proper size again, and smoothing
> Distortion down till every nerve had soothing,
>> And all lay quiet, happy and suppressed. (1996a: 103)

Browning posits this interaction as reparative, enabling a capacity to see anew 'with such different eyes' (103). In her reading of these lines, Britta Martens proposes that 'the metaphor of intellectualism as an illness implied in the (repeated) use of "healing" might refer to the supposedly too intellectual tendency in Browning's previous poetry' (2011: 102). Yet a proximately written poem, *Christmas-Eve and Easter-Day*, published in 1850, points to societal debates over biblical interpretation and scriptural authority that were much on his mind.[52]

Christmas-Eve contrasts an ordinary gathering of Dissenters at chapel, an extraordinary celebration of Jesus's birth by Catholics, and an intellectual's demystification of Christianity at a university in Germany, 'Göttingen, – most likely' (RB 1981a: 78), where higher critical hermeneutics flourished. The speaker observes the 'immense stupidity' of a clergyman delivering a sermon at a Nonconformist chapel; witnesses the 'posturings and petticoatings' of a highly stylised ceremony at Saint Peter's Basilica in Rome; and attends a lecture on the myth of Christ by a professor whose 'cranium's over-freight' (57, 95, 79). At the end of the poem, the speaker returns to what he finds most familiar, described early on as 'the hot smell and the human noises' of the Nonconformist chapel (57). Of the preacher he concludes, 'It were to be wished the flaws were fewer / . . . But the main thing is, does it hold good measure?' (95). As Charles LaPorte notes, 'An ungainly and somewhat absurd British chapel meeting reveals its true grace only through comparison with jarring and antithetical alternatives . . .' (2011: 163). In any event, the reference to the professor's enlarged brain links the poem to 'The Guardian-Angel' and to Browning's concerns with intellection.

Although he believed he was living in an age of transition, Browning could not accept the conclusions that many of his contemporaries, under the sway of modern biblical criticism, had reached. Nineteenth-century German philosophers, including David Friedrich Strauss and Ludwig Feuerbach, stressed the fragmentary, contradictory and literary elements of the Bible, hence calling into question its historicity. Mill, raised an atheist, had been introduced to this line of thought through studying Coleridge. The effect of the higher criticism on Arnold and Morley was loss of belief in the divinity of Christ as proven by prophecy and miracle. Nevertheless, Arnold, who thought tradition and ritual would persist as religion's 'poetry' (MA 1973b: 161), was agitated whenever his thought was linked 'to that of the German scholars (for whom his esteem was limited)' (Collini 2008: 101). He exalted re-embodiment, through the ministrations of culture, of a higher self with the ability to see through objective eyes. In so far as the process of seeing 'with such different eyes', to use Browning's phrase from 'The Guardian-Angel', takes place within a human frame, Arnold, too, imagined a form of re-embodiment. Unlike the modes with which Mill, Arnold and Morley were concerned (objectivisation, distantiation, impersonality), Browning's suggests that seeing properly requires restraining the overdeveloped mind to allow the fusion of sensory experience and emotion to serve as its own kind of knowledge: 'O world, as God has made it!' (RB 1996a: 103).

Thus, to sit before Guercino's painting was to feel oneself less in the presence of the image and more in the presence of the historical reality in which that image did its work. Through a process of transubstantiation, Browning saw the painting as having the power momentarily to transform or transmute, breaking down barriers between person and object, between past and present. This experience generates an epiphanic insight. For Browning *L'angelo custode* is evidence of a historically located way of perceiving the world that differs markedly from that of his own time: 'all is beauty: / And knowing this, is love, and love is duty' (1996a: 103). Apprehending reality through highly developed forms of ratiocination leading only to distortion, the contemporary mind is unable to grasp the world 'as God has made it!' In its time, the painting worked by making an affective impact on the viewer. Although Browning is subject to powerfully felt impressions while standing before the canvas, it cannot engender in him the same response its original viewers experienced. In an era in which logos has replaced pathos, one can have, instead, a modern idea of what that experience may have been like: 'I took one thought his picture struck from me, / And spread it out, translating it to song' (104).

Browning's conversion of this idea into the substance of a poem is facilitated by an act of imaginative perception. In 'House', a poem published in 1876, Browning gives this form of vision a specific name: 'spirit-sense' (1995: 173). As I noted in the introduction, 'House' depicts the reactions of passers-by to the interior of a domestic residence exposed to view following an earthquake. They make shallow observations about the life of the owner, presumably killed in the quake ('His wife and himself had separate rooms') and quick judgements about his character ('the pagan, he burned perfumes!') (173). Offering an allegory for biographical readings of poems, Browning dismisses the utility of such 'optics' (173). By contrast, the speaker urges those who wish to 'penetrate / Deeper' to activate their 'spirit-sense' (173). Denotative of imaginative perception, the 'spirit-sense' enables those seeking to understand the relationship between a work and its creator to go beyond visible, surface, ready-to-hand details. Truth, according to Browning, is more than fact. The imaginative perception necessary to attain truth may not be 'such different eyes' but is nevertheless a new optic.

For several years, Elizabeth and Robert shared the same opinion of *L'angelo custode*. In August 1848 Elizabeth described it to Mitford, in terms more aesthetic than Vasarian, as 'a divine picture of Guercino's' (*BC* 2005: 123).[53] She protested against their friend Jameson's assessment of Guercino's angels in her *Sacred and Legendary Art* as always evincing 'a touch of vulgarity' (Jameson 1848: 47). Browning had anticipated these objections by noting within the poem that it was partly written out of 'care / For dear Guercino's fame', the painter's reputation having declined 'since he did not work thus earnestly / At all times' (1996a: 103–4). 'We both cry aloud at what you say of Guercino's angels', Elizabeth wrote to Jameson in April 1850, 'and never would have said if you had been to Fano & seen his divine picture of the 'guardian angel', which affects me everytime [*sic*] I think of it' (*BC* 2007: 89). A year later, however, Elizabeth declared her earlier judgements had been faulty. Rejecting as 'soulless' the work by the Carracci family of early Baroque painters they had seen in Bologna, she admitted being partial to Renaissance art instead: 'I have even given up Guido, & Guercino too, since knowing more of them' (*BC* 2010a: 67). Although Baroque art, with its emphasis on common people, resonated with Robert, he largely came to share Elizabeth's new preference for medieval and early Italian Renaissance painting.

Historical Decoration

'The Guardian-Angel' gives some insight into Browning's sensory alertness to and perceptual engagement with historical art. Yet it is, as John Woolford, Daniel Karlin and Joseph Phelan observe, 'one of a small number of B.'s [Browning's] poems directly inspired by works of art' (2014: 15). If we think more broadly, however, including sculpture, architecture, tapestries and decorative objects as well as painting, it becomes readily apparent that the material culture of early modern Italy provided the impetus for much of *Men and Women*.

Indeed, during this period in which Browning acquired the items that decorated Casa Guidi – cast-off religious iconography and devotional paintings, Rococo chairs, brass lamps from a Catholic chapel and a hand-carved bookcase from a convent – he was also assembling the men and women to whose stories he would give voice. In 'One Word More', the poem that closes *Men and Women*, Browning exclaims:

> Love, you saw me gather men and women,
> Live or dead or fashioned by my fancy,
> Enter each and all, and use their service,
> Speak from every mouth, – the speech, a poem. (1996d: 147)

The word 'gather' is significant. Meaning 'to collect', especially from different sources or locations, 'to amass', 'to assemble in one place', 'gather' refers to the book of poems as a collection of voices. To get people to see and hear, Browning based many of the poems in *Men and Women* on artefactual and textual evidence that opened historical worlds to him. In fact, the term 'gather' also undergirds the concomitant act of collecting historical materiality ('to make a collection of'). Browning's composition of these lyrics, which invest characters with psychologies derived from the historical particularity of the ages in which they lived, is, therefore, inextricably intertwined with the poet's ongoing efforts to decorate Casa Guidi.

Two large oblong tapestries dating to the sixteenth century hung in the Casa Guidi dining room, adjacent to Browning's study. They created the effect of 'tapestry-covered walls' that Kate Field recalled (1861: 370). Elizabeth was proud of how they tied the room together. 'Did I tell you of our ancient tapestry', she asked Arabel regarding one of them, noting that 'with the carved wood & old pictures, it looks antique' (*BC* 2007: 110). Both tapestries depict scenes from Greek mythology, with an Italian coat-of-arms conspicuously included in each.

While contemplating one of these, Browning evidently derived ideas for the poem in *Men and Women* entitled '"Childe Roland to the Dark Tower Came"' (Figure 4.4). The Reverend John W. Chadwick, who visited Browning in London two years before the poet's death on 12 December 1889, was particularly struck by a prominently displayed tapestry. In a reminiscence of his visit, Chadwick notes:

> Upon the lengthwise wall of the room, above the Italian furniture, sombre and richly carved, there was a long, wide band of tapestry, on which I thought I recognized the miserable horse of Childe Roland's pilgrimage: –
>
> > 'One stiff, blind horse, his every bone astare,
> > Stood stupefied, however he came there –
> > Thrust out past service from the devil's stud!'
>
> I asked Mr. Browning if the beast of the tapestry was the beast of the poem; and he said yes, and descanted somewhat on his lean monstrosity. But only a Browning could have evolved the stanzas of the poem from the woven image. (Chadwick 1888)[54]

Unlike '"Childe Roland"', with its medieval setting, many of the poems in *Men and Women*, which take Renaissance Italy as their focus, were stimulated by the abundant reminders of early modern

Figure 4.4 Tapestry Panel.
Source: Armstrong Browning Library of Baylor University, Waco, Texas

Italian subjects that the Brownings encountered in their daily life in Tuscany. By the early winter of 1849–50 Browning had bought a number of artworks in second-hand markets, including two companion paintings, on panel, of angels that would inform the composition of his 'Old Pictures in Florence'. 'He heard, where he procured them, that they had been sawn off the sides of a great picture representing the Madonna, in a church at Arezzo', Elizabeth recounts at length to Arabel in May 1850, adding that 'the priest was reported to have said that the Madonna cd. take care of the altar alone, [. . .] saying which, he had sawn off the angels & sold them' (*BC* 2007: 110). Robert wrote to the priest, offering to purchase the Madonna, but was informed that, as the cleric had travelled to Rome for an extended period, 'nothing cd. be done until his return' (110). Then, Elizabeth continues, Robert engaged in a serendipitous shopping expedition:

> A few days since, Robert fell on some pictures in a corn shop outside the [city] walls, & was much struck by one called the 'Eterno padre', – by a Christ with an open gospel in his hand, – by a crucifixion which was curiously like Giotto, [. . .] & two smaller pictures. When he told me of them, I said [. . .] 'Oh, but I do hate those subjects [. . .] the *Eterno padre*!'. 'So do I', said he, 'but its [*sic*] a very fine picture, and we can get it for two pounds – we may be very sorry afterwards, if we dont [*sic*] take it, for even a delay may throw it into the hands of some artist, & then our chance is gone.' We agreed, then, that he shd. get the pictures. They arrived yesterday. On putting them into the light in our new drawingroom, the whole glory of the discovery became apparent. One curious thing I must tell you first. The 'Eterno padre' (so called) is surrounded with a rainbow, & sits clothed in a sort of high priest's mystical garment – an open book in the left hand, the right hand upraised – It is very grand. Robert cried out [. . .] 'How curious! the hands are painted precisely in the manner of the angels

from Arezzo, in the next room – I will go and fetch them & prove it to you.' In a moment he came back with the angels, and immediately burst out into fresh exclamations. Arabel, our angels had been sawn off that very picture. There is no doubt about it – The circle of the rainbow, and bits of the mystical garment join on line for line – Is that not surprising? Robert is in a state of rapture at the discovery – Whenever we can afford it, we shall have the pictures fastened together, and a frame to unite them. It is a fine picture of Ghirlandaio, of whom I think there is only one specimen in the Florentine gallery. (110–11)

Elizabeth's overall framing of this anecdote in religious terms – 'the whole glory of the discovery', 'state of rapture' – and her description elsewhere of her husband as having, as a shopper, an extraordinary 'artist's sense of grace', which enabled him to procure 'all manner of luxuries & glories' for their household (*BC* 2005: 64, 112), had little to do with the thematic content of these works.[55] It was not on religious grounds that these pictures appealed to the Brownings. Their contemporary Arthur Clough would have nothing of what he perceived as historical detritus: 'what do I want with this rubbish of ages departed', he writes in *Amours de Voyage* (1974: 4). Browning's anti-Catholic prejudice, like Clough's, was abiding (Melchiori 1975: 174). But Browning responded to the emotive and colouristic late medieval and early modern Italian paintings he viewed and collected, as well as the gilded decorative objects and furniture carved in high relief he acquired, because these objects were intrinsic indicators of how historical subjects attempted to shape their worlds. Thus, although Elizabeth amusingly recounts that 'Robert has walked me backwards & forwards to the next room "to see our Cimabue and Ghirlandaio" till I am quite tired today' (*BC* 2007: 111), it would be a mistake, it seems to me, to interpret this excitement as solely exhibiting pride of ownership, gratitude for one's good fortune, or astonishment at one's keen eye.

In other words, the dominant analytical terms critics mobilise to discuss decorative objects (the souvenir, the collection, the bibelot) or practices of collecting (distinction, personality, nostalgia for origins) might be employed here to form plausible accounts of this episode.[56] Because I wish to reconstruct Browning's understanding of his relationship to these artefacts, however, solely privileging any of these theories obscures his motivations. It is one thing to be able to distinguish between an article of rare value and mere household junk crowding Florentine market stalls, thereby affirming one's perceptive faculty, but quite another to transubstantiate into the present a past historical reality and to re-form into a whole what had only existed in fragments, as Browning initially sought to do with the newly discovered sixteenth-century altarpiece.

Browning ultimately decided not to fasten the pieces of Ghirlandaio's painting together but to hang them as a triptych directly over the mirror above the fireplace. From the angle Mignaty's picture provides, the panels are the most commanding presence in the room. Just below the central image, the Italian wall mirror itself is impressive. 'We have been extravagant enough', Elizabeth tells Henrietta, 'to give five guineas for a glass – above the drawingroom fire place – not very large, but with the most beautiful carved gilt frame I ever saw in my life' (*BC* 2005: 92). The frame includes on the lower sides two cupids in high relief, holding candles. Two thirteenth-century unframed Italian panels depicting male and female saints flank the mirror. Next to each panel is a bust, one of a man, the other a woman, forming a pair in circular ebonised and gilded frames. On the left, above one bust, is an oil portrait of a bishop. Above the bust on the right is a full-length oil of Saint Jerome gazing heavenward, holding a scroll and a rock with which he beats his breast, a cardinal's hat at his feet.

Robert Browning's experience of 'rapture' in Elizabeth's account occurs at the precise moment when he discovers seemingly unrelated pieces are, in fact, one. In an instant, the barrier between past and present dissolves. But in surrounding oneself with objects from the past, as Chadwick's anecdote shows, an ideational spark can take place at any time. 'Old Pictures in Florence' cites flaking frescoes and 'tempera crumbly', invoking, among other artists and works, Ghirlandaio, 'the great Bigordi' of the poem (RB 1996c: 32). These ruminations were prompted by the Florentine oil painting *Christ at the Column*, attributed by Browning to Antonio Pollaiuolo, 'My Pollajolo, the twice a craftsman . . . Of a muscular Christ . . .',[57] and by *The Penitent Saint Jerome*, which he attributes in the poem to Taddeo Gaddi (1996c: 32). Browning discovered both second hand. On the left wall of the drawing room, above the tall-back settee, Browning placed his newly purchased *Christ at the Column*, which features the Son of God in half-length tied to a column, with landscape scenes and various saints depicted in the background.

Although Rossetti thought 'Old Pictures in Florence' seemed remarkably intimate, as if 'all the pictures *desired* by the poet are in his possession *in fact*' (1897: 160–1), most scholars have not approached Browning's work by thinking of his collection. One of the few critics to do so, Leonee Ormond, dismisses his interest in art as decidedly amateurish:

> The artists who most intrigued him were either those whose pictures he believed he owned, or those with interesting psychological particularities. He sometimes seems to be making a case at the expense of the facts. His praise of the lively and bustling work of the sculptor, Nicola Pisano, is a natural enough outcome of his theories, but his choice, in the next line, of Cimabue as the supreme painter of the school, is entirely arbitrary; like so many of Browning's opinions, it was conditioned by historical and biographical factors, and not by a critical examination of the art in question. (1975: 202)

It is unfair to expect Browning to be the art critic he never purported to be, but it is certainly true that his interest in the material culture of the past had less to do with the objects themselves than with the past they made present. In Ormond's view such an admission underscores a remarkable deficiency in Browning's ability to analyse a painting. 'He has all the natural interests of the collector and antiquarian, but subservient to his creative instincts as a poet, which always lead him to seek out the man behind the work', she contends. 'None of the painter-poems reveals Browning as a poet with a true "eye for a picture", or with a pronounced visual sense' (1975: 204). But Browning worked by associations. If he ate snowdrops, it was not because he preferred them to say, polenta, but because doing so made him feel close to Tilsit.

   That Browning learned to read paintings by sitting in front of one for hours, or that he returned on multiple days to view a painting in Fano, suggests he was after something else entirely. He was intrigued by 'how history *feels*', to use Herbert Tucker's phrase (1994: 25), rather than what it means. Seymour Kirkup, on whom, as I noted earlier, the Brownings relied for attributions, was often wrong. In 'Old Pictures in Florence', Browning refers to Gaddi's *Saint Jerome* (1996c: 32). The artist was, art historians now generally agree, Fra Angelico.[58] But for Browning, the details were, in a sense, irrelevant. As Elizabeth comments regarding one of Kirkup's earlier assessments, 'if not Giotto . . . Giottesque, of his time' (*BC* 2007: 111). Looking at a painting, tapestry or decorative item from the past initiates in Browning a metonymic sequence that makes him feel, to borrow a phrase from Helena Michie and Robyn Warhol's reflections on the erotics of the archive, 'asymptotically closer to the historical reality from which the objects derive' (2015: 25). And feeling, rather than discursive reasoning, was often what he was after.

Pursuing the feeling rather than the meaning of history may necessitate relinquishing, at least temporarily, the disciplined use of reason. Meaning, under these circumstances, can only ever be provisional, conjectural, epiphanic, constructed by the reader or viewer through interpretive acts. This was, essentially, a lesson Browning learned from the higher criticism. Having accepted David Strauss's argument that the Bible's 'factual and fanciful' components could not be easily separated and the claim 'that the Bible's sacred truths were literary' (LaPorte 2011: 159, 173–4), Browning approached history in general in an intuitive rather than an analytical way. He used his 'spirit-sense'.

Yet 'Old Pictures in Florence' does give some indication as to why the Brownings gravitated away from Baroque painting and towards Renaissance art. As energetic supporters of the Risorgimento, they lived through the brief attempt to establish a republic in Tuscany in early 1849, only to see Grand Duke Leopold II restored to power in Florence, under Austrian protection, after a few months. For Browning freedom was a necessary correlative to significant artistic production. Any future republican government, he writes in 'Old Pictures', 'Shall ponder, once Freedom restored to Florence, / How Art may return that departed with her' (1996c: 35). This does not suggest, it seems to me, that Browning gives primacy to art over politics in the poem, as Martens argues (2011: 113). Rather, he insists creative activity and individual passion are vital to a dynamic, democratic body politic.

In the early modern period with which he draws parallels, many of his monologists, whose actions he subjects to critical publicity, are subject to mental and social constraints. Despite G. K. Chesterton's assertion that Browning pioneered a democratic form of poetry in which he 'let everybody talk' (1903: 173), many of his monologists live in societies not characterised by an efflorescence of free speech. As Matthew Reynolds points out, numerous speakers are, in fact, 'manifestly un-free' (2001: 183). This is especially true for women in Browning's poems. 'For only a handful of poems are actually spoken by women', Isobel Armstrong observes. 'When women appear men speak *about* or *to* them as a feminine other' (1993: 287). With no possibility of becoming active civic participants, women as well as many men are confined to private settings. Reynolds declares:

> From this point of view, the monologues look less pro-actively democratic, and more like the product of a mind focused on a country where, as the Brownings' acquaintance Edward Dicey noted in a book

of political commentary, there was 'no public life', no freedom of speech, heavy restrictions on movement, a country ruled by a group of regimes which (as the Brownings saw it) sought to stall the progress of history. (2001: 183)

Browning would have seen such conditions as inhibiting the realisation of individuality as conceived by nineteenth-century liberal thinkers, in which one privately embraced the public good. Nevertheless, as 'Old Pictures in Florence' indicates, he believed inexorable democratising tendencies fomented laudable changes in the direction taken by art, examples of which decorated his home.

'Only My Four Little Heads'

Following Elizabeth's death, Robert Browning returned to England with his and Elizabeth's son, Robert Wiedeman Barrett Browning, whom they affectionately called Pen. After spending the winter of 1861 in London in temporary accommodation at no. 1 Chichester Road, Upper Westbourne Terrace, Browning decided to lease no. 19 Warwick Crescent, a white stucco, terraced corner house with a small front garden near Paddington station. He did not intend to stay long. 'I find this house very comfortable & shall hope to make it serve my turn till I have done my work here – then I shall go home', he claimed in a letter to his good friend Isa Blagden, 'not, I think, to establish myself anywhere, but to wander about the world . . .' (1951: 137). His 'work' included overseeing Pen's education and preparation for university. Their household expanded in 1866 when Sarianna moved in after their father's death. Rather than wandering, Browning remained at Warwick Crescent for twenty-five years, from May 1862 to June 1887.[59]

His long years of residence notwithstanding, he continued to view Warwick Crescent as temporary accommodation to which he had no real attachment. 'I began by too entirely despising this little house, which has behaved well enough by me for nearly twenty years: I never condescended to consider it as other than a makeshift . . .', he confessed (1966: 120). Not until 1881 did he began taking interest in its upkeep.[60] Browning furnished it with many decorative objects that had adorned the walls or filled the large open spaces of Casa Guidi. Initially, he was not at all sure he wanted to be surrounded by reminders of Elizabeth. 'I have got my poor old things from

Florence & write this with the Bookcase beside me', he mused soon after moving in. 'It is a sad business and I hardly know – or care to think – whether I like the things best here, or there, or at the bottom of the sea' (1951: 113–14). The hand-carved chairs and sofas upholstered in velvet, the ornate escritoire and bookcases and various decorative pieces were, as several visitors noted, simply incongruous in Warwick Crescent, which lacked the lofty ceilings and spaciousness of an Italian palazzo.[61] However, as the writer and translator Helen Zimmern, who lived in both Florence and London, remarked regarding Warwick Crescent: 'Browning's conservative nature clung to it, for was it not bound up with the idyll of his life lived out in the Casa Guidi?' (1906: 44).

In the early months of 1887 Browning purchased for £5,000 a large terraced house with Italianate detail in fashionable South Kensington. Built by C. A. Daw and Son, the row of terraced houses was close to shopping areas, museums and the Royal Albert Hall. Although developed coevally with Elm Park Gardens, to which the Morleys had moved a year earlier, De Vere Gardens was the more prestigious address: Henry James, the Marquess of Carmarthen and James Fitzjames Stephen, among many notable intellectuals and officials, resided there ('De Vere Gardens' 1986). Browning was less than 400 yards from Kensington Palace, to the north, and close to Palace Gate, Kensington Gardens and Hyde Park. To the east, Belgravia, St James's and Westminster were easily accessible.

Suitably palatial and commodious, with five floors and a basement, no. 29 De Vere Gardens could accommodate Browning's antique furniture and decorative objects. As Zimmern observes, 'the fine old Italian furniture' in its new setting 'could be better seen and appreciated' (1906: 44). Sarianna, who helped manage the household, organised having the walls painted sage green, reminiscent of Casa Guidi. At Warwick Crescent, Browning had hung the two large tapestries he had acquired in Florence. As he wrote at the time: 'I am having the old tapestries put up like curtains in the drawing room: there are two large windows & I mean they shall (the tapestries) hang & *draw* their full length' (1951: 137). Against the sage-green walls at no. 29, however, the tapestries could be displayed to greater effect. In anticipation of the move, he told his friend Sarah FitzGerald, he had the precious tapestries sent to Paris for repair (1966: 194).

But De Vere Gardens would not function as a mausoleum, as in some respects Warwick Crescent had. Writing in February 1887 to his friend Katherine Bronson, a wealthy American living in Venice, to share the news of his purchase, Browning states:

> I have bought a house – Oh, sad descent in dignity – not on *Canal Grande* – the beloved and ever to be regretted – but Kensington – It is a nearly new one, and situated just where I wish: and in consequence of the temporary depreciation of that kind of property, I believe I have done very well. (1985a: 73)

The wistful beginning of this passage, with its parenthetical asides and syntactic interruptions, refers to a home in Venice he had intended to purchase for his son. Pen had fallen in love with the city in 1885, during his first visit to Italy since leaving in 1861, and was attracted to the prospect of living and working as an artist there (Orr and Kenyon 1908: 340–3). The pensive tone is replaced by a confident voice and more measured prose as Browning narrates the advantages of a new abode that might also serve as a pied-à-terre in London for his son, who was still unmarried and travelling widely.

De Vere Gardens offered the possibility of renewal, a place where Browning could 'keep house' again, something he had felt himself incapable, following Elizabeth's death, of doing (RB 1950: 133).[62] He took a more decided interest in embellishing the living spaces with both older and recently acquired furnishings. In one room he exhibited a Louis XIV-style clock he had obtained later in life. Its decorative features – an arched top carrying a fairly large gilded figure, four columns upheld by kneeling horses, white enamel hour plaques on an engraved gilt panel, and an undecorated minute hand – and the relative smallness of the clock-face call attention not to time, like the Bates of Huddersfield clock of his childhood, but to period style. He brought out from storage fine-looking antiques from Casa Guidi that it had been impossible to accommodate at Warwick Crescent (Neville-Sington 2004: 579). And he went shopping for new objects: 'The apparent delight with which he furnished his new home', notes Roma King in his study of Browning's account books, 'recalls something of the enthusiasm with which he and Mrs. Browning filled Casa Guidi with antique chairs, old tapestries, satins, and beautifully hand carved furniture years before' (1947: 28).

Between June and December of 1887 Browning, who kept detailed records of his income and expenditures, spent £275 on decorations and furniture. Over the next two years he spent another £116 (R. King 1947: 28). Some of the objects he purchased within this three-year period include a mahogany, wicker-bottomed armchair with detailed carvings on to which he had his initials embossed in silver; a Jewish Sabbath lamp; an antique mahogany bookcase, which he used to store some of his father's 6,000 books; and four gilt terracotta plaques representing the seasons. The plaques, Alexandra Orr explains, 'were to stand at intervals on brackets in a certain unsightly space on his drawing-room wall' (Orr and Kenyon 1908: 377). Conscious that his expenditures might be perceived as excessive, Browning insisted to Orr that the plaques, which she thought his son was obtaining for him, would be the final item: 'Only my four little heads, and then I shall not buy another thing for the house' (qtd in Orr and Kenyon 1908: 377). But soon a seventeenth-century Persian table, inlaid with an alternating design of mother-of-pearl and ebony and ivory, beckoned.

Browning's move to De Vere Gardens did not inaugurate a new period of intense compositional activity. Nonetheless, while he was deeply engaged in decorating his new residence, Browning presided over the publication of his last collected edition. He meticulously edited the sixteen-volume *Poetical Works*, published between April 1888 and July 1889.[63] Browning apparently contemplated adding biographical and elucidating footnotes to establish the material and historical provocations to his thought, but, owing to the press of work, ultimately decided against it: 'I am correcting them carefully, and *that* must suffice' (qtd in Hancher 1971: 25).

Object Lessons

In 1864 the banker, Liberal Party economic advisor and frequent essayist Walter Bagehot famously termed Browning's style 'grotesque' (1965b). Unlike the 'pure' style of Wordsworth, which Bagehot, like Mill before him, found able to refresh and revive a reader's mind, Browning's was entirely too jarring. Implicitly extending the definition of grotesque art – according to the *Oxford English Dictionary*, 'a kind of decorative painting or sculpture, consisting of representations of portions of human and animal forms, fantastically combined and interwoven with foliage and flowers' – to encompass Browning's poems, Bagehot argued that Browning too often focused on 'abnormal specimens' and documented 'not . . . what nature is striving to be, but . . . what by some lapse she has happened to become' (353). Acknowledging that 'grotesque objects exist in real life', Bagehot lamented that, as compositional fodder, they lead to 'ugly poems and . . . detestable stanzas' (360).

The characterisation of Browning's poetry as grotesque has been highly influential. Less attention has been paid to Bagehot's interest in the material basis of the poems' composition. Without fully understanding the implications of his argument, Bagehot makes available a way of understanding Browning's decorative practices and poetic compositions as mutually constitutive. According to Bagehot, Browning 'evidently loves what we may call the realism, the grotesque realism, of orthodox Christianity' (1965b: 360). Bagehot reflects: 'He must *see* his religion, he must have an "object-lesson" in believing' (360). Indeed, Browning 'puts together things which no one else would have put together, and produces on our minds a result which no one else would have produced, or tried to produce' (353). Although this is an assessment of the content of Browning's poems, it could as easily be a valuation of his interiors. For Browning, the act of collecting and the practice of surrounding himself with artefacts from other times and places engendered the epiphanic experience of being among objects that, in bearing their historicity, enabled the imaginative and affective dissolution of the barrier separating past from present.

Notes

1. As Stephanie Kuduk Weiner notes, during the period when Morley was editor of *The Fortnightly Review*, 'Character was an important lens of analysis in the *Fortnightly* generally' (2005: 144).
2. Meredith and Morley were frequently compared to Browning in terms of similarity of content (exploring a range of human actions and motivations, virtues and vices) and resemblance in form. Arthur Symons found Meredith and Browning 'akin in their general aim – the portrayal of living and thinking men and women' (1885: 80–1). His phrase 'men and women' invokes Browning's 1855 collection by that title. The author and positivist Frederic Harrison did not mean it as a compliment when he told his friend Morley that he was 'a prose Browning, who delights the cultured, but who is too difficult for the multitude' (qtd in Hirst 1927: I, 250).
3. Although I cite an edition of Orr's work revised and partly rewritten by Kenyon, quotations in this chapter attributed to Orr are unchanged from the original.
4. For the 1885 version, which precedes all other contributions to the volume, including William Ewart Gladstone's, see Reid 1885: 11.
5. Given the restrictions of the verse form with which he works, Browning does not elaborate on these outward circumstances, but his entire literary output suggests he viewed them as particularly decisive, often overlapping.

6. The unpublished review has been lost, but Peterson and Standley (1972) reproduce Mill's marginalia and Browning's responses.

7. On completing 'The Tomb at St. Praxed's (Rome, 15–)' in 1845, a few years after first visiting Italy, Browning declared to the writer Frederick Oldfield Ward that the poem, later retitled 'The Bishop Orders His Tomb at Saint Praxed's Church', was 'just the thing for the time – what with the Oxford business, and Camden society and other embroilments' (*BC* 1992: 83). He refers here to John Henry Newman and his followers and to Cambridge University's Camden Society, which allied itself with the Oxford Movement. But, as Matthew Reynolds points out, precisely why a poem about a sixteenth-century Catholic bishop is 'just the thing for the time' is not clear-cut. Browning may have been suggesting a contrast between the predilections of the bishop, whose deathbed wish was to be interred in an elaborate and expensive Renaissance tomb, and the Camden Society, which sought a return to medieval religious piety and Gothic architecture. Newman himself, as Reynolds notes, 'was never attacked for being a sensualist or an aesthete' (2001: 165).

8. As Isobel Armstrong observes, Browning's poems 'resist a social interpretation of evolutionary processes in terms of progress, and are fascinated instead by the randomness of evolutionary operations' (1993: 292).

9. 'I don't think, when you have read more, you will find I have "taken the man for any Hero"', Browning wrote to Edie Story, a young family friend, in January 1872. 'I rather made him confess he was the opposite, though I put forward what excuses I thought he was likely to make for himself' (1965: 167).

10. The Brownings had a complicated relationship to Napoleon III. Both disdained him when he was elected president of France in 1848. But, in 1851–5, because of his role in the Risorgimento, Elizabeth's view evolved to partial approval. From 1855 she expressed 'open admiration' (Hetzler 1977: 337). Robert began offering qualified approval only in 1856. His admiration peaked in 1859, because of the war to free Italy from Austria's rule (Hetzler 1977: 339). Thereafter, although Robert continued expressing some admiration, his approval began to wane. When he wrote *Prince Hohenstiel-Schwangau*, his feelings about Napoleon III differed considerably from what they had been a decade earlier, before Elizabeth's death.

11. Although endorsing the individualism unleashed by the Renaissance, Browning's poems ask readers to reflect critically on its extreme forms. In 'Johannes Agricola in Meditation', as Browning ultimately titled a soliloquy first published in 1836, Agricola, a German contemporary of Martin Luther and the founder of antinomianism, declares his belief that those predestined for salvation, himself included, are exempt from God's law. If 'Fra Lippo Lippi' anticipates Mill's encouragement of eccentricity, 'Johannes Agricola in Meditation' antedates Mill's belief, as well as Arnold's, that 'strong impulses are only perilous when not

properly balanced; when one set of aims and inclinations is developed into strength, while others, which ought to co-exist with them, remain weak and inactive' (JSM 1977d: 263).

12. On Browning's engagement with Vasari, see Fraser's broad consideration (2014) and Bullen's more narrowly focused study (1972). Regarding Browning's keen interest in Renaissance art and culture in Florence, see Major 1924. On Browning's study of Baldinucci, see DeVane 1927: 167–212. See DeLaura 1980 on Browning's knowledge of Rio and on Jameson's influence on the 'painter poems'.

13. See Ormond 1975 on Browning's visits to the Pitti and D. Thomas on his visits to the Uffizi (1983: 121).

14. 'Fra Lippo Lippi', published in 1855, is thought to have been composed between late 1852 and early 1853. 'We have specimens of Gaddi, Lippi [. . .] the like', Elizabeth wrote in May 1850 (*BC* 2007: 110). She went on to discuss their acquisition of works by Ghirlandaio, Cimabue and, possibly, Giotto. Subsequently, scholars have established that many of these attributions were wrong. No evidence that the Brownings owned a Lippi exists, although they believed they possessed one (*BC* 2007: 113 n. 6).

15. On Italy's significance to Browning's literary production more generally, see Korg 1983 and Melchiori 1975.

16. Alexandra Orr discusses Robert's active imagination in childhood (Orr and Kenyon 1908: 23–6). 'Though this kind of romancing', she points out, 'is common enough among intelligent children', more remarkable is 'the strong impression' that a 'flight of dramatic fancy' left on Browning's mind (1908: 23). Maynard argues that Browning possessed 'a very special power of imagination', cultivated by his parents (1977: 156).

17. Large numbers of Nonconformists and Anglican Evangelicals resided in south London, including Peckham, Herne Hill, Denmark Hill, Clapham, Camberwell, where the Brownings lived, and Walworth, where they worshipped. The family seems to have partaken liberally of this religious mixture.

18. From 1812 to April 1816 the family lived in Rainbow Cottage near the Camberwell village common; from April 1816 to November 1824 they resided a block north, next to the common; and from November 1824 to 1840 they lived in the semi-detached Hanover Cottage (Maynard 1977: 398 n. 58; Kennedy and Hair 2007: 4).

19. On the New Cross property, see also Coulter 1985–6.

20. The poet's paternal grandfather was a staunch member of the Church of England but on the Evangelical end of the spectrum. Besides owning numerous theological texts, including tracts and sermons, he read the Bible cover to cover each year. Hoping to correct a prevalent view of his grandfather as a country bumpkin, Mason insists he was a 'student of poetry' and 'a man with a taste for good literature'

(C. Mason 1983: 44, 43). He provides scant and questionable evidence for the latter assertion. Religious verse, of course, was widely read by Evangelicals. On Browning's grandfather, see also Maynard 1977: 20–4. For a contemporaneous example of the exhortation to read the Bible annually, see Emerson 1826.

21. Lilian Whiting, an American journalist who spent much of her life in Europe and knew Robert and Elizabeth's son, from whom she derived knowledge of Robert's habits, notes: 'All his life Browning was an early riser.' He began the day with a cold bath at seven and sat down for breakfast by eight – hours that, in Whiting's view, were 'heroic' (1911: 288).

22. Browning's father was raised in the Church of England but in 1820 joined his spouse, already a Dissenter, in worshipping at the York Street Congregational Church in Walworth. Several contemporaries recall the family's regular attendance and striking presence at the Reverend George Clayton's sermons (Mould 1905: 9–13). They also joined the large crowds who attended the sermons of Henry Melvill, an evangelically inclined Church of England minister, later Canon of St Paul's Cathedral. On Browning's upbringing in the religious environments of Camberwell and Walworth, see Kennedy and Hair 2007: 4–12 and Maynard 1977, especially pp. 9–162.

23. Noel Annan states that 'the more publicised memories of gloomy severity or cruelty recorded by [John] Ruskin, Samuel Butler or Augustus Hare' have overshadowed more positive accounts of Evangelical childhoods (1984: 13). Even the familiar stories of puritanical households are somewhat skewed. As Richard Altick notes, 'Ruskin's father was a devotee of Scott, and as a child Ruskin himself knew the Waverley novels and Pope's *Iliad* better than any other book except the Bible' (1998: 116). Similarly, while Hare's mother derided any work of fiction as 'wicked', his grandmother, who resided in the same household, consumed Dickens's *The Pickwick Papers* as they were published in numbers (Hare 1896: 135). On Evangelical reading practices, see Altick 1998, especially pp. 115–23.

24. Christian is the protagonist of *The Pilgrim's Progress*, John Bunyan's allegorical novel, first published in 1678, which young Browning would have known well.

25. The Irish writer and suffragist Frances Power Cobbe, a friend who visited Browning in Florence, recalls with amusement how 'he would discuss every tree and weed, and get excited about the difference between eglantine and eglatere (if there be any), and between either of them and honeysuckle' (1894: 15). See also DeVane 1955: 41 and Griffin and Minchin 1966: 39.

26. On Robert's visit to Russia, see Maynard 1977: 127–8. Writing to Elizabeth in 1846, Browning recalls having visited Holland ten years earlier (*BC* 1995: 265–6).

27. As recounted by Griffin and Minchin 1966: 17; Maynard 1977: 135–6; and Finlayson 2004: 34–5.
28. Even in early childhood Browning demonstrated unusual sensitivity to music. 'One afternoon his mother was playing in the twilight to herself. She was startled to hear a sound behind her', William Sharp relates in a biography published shortly after Browning's death. She spotted 'a little white figure distinct against an oak bookcase, and could just discern two large wistful eyes looking earnestly at her'. Sharp continues: 'The next moment the child had sprung into her arms, sobbing passionately at he knew not what, but, as his paroxysm of emotion subsided, whispering over and over, with shy urgency, "Play! play!"' (1897: 25).
29. See also Leppert 1988: 107–46.
30. On Browning's technical knowledge and appreciation of music, see Greene 1947.
31. See, for example, Browning's two 1837 letters to William Macready (*BC* 1985: 251–2) and an 1845 letter to Elizabeth (*BC* 1993: 28–31).
32. The Dulwich Picture Gallery confirmed by email on 15 May 2017 that these works were in their collection in the mid- to late-1820s.
33. A March 1846 letter to Elizabeth provides information on Browning's experience at the Dulwich (*BC* 1994: 124, 127 n. 1). For a contemporaneous overview of the gallery's collection in the late 1810s and early 1820s, see Patmore 1824. See also Griffin and Minchin 1966: 11–15 and Kennedy and Hair 2007: 37–9.
34. In September 1861, writing to his and Elizabeth's close friend Isa Blagden, Robert described the relationship between his son, Pen, and his father during a holiday in Brittany: 'He amuses himself with my father, whose kindness & simplicity make him a wonderful child's friend certainly, – they sketch together, go home & paint &c and Pen's loud merry laugh is never out of my ears' (1951: 88). In the evocatively autobiographical 'Development', published in 1889 in *Asolando*, Robert's final volume of poetry, the speaker recalls his father introducing him to the siege of Troy by utilising tables, chairs, footstools and the family's dogs and cats (2011a: 68–9). Robert and Pen were not alone in their feelings for Robert Senior. The writer Henriette Corkran deemed the 'happiest hours' of her childhood those spent with 'dear old Mr. Browning' (1902: 10).
35. Kelley and Coley inventory some of these (1984: 531–5). Maynard discusses the impact of Robert Senior's library on Browning (1977: 133–46).
36. The age requirement for admittance was fourteen, according to Whiting (1911: 11).
37. Thornton points out that 'density' is a significant historical variable in interior decoration: 'Each period of history has its own way of seeing things – its own "period eye", as it were – which, by some strange process, seems to affect pretty well everyone.' Thus, he asserts, 'people

in circles that react to fashion, even when it is only to quite a limited extent, possess a common way of viewing rooms – and, indeed, much else' (1984: 8). This shared perception extends to the 'degree of density in the arrangement of the furniture [that] is regarded as generally acceptable' and the 'number of objects [that] can be tolerated *en masse* in a room'. Consequently, 'there are variations in how much pattern the eye can assimilate' (Thornton 1984: 8).

38. Words like 'cozy' and 'comfort', Gloag notes, 'could never have been applied to the well-proportioned, elegantly furnished interiors of the Georgian period' (1962: 137).

39. For Field's accounts of her visits to Casa Guidi, see Scharnhorst 2008: 22–6, 32–4.

40. In a stimulating essay Jennifer McDonell suggests that the heterogeneous style and subject matter of Browning's dramatic monologues call to mind cabinets of curiosities, which noblemen assembled during the European Renaissance partly as testaments to their erudition (2013).

41. Lee Erickson notes that at Casa Guidi the Brownings 'led a comfortable bourgeois life' (1984: 132). Matthew Reynolds observes that 'the Brownings were surprised by a convergence between personal union and political unity' in that their first wedding anniversary occurred on the same day as 'the procession to mark the birth of the Florentine civic guard – the same celebration which was later to be described in Part I of *Casa Guidi Windows*', Elizabeth's 1851 poem (2001: 104). 'The public, in its "infinite procession", files between two domestic spaces: the home of the bourgeois married Brownings, and the palace of "the Duke & his family" . . .' (Reynolds 2001: 104).

42. See also Harris 1987: 52.

43. See Elizabeth's July 1848 letter to Arabella (*BC* 2005: 107) and the photo facing p. 112.

44. 'By the second decade of the nineteenth century, it was much less likely that middle-rank men and women would own either furniture or clothing that had previously belonged outside their family', Stana Nenadic observes, 'and it was much more likely that working people would be able to purchase second-hand goods that had once belonged to the relatively wealthy' (1994: 134). Only in the last three decades of the century, when denunciations of 'the intolerable ugliness of modern furniture' were loudest, did consumers in large numbers begin purchasing items from the past ('Art of furnishing' 1875: 536). On the rapid growth of buying relatively inexpensive used furnishings during this period, see Muthesius 1988. Ponsonby has more recently qualified this timeline by pointing to evidence that auctioneers and cabinetmakers marketed and sold used furnishings in good condition to middle-class consumers throughout the century (2007: 91). Before the 1870s, however, demand for second-hand goods was minimal.

45. Consumers in London flocked to the shops on Wardour Street, Soho, where modern furnishings with an antique appearance could be purchased (Wainwright 1989: 35–6).
46. See, for example, Kennedy and Hair's discussion of furnishing Casa Guidi (2007: 175–6).
47. As Elizabeth reported to Arabella, 'Our furnishing is nearly done – that is, everything essential is nearly provided, & waits for the arranging – the man to polish the carved wood & to put up beds and bookcases, curtains, bellropes & the like' (*BC* 2005: 103).
48. Aslet and Powers argue that Victorian middle-class housing often reproduced on a smaller scale the floor plans of country estates and aristocratic villas (1985: 214).
49. See item A 2379, Kelley and Coley 1984: 200.
50. In April 1853 Elizabeth comments that Robert 'has nearly enough lyrics to print' (*BC* 2012: 73).
51. On distinction, personality and nostalgia for origins, see Bourdieu 1984, Cohen 2006 and Baudrillard 1996.
52. These two poems are designed to be read together. I address only *Christmas-Eve. Easter-Day* is a dialogue on scepticism and belief.
53. A few months later, she used the same phrase in her part of a joint letter to another friend (*BC* 2005: 165).
54. Although Chadwick says Browning identified the horse in the poem as the one in his tapestry, Melchiori argues that the animal may also have derived from Edgar Allan Poe's story 'Metzengerstein' (1968: 208–13).
55. Elizabeth refers to Robert's 'artist's sense of grace' in *BC* 2005: 64. While she undoubtedly means an artist's appreciation of attractiveness or charm, thereby utilising a non-religious meaning, I wish to read it in conjunction with these more explicitly religious terms and phrases.
56. On the souvenir, the collection and the bibelot, see, respectively, Stewart 1993, Bal 1994 and Saisselin 1984.
57. Although Browning and others have regarded the painting as being by, or likely by, Pollaiuolo, the attribution is disputed. See, for example, Wright, who rejects it (2005: 410, 530–1).
58 Although the painting is not by Gaddi, his descendants apparently owned it before Browning purchased it. It has been attributed to Giovanni Toscani, as well as to Masolino and Masaccio, but most modern scholars agree on Fra Angelico. See Kanter and Palladino 2005: 34, 50, 52, 55–7 and Princeton University Art Museum 2007: 177.
59. Close to a major transportation link connecting London to Oxford and beyond, Warwick Crescent, unlike the scenes of his childhood and youth, had a decidedly suburban ambience without being in any sense rural. 'It was London, but London touched by some indefinite romance; the [Regent's] canal used to look cool and deep, the green trees used to shade the crescent', as Annie Thackeray Ritchie described it, adding that 'it seemed a peaceful oasis after crossing that dreary

Aeolia of Paddington, with its many despairing shrieks and whirling eddies' (1892: 853). From the upper-storey window, Browning could gaze upon the canal – with its frequent rowers, walking paths and a bridge – and a luxuriant islet in the middle of the small lake, all reminiscent of Venice.

60. 'I have *this moment* . . . desired a gardener to set the little patch of wretchedness called "our garden" in something like decent order', Robert confided to Sarah Anne FitzGerald, adding that he had not set foot in it for more than a year. 'It will be re-ordered, gravelled, and, – above all, – stocked with shrubs – plenty of green, with me, compensating for any absence of flowers – if one must choose an absence' (1966: 120).

61. 'When after his wife's death he removed to his commonplace not to say dull abode of Warwick Crescent, Paddington', Helen Zimmern notes, 'he also put it [the Casa Guidi furniture] there, where its massive carvings, heavy gildings, and valuable tapestries looked strangely out of place and overweighed the low-ceilinged English chambers' (1906: 44).

62. As Roma King notes, 'This natural love for a fireside and artistic surroundings was dormant for a long time after his wife's death . . .' (1947: 28).

63. A seventeenth volume, containing *Asolando* and biographical and historical notes, was published in 1894, five years after Browning's death.

Conclusion: 'Presentness Is Grace'

I suspect many members of the three major academic organisations on the Victorian period – the North American Victorian Studies Association (NAVSA), the British Association of Victorian Studies (BAVS) and the Australasian Victorian Studies Association (AVSA) – made the pilgrimage to Casa Guidi after a joint conference in Venice in June 2013. I had arranged to meet my friend Jennifer McDonell, a Browning scholar, to spend an afternoon there and at the so-called English Cemetery. But a series of incidents intervened: Jennifer, brave enough to make her way to Florence by car, got into an accident, and I was without a phone. I arrived promptly at three, the museum's opening time, and spent most of the afternoon waiting for Jennifer. Because only a handful of rooms are open to the public, visitors are unlikely to stay for hours. Jennifer's calamity, however, was my providence. After viewing each room, I decided to sit and wait.

Casa Guidi was the last site associated with this project I visited. In 2008 Logan Browning, publisher and executive editor of *SEL: Studies in English Literature 1500–1900*, arranged for an acquaintance to take me to the Athenaeum Club while I was doing research in London. I shared a meal with Robert Parker and several other club members in the main dining room before we ascended to the drawing room for conversation. On other London visits, I explored Leadenhall Street, where India House once stood, and walked from the Gloucester Road underground station, as John Morley would have done, to find his residences at Elm Park Gardens. Without historical markers to indicate Morley's homes, now renumbered, I was not entirely sure of their locations. On another occasion Jennifer and I, having successfully met in London, wandered through Maida Vale and Kensington searching for Browning's residences at no. 19 Warwick Crescent and no. 29 De Vere Gardens.

I undertook the expeditions after studying these places in textual and visual form. My work in local reading rooms, public records offices, archives and libraries was motivated by epistemological aspirations. I wanted to understand how the institutional and domestic spaces Mill, Arnold, Morley and Browning inhabited inflected their thinking. This kind of work engenders its own locationally specific and investigative thrills. Harriet Bradley writes eloquently about the 'pleasures' of the archive, including the enjoyment derived from partaking in the 'privileges' of conducting research in professionally sanctioned sites for producing knowledge and the pride experienced in legitimating one's authority as an interpreter of the past (1999: 109, 110). The examined materials are themselves seductive, eliciting a desire to uncover further secrets. Yet this seductive quality is illusory. Because 'the voices have been already selected and in a sense heard', one is able to generate knowledge merely from 'what has been stored', she contends. 'Only what has been pre-judged as relevant is likely to be recovered' (113). Despite these limitations, many scholars persist in believing that through scrupulous research one may obtain relatively complete knowledge of an object of study, perhaps aided by a little luck (such as stumbling on an uncatalogued or unanalysed letter, diary or manuscript). These fantasies, which I share, have been variously termed the 'seductions', 'erotics', 'romance', 'desire', 'fever' and 'sickness' of the archive.[1]

For earlier generations of material culture scholars, visual evidence was thought to provide unmediated access to Victorian interiors. Although this view is now untenable, such evidence can nevertheless profoundly affect the statements cultural historians make about historical subjects and the interiors they inhabited. For example, Elizabeth Barrett Browning does not discuss seasonal placement of furniture in her letters. But George Mignaty's commemorative portrait of Casa Guidi's salon, painted soon after her death, provides information about how the Brownings inhabited the room that textual sources alone do not divulge. As I document in Chapter 3, the visual evidence of Morley's residences at Elm Park Gardens seemingly contradicts visitors' written accounts. Paintings, photographs, illustrations and sketches can, therefore, show details of routine domestic life that went unmentioned in correspondence. They also give a sense of the organisation and arrangement of furnishings and the social use of objects (Burke 2001: 81–102). Indeed, old photographs, paintings, drawings and illustrations helped to facilitate the turn to material culture.

A promise implicit in that turn is movement from appearance to substance. In her fine study *Material Relations*, Jane Hamlett confidently asserts that, through paintings, floor plans, lists, inventories, account-books, probate records and, to a lesser extent, personal letters and diaries, because they are often mute on mundane details, we can 'uncover how the domestic interior was used and experienced in everyday life' (2010: 11). The presumption here is that we can move from text to thing and in so doing unlock history's secrets. But if domestic interiors of the past are elusive, known only in a limited way through visual and written texts, do we ever really get from text to thing?

Responding to this question, some have argued for incorporating the researcher's first-person investigations. 'Abandoning the assumption that an objective, "real" interior exists somewhere beyond the frames of our visual, and the pages of our textual evidence', Jason Edwards and Imogen Hart urge scholars of material culture to 'experience at first hand (if still extant) their chosen interiors' (2010: 17). Heeding this call if possible, I was both excited and slightly embarrassed by my expeditions. Having visited more than twenty private and public archives while researching this book, I expected to learn nothing new by traipsing through London or Florence. But, more emotionally than rationally, I wanted to 'feel' connected to the historical subjects and spaces about which I was writing: hence, both the excitement and the embarrassment. Seeking this connection was, admittedly, something of a fool's errand: of the extant sites, the Athenaeum has gone through multiple interior redecorations; Morley's Elm Park Gardens residences and Browning's De Vere Gardens home are impossible to enter; and many rooms at Casa Guidi are accessible only to students of Eton College, which owns the property, or holidaymakers renting the apartment through the Landmark Trust.

The feeling associated with visiting a home, residential district or street corner bearing little or no resemblance to its appearance in Victorian times is akin to what has been termed living or popular history. While not engaged in a re-enactment, I recognised myself to be participating in history's affective turn: 'historical representation characterized by conjectural interpretations of the past, the collapsing of temporalities and an emphasis on affect, individual experience and daily life rather than historical events, structures and processes' (Agnew 2007: 299). Affective history cannot make the past present any more than traditional forms of historical writing can, but scholars for some time were – and many still remain – wary of it. As Gareth Stedman Jones asserts, history as a field and form of writing is 'an entirely intellectual operation that takes place in the present and in the head' (1976: 296), which forecloses the possibility of apprehending the past in visceral, affective ways.

In recent years the study of history, however, has taken an affective turn, and with it new provisional interpretations, inspired by this form of writing or performing, have emerged. The methodology is not new. Within their spaces of privacy, Mill, Arnold and Morley sought to work outward from idea – produced in their own minds through thoughtful reflection – to affect by redirecting feeling from the domain of daily life to that of higher-order abstractions: 'the divine passion for seeing things as they are', which enables one to become 'a genuine lover of truth', in Morley's felicitous phrasing (1901: 201). Browning inverted this relationship: moving from affect, the feeling an object inspired in him, to idea. Although both approaches are ultimately limited in their ability to recover the past, historical writing continues to be influenced by the nineteenth-century analytical and cognitive protocols established by, among others, Mill, Arnold and Morley.[2] Thus, my desire to feel connected to the past while writing a historical account of liberalism engendered, at least initially, a feeling of shame.

But three hours in Casa Guidi is a long time to be embarrassed. After my discomfiture subsided, a feeling of grace came over me. 'Grace' is not a term often employed in academic research or, despite the sophisticated meta-historical accounts of recent years, archival research. To my recollection, I have encountered it only twice in academic scholarship apart from religious studies. The first was in Michael Fried's essay 'Art and objecthood'. Fried distinguishes between 'presence' (the proximity of a material object to a viewer) and 'presentness' (the feeling of complete visual and mental captivation) before concluding that, in elliptical phraseology, 'Presentness is grace' (1998: 142). The words have always moved me, as has James Elkins's evocation of them in *Pictures and Tears: A History of People Who Have Cried in Front of Paintings*, the second text in which I remember encountering the term 'grace'. *Pictures and Tears* seeks to understand why contemporary viewers no longer seem eager or even able to cry in front of paintings. Gallery culture with its various accoutrements (exhibition catalogues, audio-tour digital recordings, explanatory videos) may encourage a detached and disengaged approach to viewing art. Nevertheless, some people, Elkins argues, continue to experience 'presence', his term for what Fried calls 'presentness', before paintings, even if they are no longer moved to tears (2001).

I did not experience the Brownings' presence while waiting at Casa Guidi. I did, however, feel something like the presentness of the past. As I wandered from room to room, the years separating me from the Brownings seemed occasionally to disappear. The salon and the bedroom, ably reconstructed, are momentarily disorienting, appearing to offer immediate access to their lives. On closer inspection, the restoration – begun in 1971, when the Browning Institute of New York purchased Casa Guidi, and continued under Eton College and the Landmark Trust from 1992 to 1995 – only approximates the interior as it was lived by the Brownings. While Mignaty's portrait, copies of Robert's and Elizabeth's letters and the Sotheby, Wilkinson & Hodge sale catalogue of their possessions (as well of those of their son, Pen) were utilised in acquiring and placing furniture, prints and paintings, only a few originals are displayed. Parts of the home remain undocumented and cannot be reconstructed. Even if it were possible to acquire the exact objects and furnishings the Brownings owned, the residence as it was would still be elusive. From street noise to plumbing, the ambience today necessarily differs from theirs. I cannot, therefore, simply map my subjective experience on to a historical experience of the place.

When I have turned to speculation, finding through my visits to a site neither sufficient evidence to make a claim with certainty nor illumination of authentic historical experience, I have often thought of Robert Browning's approach to the material culture of the past. The entire premise of *The Ring and the Book*, often seen by critics as the successor volume to *Men and Women* because of its 'intensity and concentration' (Armstrong 1993: 316), hinges on physical materiality: a set of legal documents, bound together as a book, that Browning obtained from a Florentine bookstall, to which the speaker continually redirects the reader's attention. He asks:

> Do you see this square old yellow Book, I toss
> I' the air, and catch again, and twirl about
> By the crumpled vellum covers, – pure crude fact
> Secreted from man's life when hearts beat hard,
> And brains, high-blooded, ticked two centuries since?
>   Examine it yourselves! (RB 1985b: 8)

Yet, as Browning leads the reader through 'Pages of proof this way, and that way proof' (15), one gradually realises the ten monologues on a seventeenth-century rape and murder are not 'pure crude fact', a phrase promising complete knowledge. They offer, instead, contradictory and partial knowledge. The very arrangement of these 'facts' depends on a prior fancy to unite them. 'Fancy with fact is just one fact the more', Browning asserts (23). While fancy has connotations of 'make-believe' and 'white lies' (23), he sees it as a means of navigating the uncertainties of historical knowledge.

Despite the differences among them, Mill, Arnold and Morley would have agreed that Browning's passionate overvaluation of objects was akin to primitive fetishism. Mill thought fetishisation originated in 'the feelings'; it was 'not at all of the intelligence' (1985a: 361). Arnold believed that imaginatively ascribing power to non-human objects – to 'lend life to the dumb stones', as the speaker in 'Empedocles on Etna' puts it – was child's play (1965c: 167). Morley worried that contemporary decorative practices were leading society back to 'the worship of little domestic gods' (1873: 475). But Browning knew that, no matter how much he might write or think about the historical objects with which he surrounded himself, he could never use them to make truly present what was past. As he looked at paintings or held artefacts in his hands, Browning exuberantly and viscerally, rather than serenely, felt the presentness of the past. He experienced this presentness as grace.

Notes

1. H. Bradley 1999: 113; Michie 2009: 9; Keen 2001: 3; A. Burton 2006: 11; Derrida 1998: 12; Steedman 2002: 1–2. Drawing on Derrida, Steedman uses 'fever' and 'sickness' to connote intense longing '*for* the archive . . . not so much to enter it and use it, as to *have* it, or just for it to be there' (2002: 2).
2. Although unconcerned with liberalism or Mill, Arnold and Morley, Antoinette Burton notes that nineteenth-century 'discourses of rationalization – of archive logics – have helped to obscure', well into our time, the role desire plays in generating understandings of the past through archival research (2006: 11).

Bibliography

Abbott, L. F. (1923), 'John Morley', *The Outlook*, 135 (3 October 1923): 173–4.

Adamson, S. (1990), 'The what of the language?', in *The State of the Language*, ed. C. Ricks and L. Michaels, Berkeley: University of California Press, pp. 503–14.

Agnew, V. (2007), 'History's affective turn: historical reenactment and its work in the present', *Rethinking History: The Journal of Theory and Practice*, 11.3: 299–312.

Allen, T. and T. Wright (1839), *The History and Antiquities of London, Westminster, Southwark, and Parts Adjacent*, vol. 3, London: Virtue.

Allott, K., ed. (1965), *The Poems of Matthew Arnold*, New York: Barnes.

Altick, R. D. (1951), 'The private life of Robert Browning', *The Yale Review*, 41.2: 247–62.

Altick, R. D. (1998) [1957], *The English Common Reader: A Social History of the Mass Reading Public, 1800–1900*, 2nd edn, Columbus: Ohio State University Press.

Anderson, A. (2001), *The Powers of Distance: Cosmopolitanism and the Cultivation of Detachment*, Princeton: Princeton University Press.

Anderson, A. (2005), 'Victorian studies and the two modernities', *Victorian Studies*, 47.2: 195–203.

Anderson, J. (1835), 'Thoughts on the origin, excellencies, and defects of the Grecian and Gothic styles of architecture', *The Architectural Magazine . . .*, 2 (August 1835): 336–42.

Annan, N. G. (1984), *Leslie Stephen: The Godless Victorian*, London: Weidenfeld.

Anon. (1772), review of W. Bolts, *Considerations on India Affairs . . .*, *The Monthly Review, or Literary Journal*, 46 (March 1772): 236–43.

Anon. (1857), letter [unsigned] to J. D. Dickinson, 28 August 1857, British Library, IOR, Copy Correspondence Out [EIC], 1856–8, IOR/L/SUR/2/2, fols 353–5.

Anon. (1899), 'John Morley: a study, by a Member of Parliament', *The Century Illustrated Monthly Magazine*, October 1899: 874–80.

apRoberts, R. (1983), *Arnold and God*, Berkeley: University of California Press.

Armitage, D. (2000), *The Ideological Origins of the British Empire*, Cambridge: Cambridge University Press.

Armstrong, I. (1993), *Victorian Poetry: Poetry, Poetics and Politics*, London: Routledge.

Armstrong, I. (2008), *Victorian Glassworlds: Glass Culture and the Imagination, 1830–1880*, Oxford: Oxford University Press.

Arnold, D. (2000), *Re-presenting the Metropolis: Architecture, Urban Experience, and Social Life in London, 1800–1840*, Aldershot: Ashgate.

Arnold, D. (2005), *Rural Urbanism: London Landscapes in the Early Nineteenth Century*, Manchester: Manchester University Press.

Arnold, J. M. (1996) [1848], 'To Thomas Arnold', in MA 1996, pp. 122–5.

Arnold, M. (1867), 'Culture and its enemies', *The Cornhill Magazine*, 16.1 (July 1867): 36–53.

Arnold, M. (1952), *The Note-Books of Matthew Arnold*, ed. H. F. Lowry, K. Young and W. H. Dunn, London: Oxford University Press.

Arnold, M. (1960–77), *The Complete Prose Works of Matthew Arnold*, ed. R. H. Super, 11 vols, Ann Arbor: University of Michigan Press.

Arnold, M. (1960a) [1869], 'On the modern element in literature', in MA 1960–77, vol. 1, pp. 18–37.

Arnold, M. (1960b) [1861], 'On translating Homer', in MA 1960–77, vol. 1, pp. 97–216.

Arnold, M. (1960c) [1853], 'Preface to first edition of Poems (1853)', in MA 1960–77, vol. 1, pp. 1–15.

Arnold, M. (1962a) [1863], 'The bishop and the philosopher', in MA 1960–77, vol. 3, pp. 40–55.

Arnold, M. (1962b) [1879], 'Democracy', in MA 1960–77, vol. 2, pp. 3–29.

Arnold, M. (1962c) [1864], 'The function of criticism at the present time', in MA 1960–77, vol. 3, pp. 258–85.

Arnold, M. (1962d) [1863], 'Heinrich Heine', in MA 1960–77, vol. 3, pp. 107–32.

Arnold, M. (1962e) [1864], 'Pagan and mediaeval religious sentiment', in MA 1960–77, vol. 3, pp. 212–31.

Arnold, M. (1965a) [1869], *Culture and Anarchy*, in MA 1960–77, vol. 5, pp. 85–230.

Arnold, M. (1965b) [1867], 'Dover Beach', in MA 1965g, pp. 239–42. Note: Probably composed in 1851.

Arnold, M. (1965c) [1852], 'Empedocles on Etna', in MA 1965g, pp. 147–94.

Arnold, M. (1965d) [1852], 'Lines Written in Kensington Gardens', in MA 1965g, pp. 254–8.

Arnold, M. (1965e) [1850], 'Memorial Verses', in MA 1965g, pp. 225–9.

Arnold, M. (1965f) [1868], 'A new history of Greece', in MA 1960–77, vol. 5, pp. 257–94.

Arnold, M. (1965g), *The Poems of Matthew Arnold*, ed. K. Allott, New York: Barnes.

Arnold, M. (1965h) [1869], 'Preface [to *Culture and Anarchy*]', in MA 1960–77, vol. 5, pp. 231–56.

Arnold, M. (1965i) [1849], 'Resignation: To Fausta', in MA 1965g, pp. 84–94.

Arnold, M. (1965j) [1852], 'The Second Best', in MA 1965g, pp. 278–9.

Arnold, M. (1965k) [1849], 'Stanzas in Memory of the Author of "Obermann"', in MA 1965g, pp. 129–38.

Arnold, M. (1965l) [1852], 'A Summer Night', in MA 1965g, pp. 267–71.

Arnold, M. (1965m) [1866], 'Thyrsis: A Monody . . .', in MA 1965g, pp. 496–507.

Arnold, M. (1965n) [1848], 'To a Republican Friend', in MA 1965g, pp. 101–2.

Arnold, M. (1968a) [1873], *Literature and Dogma*, in MA 1960–77, vol. 6, pp. 139–411.

Arnold, M. (1968b) [1873], 'Preface [to *Literature and Dogma*, 1st edn]', in MA 1960–77, vol. 6, pp. 147–51.

Arnold, M. (1968c) [1870], 'Puritanism and the Church of England', in MA 1960–77, vol. 6, pp. 72–107.

Arnold, M. (1968d) [1870], *St. Paul and Protestantism* . . ., MA 1960–77, vol. 6, pp. 1–127.

Arnold, M. (1971a) [1875], 'Preface [to *God and the Bible*]', in MA 1960–77, vol. 7, pp. 374–98.

Arnold, M. (1971b) [1874], 'Preface [to *Higher Schools and Universities in Germany*, 2nd edn]', in MA 1960–77, vol. 7, pp. 90–130.

Arnold, M. (1972a) [1876], 'Bishop Butler and the zeit-geist', in MA 1960–77, vol. 8, pp. 11–62.

Arnold, M. (1972b) [1876], 'The Church of England', in MA 1960–77, vol. 8, pp. 63–86.

Arnold, M. (1972c) [1878], 'Equality', in MA 1960–77, vol. 8, pp. 277–305.

Arnold, M. (1972d) [1877], 'George Sand', in MA 1960–77, vol. 8, pp. 216–36.

Arnold, M. (1972e) [1876], 'A last word on the Burials Bill', in MA 1960–77, vol. 8, pp. 87–110.

Arnold, M. (1973a) [1880], 'The future of Liberalism', in MA, *English Literature and Irish Politics*, ed. R. H. Super, Ann Arbor: University of Michigan Press, pp. 136–60.

Arnold, M. (1973b) [1880], 'The study of poetry', in MA 1960–77, vol. 9, pp. 161–88.

Arnold, M. (1975a) [1884], 'Emerson', in MA 1960–77, vol. 10, pp. 165–86.

Arnold, M. (1975b) [1884], 'Numbers; or The Majority and the Remnant', in MA 1960–77, vol. 10, pp. 143–64.

Arnold, M. (1989) [1843–56/7], *The Yale Manuscript*, ed. S. O. A. Ullman, Ann Arbor: University of Michigan Press.

Arnold, M. (1996–2001), *The Letters of Matthew Arnold*, ed. C. Y. Lang, 6 vols, Charlottesville: University of Virginia Press.

Arnold, M. (1996), *The Letters of Matthew Arnold: Vol. 1, 1829–1859*, in MA 1996–2001.

Arnold, M. (1997), *The Letters of Matthew Arnold: Vol. 2, 1860–1865*, in MA 1996–2001.

Arnold, M. (1998), *The Letters of Matthew Arnold: Vol. 3, 1866–1870*, in MA 1996–2001.

Arnold, M. (2000), *The Letters of Matthew Arnold: Vol. 4, 1871–1878*, in MA 1996–2001.

Arnold, M. (2001), *The Letters of Matthew Arnold: Vol. 5, 1879–1884*, in MA 1996–2001.

Arnold, M. (2002), *The Letters of Matthew Arnold: Vol. 6, 1885–1888*, in MA 1996–2001.

Arnold, T. (1845) [1833], 'To the Chevalier Bunsen', in A. Stanley, *The Life and Correspondence of Thomas Arnold . . .*, 5th edn, London: Fellowes, vol. 1, pp. 358–61.

'The art of furnishing' (1875), *The Cornhill Magazine*, 31.5 (May 1875): 535–47.

Aslet, C. and A. Powers (1985), *The National Trust Book of the English House*, Harmondsworth: Viking.

Aspinall, A. (1931), *Cornwallis in Bengal: The Administrative and Judicial Reforms of Lord Cornwallis in Bengal . . .*, Manchester: Manchester University Press.

Athenaeum Club (1825–31), Reports of the Committee, TS Com. 18/1, Athenaeum Club, London.

Athenaeum Club (1828), Minute for Letter, 12 July 1828, The National Archives of the UK, Records of the Crown Estate Office, Athenaeum Club, CRES 2/710.

Athenaeum Club (1830), *An Alphabetical List of the Members, with the Rules and Regulations of the Athenaeum*, London: Athenaeum.

Athenaeum Club (1850–8), Candidate Book, 1850–8, MS Mem. 2/20, Athenaeum Club, London.

Athenaeum Club (1853), *Athenaeum: Rules and Regulations, List of Members, and Donations to the Library, 1852; with Supplement for 1853*, London: [Savill].

Athenaeum Club (1882) [1824], *Copy of the First Published List of Members (1824)*, [London]: [Athenaeum].

'Athenaeum Club House' (1830), *The Gentleman's Magazine*, April 1830: 351.

Augst, T. (2007), 'Faith in reading: public libraries, liberalism, and the civil religion', in T. Augst and K. E. Carpenter (eds), *Institutions of Reading: The Social Life of Libraries in the United States*, Amherst: University of Massachusetts Press, pp. 148–86.

Ayres, P. J. (1997), *Classical Culture and the Idea of Rome in Eighteenth-Century England*, Cambridge: Cambridge University Press.

Bagehot, W. (1965a) [1853], 'Shakespeare – the individual', in W. Bagehot, *Collected Works*, ed. N. St John-Stevas, Cambridge, MA: Harvard University Press, vol. 1, pp. 173–215.

Bagehot, W. (1965b) [1864], 'Wordsworth, Tennyson, and Browning; or, pure, ornate, and grotesque art in English poetry', in W. Bagehot, *Collected Works*, ed. N. St John-Stevas, Cambridge, MA: Harvard University Press, vol. 2, pp. 318–67.

Bailey, P. (1978), *Leisure and Class in Victorian England: Rational Recreation and the Contest for Control, 1830–1885*, London: Routledge.

Bain, A. (1882), *James Mill: A Biography*, London: Longmans.

Bain, A. (1969) [1882], *John Stuart Mill: A Criticism with Personal Recollections*, London: Longmans, 1882; repr., New York: Kelley.

Bal, M. (1994), 'Telling objects: a narrative perspective on collecting', in J. Elsner and R. Cardinal (eds), *The Cultures of Collecting*, London: Reaktion, pp. 97–115.

Banfield, F. (1884), *Biographies of Celebrities for the People . . .*, London: Maxwell.

Barker, T. C. and M. Robbins (2007) [1963], *A History of London Transport: The Nineteenth Century*, London: Routledge.

Barrell, J. (1992), *The Birth of Pandora and the Division of Knowledge*, Philadelphia: University of Pennsylvania Press.

Barrett, H. and J. Phillips (1987), *Suburban Style: The British Home, 1840–1960*, London: Macdonald.

Bashford, C. (2009), 'Learning to listen: audiences for chamber music in early-Victorian London', *Journal of Victorian Culture*, 4.1: 25–51.

Baudrillard, J. (1996), *The System of Objects*, trans. J. Benedict, London: Verso.

Bayly, C. A. (2012), *Recovering Liberties: Indian Thought in the Age of Liberalism and Empire*, Cambridge: Cambridge University Press.

Begbie, H. (1905), *Master Workers*, London: Methuen.

Begbie, H. (1909), *Broken Earthenware*, London: Hodder.

Bell, R. S. W. (1895), 'The houses of celebrated people: part III', *The Windsor Magazine*, 2, September 1895: 334–42.

Benjamin, W. (2003), *Selected Writings: Vol. 4, 1938–1940*, ed. W. Eiland and M. W. Jennings, trans. E. Jephcott and others, Cambridge, MA: Belknap–Harvard University Press.

Bennett, T. (1995), *The Birth of the Museum: History, Theory, Politics*, London: Routledge.

Bentham, J. (1838–43), *The Works of Jeremy Bentham . . .*, ed. John Bowring, 11 vols, Edinburgh: Tait.

Bentinck, W. C. (1977), *The Correspondence of Lord William Cavendish Bentinck, Governor-General of India, 1828–1835: Vol. 1, 1828–1831*, ed. C. H. Philips, Oxford: Oxford University Press.

Bernstein, J. (2000), *Dawning of the Raj: The Life and Trials of Warren Hastings*, Chicago: Dee.

Bernstein, S. D. (2013), *Roomscape: Women Writers in the British Museum from George Eliot to Virginia Woolf*, Edinburgh: Edinburgh University Press.

Biagini, E. F. (1992), *Liberty, Retrenchment, and Reform: Popular Liberalism in the Age of Gladstone, 1860–1880*, Cambridge: Cambridge University Press.

Biagini, E. F. (2003), 'Neo-Roman liberalism: "republican" values and British liberalism, ca. 1860–1875', *History of European Ideas*, 29.1: 55–72.

Birdwood, G. C. M. (1890), 'Illustrations from the records and relics of the late Honourable East India Company', *The Journal of Indian Art*, 3.31: 41–115.

Black, A. (1887), 'The amateur photographer', *The Century Illustrated Monthly Magazine*, 34 (May–October 1887): 722–9.

Black, B. (2000), *On Exhibit: Victorians and Their Museums*, Charlottesville: University Press of Virginia.

Black, B. (2012), *A Room of His Own: A Literary-Cultural Study of Victorian Clubland*, Athens: Ohio University Press.

Black, M. E. (1987), 'Matthew Arnold as school inspector: a revaluation', *Pacific Coast Philology*, 22.1–2: 15–21.

Boman-Behram, B. K. (1943), *Educational Controversies in India: The Cultural Conquest of India under British Imperialism*, Bombay: Taraporevala.

Boswell, J. (1826) [1791], *The Life of Samuel Johnson, LL.D.*, vol. 1, Oxford: Talboys.

Boucher, B. (2001), 'Antiquity writ large: Alma-Tadema, Poynter and the redecoration of the Athenaeum', *Armchair Athenians: Essays from Athenaeum Life*, London: Athenaeum, pp. 55–74.

Bourdieu, P. (1980), *The Logic of Practice*, trans. R. Nice, Stanford: Stanford University Press.

Bourdieu, P. (1984), *Distinction: A Social Critique of the Judgement of Taste*, trans. R. Nice, Cambridge, MA: Harvard University Press.

Bowen, H. V. (2006), *The Business of Empire: The East India Company and Imperial Britain, 1756–1833*, Cambridge: Cambridge University Press.

Bowran, T. (1900), 'John Morley', *The Westminster Review*, 154.2: 117–32.

Bradley, H. (1999), 'The seductions of the archive: voices lost and found', *History of the Human Sciences*, 12.2: 107–22.

Bradley, I. (1976), *The Call to Seriousness: The Evangelical Impact on the Victorians*, 1st American edn, New York: Macmillan.

Brent, R. (1987), *Liberal Anglican Politics: Whiggery, Religion, and Reform, 1830–1841*, Oxford: Clarendon.

Brightfield, M. F. (1940), *John Wilson Croker*, Berkeley: University of California Press.

Britton, J., A. Pugin and W. H. Leeds (1838), *Illustrations of the Public Buildings of London . . .*, 2nd edn enl., vol. 2, London: Weale.

Brown, W. (1995), *States of Injury: Power and Freedom in Late Modernity*, Princeton: Princeton University Press.

Brown, W. (2009), *Regulating Aversion: Tolerance in the Age of Identity and Empire*, Princeton: Princeton University Press.

Browning, R. (1863), *Sordello, Strafford, Christmas-Eve and Easter-Day*, Boston: Houghton.

Browning, R. (1933) [1888], *Letters of Robert Browning: Collected by Thomas J. Wise*, ed. T. Hood, New Haven: Yale University Press.

Browning, R. (1937), *Robert Browning and Julia Wedgwood: A Broken Friendship as Revealed by Their Letters*, ed. R. Curle, New York: Stokes.

Browning, R. (1950) [1861], *New Letters of Robert Browning*, ed. W. C. DeVane and K. L. Knickerbocker, New Haven: Yale University Press.

Browning, R. (1951), *Dearest Isa: Robert Browning's Letters to Isabella Blagden*, ed. E. C. McAleer, Austin: University of Texas Press.

Browning, R. (1965), *Browning to His American Friends: Letters between the Brownings, the Storys and James Russell Lowell, 1841–1890*, ed. G. R. Hudson, New York: Barnes.

Browning, R. (1966), *Learned Lady: Letters from Robert Browning to Mrs. Thomas FitzGerald, 1876–1889*, ed. E. C. McAleer, Cambridge, MA: Harvard University Press.

Browning, R. (1969–2011), *The Complete Works of Robert Browning: With Variant Readings & Annotations*, ed. R. A. King, 17 vols, Athens: Ohio University Press.

Browning, R. (1973a) [1845], 'The Bishop Orders His Tomb at Saint Praxed's Church', in RB 1969–2011, vol. 4, ed. R. A. King, M. Peckham, P. Honan and W. Barnes, pp. 189–93.

Browning, R. (1973b) [1845], 'Pictor Ignotus', in RB 1969–2011, vol. 4, ed. R. A. King, M. Peckham, P. Honan and W. Barnes, pp. 164–6.

Browning, R. (1981a) [1850], *Christmas-Eve and Easter-Day*, in RB 1969–2011, vol. 5, ed. R. A. King, J. W. Herring, P. Honan, A. N. Kincaid and A. C. Dooley, pp. 49–133.

Browning, R. (1981b) [1855], 'Fra Lippo Lippi', in RB 1969–2011, vol. 5, ed. R. A. King, J. W. Herring, P. Honan, A. N. Kincaid and A. C. Dooley, pp. 183–96.

Browning, R. (1985a), *More Than Friend: The Letters of Robert Browning to Katherine de Kay Bronson*, ed. M. Meredith and R. S. Humphrey, Waco: Armstrong Browning Library of Baylor University.

Browning, R. (1985b) [1868–9], *The Ring and the Book* [Books 1–4], in RB 1969–2011, vol. 7, ed. J. W. Herring, R. A. King, P. Honan, A. N. Kincaid and A. C. Dooley.

Browning, R. (1995) [1876], 'House', in RB 1969–2011, vol. 13, ed. A. B. Crowder, pp. 172–3.

Browning, R. (1996a) [1855], 'The Guardian-Angel: A Picture at Fano', in RB 1969–2011, vol. 6, ed. J. C. Berkey, A. C. Dooley and S. E. Dooley, pp. 102–4.

Browning, R. (1996b) [1864], 'A Likeness', in RB 1969–2011, vol. 6, ed. J. C. Berkey, A. C. Dooley and S. E. Dooley, pp. 282–4.

Browning, R. (1996c) [1855], 'Old Pictures in Florence', in RB 1969–2011, vol. 6, ed. J. C. Berkey, A. C. Dooley and S. E. Dooley, pp. 24–36.

Browning, R. (1996d) [1855], 'One Word More', in RB 1969–2011, vol. 6, ed. J. C. Berkey, A. C. Dooley and S. E. Dooley, pp. 141–50.

Browning, R. (1999) [1871], *Prince Hohenstiel-Schwangau, Saviour of Society*, in RB 1969–2011, vol. 10, ed. A. C. Dooley and S. E. Dooley, pp. 119–211.

Browning, R. (2011a) [1889], 'Development', in RB 1969–2011, vol. 17, ed. A. B. Crowder and A. C. Dooley, pp. 68–71.

Browning, R. (2011b) [1889], 'Reverie', in RB 1969–2011, vol. 17, ed. A. B. Crowder and A. C. Dooley, pp. 77–85.

Browning, R. (2011c) [1885], 'Why I Am a Liberal', in RB 1969–2011, vol. 17, ed. A. B. Crowder and A. C. Dooley, p. 131.

Browning, R. and E. B. Browning (1984–), *The Brownings' Correspondence*, ed. P. Kelley and R. Hudson, 24 vols to date, Winfield, KS: Wedgestone.

Browning, R. and E. B. Browning (1985), *BC: Vol. 3, 1832–1837, Letters 435–601*, ed. P. Kelley and R. Hudson.

Browning, R. and E. B. Browning (1986), *BC: Vol. 4, 1838–1840, Letters 602–783*, ed. P. Kelley and R. Hudson.

Browning, R. and E. B. Browning (1992), *BC: Vol. 10, January 1845–July 1845, Letters 1799–1981*, ed. P. Kelley and S. Lewis.

Browning, R. and E. B. Browning (1993), *BC: Vol. 11, July 1845–January 1846, Letters 1982–2177*, ed. P. Kelley and S. Lewis.

Browning, R. and E. B. Browning (1994), *BC: Vol. 12, January 1846–May 1846, Letters 2178–2383*, ed. P. Kelley and S. Lewis.

Browning, R. and E. B. Browning (1995), *BC: Vol. 13, May 1846–September 1846, Letters 2384–2615*, ed. P. Kelley and S. Lewis.

Browning, R. and E. B. Browning (1998), *BC: Vol. 14, September 1846–December 1847, Letters 2616–2716*, ed. P. Kelley and S. Lewis.

Browning, R. and E. B. Browning (2005), *BC: Vol. 15, January 1848–August 1849, Letters 2717–2812*, ed. P. Kelley, S. Lewis and E. Hagan.

Browning, R. and E. B. Browning (2007), *BC: Vol. 16, September 1849–January 1851, Letters 2813–2900*, ed. P. Kelley, S. Lewis and E. Hagan.

Browning, R. and E. B. Browning (2010a), *BC: Vol. 17, February 1851–January 1852, Letters 2901–3000*, ed. P. Kelley, S. Lewis and E. Hagan.

Browning, R. and E. B. Browning (2010b), *BC: Vol. 18, February 1852–March 1853, Letters 3001–3173*, ed. P. Kelley, S. Lewis and E. Hagan.

Browning, R. and E. B. Browning (2012), *BC: Vol. 19, March 1853–November 1853, Letters 3174–3290*, ed. P. Kelley, S. Lewis and E. Hagan.

Buchanan, R. (1871), 'Mr. John Morley's essays', *The Contemporary Review*, 17 (April–July 1871): 319–37.

Buffon, G. L. L. (1992), *Discours sur le style: Suivi de l'*Art d'écrire *du même et de* Visite à Buffon *d'Hérault de Séchelles*, Castelnau-le-Nez: Climats.

Bullen, J. B. (1972), 'Browning's "Pictor Ignotus" and Vasari's "Life of Fra Bartolommeo di San Marco"', *The Review of English Studies*, new ser., 23: 313–19.

Burke, P. (2001), *Eyewitnessing: The Uses of Images as Historical Evidence*, Ithaca: Cornell University Press.

Burrow, J. W. (1985), *Whigs and Liberals: Continuity and Change in English Political Thought*, Oxford: Clarendon.

Burton, A. (2006), 'Archive fever, archive stories', in A. Burton (ed.), *Archive Stories: Facts, Fictions, and the Writing of History*, Durham, NC: Duke University Press, pp. 1–24.

Burton, J. H. (1861), 'The book-hunter again', *Blackwood's Edinburgh Magazine*, 90 (July 1861): 55–76.

The Cabinet Portrait Gallery: 1st series (1890), photographs by W. and D. Downey, London: Cassell.

Calder, J. (1977), *The Victorian Home*, London: Batsford.

Campbell, J. W. P. (2014), 'The British staircase', in J. W. P. Campbell, M. Tutton and J. Pearce (eds), *Staircases: History, Repair and Conservation*, Abingdon: Routledge, pp. 75–140.

Capaldi, N. (2004), *John Stuart Mill: A Biography*, Cambridge: Cambridge University Press.

Carnac, J. R. (1836), letter to J. C. Hobhouse, 14 December 1836, British Library, IOR, Papers of John Cam Hobhouse [EIC], 1827–52, MSS Eur F213/2, fol. 56.

Carpentry and Building: A Monthly Journal (1885), 7.11 (November 1885): 211.

Casid, J. H. (2003), 'Commerce in the boudoir', in M. Hyde and J. Milam (eds), *Women, Art and the Politics of Identity in Eighteenth-Century Europe*, Aldershot: Ashgate, pp. 91–114.

Cassell's Universal Portrait Gallery: A Collection of Portraits of Celebrities . . . (1895), London: Cassell.

Chadwick, J. W. (1888), 'An eagle-feather', *The Christian Register*, 19 January 1888: 37.

Chase, K. and M. Levenson (2000), *The Spectacle of Intimacy: A Public Life for the Victorian Family*, Princeton: Princeton University Press.

Chaudhuri, K. N. (1978), *The Trading World of Asia and the English East India Company, 1660–1760*, Cambridge: Cambridge University Press.

'Chelsea electric lighting' (1890), *The Electrical Engineer: A Weekly Journal . . .*, new ser., 6, 26 September 1890: 271–2.

Chelsea Society (1962), *Annual Report, 1962*.

Chesterton, G. K. (1903), *Robert Browning*, London: Macmillan.

Chesterton, G. K. (1906), introduction in MA, *Essays Literary and Critical*, London: Dent, pp. ix–xiv.

'Civil architecture' (1837), in *The Penny Cyclopaedia of the Society for the Diffusion of Useful Knowledge: Vol. 7, Charleston-Copyhold*, London: Knight, pp. 217–24.

Clive, J. (1975), *Macaulay: The Shaping of the Historian*, New York: Vintage.

Clough, A. H. (1974) [1858], *Amours de Voyage*, ed. P. Scott, St Lucia: University of Queensland Press.

Cobbe, F. P. (1894), *Life of Frances Power Cobbe: By Herself*, vol. 2, London: Bentley.

Cohen, D. (2006), *Household Gods: The British and Their Possessions*, New Haven: Yale University Press.

Coleridge, S. T. (1983) [1817], *Biographia Literaria, or Biographical Sketches of My Literary Life and Opinions: I*, ed. J. Engell and W. J. Bate, London: Routledge.

Collini, S. (1991), *Public Moralists, Political Thought and Intellectual Life in Britain, 1850–1930*, Oxford: Clarendon.

Collini, S. (2008), *Matthew Arnold: A Critical Portrait*, Oxford: Clarendon.

Committee of Correspondence [EIC] (1719–1834), Reports, British Library, IOR, Correspondence Reports: Reports and resolutions of the Committee of Correspondence, IOR/D/18–90.

Connerton, P. (1989), *How Societies Remember*, Cambridge: Cambridge University Press.

Conrad, J. (2002), *The Collected Letters of Joseph Conrad: Vol. 6, 1917–1919*, ed. L. Davies, F. R. Karl and O. Knowles, Cambridge: Cambridge University Press.

Conrad, P. (1973), *The Victorian Treasure-House*, London: Collins.

Cordery, L. (2009), 'Beautiful freedom: Elizabeth Barrett Browning's *Casa Guidi Windows*', in A. Vescovi, L. Villa and P. Vita (eds), *The Victorians and Italy: Literature, Travel, Politics and Art*, Milan: Polimetrica, pp. 83–98.

Corkran, H. (1902), *Celebrities and I*, London: Hutchinson.

Cosgrove, D. E. (1985), *Social Formation and Symbolic Landscape*, Totowa, NJ: Barnes.

Coulter, J. (1985–6), 'The Browning house at New Cross', *Browning Society Notes*, 15 (Winter–Spring 1985–6): 2–19.

Court of Directors (1599–1858), Minutes, British Library, IOR, Minutes of the East India Company's Directors and Proprietors, IOR/B/1–236.

Cowan, P. and D. Fine (1969), *The Office: A Facet of Urban Growth*, London: Heinemann.

Cowell, F. R. (1975), *The Athenaeum: Club and Social Life in London, 1824–1974*, London: Heinemann.

Croker, J. W. (1816), 'Lord Elgin's collection of sculptured marbles', *The Quarterly Review*, 14.28 (January 1816): 513–47.

Croker, J. W. (1884), *The Croker Papers: The Correspondence and Diaries of the Late Right Honourable John Wilson Croker . . .*, ed. L. J. Jennings, vol. 1, London: Murray.

Crook, J. M. (2001), 'Locked out of paradise: blackballing at the Athenaeum, 1824–1935', *Armchair Athenians: Essays from Athenaeum Life*, London: Athenaeum, pp. 19–30.

Crook, M. and T. Crook (2007), 'The advent of the secret ballot in Britain and France, 1789–1914: from public assembly to private compartment', *History*, 92 (October 2007): 449–71.

Crook, T. (2006), '"Schools for the moral training of the people": public baths, liberalism and the promotion of cleanliness in Victorian Britain', *European Review of History*, 13.1: 21–47.

Croot, P. E. C., ed. (2004), *A History of the County of Middlesex: Vol. 12, Chelsea*, Woodbridge: Boydell for Institute of Historical Research.

Csikszentmihalyi, M. and E. Rochberg-Halton (1981), *The Meaning of Things: Domestic Symbols and the Self*, Cambridge: Cambridge University Press.

Culler, A. D. (1985), *The Victorian Mirror of History*, New Haven: Yale University Press.

Curgenven, J. P. (1946), 'Mathew Arnold in two scholarship examinations', *The Review of English Studies*, 22.85: 54–5.

Curthoys, M. C. (1997), 'The examination system', in M. G. Brock and M. C. Curthoys (eds), *The History of the University of Oxford, Vol. 6: Nineteenth-Century Oxford, Part I*, Oxford: Oxford University Press, pp. 339–74.

Cust, L., comp. (1898), *History of the Society of Dilettanti*, ed. S. Colvin, London: Macmillan.

Davidoff, L. and C. Hall (1987), *Family Fortunes: Men and Women of the English Middle Class, 1780–1850*, Chicago: University of Chicago Press.

Davies, A. M. (1935), *Strange Destiny: A Biography of Warren Hastings*, New York: Putnam.

Davis, N. Z. (1988), 'On the lame', *The American Historical Review*, 93.3: 572–601.

DeLaura, D. J. (1965), 'Matthew Arnold and John Henry Newman: the "Oxford Sentiment" and the religion of the future', *Texas Studies in Literature and Language*, 6 (Supplement): 571–702.

DeLaura, D. J. (1969a), 'Arnold, Clough, Dr. Arnold, and "Thyrsis"', *Victorian Poetry*, 7.3: 191–202.

DeLaura, D. J. (1969b), *Hebrew and Hellene in Victorian England: Newman, Arnold, and Pater*, Austin: University of Texas Press.

DeLaura, D. J. (1980), 'The context of Browning's painter poems: aesthetics, polemics, historics', *PMLA*, 95.3: 367–88.

Derrida, J. (1998), *Archive Fever: A Freudian Impression*, trans. E. Prenowitz, Chicago: University of Chicago Press.

DeVane, W. C. (1927), *Browning's Parleyings: The Autobiography of a Mind*, New Haven: Yale University Press.

DeVane, W. C. (1955) [1935], *A Browning Handbook*, 2nd edn, New York: Appleton.

'De Vere Gardens area' (1986), in H. Hobhouse (ed.), *Survey of London: Vol. 42, Kensington Square to Earl's Court*, London: London County Council, pp. 121–9. Available at <http://www.british-history.ac.uk/survey-london/vol42/pp121-129> (last accessed 30 June 2017).

Dirks, N. B. (2006), *The Scandal of Empire: India and the Creation of Imperial Britain*, Cambridge, MA: Belknap–Harvard University Press.

Doherty, J. (1869), 'The Ring and the Book', review of RB, *The Ring and the Book*, *The Dublin Review*, 65 (July 1869): 48–62.

Dohme, R. (1888), *Das englische Haus: Eine kultur- und baugeschichtliche Skizze*, Braunschweig: Westermann.

Dyos, H. J. (1961), *Victorian Suburb: A Study of the Growth of Camberwell*, Leicester: Leicester University Press.

Easley, A. (2006), 'The woman of letters at home: Harriet Martineau and the Lake District', *Victorian Literature and Culture*, 34.1: 291–310.

East India Company (1814), *Proceedings of the Select Committee Appointed by the General Court of Proprietors on the 6th October 1813 . . .*, London: General Court.

'The East India docks: historical development' (1994), in H. Hobhouse (ed.), *Survey of London: Vols 43 and 44, Poplar, Blackwall and Isle of Dogs*, London: London County Council, pp. 575–82. Available at <http://www.british-history.ac.uk/survey-london/vols43-4/pp575-582> (last accessed 30 June 2017).

'Echoes of the week' (1891), *The Leeds Mercury*, 21 November 1891: 12.

Edwards, C. and M. Ponsonby (2008), 'Desirable commodity or practical necessity?: the sale and consumption of second-hand furniture, 1750–1900', in D. Hussey and M. Ponsonby (eds), *Buying for the Home: Shopping for the Domestic from the Seventeenth Century to the Present*, Aldershot: Ashgate, pp. 117–38.

Edwards, J. and I. Hart (2010), 'The Victorian interior: a collaborative, eclectic introduction', in J. Edwards and I. Hart (eds), *Rethinking the Interior, c. 1867–1896: Aestheticism and Arts and Crafts*, Farnham: Ashgate, pp. 1–24.

Elkins, J. (2001), *Pictures and Tears: A History of People Who Have Cried in Front of Paintings*, London: Routledge.

Embree, A. T. (1962), *Charles Grant and British Rule in India*, New York: Columbia University Press.

Emerson, J. (1826), *The Evangelical Primer: Containing a Minor Doctrinal Catechism . . .*, new edn, Boston: Crocker.

Erickson, L. (1984), *Robert Browning: His Poetry and His Audiences*, Ithaca: Cornell University Press.

'Failure of a contractor' (1886), *Edinburgh Evening News*, 3 November 1886: 3.

Farge, A. (2013), *The Allure of the Archives*, trans. T. Scott-Railton, New Haven: Yale University Press.

Field, K. (1861), 'Elizabeth Barrett Browning', *The Atlantic Monthly*, September 1861: 368–76.

Fields, J. T. (1872), *Yesterdays with Authors*, London: Sampson.

'53 GEORGII III, cap. 155' (1841) [1813], *The Law Relating to India and the East-India Company . . .*, 2nd edn, London: Allen, pp. 167–99.

Filon, A. (1891), 'John Morley: critique, journaliste et homme d'état', *Revue des deux mondes*, November 1891: 154–92.

Finance and Home Committee [EIC] (1849), Minutes/Record of Meeting, 22 August 1849, British Library, IOR, Selected Minutes (1847–52), IOR/L/SUR/1/1, fol.78.

Finance and Home Committee [EIC] (1851), Minutes/Record of Meeting, 3 September 1851, British Library, IOR, Selected Minutes (1847–52), IOR/L/SUR/1/1, fols 142–3.

Findlen, P. (1998), 'Possessing the past: the material world of the Italian Renaissance', *The American Historical Review*, 103.1: 83–114.

Finlayson, I. (2004), *Browning: A Private Life*, London: Harper.

Flanders, J. (2004), *Inside the Victorian Home: A Portrait of Domestic Life in Victorian England*, 1st American edn, New York: Norton.

Forbes, D. (1951), 'James Mill and India', *The Cambridge Journal*, 5.1: 19–33.

Ford, I. N. (1908), 'John Morley in politics', *The Outlook*, 90.4 (26 September 1908): 210–15.

Forty, A. (1992), *Objects of Desire: Design and Society since 1750*, New York: Thames.

Foster, W. (1917), 'The India Board (1784–1858)', *Transactions of the Royal Historical Society*, 3rd ser., 11: 61–85.

Foster, W. (1919), *A Guide to the India Office Records, 1600–1858*, London: India Office.

Foster, W. (1924), *The East India House: Its History and Associations*, London: Bodley.

Fox, C. (1883), *Memories of Old Friends: Being Extracts from the Journals and Letters of Caroline Fox . . .*, ed. H. N. Pym, new and rev. edn, London: Smith.

Franklin, M. J. (2011), *Orientalist Jones: Sir William Jones, Poet, Lawyer, and Linguist, 1746–1794*, Oxford: Oxford University Press.

Fraser, H. (2014), 'Vasari's *Lives* and the Victorians', in D. J. Cast (ed.), *The Ashgate Research Companion to Giorgio Vasari*, Farnham: Ashgate, pp. 277–94.

'A French view of Mr. John Morley' (1891), *The Pall Mall Gazette*, 14 November 1891: 1–2.

Fried, M. (1998), 'Art and objecthood', in M. Fried, *Art and Objecthood: Essays and Reviews*, Chicago: University of Chicago Press, pp. 148–72.

Fuss, D. (2004), *The Sense of an Interior: Four Writers and the Rooms That Shaped Them*, New York: Routledge.

Gardiner, A. G. (1914), *Prophets, Priests, and Kings*, London: Dent.

Gascoigne, J. (1989), *Cambridge in the Age of the Enlightenment: Science, Religion and Politics from the Restoration to the French Revolution*, Cambridge: Cambridge University Press.

Gaunt, W. (1952), *Victorian Olympus*, London: Cape.

Gere, C. (1989), *Nineteenth-Century Decoration: The Art of the Interior*, London: Weidenfeld.

Gibbs, R. W., Jr (1994), *The Poetics of Mind: Figurative Thought, Language, and Understanding*, Cambridge: Cambridge University Press.

Gibson, M. E. (1987), *History and the Prism of Art: Browning's Poetic Experiments*, Columbus: Ohio State University Press.

Girouard, M. (1977), *Sweetness and Light: The Queen Anne Movement, 1860–1900*, New Haven: Yale University Press.

Girouard, M. (1978), *Life in the English Country House: A Social and Architectural History*, New Haven: Yale University Press.

Gleig, G. R. (1841), *Memoirs of the Life of the Right Hon. Warren Hastings, First Governor-General of Bengal . . .*, vol. 1, London: Bentley.

Gloag, J. (1962), *Victorian Taste: Some Social Aspects of Architecture and Industrial Design, from 1820–1900*, London: Black.

Gonzales, M. [D. Defoe?] (1888) [1745: *The Voyage of Don Manoel Gonzales*], *London in 1731*, London: Cassell.

Goodlad, L. M. E. (2003), *Victorian Literature and the Victorian State: Character and Governance in a Liberal Society*, Baltimore: Johns Hopkins University Press.

Goodlad, L. M. E. (2008), '"Character worth speaking of": individuality, John Stuart Mill, and the critique of liberalism', *Victorians Institute Journal*, 36: 7–45.

Goodlad, L. M. E. (2015), *The Victorian Geopolitical Aesthetic: Realism, Sovereignty, and Transnational Experience*, Oxford: Oxford University Press.

Grant, C. [1797], *Observations on the State of Society among the Asiatic Subjects of Great-Britain . . .*, [London]: n.p. Available at <https://archive.org/stream/observationsonst00gran#page/n5/mode/2up> (last accessed 30 June 2017).

'A great English man of letters: the life story and memoirs of Viscount Morley', *The Graphic* [London], 17 November 1917: 606–7, 634.

Greene, H. E. (1947), 'Browning's knowledge of music', *PMLA*, 62: 1095–9.

Greville, V. (1893), 'Place aux dames', *The Graphic* [London], 1 April 1893: 346.

Griffin, W. H. and H. C. Minchin (1966) [1910], *The Life of Robert Browning: With Notices of His Writings, His Family, and His Friends*, Hamden, CT: Archon.

Grob, A. (2002), *A Longing Like Despair: Arnold's Poetry of Pessimism*, Newark: University of Delaware Press.

Gronow, R. H. (1862), *Reminiscences of Captain Gronow . . . : Being Anecdotes of the Camp, the Court, and the Clubs . . .*, 2nd rev. edn, London: Smith.

Grove, W. H. (2000), 'My memories of Robert Browning', *Browning Society Notes*, 26 (May 2000): 69–72.

Günther, T. (2010), 'Apollo', trans. P. Baker, in A. Grafton, G. W. Most and S. Settis (eds), *The Classical Tradition*, Cambridge, MA: Belknap–Harvard University Press, pp. 54–5.

Hadley, E. (2010), *Living Liberalism: Practical Citizenship in Mid-Victorian Britain*, Chicago: University of Chicago Press.

Hall, L. (1997), *Athena: A Biography*, Reading, MA: Addison-Wesley.

Hamburger, J. (1963), *James Mill and the Art of Revolution*, New Haven: Yale University Press.

Hamer, D. A. (1968), *John Morley: Liberal Intellectual in Politics*, Oxford: Clarendon.

Hamilton, I. (1999), *A Gift Imprisoned: The Poetic Life of Matthew Arnold*, New York: Basic.

Hamlett, J. (2010), *Material Relations: Domestic Interiors and Middle-Class Families in England, 1850–1910*, Manchester: Manchester University Press.

Hamlett, J. (2015), *At Home in the Institution: Material Life in Asylums, Lodging Houses and Schools in Victorian and Edwardian England*, Basingstoke: Palgrave.

Hancher, M. (1971), 'Browning and the *Poetical Works* of 1888–1889', *Browning Newsletter*, (Spring 1971): 25–7.

Hanley, K. (2015), 'Edinburgh–London–Oxford–Coniston', in F. O'Gorman (ed.), *The Cambridge Companion to John Ruskin*, Cambridge: Cambridge University Press, pp. 17–31.

Hansard, B. ([1912?]), *Leaders of the Empire: A Roll of Fame . . .*, vol. 4, London: Virtue.

Harcourt, L. H. (2006), *Loulou: Selected Extracts from the Journals of Lewis Harcourt (1880–1895)*, ed. P. Jackson, Madison, NJ: Fairleigh Dickinson University Press.

Hare, A. J. C. (1896), *The Story of My Life*, vol. 1, London: Allen.

Harris, C. (1987), *Portraiture in Prints*, Jefferson, NC: McFarland.

Harrison, H. (1952), 'John Morley's wife', *The Spectator*, 31 October 1952: 570.

Harrison, R. (1888), *Catalogue of the London Library . . .*, London: London Library.

Haskell, F. and N. Penny (1981), *Taste and the Antique: The Lure of Classical Sculpture, 1500–1900*, New Haven: Yale University Press.

Hassan, J. (2003), *The Seaside, Health and Environment in England and Wales since 1800*, Aldershot: Ashgate.

Haweis, M. E. (1881), *The Art of Decoration*, London: Chatto.

Haweis, M. E. (1889), *The Art of Housekeeping: A Bridal Garland*, London: Sampson.

Hay, C. (1870), *The Club and the Drawing Room: Being Pictures of Modern Life . . .*, vol. 1, London: Hardwicke.

Helps, A. (1917), *Correspondence of Sir Arthur Helps . . .*, ed. E. A. Helps, London: Lane.

Helsinger, E. K. (2008), *Poetry and the Pre-Raphaelite Arts: Dante Gabriel Rossetti and William Morris*, New Haven: Yale University Press.

Hepworth, M. (1999), 'Privacy, security and respectability: the ideal Victorian home', in T. Chapman and J. Hockey (eds), *Ideal Homes?: Social Change and Domestic Life*, London: Routledge, pp. 17–29.

Hersey, G. L. (1972), *High Victorian Gothic: A Study in Associationism*, Baltimore: Johns Hopkins University Press.

Hetzler, L. A. (1977), 'The case of Prince Hohenstiel-Schwangau: Browning and Napoleon III', *Victorian Poetry*, 15.4: 335–50.

Hilton, B. (1988), *The Age of Atonement: The Influence of Evangelicalism on Social and Economic Thought, 1795–1865*, Oxford: Clarendon.

Himmelfarb, G. (1974), *On Liberty and Liberalism: The Case of John Stuart Mill*, New York: Knopf.

Himmelfarb, G. (2004) [1987], *The New History and the Old: Critical Essays and Reappraisals*, rev. edn, Cambridge, MA: Belknap–Harvard University Press.

Hinton, D. (1967), 'High Victorian: 1840–80', in I. Grant (ed.), *Great Interiors*, New York: Dutton, pp. 172–213.

Hirst, F. W. (1927), *Early Life and Letters of John Morley*, 2 vols, London: Macmillan.

Hobhouse, J. C. (1836), letter to J. R. Carnac, appendix to PC 1828, 12 December 1836, British Library, IOR, Revenue, Judicial and Legislative Committee Papers [EIC] (1824–43), IOR/L/PJ/1/92.

Hobhouse, L. T. (1994) [1911], *Liberalism*, in L. Hobhouse, *Liberalism and Other Writings*, ed. J. Meadowcroft, Cambridge: Cambridge University Press, pp. 1–23.

Honan, P. (1981), *Matthew Arnold: A Life*, London: Weidenfeld.

Hood, T. L. (1933), introduction in RB, *Letters of Robert Browning: Collected by Thomas J. Wise*, ed. T. L. Hood, New Haven: Yale University Press, pp. xi–xx.

Hopper, R. J. (1971), *The Acropolis*, 1st American edn, New York: Macmillan.

Houghton, W. E. (1957), *The Victorian Frame of Mind, 1830–1870*, New Haven: Yale University Press.

Hughson, D. [D. Pugh] (1805), *London: Being an Accurate History and Description of the British Metropolis . . .*, vol. 2, London: Stratford.

Hughson, D. [Pugh, D.] (1817), *Walks through London: Including Westminster and the Borough of Southwark . . .*, vol. 1, London: Sherwood.

'The humble petition of the Moosliman inhabitants of Bengal to the Right Honorable the Governor General in Council' (1836), n.d. [1836], British Library, IOR, Papers regarding the promotion of native education in India [EIC], vol. 4, IOR/F/4/1846/77636, pp. 11–21.

'The humble petition of the students of the Sanscrit College of Calcutta, to the Right Honorable Lord George Auckland, K. G. C. B., Governor-General of India in Council' (1836), 9 August 1836, British Library, IOR, Papers regarding the promotion of native education in India [EIC], vol. 4, IOR/F/4/1846/77636, pp. 23–6.

Huxley, M. (2007), 'Geographies of governmentality', in J. W. Crampton and S. Elden (eds), *Space, Knowledge and Power: Foucault and Geography*, Aldershot: Ashgate, pp. 185–204.

Huxley, T. H. (1882), *Science and Culture and Other Essays*, New York: Appleton.

'Imaginary conversation' (1858), *Punch's Almanack for 1858, Punch* 34 (January–June 1858): n.p.

Isacoff, S. (2011), *A Natural History of the Piano: The Instrument, the Music, the Musicians – from Mozart to Modern Jazz, and Everything in Between*, New York: Knopf.

Jameson, A. (1848), *Sacred and Legendary Art: Vol. 1, Containing Legends of the Angels and Archangels . . .*, London: Longman.

Janus [W. Harris] (1952), 'A spectator's notebook', *The Spectator*, 24 October 1952: 525.

Jenkins, I. (1992), *Archaeologists and Aesthetes: In the Sculpture Galleries of the British Museum, 1800–1939*, London: British Museum.

Jenkins, I. (1994), *The Parthenon Frieze*, Austin: University of Texas Press.

Jenkins, T. A. (1994), *The Liberal Ascendancy, 1830–1886*, New York: St Martin's.

Jenkyns, R. (1980), *The Victorians and Ancient Greece*, Cambridge, MA: Harvard University Press.

Jensen, J. V. (1991), *Thomas Henry Huxley: Communicating for Science*, Newark: University of Delaware Press.

'John Morley as others see him' (1891), *The Review of Reviews*, 4 (December 1891): 588.

Jones, G. S. (1976), 'From historical sociology to theoretical history', *The British Journal of Sociology*, 27.3: 295–305.

Jones, H. S. (2007), *Intellect and Character in Victorian England: Mark Pattison and the Invention of the Don*, Cambridge: Cambridge University Press.

Jones, R. P. (1905), 'The life and works of Decimus Burton, II: conclusion', *The Architectural Review* [UK], 17 (January–June 1905): 155–64.

Joyce, P. (2001), *The Rule of Freedom: Liberalism and the Modern City*, London: Verso.

Joyce, P. (2010), 'Filing the Raj: political technologies of the imperial British state', in T. Bennett and P. Joyce (eds), *Material Powers: Cultural Studies, History and the Material Turn*, London: Routledge, pp. 102–23.

Kahan, A. S. (2001), *Aristocratic Liberalism: The Social and Political Thought of Jacob Burckhardt, John Stuart Mill, and Alexis de Tocqueville*, New Brunswick, NJ: Transaction.

Kanter, L. and P. Palladino (2005), *Fra Angelico*, New York: Metropolitan Museum of Art.

Karlin, D. (2009), 'Robert Browning's pleasure-house', in RB, *The Major Works*, ed. A. Roberts, Oxford: Oxford University Press, pp. xi–xxvii.

[Kaye, J. W.] (1860), 'The house that John built', *The Cornhill Magazine*, 2.1 (July 1860): 113–21.

Keen, S. (2001), *Romances of the Archive in Contemporary British Fiction*, Toronto: University of Toronto Press.

Kellett, J. R. (1969), *The Impact of Railways on Victorian Cities*, London: Routledge.

Kelley, P. and B. A. Coley, comps (1984), *The Browning Collections: A Reconstruction with Other Memorabilia*, Waco: Armstrong Browning Library of Baylor University.

Kennedy, R. S. and D. S. Hair (2007), *The Dramatic Imagination of Robert Browning: A Literary Life*, Columbia: University of Missouri Press.

Kerr, R. (1871), *The Gentleman's House: Or, How to Plan English Residences . . .*, 3rd rev. edn, London: Murray.

King, A. (1976), 'Architectural journalism and the profession: the early years of George Godwin', *Architectural History*, 19 (January 1976): 32–53.

King, R. A. (1947), *Robert Browning's Finances from His Own Account Book*, Waco: Baylor University Press.

Kipling, R. (1990) [1937], *Something of Myself and Other Autobiographical Writings*, ed. T. Pinney, Cambridge: Cambridge University Press.

Knight, C., ed. (1843), *London*, vol. 5, London: Knight.

Knights, B. (1978), *The Idea of the Clerisy in the Nineteenth Century*, Cambridge: Cambridge University Press.

Kopf, D. (1969), *British Orientalism and the Bengal Renaissance: The Dynamics of Indian Modernization, 1773–1835*, Berkeley: University of California Press.

Korg, J. (1983), *Browning and Italy*, Athens: Ohio University Press.

Koven, S. (2014), *The Match Girl and the Heiress*, Princeton: Princeton University Press.

Kuduk Weiner, S. (2005), *Republican Politics and English Poetry, 1789–1874*, Houndmills: Palgrave.

Lakoff, G. and M. Johnson (2003), *Metaphors We Live By*, Chicago: University of Chicago Press.

Lamb, C. (1870), *Complete Correspondence and Works of Charles Lamb . . .*, vol. 3, London: Moxon.

Lamb, C. (1875), *The Complete Works in Prose and Verse of Charles Lamb: From the Original Editions . . .*, ed. R. H. Shepherd, London: Chatto.

Lamb, C. (1876), *Life, Letters and Writings of Charles Lamb*, ed. P. Fitzgerald, vol. 1, London: Moxon.

LaPorte, C. (2011), *Victorian Poets and the Changing Bible*, Charlottesville: University of Virginia Press.

Laqueur, T. W. (1979), *Religion and Respectability: Sunday Schools and Working Class Culture, 1780–1850*, 2nd edn, New Haven: Yale University Press.

Latour, B. (2005), *Reassembling the Social: An Introduction to Actor-Network-Theory*, Oxford: Oxford University Press.

Le Corbusier (1931), *Towards a New Architecture*, trans. F. Etchells, London: Rodker.

Lemann, K. (1904), letter to W. Hall Griffin, 8 November 1904, British Library, Hall Griffin Papers, Add MS 45564, fol. 91.

Lepore, J. (2001), 'Historians who love too much: reflections on microhistory and biography', *The Journal of American History*, 88.1: 129–44.

Leppert, R. (1988), *Music and Image: Domesticity, Ideology and Socio-Cultural Formation in Eighteenth-Century England*, Cambridge: Cambridge University Press.

'Lessons from a family album' (1901), *The British Journal of Photography*, 48 (27 September 1901): 612–13.

Levi, A. W. (1945), 'The "Mental Crisis" of John Stuart Mill', *The Psychoanalytic Review*, 32 (January 1945): 86–101.

Levine, G. (2002), *Dying to Know: Scientific Epistemology and Narrative in Victorian England*, Chicago: University of Chicago Press.

Lewes, G. H. (1879), *Problems of Life and Mind: Third Series . . .*, 2 vols, London: Trübner.

[Lewes, G. H.] (1865), 'The Fortnightly Review', *The Publishers' Circular and General Record . . .*, 28 (15 April 1865): 218.

Lewis, S. (1831), *A Topographical Dictionary of England . . .*, vol. 3, London: Lewis.

Lightman, B. (1987), *The Origins of Agnosticism: Victorian Unbelief and the Limits of Knowledge*, Baltimore: Johns Hopkins University Press.

Logan, T. (2001), *The Victorian Parlour*, Cambridge: Cambridge University Press.

London County Council (1912), *London Statistics: Vol. 22, 1911–12*, London: London County Council.

Lorsch, S. E. (1983), *Where Nature Ends: Literary Responses to the Designification of Landscape*, London: Associated University Presses.

Lüdtke, A. (1995), 'What is the history of everyday life and who are its practitioners?', in A. Lüdtke (ed.), *The History of Everyday Life: Reconstructing Historical Experiences and Ways of Life*, trans. W. Templer, Princeton: Princeton University Press, pp. 3–40.

Lynch, H. R. (1970), *Edward Wilmot Blyden: Pan-Negro Patriot, 1832–1912*, London: Oxford University Press.

Macaulay, T. B. (1935) [1835], *Speeches by Lord Macaulay: With His Minute on Indian Education*, ed. G. M. Young, London: Oxford University Press.

Machann, C. (1998), *Matthew Arnold: A Literary Life*, New York: St Martin's.

Majeed, J. (1992), *Ungoverned Imaginings: James Mill's* The History of British India *and Orientalism*, Oxford: Clarendon.

Majeed, J. (2005), 'James Mill's *The History of British India*: the question of utilitarianism and empire', in B. Schultz and G. Varouxakis (eds), *Utilitarianism and Empire*, Lanham, MD: Lexington-Rowman, pp. 93–106.

Major, M. (1924), *Browning and the Florentine Renaissance*, Fort Worth: Texas Christian University.

Makepeace, M. (2010), *The East India Company's London Workers: Management of the Warehouse Labourers, 1800–1858*, Woodbridge: Boydell.

Malachuk, D. S. (2005), *Perfection, the State, and Victorian Liberalism*, Basingstoke: Palgrave.

Mansel, H. L. (1858), *The Limits of Religious Thought Examined in Eight Lectures . . .*, 2nd edn, London: Murray.

Marcus, S. (1999), *Apartment Stories: City and Home in Nineteenth-Century Paris and London*, Berkeley: University of California Press.

Martens, B. (2011), *Browning, Victorian Poetics and the Romantic Legacy: Challenging the Personal Voice*, Farnham: Ashgate.

Mason, A. W., J. S. Kingston and G. Owen ([1817]), *The East-India Register and Directory for 1817 . . .*, 2nd edn, London: Cox.

Mason, C. (1983), *The Poet Robert Browning and His Kinsfolk*, ed. W. C. Turner, Waco: Baylor University Press.

Matthew, H. C. G. (1986), *Gladstone, 1809–1874*, Oxford: Clarendon.

'Matthew Arnold' (1888), *The Journal of Education* [UK], new ser., 10 (1 May 1888): 241–2.

Maynard, J. (1977), *Browning's Youth*, Cambridge, MA: Harvard University Press.

Mazlish, B. (1975), *James and John Stuart Mill: Father and Son in the Nineteenth Century*, New York: Basic.

McAleer, E. C. (1979), *The Brownings of Casa Guidi*, New York: Browning Institute.

McCarthy, J. (1880), *A History of Our Own Times from the Accession of Queen Victoria to the General Election of 1880*, vol. 2, New York: Harper.

McCormack, K. (2013), *George Eliot in Society: Travels Abroad and Sundays at the Priory*, Columbus: Ohio State University Press.

McCully, B. T. (1966), *English Education and the Origins of Indian Nationalism*, Gloucester, MA: Smith.

McDonell, J. (2013), 'Browning's curiosities: *The Ring and the Book* and the "democracy of things"', in J. Shears and J. Harrison (eds), *Literary Bric-à-Brac and the Victorians: From Commodities to Oddities*, Aldershot: Ashgate, pp. 67–83.

McKechnie, S. (1946), 'Charles Lamb of the India House', *Notes and Queries*, 191.11: 225–30.

McLeod, H. (1995), introduction in H. McLeod (ed.), *European Religion in the Age of Great Cities: 1830–1930*, London: Routledge, pp. 1–40.

Meacham, S. (1970), *Lord Bishop: The Life of Samuel Wilberforce, 1805–1873*, Cambridge, MA: Harvard University Press.

Meadmore, D. (1993), 'The production of individuality through examination', *British Journal of Sociology of Education*, 14.1: 59–73.

Melchiori, B. (1968), *Browning's Poetry of Reticence*, Edinburgh: Oliver.

Melchiori, B. (1975), 'Browning in Italy', in I. Armstrong (ed.), *Robert Browning*, Athens: Ohio University Press, pp. 168–83.

Metcalf, T. R. (1994), *Ideologies of the Raj*, New York: Cambridge University Press.

Michie, H. (2009), *Victorian Honeymoons: Journeys to the Conjugal*, Cambridge: Cambridge University Press.

Michie, H. and R. Warhol (2015), *Love among the Archives: Writing the Lives of Sir George Scharf, Victorian Bachelor*, Edinburgh: Edinburgh University Press.

Miles, H. K. E. (1911), *The Ideal Home and Its Problems*, London: Methuen.

Mill, H. T. (1998), *The Complete Works of Harriet Taylor Mill*, ed. J. E. Jacobs and P. H. Payne, Bloomington: Indiana University Press.

Mill, J. (1824), Revenue Department dispatch to Bengal [EIC], 18 February 1824, British Library, IOR, Correspondence with India, 1703–1858 (December 1823–February 1824), IOR/E/4, vol. 710/1066, pp. 867–1149.

Mill, J. (1840) [1817], *The History of British India*, ed. H. H. Wilson, 4th edn, 6 vols, London: Madden.

Mill, J. (1878) [1829], *Analysis of the Phenomena of the Human Mind . . .*, ed. JSM, 2nd edn, vol.1, London: Longmans.

Mill, J. (1992) [1819–23], *Political Writings*, ed. T. Ball, Cambridge: Cambridge University Press.

Mill, J. S. (1825), Public Department dispatch to Bengal [EIC], 9 March 1825, British Library, IOR, Correspondence with India, 1703–1858 (February–June 1825), IOR/E/4, vol. 714, pp. 167–217.

Mill, J. S. (1826), Public Department dispatch to Bengal [EIC], 13 December 1826, British Library, IOR, Correspondence with India, 1703–1858 (October 1826–March 1827), IOR/E/4, vol. 718, pp. 447–56.

Mill, J. S. (1830), Public Department dispatch to Bengal [EIC], 29 September 1830, British Library, IOR, Correspondence with India, 1703–1858 (August–November 1830), IOR/E/4, vol. 729, pp. 357–485.

Mill, J. S. (1836), India Public Department PC 1828: 'Recent changes in native education' [EIC], n.d. (submitted to Board of Control October 1836), British Library, IOR, Revenue, Judicial and Legislative Committee Papers, IOR/L/PJ/1/92, unpaginated.

Mill, J. S. (1899) [1866], letter of 20 March 1866, in 'Letters from a portfolio', *Literature* [London], 5 (12 August 1899): 160.

Mill, J. S. (1945), *Bibliography of the Published Writings of John Stuart Mill . . .*, ed. N. MacMinn, J. R. Hainds and J. M. McCrimmon, Evanston: Northwestern University.

Mill, J. S. (1963–91), *The Collected Works of John Stuart Mill*, ed. J. M. Robson, 33 vols, Toronto: University of Toronto Press.

Mill, J. S. (1963a), *The Earlier Letters of John Stuart Mill: 1812–1848 [Part 1]*, JSM 1963–91, vol. 12, ed. F. E. Mineka.

Mill, J. S. (1963b), *The Earlier Letters of John Stuart Mill: 1812–1848 [Part 2]*, JSM 1963–91, vol. 13, ed. F. E. Mineka.

Mill, J. S. (1965) [1848], *Principles of Political Economy: With Some of Their Applications to Social Philosophy [Part 2]*, JSM 1963–91, vol. 3, ed. J. M. Robson.

Mill, J. S. (1972a), *The Later Letters of John Stuart Mill, 1849–1873 [Part 3]*, JSM 1963–91, vol. 16, ed. F. E. Mineka and D. N. Lindley.

Mill, J. S. (1972b), *The Later Letters of John Stuart Mill, 1849–1873 [Part 4]*, JSM 1963–91, vol. 17, ed. F. E. Mineka and D. N. Lindley.

Mill, J. S. (1974) [1843], *A System of Logic Ratiocinative and Inductive: Being a Connected View of the Principles of Evidence and the Methods of Scientific Investigation [Part 2]*, JSM 1963–91, vols 7–8, ed. J. M. Robson.

Mill, J. S. (1977a) [1836], 'Civilization', in *Essays on Politics and Society [Part 1]*, JSM 1963–91, vol. 18, ed. J. M. Robson, pp. 116–47.

Mill, J. S. (1977b) [1861], *Considerations on Representative Government*, in *Essays on Politics and Society [Part 2]*, JSM 1963–91, vol. 19, ed. J. M. Robson, pp. 371–577.

Mill, J. S. (1977c) [1840], 'De Toqueville on democracy in America [II]', in *Essays on Politics and Society, Part I*, JSM 1963–91, vol. 18, ed. J. M. Robson, pp. 153–204.

Mill, J. S. (1977d) [1859], *On Liberty*, in *Essays on Politics and Society [Part 1]*, JSM 1963–91, vol. 18, ed. J. M. Robson, pp. 212–310.

Mill, J. S. (1978a) [1846], 'Grote's History of Greece [I], in *Essays on Philosophy and the Classics*, JSM 1963–91, vol. 11, ed. J. M. Robson, pp. 271–304.

Mill, J. S. (1978b) [1853], 'Grote's History of Greece [II]', in *Essays on Philosophy and the Classics*, JSM 1963–91, vol. 11, ed. J. M. Robson, pp. 307–36.

Mill, J. S. (1978c) [1834–5], 'Notes on some of the more popular dialogues of Plato', in *Essays on Philosophy and the Classics*, JSM 1963–91, vol. 11, ed. J. M. Robson, pp. 37–238.

Mill, J. S. (1979) [1865], *An Examination of Sir William Hamilton's Philosophy and of The Principle Philosophical Questions Discussed in His Writings*, JSM 1963–91, vol. 9, ed. J. M. Robson.

Mill, J. S. (1981) [1873], *Autobiography*, in *Autobiography and Literary Essays*, JSM 1963–91, vol. 1, ed. J. M. Robson and J. Stillinger, pp. 1–290.

Mill, J. S. (1982) [1834], 'Notes on the newspapers: no. 1, March, 1834', in *Essays on England, Ireland, and the Empire*, JSM 1963–91, vol. 6, ed. J. M. Robson, pp. 151–68.

Mill, J. S. (1984) [1869], *The Subjection of Women*, in *Essays on Equality, Law, and Education*, JSM 1963–91, vol. 21, ed. J. M. Robson, pp. 259–340.

Mill, J. S. (1985a) [1865], *Auguste Comte and Positivism*, in *Essays on Ethics, Religion and Society*, JSM 1963–91, vol. 10, ed. J. M. Robson, pp. 262–368.

Mill, J. S. (1985b) [1840], 'Coleridge', in *Essays on Ethics, Religion and Society*, JSM 1963–91, vol. 10, ed. J. M. Robson, pp. 117–63.

Mill, J. S. (1985c) [1861], *Utilitarianism*, in *Essays on Ethics, Religion and Society*, JSM 1963–91, vol. 10, ed. J. M. Robson, pp. 203–59.

Mill, J. S. (1986a) [1831], 'The spirit of the age, I', in *Newspaper Writings, December 1822–July 1831[Part I]*, JSM 1963–91, vol. 22, ed. A. P. Robson and J. M. Robson, pp. 227–34.

Mill, J. S. (1986b) [1831], 'The spirit of the age, II', in *Newspaper Writings, December 1822–July 1831[Part 1]*, JSM 1963–91, vol. 22, ed. A. P. Robson and J. M. Robson, pp. 238–45.

Mill, J. S. (1988) [1867], 'East India revenue', 12 August 1867, in *Public and Parliamentary Speeches, November 1850–November 1868*, JSM 1963–91, vol. 28, ed. J. M. Robson and B. L. Kinzer, pp. 233–6.

Mill, J. S. (1990) [1852], 'The East India Company's charter', in *Writings on India*, JSM 1963–91, vol. 30, ed. J. M. Robson, M. Moir and Z. Moir, pp. 31–74.

Mill, J. S. (1991) [1840], *Additional Letters of John Stuart Mill*, JSM 1963–91, vol. 32, ed. M. Filipiuk, M. Laine and J. Robson.

Miller, B. (1953), *Robert Browning: A Portrait*, New York: Scribner.

Miller, J. H. (2000) [1963], *The Disappearance of God: Five Nineteenth-Century Writers*, Urbana: University of Illinois Press.

Milne-Smith, A. (2011), *London Clubland: A Cultural History of Gender and Class in Late Victorian Britain*, New York: Palgrave.

Moir, M. (1979), 'The Examiner's Office: the emergence of an administrative elite in East India House (1804–58)', in *India Office Library and Records: Report for the Year, 1977*, London: HMSO, pp. 25–42.

Moir, M. (1986), 'The Examiner's Office and the drafting of East India Company despatches', in K. Ballhatchet and J. Harrison (eds), *East India Company Studies: Papers Presented to Professor Sir Cyril Philips*, Hong Kong: Asian Research, pp. 123–52.

Moir, M. (1990), introduction in *Writings on India*, JSM 1963–91, vol. 30, ed. J. M. Robson, M. Moir and Z. Moir, pp. vii–liv.

Moir, M. (1999), 'John Stuart Mill's draft despatches to India and the problem of bureaucratic authorship', in M. I. Moir, D. M. Peers and L. Zastoupil (eds), *J. S. Mill's Encounter with India*, Toronto: University of Toronto Press, pp. 72–86.

Moore, R. J. (1983), 'John Stuart Mill at East India House', *Historical Studies*, 20.81: 497–519.

Moore, T. (1984), *The Journal of Thomas Moore: Vol. 2, 1821–1825*, ed. W. S. Dowden, B. G. Bartholomew and J. L. Linsley, Newark: University of Delaware Press.

Morgan, D. (1998), *Visual Piety: A History and Theory of Popular Religious Images*, Berkeley: University of California Press.

Morgan, D. (2010a), 'The Matter of Belief', in D. Morgan (ed.), *Religion and Material Culture: The Matter of Belief*, London: Routledge, pp. 1–18.

Morgan, D. (2010b), preface in D. Morgan (ed.), *Religion and Material Culture: The Matter of Belief*, London: Routledge, pp. xiii–xiv.

Morley, J. (n.d.), Annotated floor plan, Bodleian Library, Oxford, Papers of John Morley, Miscellaneous family correspondence and papers, 1829–1921, MS. Eng. c. 7090, fol. 4.

Morley, J. (1865a), 'Authors and books', in J. Morley 1865d, pp. 206–15.

Morley, J. (1865b), 'The companions of our pleasures', in J. Morley 1865d, pp. 114–24.

Morley, J. (1865c), 'Husbands', in J. Morley 1865d, pp. 103–13.

Morley, J. (1865d), *Modern Characteristics: A Series of Short Essays from the* Saturday Review, London: Tinsley.

Morley, J. (1865e), 'Thrift', in J. Morley 1865d, pp. 71–81.

Morley, J. (1865f), 'The uses of dignity', in J. Morley 1865d, pp. 11–20.

Morley, J., (1866a), 'George Eliot's novels', *Macmillan's Magazine*, 14 (August 1866): 272–9.

Morley, J. (1866b), 'Social responsibilities', *Macmillan's Magazine*, 14 (September 1866): 377–86.

Morley, J. (1867a), "The capacity for pleasure', in J. Morley 1867f, pp. 1–10.

Morley, J. (1867b), *Edmund Burke: A Historical Study*, London: Macmillan.

Morley, J. (1867c), 'Favourite authors', in J. Morley 1867f, pp. 174–86.

Morley, J. (1867d), 'The leopard and his spots', in J. Morley 1867f, pp. 14–51.

Morley, J. (1867e), 'Mental ripeness', in J. Morley 1867f, pp. 164–73.

Morley, J. (1867f), *Studies in Conduct: Short Essays from the* 'Saturday Review', London: Chapman.

Morley, J. (1869), 'On "The Ring and the Book"', *The Fortnightly Review*, new ser., 5.27: 331–43.

Morley, J. (1871a), 'Carlyle', in J. Morley, *Critical Miscellanies*, London: Chapman, pp. 195–248.

Morley, J. (1871b), 'Some Greek conceptions of social growth', in J. Morley, *Critical Miscellanies*, London: Chapman, pp. 293–348.

Morley, J. (1873), 'Mr. Pater's essays', *The Fortnightly Review*, new ser., 13.76: 469–77.

Morley, J. (1874–1918), Correspondence with Grace Morley, Bodleian Library, Oxford, Papers of John Morley, MSS. Eng. e. 3433–6.

Morley, J. (1878), 'Lancashire', *The Fortnightly Review*, ns 24.139: 1–25.

Morley, J. (1882–92), Letts Diaries, 1882–92, Bodleian Library, Oxford, Papers of John Morley, MSS. Eng. d. 3437–47.

Morley, J. (1883), 'Genius and versatility', *Macmillan's Magazine*, 49 (December 1883): 87–94.

Morley, J. (1887), *On the Study of Literature: The Annual Address to the Students of the London Society for Extension of University Teaching* . . ., London: Macmillan.

Morley, J. (1901) [1874], *On Compromise*, London: Macmillan.

Morley, J. (1917), *Recollections*, New York: Macmillan, vol. 1.

Morley, J. (1923a), Last will and testament of John Morley, 29 March 1923, London Probate Department, Principal Registry of the Family Division.

Morley, J. (1923b) [1872], *Voltaire*, London: Macmillan.

Morison, J. C. (1878), 'La révolution', *Macmillan's Magazine*, 38 (July 1878): 235–45.

Morrison, K. A. (2010), '"Whose injury is like mine?": Emily Brontë, George Eliot, and the sincere postures of suffering men', *Novel: A Forum on Fiction*, 43.2: 271–93.

Morrison, K. A. (forthcoming) 'Matthew Arnold: Sir Thomas Bodley's librarian?' *Notes & Queries*.

Morrison, K. A. (forthcoming) *A Microhistory of Victorian Liberal Parenting: John Morley's 'Discrete Indifference'*, Houndmills: Palgrave.

Mould, R. W. (1905), *Southwark Men of Mark, Past and Present: A Contribution towards a Dictionary of Southwark Biography*, ed. R. W. Bowers, London: Bowers.

[Mozley, J. R.] (1869), 'Modern English poets', *The Quarterly Review*, 126.252 (April 1869): 328–59.

'Mr. John Morley's London home' (1892), *The Penny Illustrated Paper and Illustrated Times*, 3 September 1892: 157.

'Mr. Nash's report on the new park and street' (1813), *The Monthly Magazine: Or, British Register*, 36 (1 August 1813): 26–32.

Müller, F. M. (1901), *My Autobiography: A Fragment*, New York: Scribner's.

Munro, T. (1987) [1824], 'Minute, 31 December 1824', in F. Madden and D. Fieldhouse (eds), *Imperial Reconstruction, 1763–1840: The Evolution of Alternative Systems of Colonial Government*, Westport, CT: Greenwood, pp. 239–42.

Murray, N. (1997), *A Life of Matthew Arnold*, 1st US edn, New York: St Martin's.

Muthesius, S. (1982), *The English Terraced House*, New Haven: Yale University Press.

Muthesius, S. (1988), 'Why do we buy old furniture?: aspects of the authentic antique in Britain, 1870–1910', *Art History*, 11.2: 231–54.

Muthesius, S. (2009), *The Poetic Home: Designing the 19th-Century Domestic Interior*, New York: Thames.

Neiswander, J. A. (2008), *The Cosmopolitan Interior: Liberalism and the British Home, 1870–1914*, New Haven: Yale University Press.

Nenadic, S. (1994), 'Middle-rank consumers and domestic culture in Edinburgh and Glasgow, 1720–1840', *Past and Present*, 145: 122–56.

Nevill, R. and C. E. Jerningham (1909), *Piccadilly to Pall Mall: Manners, Morals, and Man*, New York: Dutton.

Neville-Sington, P. (2004), *Robert Browning: A Life after Death*, London: Weidenfeld.

'New grand entrance into Hyde Park' (1827), *The Mechanics' Magazine . . .*, 8 (18 August 1827): 66–8.

Nielssen, H., I. M. Okkenhaug and K. H. Skeie (2011), introduction in H. Nielssen, I. M. Okkenhaug and K. H. Skeie (eds), *Protestant Missions and Local Encounters in the Nineteenth and Twentieth Centuries: Unto the Ends of the World*, Leiden: Brill, pp. 1–22.

[Obituary notice of Decimus Burton] (1883), *Proceedings of the Royal Society of London*, 34 (25 January1883): viii–x.

'Ollendorfiana' (1892), *Moonshine*, 20 August 1892: 96.

Olsen, D. J. (1986), *The City as a Work of Art: London, Paris, Vienna*, New Haven: Yale University Press.

Ormond, L. (1975), 'Browning and painting', in I. Armstrong (ed.), *Robert Browning*, Athens: Ohio University Press, pp. 184–210.

Orr, A. [Mrs S.], and F. G. Kenyon (1908), *Life and Letters of Robert Browning*, new rev. edn, London: Smith.

Orrinsmith, L. (1878), *The Drawing-Room: Its Decorations and Furniture*, London: Macmillan.

Osborne, T. (1994), 'Bureaucracy as a vocation: governmentality and administration in nineteenth-century Britain', *Journal of Historical Sociology*, 7.3: 289–313.

Otter, C. (2008), *The Victorian Eye: A Political History of Light and Vision in Britain, 1800–1910*, Chicago: University of Chicago Press.

Owen, R. (1970) [1813–4; 1821], *A New View of Society; and Report to the County of Lanark*, ed. V. Gatrell, Harmondsworth: Penguin.

'Pall Mall, south side, existing buildings: the United Service Club, the Athenaeum' (1960), in F. H. W. Sheppard (ed.), *Survey of London: Vols 29 and 30: St James Westminster, Part 1*, London: London County Council, pp. 386–99. Available at <http://www.british-history.ac.uk/survey-london/vols29-30/pt1/pp386-399> (last accessed 30 June 2017).

Panton, J. E. (1888), *From Kitchen to Garret: Hints for Young Householders*, 4th edn, London: Ward.

Panton, J. E. (1889), *Nooks and Corners: Being the Companion Volume to 'From Kitchen to Garret'*, London: Ward.

Parkinson, C. N. (1937), *Trade in the Eastern Seas, 1793–1813*, Cambridge: The University Press.

Parry, J. P. (1986), *Democracy and Religion: Gladstone and the Liberal Party, 1867–1875*, Cambridge: Cambridge University Press.

Parry, J. P. (1993), *The Rise and Fall of Liberal Government in Victorian Britain*, New Haven: Yale University Press.

[Patmore, P. G.] (1824), *Beauties of the Dulwich Picture Gallery*, London: Wetton.

Pattison, M. (1884), letter to J. R. Thursfield, 2 January 1884, Bodleian Library, Oxford, Papers of Mark Pattison, Pattison MS 139, fol. 17.

Peers, D. M. (1999), 'Imperial epitaph: John Stuart Mill's defence of the East India Company', in M. I. Moir, D. M. Peers and L. Zastoupil (eds), *J. S. Mill's Encounter with India*, Toronto: University of Toronto Press, pp. 198–220.

Peirce, C. S. (1992), *The Essential Peirce: Selected Philosophical Writings, Vol. 1, 1867–1893*, ed. N. Houser and C. Kloesel, Bloomington: Indiana University Press.

Pelégrin-Genel, E. (1996), *The Office*, Paris: Flammarion.

Perkin, H. J. (1969), *The Origins of Modern English Society, 1780–1880*, London: Routledge; Toronto: University of Toronto Press.

Perks, S. (1905), *Residential Flats of All Classes, Including Artisans' Dwellings: A Practical Treatise . . .*, London: Batsford.

Peterson, W. S. and F. L. Standley (1972), 'The J. S. Mill marginalia in Robert Browning's *Pauline*: a history and transcription', *Papers of the Bibliographical Society of America*, 66.2: 135–70.

Philip, I. G. (1997), 'The Bodleian Library', in M. G. Brock and M. C. Curthoys (eds), *The History of the University of Oxford: Vol. 6*,

Nineteenth-Century Oxford, Part I, Oxford: Oxford University Press, pp. 585–97.

Philips, C. H. (1940a), *The East India Company, 1784–1834*, Manchester: Manchester University Press.

Philips, C. H. (1940b), 'The Secret Committee of the East India Company', *Bulletin of the School of Oriental and African Studies*, 10.2: 299–315.

Philips, C. H. (1940c), 'II. The Secret Committee of the East India Company, 1784–1858', *Bulletin of the School of Oriental and African Studies*, 10.3: 699–716.

Phillips, P. T. (1982), *The Sectarian Spirit: Sectarianism, Society, and Politics in Victorian Cotton Towns*, Toronto: University of Toronto Press.

Picker, J. M. (2003), *Victorian Soundscapes*, Oxford: Oxford University Press.

Pollen, J. H. (1885), 'Cantor Lectures: carving and furniture: lecture IV. – delivered March 30, 1885', *The Journal of the Society of Arts*, 33 (4 September 1885): 983–8.

Ponsonby, M. (2007), *Stories from Home: English Domestic Interiors, 1750–1850*, Aldershot: Ashgate.

Postlethwaite, D. (1984), *Making It Whole: A Victorian Circle and the Shape of Their World*, Columbus: Ohio State University Press.

Prettejohn, E. (1997), *Rossetti and His Circle*, London: Tate Gallery.

'Princes Gate and Ennismore Gardens: the Kingston House Estate: development by Peter and Alexander Thorn, 1868–74' (2000), in J. Greenacombe (ed.), *Survey of London: Vol. 45, Knightsbridge*, London: London County Council, pp. 171–4. Available at <http://www.british-history.ac.uk/survey-london/vol45/pp171-174> (last accessed 30 June 2017).

Princeton University Art Museum (2007), *Princeton University Art Museum: Handbook of the Collections*, New Haven: Yale University Press.

'Private correspondence' (1877), *The Birmingham Daily Post*, 8 January 1877: n.p.

Quiller-Couch, A. (1893), 'A literary causerie: the country as "copy"', *The Speaker* [London], 30 September 1893: 357–8.

Raman, K. K. (1994), 'Utilitarianism and the criminal law in colonial India: a study of the practical limits of utilitarian jurisprudence', *Modern Asian Studies*, 28.4: 739–91.

Ramsey, S. C. (1913), 'London clubs – IV: the Athenaeum', *The Architectural Review* [UK], 34 (September 1913): 54–8, plates I–IV.

Raumer, F. von. (1836), *England in 1835: Being a Series of Letters Written to Friends in Germany . . .*, trans. and ed. S. Austin, vol. 1, London: Murray.

Reid, A., comp. and ed. (1885), *Why I Am a Liberal: Being Definitions and Confessions of Faith by the Best Minds of the Liberal Party*, London: Cassell.

Reid, T. W. (1891), *The Life, Letters, and Friendships of Richard Monckton Milnes . . .*, 3rd edn, vol. 2, London: Cassell.

'A returned empty (gleanings from the field of memory)' (1900), *The Calcutta Review*, 221 (July 1900): 29–49.

Reynolds, M. (2001), *The Realms of Verse, 1830–1870: English Poetry in a Time of Nation-Building*, Oxford: Oxford University Press.

Reynolds, N. (2010), *Building Romanticism: Literature and Architecture in Nineteenth-Century Britain*, Ann Arbor: University of Michigan Press.

Rhodes, R. F. (1995), *Architecture and Meaning on the Athenian Acropolis*, Cambridge: Cambridge University Press.

Rice, C. (2007), *The Emergence of the Interior: Architecture, Modernity, Domesticity*, London: Routledge.

Rice, C. and B. Penner (2004), 'Constructing the interior – introduction', *The Journal of Architecture*, 9.3: 267–73.

Ritchie, A. T. (1892), 'Robert and Elizabeth Barrett Browning', *Harper's New Monthly Magazine*, May 1892: 832–55.

Robertson Scott, J. W. (1952), *The Life and Death of a Newspaper . . .*, London: Methuen.

Robinson, H. C. (1870), *Diary, Reminiscences, and Correspondence of Henry Crabb Robinson . . .*, ed. T. Sadler, vol. 2, Boston: Fields.

Robson, J. M. (1968), *The Improvement of Mankind: The Social and Political Thought of John Stuart Mill*, Toronto: University of Toronto Press.

Robson, J. M., M. Moir and Z. Moir, eds (1990), 'Check list of Mill's Indian despatches (1823–58)', appendix A of *Writings on India*, JSM 1963–91, vol. 30, ed. J. M. Robson, M. Moir and Z. Moir, pp. 238–96.

Roper, A. (1969), *Arnold's Poetic Landscapes*, Baltimore: Johns Hopkins University Press.

Rose, N. (1999), *Powers of Freedom: Reframing Political Thought*, Cambridge: Cambridge University Press.

Rosenhain, W. (1908), *Glass Manufacture*, New York: Van Nostrand.

Rosman, D. (2011) [1984], *Evangelicals and Culture*, 2nd edn, Eugene: Pickwick.

Rosner, V. (2005), *Modernism and the Architecture of Private Life*, New York: Columbia University Press.

Rossetti, D. G. (1897) [1856], *Letters of Dante Gabriel Rossetti to William Allingham, 1854–1870*, ed. G. B. Hill, London: Unwin.

Rössler, B. (2005), *The Value of Privacy*, trans. R. D. V. Glasgow, Cambridge: Polity.

Rothblatt, S. (1968), *The Revolution of the Dons: Cambridge and Society in Victorian England*, New York: Basic.

Rowell, D. (2012), *Paris: The 'New Rome' of Napoleon I*, London: Bloomsbury.

Ruskin, J. (1904) [1854], *The Works of John Ruskin*, ed. E. T. Cook and A. Wedderburn, vol. 12, London: Allen.

Ruskin, J. (1905) [1865], *The Works of John Ruskin*, ed. E. T. Cook and A. Wedderburn, vol. 18, London: Allen.

Russell, B. (2009), *The Basic Writings of Bertrand Russell*, ed. R. Egnan and L. E. Denonn, London: Routledge.

Russell, G. W. E. (1895), 'Prefatory note', in MA, *Letters of Matthew Arnold, 1848–1888*, ed. G. W. E. Russell, vol. 1, New York: Macmillan, pp. vii–xi.

Russell, G. W. E. (1904), *Matthew Arnold*, 2nd edn, London: Hodder.

Ryan, A. (1972), 'Utilitarianism and bureaucracy: the views of J. S. Mill', in G. Sutherland (ed.), *Studies in the Growth of Nineteenth-Century Government*, London: Routledge, pp. 33–62.

Ryan, W. P. (1923), 'John Morley as a man of letters', *The Bookman* [London], November 1923: 92–4.

Said, E. W. (1978), *Orientalism*, New York: Pantheon.

Saisselin, R. G. (1984), *The Bourgeois and the Bibelot*, New Brunswick, NJ: Rutgers University Press.

Sampson, R. V. (1959), 'The limits of religious thought: the theological controversy', in P. Appleman, W. A. Madden and M. Wolff (eds), *1859: Entering an Age of Crisis*, Bloomington: Indiana University Press, pp. 63–80.

Samuel, H. (1951), 'Lord Samuel on John Morley', *London Calling*, 1 November 1951: 13.

Scharnhorst, G. (2008), *Kate Field: The Many Lives of a Nineteenth-Century American Journalist*, Syracuse: Syracuse University Press.

Shapin, S. and B. Barnes (1976), 'Head and hand: rhetorical resources in British pedagogical writing, 1770–1850', *Oxford Review of Education*, 2.3: 231–54.

Sharp, H., ed. (1920), *Selections from Educational Records: Part 1, 1781–1839*, Calcutta: Superintendent, Government Printing, 1920.

Sharp, W. (1897), *Life of Robert Browning*, London: Scott.

Sharrock, R. (1975), 'Browning and history', in I. Armstrong (ed.), *Robert Browning*, Athens: Ohio University Press, pp. 77–103.

Shonfield, Z. (1987), *The Precariously Privileged: A Professional Family in Victorian London*, Oxford: Oxford University Press.

Sirkin, G. and N. R. Sirkin (1974), 'Mill in India House: a little bureaucratic tale in two letters', *The Mill Newsletter*, 9.2: 3–7.

Smith, A. (1767) [1759], *The Theory of Moral Sentiments . . .*, 3rd edn, London: Millar.

Smith, G. (1874), 'Female suffrage', *Macmillan's Magazine*, 30 (May 1874): 139–50.

Smith, J. (1808), 'Endymion the exile: letter III', *The Monthly Mirror*, new ser., 3 (March 1808): 212–15.

Soros, S. W. (1999), 'E. W. Godwin and interior design', in S. W. Soros (ed.), *E. W. Godwin: Aesthetic Movement Architect and Designer*, New Haven: Yale University Press, pp. 185–223.

Sousa Correa, D. da (2003), *George Eliot, Music and Victorian Culture*, Houndmills: Palgrave.

Spear, P. (1958), 'India in the British period', in V. A. Smith, *The Oxford History of India*, ed. P. Spear, 3rd edn, Oxford: Clarendon, pp. 446–838.

Spear, P. (1963), *The Nabobs: A Study of the Social Life of the English in Eighteenth-Century India*, rev. edn, London: Oxford University Press.

Spencer, H. (1910) [1864], *The Principles of Biology*, vol. 1, New York: Appleton.

Staebler, W. (1943), *The Liberal Mind of John Morley*, Princeton: Princeton University Press.

Stafford, W. (1998), *John Stuart Mill*, Houndmills: Macmillan.

Stead, W. T. (1890), 'Right Hon. John Morley, M.P.', *The Review of Reviews*, 2 (November 1890): 423–37.

Steedman, C. (2002), *Dust: The Archive and Cultural History*, New Brunswick, NJ: Rutgers University Press.

Steedman, C. (2007), *Master and Servant: Love and Labour in the English Industrial Age*, Cambridge: Cambridge University Press.

Stephen, L. (1950) [1900], *The English Utilitarians*, vol. 3, London: Duckworth, 1900; facs. edn, London: LSE.

Stewart, S. (1993), *On Longing: Narratives of the Miniature, the Gigantic, the Souvenir, the Collection*, Durham, NC: Duke University Press.

St John, I. (2012), *The Making of the Raj: India under the East India Company*, Santa Barbara: Praeger.

Stokes, E. (1959), *The English Utilitarians and India*, Oxford: Clarendon.

Stray, C. (1998), *Classics Transformed: Schools, Universities, and Society in England, 1830–1960*, Oxford: Oxford University Press.

Stray, C. (2007a), 'Non-identical twins: classics in nineteenth-century Oxford and Cambridge', in C. Stray (ed.), *Oxford Classics: Teaching and Learning, 1800–2000*, London: Bloomsbury, pp. 1–13.

Stray, C. (2007b), 'Politics, culture, and scholarship: classics in the *Quarterly Review*', in J. Cutmore (ed.), *Conservatism and the Quarterly Review: A Critical Analysis*, London: Pickering, pp. 87–106.

Styles, J. (1815), *The Temptations of a Watering-Place, and the Best Means of Counteracting Their Influence . . .*, Brighton: Fleet.

Sullivan, E. P. (1983), 'Liberalism and imperialism: J. S. Mill's defense of the British Empire', *Journal of the History of Ideas*, 44.4: 599–617.

Summerson, J. (1980), *The Life and Work of John Nash, Architect*, Cambridge, MA: MIT Press, 1980.

Symons, A. (1885), 'Browning notes and queries no. 81: Robert Browning and George Meredith', *Monthly Abstract of Proceedings (Browning Society, London)*: Vol. 2, 1885–89, London: Browning Society, pp. 80–2.

Tange, A. K. (2010), *Architectural Identities: Domesticity, Literature and the Victorian Middle Classes*, Toronto: University of Toronto Press.

Tarlo, E. (1996), *Clothing Matters: Dress and Identity in India*, Chicago: University of Chicago Press.

Thesing, W. B. (1982), *The London Muse: Victorian Poetic Responses to the City*, Athens: University of Georgia Press.

Thomas, D. (1983), *Robert Browning: A Life Within*, New York: Viking.

Thomas, D. W. (2004), *Cultivating Victorians: Liberal Culture and the Aesthetic*, Philadelphia: University of Pennsylvania Press.

Thomas, W. (1979), *Philosophic Radicals: Nine Studies in Theory and Practice, 1817–1841*, Oxford: Clarendon.

Thomas, W. (2000), *The Quarrel of Macaulay and Croker: Politics and History in the Age of Reform*, Oxford: Oxford University Press.

Thompson, S. R. (1889), 'Robert Browning, teacher of music', *The Musical World*, 11 May 1889: 296–7.

Thomson, J. (2001), '*The Edinburgh, The Quarterly*, and the Athenaeum', *Armchair Athenians: Essays from Athenaeum Life*, London: Athenaeum, pp. 3–18.

Thorne, R. (1987), 'Building bridges: George Godwin and architectural journalism', *History Today*, 37.8: 11–17.

Thornton, P. (1984), *Authentic Decor: The Domestic Interior, 1620–1920*, New York: Viking.

Thornton, P. (1998), *Form and Decoration: Innovation in the Decorative Arts, 1470–1870*, London: Weidenfeld.

Timbs, J. (1866), *Club Life of London: With Anecdotes of the Clubs, Coffee-Houses and Taverns of the Metropolis . . .*, vol. 1, London: Bentley.

Tosh, J. (1999a), *A Man's Place: Masculinity and the Middle-Class Home in Victorian England*, New Haven: Yale University Press.

Tosh, J. (1999b), 'The old Adam and the new man: emerging themes in the history of English masculinities, 1750–1850', in T. Hitchcock and M. Cohen (eds), *English Masculinities, 1660–1800*, London: Longman, pp. 217–38.

Tristram, P. (1989), *Living Space in Fact and Fiction*, London: Routledge.

Trollope, A. (1999) [1883], *An Autobiography*, ed. M. Sadleir and F. Page, Oxford: Oxford University Press.

Tucker, H. F. (1994), 'Wanted dead or alive: Browning's historicism', *Victorian Studies*, 38.1: 25–39.

Turner, F. M. (1981), *The Greek Heritage in Victorian Britain*, New Haven: Yale University Press.

Tutton, M. (2014), 'An outline of the history and development of the staircase', in J. Campbell, M. Tutton and J. Pearce (eds), *Staircases: History, Repair and Conservation*, Abingdon: Routledge, pp. 13–74.

Tyack, G. (1992), *Sir James Pennethorne and the Making of Victorian London*, Cambridge: Cambridge University Press.

Unger, R. (1978), 'Arnold and Winckelmann', in J. L. Cutler and L. S. Thompson (eds), *Studies in English and American Literature*, Troy, NY: Whitston, pp. 207–9.

Unwin, S. (2007), *Doorway*, London: Routledge.

Vasari, G. (1850–2) [1568], *Lives of the Most Eminent Painters, Sculptors, and Architects . . .*, trans. and ed. Mrs J. Foster, 5 vols, London: Bohn.

Vernon, J. (1993), *Politics and the People: A Study in English Political Culture, c. 1815–1867*, Cambridge: Cambridge University Press.

Vickery, A. (2010), *Behind Closed Doors: At Home in Georgian England*, New Haven: Yale University Press.

Vincent, J. R. (1972), *The Formation of the British Liberal Party, 1857–1868*, Harmondsworth: Penguin.

Viswanathan, G. (1989), *Masks of Conquest: Literary Study and British Rule in India*, New York: Columbia University Press.

Waddy, F. (1873), *Cartoon Portraits and Biographical Sketches of Men of the Day . . .*, London: Tinsley.

Wainwright, C. (1989), *The Romantic Interior: The British Collector at Home, 1750–1850*, New Haven: Yale University Press.

Walker, T. (1835), 'Clubs', *The Original*, 17 (9 September 1835): 253–63.

Waller, P. J. (1983), *Town, City, and Nation: England, 1850–1914*, Oxford: Oxford University Press.

Ward, A. W. (1882), *Dickens*, London: Macmillan.

Ward, H. (1926), *History of the Athenaeum, 1824–1925*, London: Athenaeum.

Ward, M. (1967), *Robert Browning and His World: The Private Face [1812–1861]*, New York: Holt.

Waugh, F. G. (1893), 'In clubland III: the Athenaeum', *The Illustrated London News*, 11 March 1893: 305–10.

Waugh, F. G. (1900), *The Athenaeum Club and Its Associations*, new edn, London: privately printed.

Webb, A. (1878), 'Windows', *The British Architect and Northern Engineer*, 10.23: 212, 221–2.

Whinney, M. (1992), *Sculpture in Britain, 1530–1830*, 2nd edn, New Haven: Yale University Press.

Whiting, L. (1911), *The Brownings: Their Life and Art*, London: Hodder.

Wigley, M. (2001), *White Walls, Designer Dresses: The Fashioning of Modern Architecture*, 1st MIT paperback edn, Cambridge, MA: MIT Press.

Willey, B. (1949), *Nineteenth-Century Studies: Coleridge to Matthew Arnold*, London: Chatto.

Willey, B. (1956), *More Nineteenth-Century Studies: A Group of Honest Doubters*, London: Chatto.

Williams, G. (1990), *Augustus Pugin versus Decimus Burton: A Victorian Architectural Duel*, London: Cassell.

[Williams, T.?] (1821), 'Spiritual arithmetic', *The Evangelical Magazine and Missionary Chronicle*, 29 (January 1821): 9–11.

Wilson, H. H. (1836), 'Education of the natives of India', *The Asiatic Journal and Monthly Register . . .*, new ser., 19.73: 1–16.

Windscheffel, R. C. (2008), *Reading Gladstone*, New York: Palgrave.

Winstanley, M. J. (1990), *Gladstone and the Liberal Party*, London: Routledge.

Wolfreys, J. (1994), *Being English: Narratives, Idioms, and Performances of National Identity from Coleridge to Trollope*, Albany: State University of New York Press.

Woolford, J. (1988), *Browning the Revisionary*, New York: St Martin's.

Woolford, J., D. Karlin and J. Phelan (eds) (2014), *The Poems of Browning: Vol. 3, 1847–1861*, London: Routledge.

Wordsworth, W. (1892) [1798], 'Lines Composed a Few Miles above Tintern Abbey . . .', in W. Wordsworth, *Tintern Abbey, Ode to Duty, Ode on Intimations of Immortality . . .*, ed. A. M. Trotter, London: Chambers, pp. 5–13.

Wright, A. (2005), *The Pollaiuolo Brothers: The Arts of Florence and Rome*, New Haven: Yale University Press.

Young, W. (1879), *Town and Country Mansions and Suburban Houses . . .*, London: Spon.

Zastoupil, L. (1994), *John Stuart Mill and India*, Stanford: Stanford University Press.

Zastoupil, L. and M. Moir (eds) (1999), *The Great Indian Education Debate: Documents Relating to the Orientalist-Anglicist Controversy, 1781–1843*, Richmond: Curzon.

Zegger, R. E. (1973), *John Cam Hobhouse: A Political Life, 1819–1852*, Columbia: University of Missouri Press.

Zemka, S. (1997), *Victorian Testaments: The Bible, Christology, and Literary Authority in Early-Nineteenth-Century British Culture*, Stanford: Stanford University Press.

Zimmerman, C. (2004), 'Photographic modern architecture: inside "the New Deep"', *The Journal of Architecture*, 9.3: 331–54.

Zimmern, H. (1906), 'The Brownings', in H. B. Baildon, W. G. Collingwood, E. Dowden and A. Lang (eds), *Homes and Haunts of Famous Authors*, London: Wells, pp. 35–54.

Index